Nina Käsehage (ed.)
Religious Fundamentalism in the Age of Pandemic

I0616417

Religious Studies | Volume 21

Acknowledgement: A special thank goes to Donja ben Mcharek with regard to her intensive proofreading, my husband for his precise support in terms of the finishing process and to Annika Linnemann for being a wonderful project coordinator. In addition, I would like to thank all of the contributors in view of their trust in my idea regarding this project and for their great contributions.

Nina Käsehage, born in 1978, is an historian and religious scholar. Since 2017, she is a senior lecturer at the Department for Religious Studies and Intercultural Theology (Faculty of Theology) at the University of Rostock. In 2018, she received her Ph.D. for her basic research about the contemporary Salafist and Jihadist milieu in Germany from the Department of Religious Studies (Faculty of Philosophy) at the Georg-August-University of Göttingen. Her main research interests are Islamic Radicalization, New Religious Movements, Qualitative Religious Research, Religious Fundamentalism, Psychology and Sociology of Religion.

Nina Käsehage (ed.)
Religious Fundamentalism in the Age of Pandemic

Funding: The Open Access publication of this volume was supported by Rostock University Library.

Bibliographic information published by the Deutsche Nationalbibliothek
The Deutsche Nationalbibliothek lists this publication in the Deutsche Nationalbibliografie; detailed bibliographic data are available in the Internet at http://dnb.d-nb.de

Cover layout: Maria Arndt, Bielefeld
Copy-editing: Nina Käsehage
Proofread by: Donja ben Mcharek and Anna P. Korula (Nina Käsehage's chapters)

Print-ISBN 978-3-8376-5485-1
PDF-ISBN 978-3-8394-5485-5
https://doi.org/10.14361/9783839454855

Contents

Introduction

Nina Käsehage

Since the Coronavirus (Covid-19) was first identified in 2019 in the Chinese province of Hubei its impact around the world has been unprecedented. Apart from the millions of infections and several thousand deaths worldwide, the continuing uncertainty about its mutations and transmission modes, and in the absence of an effective vaccine, there is persistent fear of this poorly understood and invisible 'enemy'.

Fear often causes mistrust of the unknown and what is alien or foreign, and when it is an undefinable, ever-present, persistent or enduring fear, it can lead to a climate of insecurity, resultant injustices, and – in the end – to misguided decisions that could have far-reaching impacts on societies.

Secondly, and not less adversely, the effects of Covid-19 on social life are evident, where normal, everyday activities and interactions have changed drastically and fundamentally: Yesterday's daily life is inconceivable today.

Despite the innumerable negative impacts of Covid-19 on health, social, political and the private sphere, such as the loss of well-being, social contacts, individual deprivation, poverty, financial insecurity and fear of the future, several groups have become more vulnerable in terms of the pandemic than others. According to a report of *UN Women*, women and children around the world have suffered physical, psychological and other forms of (domestic) violence that increased as a consequence of the lockdown.[1] Working female employees with children "were relieved of their professional duties to care for their children, reinforcing gender stereotypes that expect women to be caregivers and men to be breadwinners."[2] The

---

1   Cf. UN Women (2020). 'New report from UN Women brings forth voices of Palestinian women under COVID-19 lockdown'. June 9. See: https://www.unwomen.org/en/news/stories/2020/6/f eature-voices-of-palestinian-women-under-covid-19-lockdown, accessed on June 17, 2020.; In April 2020 *"France 24* reported a 30% increase in domestic violence, with abused partners unable to escape their abusers during quarantine." In: The Soufan Center (2020): *Intelbrief: The Plague of Domestic Violence during Covid-19.* April 17. See: https://thesoufancenter.org/intel brief-the-plague-of-domestic-violence-during-covid-19/, accessed on April 17.

2   Cf. UN Women (2020).; Cf. UN Nations (2020). *Policy Brief: The Impact of COVID-19 on Women,* pp. 1-21.

confinement measures illustrated the fact that the "burden of domestic work and childcare" in emergency situations still remains with women.[3]

Beside this gender-lens perspective,[4] another group that is specifically vulnerable towards the consequences of the pandemic are people at risk of various forms of radicalization or radical mindsets. According to *Counter Terrorism Policing* (CTP) "the impact of Covid-19 and social isolation could make some of society's most vulnerable people more susceptible to radicalization and other forms of grooming."[5]

With respect to a report of the Department of Homeland Security (DHS), "the coronavirus pandemic and its social repercussions are fueling violence by both frustrated individuals and domestic terrorists."[6] Some cases are well known, such as the one of a white supremacist extremist in Missouri who wanted – beside other plans – to blow up a local hospital, a mosque, a synagogue and a school with a high population of black students, and was killed after a failed arrest.[7] The reasons for politically motivated radicalization of individuals in the Covid-19 context are identifiable in social distancing as a consequence of "the pandemic [that therefore] has created a new source of anger and frustration for some individuals. As a result, violent extremist plots will likely involve individuals seeking targets symbolic to their personal grievances."[8]

According to the *The Council conclusions on EU External Action on Preventing and Countering Terrorism and Violent Extremism* of June 2020, the threat of terrorism and the prevention of radicalization remain high on the European Union's Agenda despite the pandemic.[9]

Various authors and researchers have constructed a link or rather similarities between Covid-19 and terrorism, by marking it as a new actor in the theatre of

---

3   Ib.; Cf. UN Nations (2020).

4   Cf. CGDEV (2020). *Approaching Covid-19. Risk and response through gender-lens.* See: https://www.cgdev.org/event/approaching-covid-19-risk-and-response-through-gender-lens#.Xoc_3hXaQxo.linkedin, accessed on April 3rd, 2020.

5   Cf. Police UK (2020). *Counter Terrorism Police highlight support services as COVID-19 pandemic is linked to greater risk of radicalization.* April, 22nd. See: https://www.counterterrorism.police.uk/ctp-look-to-bolster-prevent-referrals-during-lockdown/, accessed on April 23rd.

6   Cf. Ken Dilanian (2020). 'The coronavirus pandemic and its social repercussions are fueling violence by both frustrated individuals and domestic terrorists, according to a new intelligence report by DHS'. *NBC News.* April 23. See: https://www.nbcnews.com/politics/national-security/coronavirus-its-social-effects-fueling-extremist-violence-says-government-report-n1190921, accessed on April 24, 2020.

7   Cf. Dilanian (2020).

8   Ib.

9   See General Secretariat of the Council (2020). *Council Conclusions on EU External Action on Preventing and Countering Terrorism and Violent Extremism.* In Council of the European Union (Ed.). No. prev. doc.: 8742/20 + COR 1. Brussels, June 16, pp. 1-16.

global terrorism.[10] Others underline the difference[11] between terrorism as a man-made strategy with specific purposes on individual actors or certain states in comparison to Covid-19 as "a natural threat" and "an infectious disease [that] does not occur in separate individual actions, but rather more in waves of propagation."[12] Marone points out that

> "Terrorism is visible by definition. Still, the fear of COVID-19 is fueled precisely by invisibility: the pathogen is undetectable to the naked eye and for this reason contagion is, at this stage, practically not avoidable, except through social distancing. This aspect of the epidemic could lead to the risk of a state of fear that is even deeper compared to terrorism because it is invisible, faceless, without references, close to unfocused anguish."[13]

In this sense, the speech of the French President Emanuel Macron on March 16, 2020 "Nous sommes en guerres" ['We are at war.'] can be seen as a bad example of warfare related rhetoric that doesn't impart the public an enhanced feeling of security, but fuels the fear and anger towards a more readily identifiable enemy:

> "Nous sommes en guerre, toute l'action du gouvernement et du parlament doit être tournée désormais vers le combat contre l'épidémié, de jour comme de nuit, rien ne doit nous en diverter. [...] Nous sommes en guerre. Et la Nation soutiendra ses enfants qui [...] se trouvent en première ligne dans un combat qui va leur demander énergie, détermination, solidarité."[14]

In the video, just six minutes and 8 seconds long Macron uses the sentence "Nous sommes en guerre" ('We are at war') four times and calls on French inhabitants to battle against the so-called 'enemy', Covid-19. His demand for the solidarity of the whole "Nation" in terms of the fight ("combat") ends with the 'assurance' that "nous gagnerons" ('we will win'). The warfare-related rhetoric that the French President

---

10 Cf. Bruce Magnusson and Zahi Zalloua (Eds.) (2012). *Contagion: Health, Fear, Sovereignty*. Seattle, WA: University of Washington Press.

11 Cf. D. Pratt (2007). Religious Fundamentalism: A Paradigm for Terrorism? *Australian Religion Studies Review* 20(2), 195-215.

12 Cf. Francesco Marone (2020). 'A Tale of Two Fears: Comparing Terrorism and the Coronavirus'. *Eeradicalization*. May 29. See: https://eeradicalization.com/a-tale-of-two-fears-comparing-terrorism-and-the-coronavirus/, accessed on May 29, 2020.

13 Cf. Marone (2020).

14 Le Monde (2020). *"Nous sommes en guerre". Le discours de Macron face au coronavirus*. Élysée, March 16. See: https://www.youtube.com/watch?v=N5lcMoqA1XY Minute 1:13-2:06; 2:24-2:42. This is the author's English translation of the French original: "We are at war. All governmental and parliamentary actions must now concentrate on the fight against the pandemic, day and night, nothing can stop us. [...] We are at war. And the Nation will support its children, who will find themselves at the frontline of a fight that will demand their energy, determination and solidarity."

used in his speech reminds the audience of the call of religious fundamentalist groups for a battle against the non-believers and for the values of 'true' Islam. The military jargon creates a war scenario that should empower the French population to join this 'fight' towards a national opponent and impart a feeling of action possibilities towards a virus whose therapies or vaccines have not been developed yet. Macron's speech indicates the attempt to give a faceless fear a name and to fake the fight against it, by assuring the French that the government and the individuals aren't helpless towards this unknown 'enemy'.

With respect to Marone, "Terrorism is defined by definition",[15] but it does not assess its origins nor provide appropriate methods for how best to combat it – or in case of Covid-19 – how to develop a suitable cure for a disease that will infect all individuals, regardless of nationality or borders.

Against this background, it might be much wiser to search for appropriate measures of healing the infected and finding an effective vaccine against the virus in order to avoid an increase of the pandemic, instead of constructing a new (national) 'enemy'.

Nevertheless, the individual's powerlessness in the face of Covid-19 leads political leaders such as the U.S. President Donald Trump[16] or the President of Brazil Jair Bolsonaro[17] to impulsive activism instead of long-term, carefully evaluated solutions for the inhabitants of the countries they control.[18] Brazil has been hit the hardest after the USA by the pandemic. Nevertheless, both presidents refused to wear protection masks until recently. Because of his refusal to wear a protection mask in one Brazilian district where specific hygienic regulations such as the wearing of protection masks had to be observed, President Bolsonaro was sentenced by a regional court to wear a mask, before stepping further into this area. Bolsonaro, who called Covid-19 a 'little cold', fell ill himself from the virus, but recovered in the meantime.

History appears to repeat itself, as specific prejudices against religious minorities such as Jews or Muslims are in evidence in Western countries such as Great

---

15   Cf. Marone (2020).

16   Cf. Steffen Schwarzkopf (2020). ‚Zahlreiche Notrufe bei der US-Giftzentrale und ein beleidigter Präsident'. *Die Welt*. April 26. See: https://www.welt.de/politik/ausland/article207529489/Corona-USA-Mehr-Notrufe-nach-Trumps-wirrer-Idee-bei-US-Giftzentrale.html, accessed on August 9, 2020. - This article was closed before the end of August 2020, when Donald Trump was the official President of the United States of America.

17   Cf. Ivo Marusczyk (2020). ‚Bolsonaro und die „Coronagrippe". Ein Rechtspopulist stürzt Brasilien ins Verderben'. *Deutschlandfunk Kultur*. July 16. See: https://www.deutschlandfunkkultur.de/bolsonaro-und-die-coronagrippe-ein-rechtspopulist-stuerzt.979.de.html?dram:article_id=480606, accessed on August, 9 2020.

18   Cf. BR (2020). ‚Bolsonaro: Ein Populist stürzt Brasilien ins Verderben'. July 17. See: https://www.br.de/nachrichten/deutschland-welt/bolsonaro-hat-grippe-ein-populist-stuerzt-brasilien-ins-verderben,S4thfGl, accessed on August, 9 2020.

Britain since the current pandemic.[19] Sometimes these prejudices are fueled by specific political or ideological movements and even heads of State and Government.[20] President Trump called Covid-19 'Kung Flu' and noted that 99 percent of the cases related to Covid-19 were 'completely harmless'.[21] The Indian Prime Minister Narendra Modi launched a political programme of Hindu primacy since the rise of the pandemic. In February 2020, New Delhi has witnessed large violent conflicts between Muslims and Hindus where 50 people were killed. These riots were a result of the scapegoating of the Muslim minority practised by the Hindu-majority. Many Hindus blamed the Muslim communities in India as Covid-19-superspreaders because of the celebration of Islamic holidays.[22]

According to Meyer, the "impulse to associate the outbreak and spread of the virus with supposedly less advanced Others (be they Chinese eating wild animals or religious fundamentalists) and to close the endangered "body" of the nation – or Europe as a whole – is a symptom of the will to keep such a narrative alive."[23] The idea of the nation being threatened "by intruders from outside" is defined as a "breeding ground for conspiracy ideas that attribute the spread of the Sars-CoV-2-to the new 5G-wireless network, going viral" in violent extremist networks. Therefore, it is noteworthy, "to deconstruct the use of body metaphors in discourses around Corona that naturalize a sense of the "body social" as endangered by out-

---

19   Cf. Lizzie Dearden (2020). 'Neo-Nazis telling followers to deliberately infect Jews and Muslim with coronavirus, report warns.' *The Independent.* July 9. See: https://www.independent.co.uk./news/uk/home-news/neo-nazis-coronavirus-muslims-racism-antisemitism-islamophobia.a96608851.html; Cf. Arab News (2020). 'British Asians fear blame for rise in COVID-19 cases, racial abuse during Eid Al-Adha'. July 30. See: https://www.arabnews.com/mode/1712281/world

20   Cf. JoannaSlater and NihaMasih (2020). 'As the world looks for coronavirus scapegoats, Muslims are blamed in India.' *The Washington Post.* April 23. See: https://www.washingtonpost.com/world/asia_pacific/as-world-looks-for-coronavirus-scapegoats-india-pins-blame-on-muslims/2020/04/22/3cb43430-7f3f-11ea-84c2-0792d8591911_story.html, accessed on August 9, 2020.

21   Cf. Patrick Mayer and Andreas Schmid (2020). ,Corona in den USA: Trump bezeichnet Virus als ,Kung Flu' - Publikum feiert ihn dafür'. *Merkur.* July 9. See: https://www.merkur.de/welt/coronavirus-usa-donald-trump-twitter-schwarzenegger-lockerungen-new-york-tote-zahlen-tests/covid-19-zr-13803461.html, accessed on August 9, 2020.; Cf. *Tagesspiegel* (2020). 'Trump erklärt 99 Prozent der Covid-19-Fälle für „komplett harmlos". July 7. See: https://www.tagesspiegel.de/politik/coronakrise-in-den-usa-trump-erklärt-99-prozent-der-covid-19-faelle-fuer-komplett-harmlos-25976986.html

22   Cf. Slater & Masih (2020).

23   Birgit Meyer (2020). *Religious matters. 'Dossier Corona'. Religious Matters in an Entangled World research project.* April 21. URL: https://religiousmatters.nl/dossier-corona/, accessed on May 16, 2020.

side, malevolent intruders." [24] Though "the virus is real; it cannot be deconstructed away, but [...] challenge us to re-think well-trodden assumptions and biases."[25]

In this sense, the anthology *Religious Fundamentalism in the Age of Pandemic* tries to provide an objective approach towards the impact of the pandemic in religious environments with a fundamental notion of religion. Eight well-known scholars from the field of Buddhist, Islamic, Jewish, Christian, Religious and Political Studies and Sociology discuss the influence of Covid-19 on (militant) Buddhist, Christian, Jewish and Islamic movements in Central Asia, Europe, Israel, Mali, Russia, Syria and Tibet.

The results of their investigations of the possible impact of Covid-19 on the religious groups examined vary widely: While for instance Uran Botobekov could identify an instrumentalization of the pandemic in the field of radical Islam by Salafi and Jihadi groups in Central Asia, Miguel Álvarez Ortega underlines the positive impact of teachers within the Tibetan Buddhism tradition who support their adherents in terms of balanced and peaceful reactions towards the challenges that occur due to the spread of Covid-19.

The present anthology focusses on *Religious Fundamentalism in the Age of Pandemic* and is based on the terminological understanding that

"Fundamentalism [...] refers to a discernible pattern of religious militance by which self-styled "true believers" attempt to arrest the erosion of religious identity, fortify the borders of the religious community, and create viable alternatives to secular institutions and behaviors."[26]

It aims to examine and to describe, why and how certain groups and actors could make use of individual fears of Covid-19 and frame these worries for their religious purposes. Although different religions are discussed in this book, their shared (and sometimes fundamentalist) notion of the criteria that should be essential for a 'strong religion' – as the opposite of a "mainstream religious establishment" with "conventional religious authorities" – is designed by their unified claim for "purity" characterized by "uniformity of belief and practice."[27]

Religious fundamentalist movements distinguish themselves from other religious movements in terms of their actions, because "they are inherently interactive, reactive, and oppositional [and] are inexorably drawn to some form of antagonistic engagement with the world outside the enclave."[28]

The religious dimension of fundamentalism occurs in its various forms such as

---

24   Meyer (2020).

25   Ib.

26   G. A. Almond, R. Scott Appleby and E. Sivan (2003) (Eds.).*Strong Religion. The Rise of Fundamentalism around the World.* Chicago; London: The University of Chicago Press, p. 17.

27   Almond et al., 2003, p. 17.

28   Ib., p. 218.

"...the charismatic leader whose authoritative interpretations of the religious tra-dition legitimates his religiopolitical diagnoses and prescriptions and guides his associates and assistants in setting and implementing policy. Militance, coalition building, "diplomacy" – all of the "ordinary" pursuits of minority political move-ments – take on unique rhythms and patterns in fundamentalisms due to their religious character."[29]

While some experts suggest that the term 'fundamentalism' should solely be applied to the three monotheistic religions Judaism, Islam or Christianity[30] because of the aforementioned definition of its elements and its origin in the field of an alliance of an orthodox Protestant group who strongly adhere to the *five fundamentals*,[31] others such as Almond et al. point out that religious entities are constrained by both, "the boundaries of the host religion and by their own antitraditional character."[32]

In his chapter *Cultural Wars and Communal Perseverance: Jewish Fundamentalism in Our Time*, Yaakov Ariel points out, that Jewish fundamentalists could be defined "as those taking affirmative religious stands in face of secularization and liberalization of Jewish life; those upholding and strengthening tradition in face of other options in Jewish culture." In view of Zionist-Orthodox and ultra-Orthodox groups, Ariel describes how "Jewish fundamentalists insist on the validity and authority of the Jewish sacred scriptures, see special merits in studying the texts as central to Jewish life and identity, and are protective of the narratives the texts offer" with regard to the pandemic. Similar to some reactions of Islamic fundamentalists, "a number of *Haredi*, ultra-Orthodox, leaders expressed their opinion that the pandemic came as a punishment, a retribution for the lax morality of women and other members of the community".

Ariel discusses the development of "movements within a larger social, cultural and religious context in which they have evolved and to which they have reacted", for instance with regard to their support of Right-wing governments and various reactions according to Covid-19.

Though Zionist- and ultra-Orthodox groups both "believe in the need to main-tain the *Halacha*, and observe Jewish law and Jewish rituals", their approaches to

---

29   Ib., p. 219.
30   See the discussion of this position for instance in: Martin Riesebrodt (2001). *Die Rückkehr der Religionen. Fundamentalismus und der ,Kampf der Kulturen'.* 2. Aufl., München: Beck Verlag, p. 52.
31   Martin Riesebrodt (2004). Was ist "religiöser Fundamentalismus"? In Clemens Six, Martin Riesebrodt und Siegfried Haas (Eds.). *Religiöser Fundamentalismus. Vom Kolonialismus zur Glob-alisierung.* Wien: StudienVerlag, p. 16. The *five fundamentals* are the absolute inerrancy of the Scripture, the virgin birth, the representative sin offering, the physical resurrection and the return of Christ in terms of establishing of his millennial reign before the Last Judgement. In: Klaus Kienzler (2007). *Der Religiöse Fundamentalismus. Christentum, Judentum, Islam.* 5. Aufl., München, p. 30.
32   Almond et al., 2003, p. 219.

achieve these aims varied widely since the rise of the virus and the need for modifying religious rituals in order to care for their adherents and to protect their private from public spheres arose. High numbers of sick and dying in the ultra-Orthodox communities have been a result of the refusal to follow governmental rules in the first time since Covid-19 occurred. This development fueled the anger of groups such as the Orthodox and the Zionist Orthodox towards the ultra-Orthodox communities. For Ariel, "the Corona pandemic created a dramatic rift between the Zionist Orthodox and the ultra-Orthodox", in terms of separatism and modernity and highlighted "the character of the Orthodox communities as well as altered it in some measures". This development will have deep impacts on the future cohabitation and "the inner life of the communities".

Almond et al. describe the "willingness [of religious fundamentalists] to manipulate the religious tradition and [to] introduce innovation for political rather than strictly spiritual purposes"[33] as one reason for the loss of reputation of the self-declared 'true believers'. By doing so, they delegitimize their 'religious' claims in the eyes of other believers.[34] As a consequence, the term fundamentalism was applied on religious movements of other religions such as Buddhism as well, because some Buddhists have been involved in bloody conflicts with individuals of other religious heritage, for instance the Tamils in Sri Lanka.[35]

In his chapter *Global virus, international lamas: Tibetan religious leaders in the face of the Covid-19 crisis* Miguel Álvarez Ortega discusses the question if the extension of the term fundamentalism in view of Tibetan Buddhism might be appropriate. Álvarez Ortega "attempts to analyze how the Covid-19 crisis has been treated by leading Tibetan teachers in the global media". He examines the Buddhist concepts in terms of sickness that contains "a depiction of time cycles in which the notion of degenerate times or decline of the Dharma" is essential and sets them in relation to public statements of well-known Tibetan Buddhist teachers such as Dzongsar Jamyang Khyentse who sees "our present time as "kaliyuga" (the Hindu Age of Quarrel) and "dark age".

---

33   Ib.

34   Ib.

35   Riesebrodt, 2004, p. 17.; Cf. Martin E. Marty and R. Scott Appleby (Eds.) (1991). *Fundamentalisms Observed. (The Fundamentalism Project)*, Vol. I. Chicago [et al.]: University of Chicago Press.; Cf. Martin E. Marty. and R. Scott Appleby (Eds.) (1993/1). *Fundamentalisms and Society: Reclaiming the Sciences, the Family and Education (The Fundamentalism Project)*, Vol. II. Chicago [et al.]: University of Chicago Press.; Cf. Martin E. Marty and R. Scott Appleby (Eds.) (1993/2). *Fundamentalisms and the State: Remaking Polities, Economies, and Militance (The Fundamentalism Project)*, Vol. III. Chicago [et al.]: University of Chicago Press.; Cf. Martin E. Marty and R. Scott Appleby (Eds.) (1994). *Fundamentalisms Observed.* Chicago [et al.]: University of Chicago Press.; Cf. Martin E. Marty and R. Scott Appleby (Eds.) (1995). *Fundamentalisms Comprehended.* Chicago [et al.]: University of Chicago Press.

Álvarez Ortega's conclusion of the Tibetan Buddhists' response to Covid-19 is defined by "an appeal to an external compliance with the authorities, and an internal plural interpretation that reflects a common tension between a symbolic and a transcendental construal of religious categories." In addition, he tries to enable the reader to comprehend why Tibetan Buddhism lacks "successful fundamentalist or millennialist reaction" but offers a "particular suitability of Buddhism to accommodate to the crisis." In this context, he underlines the dichotomy of Buddhist discourses in view of the pandemic that tries to respond to this demanding situation appropriately in terms of "a native and an international audience in a context where Science arguably tends to hold, so far, the epistemological monopoly." This balancing act is characterized by Álvarez Ortega as follows: "On the one hand, there is this idea that practice helps us be calm and focused, and also gives us courage, but that prayer is no counterfeit to the virus and the "mamos" are but a metaphor for our relationship with nature; on the other hand, there is this call for rituals, for specific prayers that can tame the virus and appease real evil forces unleashed by humans."

In contrast to Álvarez Ortega, Uran Botobekov's contribution *How Central Asian Salafi-Jihadi Groups are Exploiting the Covid-19 Pandemic: New Opportunities and Challenges* deals with the misuse of the crisis in the field of Islam by global Salafi-Jihadi-Movements. Botobekov analyses the impact of the virus on Central Asian Salafi-Jihadi groups such the Uighur jihadists of the Turkestan Islamist Party (TIP) and on its "parent organizations such as the Taliban, al Qaeda and Hayat Tahrir al-Sham". He points out that the motives to use Covid-19 as a propaganda tool of "the Uighur and Uzbek Islamist extremist groups from Chinese Xinjiang region and post-Soviet Central Asia are affiliated precisely with these major players of the Sunni jihadist world, such as ISIS and al Qaeda, which are their military patron[s] and ideological banner[s]."

Botobekov aims to underline the strategy of various Salafi-Jihadi groups in Afghanistan, the five former post-Soviet republics of Central Asia, and the Middle East to make use of the pandemic, e.g. as an "invisible soldier of Allah" sent to weaken the enemies of Islam and punish the disbelievers" in the sense of Al Qaeda, with regard to their specific political goals towards the Afghan government, the suppression by the Chinese government and their opponent Bashar al-Assad in Syria as well as his main allies from Russia and Iran.

The mutual goal of these religious fundamentalists is to establish a strict form "of Islamic rule in their controlled areas" by drawing a picture of themselves "as the only military and religious-political force in the region, caring for the health of Muslims in "Islamic territories".

The focus of Botobekov's examination lies on the role of Central Asian Salafist communities whose influence in the region is still unbroken, but had currently been overtaken by the threat of Covid-19. He assumes that they aim to gather their strength by using the pandemic for their "violent extremism and terrorism, associated with Salafi-Takfiri ideologies", is a strategy that might "have huge implications and effects on the security of the world in the medium and long term."

The need for the distinction between traditional and fundamentalist approaches to religion is crucial in the field of religious studies, though fundamentalism is often taken as a strike against modernity or the return to the Middle Ages. According to Riesebrodt, these definitions are misleading, because fundamentalism is neither anti-modernistic nor purely traditional but represents a process of a conscious revitalization of the tradition that arises from the tension between tradition and modernity and tries to incorporate both aspects.[36]

Olga Torres Díaz describes in her chapter *Islamic Fundamentalism Framing Politics in Mali: From the Middle Ages to the Age of Pandemic* the amalgamation of tradition and fundaments in Mali in terms of "the imported and the purely local beliefs of the country." She points out that "alternating between periods of peaceful cohabitation and others of open confrontation, has not concealed a basic distinction between what is foreign and what is indigenous, what is revolutionary – in the sense of bringing a major change – and what is traditional."

Torres Díaz draws a picture of "the centuries-long path of the mutualistic relationship between political power and Islam represented by two fundamentalist tendencies clearly discernible in Mali until today." One of these two types of Malian fundamentalism is "a textual and Arabic fundamentalism while the other is an oral and vernacular fundamentalism, but both remain attached to what is settled as original and essential in their respective realms." Though the first one has been related "historically as at present, to educated and Arabised minority elites; the other [one is associated with] the less favoured majority of common people." Against this background, the impact of "Frenchification and later Arabisation" concerning the Malian society and its roots of religious fundamentalism are discussed by Torres Díaz in order to facilitate a "comprehension of current [Islamic] movements – personified by imams and preachers such as Muḥammad Dicko and Sheikh Madani Haïdara – now that the emergence of the Wahhabi trend has begun to compete again with the prevalent traditional Malian Islam in modulating the orientation of the government."

In her conclusion, she calls for a more differentiated approach to the term 'Islamic fundamentalism' in view of Mali, based on the differences of Islamic terrorist extremism and Wahabi fundamentalism that can be observed currently[37] and will pose challenges for the area in the long-term.

---

36   Riesebrodt, 2004, p.19.
37   Cf. Deutsche Welle (2020). ,Präsident und Regierungschef Malis festgenommen'. August 18. See: https://www.dw.com/de/p%C3%A4sident-und-regierungschef-malis-festgenommen/a-5 4608659

The possible interlinking between jihadism and millenialism in terms of the current pandemic is discussed by Nina Käsehage in her contribution *Towards a Covid-Jihad – Millenialism in the field of Jihadism*. Käsehage selected two groups that might be specifically vulnerable towards jihadist narratives since Covid-19 occurred: former Foreign Terrorist Fighters (FTFs) who have already returned to their countries of origin as well as female inhabitants of detention camps in Syria and their children who (still) cannot return to their 'home' countries. For different reasons, both groups join the jihadistic narratives regarding an end time battle between the 'good' and the 'evil' that is supposed to be announced by the rise of the pandemic. Mobilizing supporters in terms of 'the end of all days' is explained by Käsehage as also "a well-known tradition in the field of millennialism" that helps to convince adherents to fight for a particular purpose. With respect to the concerned groups, it assures both, adults and children, a bright future in paradise, if they will join the fight.

By observing the use of "elements of religious fundamentalism, especially in view of its millennialist and apocalyptic elements" with regard to jihadist narrative of groups such as AQ and IS, Käsehage points out that "[w]hereas IS could be defined as a religious movement that strives to obtain the *world domination* with the support of its adherents, the female detainees who have unsuccessfully tried to *escape* the camps in *reality*, abandoned their plans and *escaped symbolically* within the camps by remaining among their religious peer group, the other female IS members."

For Käsehage, the strategy of AQ and IS to misuse the pandemic for a 'Covid-Jihad' towards their self-declared 'enemies' is accompanied by "the increased attempts of the use of biological weapons for terrorist attacks by jihadist groups and actors [and] seems to mark just the beginning of an era of bio-warfare that will be fought by various fundamentalist and extremist groups in the upcoming years."

In her contribution *The impact of Covid-19 on Orthodox Groups and Believers in Russia* Anastasia V. Mitrofanova concentrates on the reactions of various Orthodox groups and individuals from the field of the Russian Orthodox Church (ROC) in view of the pandemic. Apart from the responses of the fundamentalist milieus to Covid-19, who assume for instance that the origin of the virus might be a "special operation" against Russia" and spread the conspiracy of the 5G-wireless network as the 'real' source of the pandemic, other ROC voices arose that sympathized with the fundamentalist approaches towards an ecclesiastical lockdown, that were subsumed by Mitrofanova under the name of the "so called "corona-dissidents" within the Church." This group includes moderate traditionalists, liberals and other believers that usually corresponded with the official ecclesiastical opinion.

The mutual starting point of these groups' refusal of the national and ecclesiastical lockdown is their collective remembrance of the religious suppression in Russia within the 20th century. During this period, the conditions within churches have been blamed as harmful in view of the individual health. The current resistance of different Orthodox believers and groups towards the solidarity of the Patriarch in terms of the ecclesiastical lockdown and his call for the disinfection of sacred objects reflect their traumatic experiences with the Soviet anti-religious strategy in the past.

Another reason for inner-church resistances is located in the transfer of the communion in the virtual room. Beside formal aspects such as the necessity of technological skills, the presence of technical equipment and the money to buy such in order to participate in the digital communion, Mitrofanova explains that "for the first time in the post-Soviet history of the ROC, its speakers officially declared that the communion and the church attendance in general were not necessary conditions with regard to the salvation." Therefore, the term «self-isolation» became popular within Russia instead of the term 'lockdown', "because this approach implies a voluntary subjugation to the antichrist."

The major content-related difference between the live and videoconference is located in the Liturgy: since the attendees of a videoconference Liturgy remain *observers* of the performance of the sacrament, the assembly of the live Liturgy becomes *a part* of it.

In the eyes of the fundamentalists, the compliance to the lockdown indicates a return to former political times. They associated the virus with a "corona-posession" (*koronabesie*) accompanied by worldwide lockdowns and "safety measures as an analogy to being possessed by evil spirits." In addition, they doubt the need of the governmental measurements that "represent the real threat in their eyes [...] a pandemic of fear created with the help of the mass media."

Furthermore, the rise of the pandemic and its appropriate handling visualized the inner-church problems between canonical and non-canonical voices and between an 'official' and a 'folk' religion and religious practice.

Against the background of "Soviet policy of state-imposed atheism" the mistrust within the Russian Orthodox community seems to be a major factor for the interlinking between various religious groups that are commonly not representing the same religious position, unified in terms of their fear that contemporary Russia has become "a godless state" such as the Soviet Union was. Mitrofanova's contribution with regard to the *Impact of Covid-19 on Orthodox Groups and Believers in Russia* could therefore been seen more as an attempt to dismantle the deeper societal problems within former (religiously) 'suppressed' societies that will occur whenever a possible relapse into governmental old habits, for instance in the context of nationwide lockdowns with regard to the pandemic, might appear rather than just the description of the impact of Covid-19 on specific Orthodox believers in Russia.

The present anthology aims to deconstruct the stereotyping of all adherents of certain religions for instance such as Islam as religious fundamentalists as a consequence of selected reactions towards Covid-19 of *some* believers.

The rise of the virus caused most of the losses within Europe in Italy and had a deep impact on Italian society. As we can see in Barbara Lucini's contribution *Dismantling prejudices on Muslim Communities in Italy in Times of Pandemic: not just Religious Fundamentalism*, it is important to examine "the role that perceptions and cultural aspects of a crisis, such as that cause from Covid-19 virus can generate in ethnic communities such as the Muslim one."

Therefore, Lucini explores the interaction "of perception and interpretation [...] between [a] possible exploitation of the pandemic by Islamic extremism and the way in which the Muslim community in Italy is facing the crisis from Covid-19." During this process she observed that "the sense of identity of the Muslim community in Italy" is "complex and fragmented" and varies between the call for respect towards the nation-state as a "religious duty for Muslims" and their perception as a "threat" linked with the prejudices that all Muslims are terrorists and sympathizers of Daesh which is often fueled by (social) media. One of her findings is the result that "the characteristics of the context before the pandemic caused by the Covid-19 virus affected not only the perceptions of such crises, but also the interpretations, thus going to better delineate the specific fragmentary and complexity of the Islamic experience in Italy." That shows the "lack of explicit reference to Islamic fundamentalism" that is primarily linked with 9/11 and not in view of Covid-19 in Italy.

In addition, Lucini observed an increased solidarity "during the emergency and in the first months of the pandemic: at the local level among Muslims, while at the national level the offers have also spread to Italian institutions and organizations."

The use of the term religious fundamentalism is discussed controversially within scientific discourses. Though a detailed debate on the various pros and cons of the systematic use of this term would lead too far (in this context) and can be found in the work of other authors,[38] the two major critical aspects regarding the term fundamentalism are mentioned in the following. The first critique of this term deals with its misuse within political debates where ideological 'enemies' make use of the term fundamentalism in order to destroy the political and individual reputation of their opponents.[39] The second critical aspect concerning the word fundamentalism is found for instance in authoritarian countries that discriminate against religious minorities and are willing to blame these groups

---

38   Cf. Marty & Appleby (1991).; Cf. Marty & Appleby (1993/1).; Cf. Marty & Appleby (1993/2).; Cf. Marty & Appleby (1995).; Cf. Almond et al.(2003).

39   Riesebrodt, 2004, p. 17.

as 'fundamentalists' in order to delegitimize their role and weaken their position within society.[40]

In his contribution Peter Antes discusses the question, if *Religious Fundamentalism* could be seen as *a misleading concept* in itself, in the sense of a category that itself becomes an actor. Starting by the description of the religious roots of fundamentalism, Antes explains the various (mis-)uses of this term that might lead to "at least four major consequences of such general interpretative terms: the addressees, protest as a moral claim against the economy worldwide, the local differences, and the historicity and ambiguity of terms and texts." With the help of examples of different religious developments e.g. in Iran, Algeria and Chechnya, Antes underlines the importance of "a close look at local problems and reasons for protest, in order to avoid thinking that all is embedded in the interpretative framework of global protest as a general trend typical of each of the great religions in the world".

Antes' approach is seen as very important in terms of the need for a multifaceted understanding of religions and religious practices, especially *in the age of pandemic* when discrimination against and othering of religious groups are en vogue (again) in certain societal and political circles.

Therefore and with regard to Riesebrodt, the term religious fundamentalism should not be avoided in scientific discourses but should go through continuous specification and become a part of systematic further development.[41]

This edited volume offers a selection of multidisciplinary approaches towards the questions, if religious fundamentalism is conceptually and semantically applicable to the concerned religions and religious groups and how these groups' reactions in view of Covid-19 might differ from each other and could be shaped by both societal and political impacts.[42]

Though 'the rise of the pandemic' has just begun, we do not know at present if and how other forms of this or other types of viruses might occur in the future and jeopardize world health, but we can imagine how much our lives could change in comparison to the status quo. As far as the future development of the global health crises is not predictable, the responses from religious groups or individuals in terms of this development are not estimable either. The misuse of the pandemic – coming from political, religious or other types of ideological groups – is nothing new, but appeared before as a negative accompaniment of global catastrophes.

Another positive side effect of the pandemic might be the growing solidarity for people at risk or in need and the increased care for each other within the crisis, as

40   Cf. Mark Jürgensmeyer (1993). *The New Cold War? Religious Nationalism Confronts the Secular State.* Berkeley.; This strategy is also followed in terms of the blaming of individual or political opponents as 'terrorists'.

41   Riesebrodt, 2004, pp. 18-31.

42   The present anthology provides no uniformity with regard to the diacritical characters in view of the Arabic terms.

described by Lucini. This could also underline the calming and harmonizing effects of religions in terms of their adherents to face the pandemic together, peacefully, and to receive positive energy through faith as Álvarez Ortega points out.

In this sense, the discussion about the development of *religious fundamentalism in the age of pandemic* might become our constant companion in the future, although it is not possible at present to predict if the violent or the peaceful intentions of religious groups or actors will gain the upper hand.

Bibliography

Almond, G. A.; Appleby, R. Scott, and Sivan, Emmanuel (2003) (Eds.). *Strong Religion. The Rise of Fundamentalism around the World*. Chicago; London: The University of Chicago Press.

Arjomand, Said A. (1984). Traditionalism in the Twentieth-century Iran. In Said A. Arjomand (Ed.). *From Nationalism to Revolutionary Islam*. Albany.

General Secretariat of the Council (2020). *Council Conclusions on EU External Action on Preventing and Countering Terrorism and Violent Extremism*. In Council of the European Union (Ed.). No. prev. doc.: 8742/20 + COR 1. Brussels, June 16, pp. 1-16.

Jürgensmeyer, Mark (1993). *The New Cold War? Religious Nationalism Confronts the Secular State*. Berkeley.

Jürgensmeyer, Mark (1995). Antifundamentalism. In Martin E. Martin and R. Scott Appleby (Eds.). *Fundamentalisms Observed*. Chicago [et al.]: University of Chicago Press, pp. 353-366.

Kienzler, Klaus (2007). *Der Religiöse Fundamentalismus. Christentum, Judentum, Islam*. 5. Aufl., München: C.H. Beck.

Magnusson, Bruce, and Zalloua, Zahi. (Eds.) (2012). *Contagion: Health, Fear, Sovereignty*. Seattle, WA: University of Washington Press.

Marty, Martin E., and Appleby, R. Scott (Eds.) (1991). *Fundamentalisms Observed. (The Fundamentalism Project)*, Vol. I., Chicago [et al.]: University of Chicago Press.

Marty, Martin E., and Appleby, R. Scott (Eds.) (1993/1). *Fundamentalisms and Society: Reclaiming the Sciences, the Family and Education (The Fundamentalism Project)*, Vol. II., Chicago [et al.]: University of Chicago Press.

Marty, Martin E., and Appleby, R. Scott (Eds.) (1993/2). *Fundamentalisms and the State: Remaking Polities, Economies, and Militance (The Fundamentalism Project)*, Vol. III., Chicago [et al.]: University of Chicago Press.

Marty, Martin E., and Appleby, R. Scott (Eds.) (1994). *Fundamentalisms Observed*. Chicago [et al.]: University of Chicago Press.

Marty, Martin E., and Appleby, R. Scott (Eds.) (1995). *Fundamentalisms Comprehended*. Chicago [et al.]: University of Chicago Press.

Pratt, D. (2007). Religious Fundamentalism: A Paradigm for Terrorism? *Australian Religion Studies Review* 20(2), 195-215.

Riesebrodt, Martin (1990). *Fundamentalismus als patriachalische Protestbewegung, Amerikanische Protestanten (1910-1928) und iranische Schiiten (1961-1979) im Vergleich.* Tübingen.

Riesebrodt, Martin (2001). *Die Rückkehr der Religionen. Fundamentalismus und der ,Kampf der Kulturen'.* 2. Aufl., München: Beck Verlag.

Riesebrodt, Martin (2004). Was ist "religiöser Fundamentalismus"? In Clemens Six, Martin Riesebrodt und Siegfried Haas (Eds.). *Religiöser Fundamentalismus. Vom Kolonialismus zur Globalisierung.* Wien: StudienVerlag, pp. 13-32.

United Nations (2020). *Policy Brief: The Impact of COVID-19 on Women*, pp. 1-21.

Online Open Sources

Arab News (2020). 'British Asians fear blame for rise in COVID-19 cases, racial abuse during Eid Al-Adha'. July 30. URL: https://www.arabnews.com/mode/17 12281/world

BR (2020). ,Bolsonaro: Ein Populist stürzt Brasilien ins Verderben'. July 17. URL: https://www.br.de/nachrichten/deutschland-welt/bolsonaro-hat-grippe-ein-populist-stuerzt-brasilien-ins-verderben,S4thfGl, accessed on August 9, 2020.

CGDEV (2020). *Approaching Covid-19. Risk and response through gender-lens.* URL: http s://www.cgdev.org/event/approaching-covid-19-risk-and-response-through-gender-lens#.Xoc_3hXaQxo.linkedin, accessed on April 3rd, 2020.

Dearden, Lizzie (2020). 'Neo-Nazis telling followers to deliberately infect Jews and Muslim with coronavirus, report warns.' *The Independent.* July 9. URL: https://www.independent.co.uk./news/uk/home-news/neo-nazis-coron avirus-muslims-racism-antisemitism-islamophobia.a96608851.html

Dilanian, Ken (2020). 'The coronavirus pandemic and its social repercussions are fueling violence by both frustrated individuals and domestic terrorists, according to a new intelligence report by DHS'. *NBC News.* April 23. URL: https://www.nbcnews.com/politics/national-security/coronavirus-its-so cial-effects-fueling-extremist-violence-says-government-report-n1190921, accessed on April 24, 2020.

Deutsche Welle (2020). ,Präsident und Regierungschef Malis festgenommen'. August 18. URL: https://www.dw.com/de/p%C3%A4sident-und-regierungschef-malis-festgenommen/a-54608659

Knoppe, Peter (2020). 'From Terrorism to Pandemic: Fear needs an enemy'. *Spectator. Clingendael.* May 14. URL: https://spectator.clingendael.org/nl/publicatie/ terrorism-pandemics-fear-needs-enemy, accessed on May 27, 2020.

Le Monde (2020). *"Nous sommes en guerre." Le discours de Macron face au coronavirus.* Élysée, March 16. URL: https://www.youtube.com/watch?v=N5IcMoqA1XY

Marone, Francesco (2020). 'A Tale of Two Fears: Comparing Terrorism and the Coronavirus'. *Eeradicalization.* May 29. URL: https://eeradicalization.com/a-tale-of-two-fears-comparing-terrorism-and-the-coronavirus/, accessed on May 29, 2020.

Marusczyk, Ivo (2020). ,Bolsonaro und die „Coronagrippe". Ein Rechtspopulist stürzt Brasilien ins Verderben.' *Deutschlandfunk Kultur.* July 16. URL: https://www.deutschlandfunkkultur.de/bolsonaro-und-die-coronagrippe-ein-rechtspopulist-stuerzt.979.de.html?dram:article_id=480606, accessed on August 9, 2020.

Meyer, Birgit (2020). *Religious matters. 'Dossier Corona'. Religious Matters in an Entangled World.* April 21. URL: https://religiousmatters.nl/dossier-corona/, accessed on May 16, 2020.

Mayer, Patrick, and Schmid, Andreas (2020). ,Corona in den USA: Trump bezeichnet Virus als ,Kung Flu' – Publikum feiert ihn dafür'. *Merkur.* July 9. URL: https://www.merkur.de/welt/coronavirus-usa-donald-trump-twitter-schwarzenegger-lockerungen-new-york-tote-zahlen-tests/covid-19-zr-13803461.html, accessed on August 9, 2020.

Police UK (2020). *Counter Terrorism Police highlight support services as COVID-19 pandemic is linked to greater risk of radicalization.* April, 22nd. URL: https://www.counterterrorism.police.uk/ctp-look-to-bolster-prevent-referrals-during-lockdown/, accessed on April 23rd.

Slater, Joanna, and Masih, Niha (2020). 'As the world looks for coronavirus scapegoats, Muslims are blamed in India.' *The Washington Post.* April 23. URL: https://www.washingtonpost.com/world/asia_pacific/as-world-looks-for-coronavirus-scapegoats-india-pins-blame-on-muslims/2020/04/22/3cb43430-7f3f-11ea-84c2-0792d8591911_story.html, accessed on August 9, 2020.

Schwarzkopf, Steffen (2020). ,Zahlreiche Notrufe bei der US-Giftzentrale und ein beleidigter Präsident'. *Die Welt.* April 26. URL: https://www.welt.de/politik/ausland/article207529489/Corona-USA-Mehr-Notrufe-nach-Trumps-wirrer-Idee-bei-US-Giftzentrale.html, accessed on August 9, 2020.

Tagesspiegel (2020). 'Trump erklärt 99 Prozent der Covid-19-Fälle für „komplett harmlos". July 7. URL: https://www.tagesspiegel.de/politik/coronakrise-in-den-usa-trump-erklärt-99-prozent-der-covid-19-faelle-fuer-komplett-harmlos-25976986.html

The Soufan Center (2020). *Intelbrief: The Plague of Domestic Violence during Covid-19.* April 17. URL: https://thesoufancenter.org/intelbrief-the-plague-of-domestic-violence-during-covid-19/, accessed on April 17.

UN Women (2020). *New report from UN Women brings forth voices of Palestinian women under COVID-19 lockdown.* June 9. URL: https://www.unwomen.org/en/

news/stories/2020/6/feature-voices-of-palestinian-women-under-covid-19-lockdown, accessed on June 17, 2020.

Cultural Wars and Communal Perseverance: Jewish Fundamentalism in Our Time

Yaakov Ariel

Abstract

The Corona epidemic highlighted the position of the Orthodox communities within the larger Jewish, and non-Jewish, populations. It exacerbated Jewish cultural wars, and the divisions between the ultra-Orthodox and other groups, including the other fundamentalist Jewish camp, the Nationalist Orthodox. The article explores the rise of the fundamentalist movements, their developments, beliefs, and characteristics, and places the reaction of the different camps to the pandemic within larger cultural contexts.

Keywords: Judaism, Orthodoxy, Haredim, Ultra-Orthodoxy, Zionism, Nationalism.

1. Introduction

As the Corona epidemic began unfolding in March 2020, a number of *Haredi*, ultra-Orthodox, leaders expressed their opinion that the pandemic came as a punishment, a retribution for the lax morality of women and other members of the community. "The Corona Pandemic-Measure for Measure" announced posters in Haredi neighborhoods in Jerusalem. "You have taken your crowns of your heads and replaced them with wigs, and retribution came swiftly – measure for measure. You have walked the streets exposed, instead of wearing dresses that fully cover your entire bodies..."[1] To those who read the ultra-Orthodox *pashkvils*, wall posters, such public chastising does not seem out of line. They fit well with the language and content of public discourses in ultra-Orthodox neighborhoods, where the writers

---

1   Cf. Anshel Pfeffer (2020). *Haaretz.* April 28. See: https://www.haaretz.co.il/health/corona/.premium-MAGAZINE-1.8803930

refrain from using electronic means of communications and often air their concerns and arguments via wall posters. With the appearance and proliferation of the Corona virus, the posters made use of Covid-19 to promote a message of austerity and modesty, in line with the values of the community.

The epidemic highlighted the position of the ultra-Orthodox communities within the larger Jewish population, the cultural wars among Jews and the divisions between the ultra-Orthodox and other groups in the Orthodox community, including the other fundamentalist Jewish camp, the Nationalist Orthodox. The chastising and arguments that developed have drawn on a long history of Jewish fundamentalism that started in the early nineteenth century.

This article will explore the two Jewish fundamentalist communities: the separatist ultra-Orthodox, and the more culturally acculturated but politically radical Nationalist Orthodox groups. Those segments of Judaism have been on the rise in the last generation, demographically, institutionally and politically. They have attracted much media attention as well as made their way, in fictionalized forms to popular Jewish literature, TV series and movies.

Jewish fundamentalists are currently prominent on the Israeli political scene, supporting Right Wing governments and affecting national policies. Declarations and actions of some members of the groups in relation to Israeli society and policies have gone even beyond the Jewish community, affecting the image of Israel on a global level. Likewise, the ultra-Orthodox reaction to Corona public regulations has reinforced their image as separatist group among Jews and non-Jews alike.

While many have paid attention to Jewish fundamentalism, especially in its depiction in popular TV series, movies, and novels,[2] few have been aware of the history and development of the Jewish fundamentalist movements and the varied characteristics of the many groups that make up these camps. This paper aims to place the movements within a larger social, cultural and religious context in which they have evolved and to which they have reacted. The paper will point to two major camps of contemporary Jewish fundamentalists that differ from each other in their theologies, communal structures, lifestyles, and political choices. This has been evident, perhaps as never before, in their different reactions to the Covid-19 epidemic.

One can define Jewish fundamentalists as those taking affirmative religious stands in face of secularization and liberalization of Jewish life: those upholding and strengthening tradition in face of other options in Jewish culture. Jewish fundamentalists insist on the validity and authority of the Jewish sacred scriptures, see special merits in studying the texts as central to Jewish life and identity, and

---

2   See, for example, the global success of the mini-series *Unorthodox*, which aired on Netflix, in 2020, during the Corona epidemic: https://www.imdb.com/title/tt9815454/

are protective of the narratives the texts offer. Both groups are eschatologically oriented, but while the Zionist-Orthodox believe in taking an active role in history, the ultra-Orthodox have often objected to such attempts.[3] While the ultra-Orthodox take their model from the *alter heim*, Eastern European Jewish society before Communism, Nazism and emigration brought it to an end, Zionist Orthodox groups have come instead to promote the Land of Israel as a focal point of their political vision.[4]

2. Fundamentalist Ultra-Orthodoxy

The demographically largest of the religious fundamentalist movements within contemporary Judaism is ultra-Orthodoxy.[5] This diverse fundamentalist movement started in Central Europe, in the nineteenth century, in reaction to movements of acculturation and liberalization.[6] It spread to Jewish communities in other parts of the world, changing and evolving in response to new environments and challenges.

Until the turn of the nineteenth century, Jews did not define themselves as 'orthodox.' Matters changed in the early nineteenth century when leaders of more militant forms of reactive traditional Judaism appeared on the scene and declared themselves 'orthodox' in contrast to what they considered to be the erring reformers. Until secular and liberal alternatives appeared in Jewish society, Jews could move away from the faith by converting to another religion, but they could not choose, on an individual basis, how they defined their tradition and in what forms they observed it. Now, such choices became possible. In Western and Central Europe, as well as in the New World, many Jews liberalized, easing up or giving up completely on daily observance of their tradition. A number of rabbis and layperson made deliberate efforts to bring Judaism to par with the cultural norms of urban Christian European societies.[7] Those deciding to uphold traditional Jewish forms considered such liberal reformers misguided, if not outright traitors. They set out to create a more stern and uncompromising version of traditional Judaism that would save the Jewish community from disintegration.

---

3   Cf. Aviezer Ravitzky (1996). *Messianism, Zionism, and Jewish Religious Radicalism*. Chicago: Chicago University Press, chapter 4.

4   On the ethos of ultra-Orthodox society, see Menachem Friedman (1991). The Haredi (ultra-Orthodox) Society. Jerusalem: Jerusalem Institute.

5   Cf. Friedman (1991).

6   Cf. Jacob Katz (1973). *Out of the Ghetto: the Social Background of Jewish Emancipation*. Syracuse: Syracuse University Press.

7   Cf. Michael Mayer (1995). *Response to Modernity: A History of the Reform Movement in Judaism*. Detroit: Wayne State University Press.

The term ultra-Orthodoxy has not been a self-designation. Most members of this camp prefer instead terms that express their understanding of themselves as the most loyal followers of the Jewish faith, using at times 'Torah Camp,' or *Haredim*, Eager to Follow God, to emphasize their zealous commitment to the highest standards of Jewish observance. Michael Silber has pointed out that the ultra-Orthodox reacted not only to the rise of Reform or secular forms of Jewish life, but also to the appearance of acculturated forms of Orthodoxy whose holders had wished to make observant forms of Judaism compatible with modern life.[8] The ultra-Orthodox believe that even minor attempts at acculturation or reform could be the beginning of a slippery slope, decline in commitment and deterioration in the standards of observing the faith that would eventually lead to the complete disintegration of the tradition. The first ultra-Orthodox leaders lashed out at early Orthodox thinkers, such as Moses Mendelssohn, and even at Samson Raphael Hirsch and Azriel Hildesheimer, who were, in fact, founders of firm forms of Judaism and militated against reforms of the faith.[9]

If Moses Mendelssohn was the thinker most associated with the beginning of a moderate, acculturated form of Jewish Orthodoxy, Moses Sofer (Schreiber) of Pressburg (Bratislava), known as the Hatam Sofer (1762-1839), was the early founder of ultra-Orthodoxy. Spiritual leader of the utmost Eastern urban center of the Habsburg Empire, Sofer established a yeshiva that became a bastion of anti-modernism in Central and Eastern Europe. The Hatam Sofer pun on a Talmudic ruling, "Kol hadash asur min ha Torah," the Torah forbids all new things, became a battle cry of ultra-Orthodoxy. It has reflected the dialectics of the new movement, which has come about within the context of modernity yet carried a banner of opposition to modernism and acculturation, and while thoroughly opposing reforms, made profound theological and practical changes in the tradition. It was perhaps not surprising that the Hatam Sofer held expectations for the imminent arrival of the Messiah to usher in a global righteous age and bring about the redemption of Israel. It stood in contrast to the views and hopes of newly emerging circles of liberal Jews, who adopted progressive millennial views and hoped to build the Kingdom of God on Earth through education, the spreading of the values of the Enlightenment, technological advancement, and political reforms. The Hatam Sofer believed that the Messianic era would not be ushered in through human efforts, but rather

---

8   Michael Silber (1992). The Invention of Ultra-Orthodoxy: the Emergence of a Tradition. In edited by Jack Wertheimer (Ed.) *The Uses of Tradition: Jewish Community in the Modern Era.* New York: Jewish Theological Seminary, pp. 23-82.

9   Cf. Maoz Kahana (2015). *From the Noda BeYehuda to the Hatam Sofer: Halacha and Thought in Response to the Challenges of the Time.* Jerusalem: Zalman Shazar.; On Hirsch, Hildsheimer and the rise of German Jewish neo-Orthodoxy, see Mordechai Breuer (1992). *Modernity within Tradition.* New York: Columbia University Press.

through divine intervention and busied himself in trying to calculate the exact date of its arrival.

In that, ultra-Orthodoxy has been similar to the ideologies and attitudes of fundamentalist movements that have come about in other religious traditions in the late Modern era. Like other such movements, ultra-Orthodoxy should be understood as a reaction to modernism, liberalism, and pluralism. If in previous generations, there was more leeway for rabbis, and laypersons, to balance the demands of day to day life with those of tradition and the *halakha*, now regulations and standards have become more stringent and greater emphasize put on separation from outside cultures including other groups of Jews.[10]

In their declared ideology as well as in their own minds, the ultra-Orthodox created nothing new. They have seen themselves as merely preserving the customs and faith of their fathers and forefathers, which, they have asserted, had remained unaltered throughout the ages. Religious traditions, however, are dynamic by nature and fundamentalist groups, such as the ultra-Orthodox, tend to be particularly active in re-designing their traditions in order to make them more insular and immune to outside influences. While opposing innovations, ultra-Orthodox leaders and groups have implemented huge changes in Jewish customs and standards of observance as well as in the relation between different groups of Jews.[11] For example, the ultra-Orthodox unwillingness to recognize more acculturated or accommodating rabbis as legitimate has brought the older concept of, *More deAtra*, local rabbis as the authoritative halachic figures in their own territories, to an end. The dynamic nature of fundamentalism is also evident in the significant developments that have taken place as new generations of ultra-Orthodox have come on the scene. As a generalization, the movement has become increasingly stricter and demanding throughout the nineteenth and twentieth centuries. Its leaders have militated against, and partially withstood, within their communities, the influence of a number of central ideological movements of the late modern era, such as nationalism, or equality for women. In July 2020, the Israeli Institute for Democracy released the findings of a survey it has taken among ultra-Orthodox Jews in Israel. A vast majority among the 863 members of the community, who participated in the survey, expressed, in different degrees, separatist and non-egalitarian views on the roles of women and men in the community.[12]

---

10 For similar attitudes among Christian fundamentalists, see George Marsden (1982). *Fundamentalism and American Culture: the Shaping of Twentieth Century Evangelicalism, 1870-1925*. New York: Oxford University Press.; Cf. Timothy Weber (1983). *Living in the Shadow of the Second Coming: American Premillennialism*. Grand Rapids: Zondervan

11 Cf. Jacob Katz (1998). *A House Divided: Orthodoxy and Schism in Nineteenth Century Judaism*. Waltham: Brandeis University Press.

12 Cf. Or Kashti (2020). *Haaretz*. See: https://www.haaretz.co.il/news/education/.premium-1.899 9355

At the same time, the movement also manifests enormous inner diversity. While for many observers ultra-Orthodoxy seem, from the outside, like a homogeneous camp, it is in fact a large and diverse religious-cultural movement. Divisions have to do with the areas from which the ultra-Orthodox have arrived from, as well as between Hasidic and non-Hasidic forms of leadership, authority and worship. The camp is composed of numerous communities that share the basic cultural values and adhere to the same narratives on the course of Jewish history, yet differ in the leaders they follow, as well as small details of appearance and customs. There are also varying shades of separatism from the outside culture. These communal divisions often result in inner struggles, the building and dissolving of coalitions and public institutions, and even verbal and physical skirmishes. For example, most ultra-Orthodox Jews in Israel lend their support to political parties that represent their interests vis a vis the Israeli government. However, a minority group considers such political maneuvers to be in violation of the community's values and boycotts the elections.[13]

While positioning themselves in opposition to modernity and the general culture, the ultra-Orthodox have chosen, especially since World War II, to live their lives in large cities. They have made extensive usage of modern technology and international transportation. This has allowed them to build global networks and unite over common causes. Most ultra-Orthodox Jews are of Eastern-European origins, and many of them consider traditional Eastern-European customs to represent normative Judaism. The separatist communities in Germany were more acculturated than the ultra-Orthodox groups in Eastern-Europe, and they encouraged their male members to obtain general education and professional training, alongside Jewish traditional schooling, a reality that made some Eastern European leaders treat them with suspicion.

By the turn of the twentieth century, the Germans and Eastern-Europeans cooperated in establishing political bodies that came to represent the conservative elements of Orthodox Judaism in the public and political spheres. By that time, the ultra-Orthodox were reacting strongly to the rise of the Zionist movement, and especially to its Orthodox wing, *Hamizrahi*.[14] Leaders of ultra-Orthodox communities, such as the *Munkatcher Rebbe*, Chaim Elazar Spira (1868-1937) and the *Satmar Rebbe*, Joel Teitelbaum (1887-1979) shared the conviction that the Jews were forbidden 'La'alot Bahoma,' to re-enter history as active agents. They therefore opposed the Zionist agenda vehemently, viewing it as a futile and dangerous attempt. The

---

13   Cf. Friedman (1991).

14   Michael Silber (1992). See also Motti Inbari (2016). *Jewish Radical ultra-Orthodoxy Confronts Modernity*. New York: Cambridge University Press. On ultra-Orthodox life and institutions, see Samuel Heilman (2000). *Defenders of the Faith: Inside Ultra-Orthodox Jewry*. Berkley: University of California Press.

founding of an ultra-Orthodox party, Agudat Israel, came to present a political alternative to Zionist voices.[15] While inner divisions, such as between Hasidic Jews and 'opponents,' non-Hasidic ultra-Orthodox did not disappear, Eastern and Central European traditionalists were now willing to put aside some of their differences and cooperate in order to fight the modernists and strengthen the ideological and spiritual walls around their communities.

After World War I, Agudat-Israel became active in a number of Eastern and Central European countries and in Palestine, expressing opposition to the Zionist movement in international forums. Still, in the mid-1920s, the ultra-Orthodox party begun, on a pragmatic basis, to cooperate with the Zionist establishment. Its leaders wished to get their share of certificates for immigration to Palestine, as well as budgets and allocations of land.[16] This created a backlash among the more radical elements of the ultra-Orthodox in Jerusalem. In 1937, Amram Blau (1894-1974) and others, established *Neturei Karta*, Defenders of the City, a group that in the 1950s-1960s galvanized ultra-Orthodox antagonists of the newly created State of Israel and organized demonstrations in Jerusalem against the desecration of the Sabbath. This group gave voice to a minority within the ultra-Orthodox. Most chose to operate within the system in order to protect their community's interests, including its growing separatist educational institutions. Avraham Yishaya Karelitz (1878-1953), known as the *Hazon Ish*, emerged as a spiritual leader, giving voice to ultra-Orthodoxy at large, in opposing the conscription of women, as well as of male yeshiva students, to the Israeli military.

The deferment from conscription of yeshiva students and young women, which the Israeli governments granted to its ultra-Orthodox coalition partners, proved crucial to the educational, occupational, and economic development of the community. Since the 1950s, studies in *yeshivot*, rabbinical academies, previously a privilege of a small elite, became routine for all young men. While Zionist Orthodox also engage in some rabbinical studies, for the ultra-Orthodox it has become a way of life. Men continue their studies after marriage, while their wives work for a living.[17] As a rule, the ultra-Orthodox remain in coalition governments, whoever heads them, to ensure the continuation of this arrangement and the integrity of their communities.

Many observers thought, in the aftermath of WWII, and the Holocaust, that ultra-Orthodoxy would not be able to overcome the deadly blows that the Nazi death machine and the Communist regimes have dealt the traditionalist Jewish

---

15   On Agudat Israel, see Gershon Bacon (1996). *The Politics of Tradition: Agudat Yisrael in Poland.* Jerusalem: Magness Press.

16   On Agudat Israel, see Gershon Bacon (1996). *The Politics of Tradition: Agudat Yisrael in Poland.* Jerusalem: Magness Press.

17   On ultra-Orthodox life and institutions, see Samuel Heilman (2000). *Defenders of the Faith: Inside Ultra-Orthodox Jewry.* Berkley: University of California Press.

communities in Eastern Europe. However, to the amazement of many, including the ultra-Orthodox themselves, the community has risen up, like a phoenix, from the ashes of destruction and suppression, showing signs of vitality and growth. Contrary to warnings, America, Israel and centers in Australia, Canada, England and Belgium, proved to be congenial to the reconstruction and thriving of ultra-Orthodox communities. While previously traditionalist Jews, who settled in the New World, saw a need to acculturate quickly in order to accommodate success-fully to their new environments, the post-Holocaust ultra-Orthodox migrants saw matters differently. They wished to maintain many of their customs, including their distinctive attire, and build an independent educational infrastructure that has en-hanced the community's ability to retain most of its children within the fold.[18]

The separatist, seemingly archaic, character of ultra-Orthodox societies brought sociologists and anthropologists, as well as journalists, writers, and film producers, to take special interest in the various aspects of their lives.[19] Some are fascinated by the arranged marriages that are the norm in the community, while renegade female writers, such as Yochi Brandeis or Judith Rotem, point to the sometimes difficult position of women, who are married of young, and who carry most of the burden of raising large families.[20] Ultra-Orthodox women give birth to averagely five and a half children in the United States and seven children in Israel, about three times more than liberal Jewish women in these countries. Es-pecially in Israel, most ultra-Orthodox live economically frugal existence. In spite of an impressive network of mutual aid and extensive government support, many in community live in poverty, depriving themselves of the luxuries of Western consumer societies.[21]

Relationships between the ultra-Orthodox community and the liberal segments of Israeli society have become strenuous. Many secular Jews resent the separatist nature of the ultra-Orthodox community, and the refraining from economic ac-tivity of so many ultra-Orthodox men. Likewise, the ultra-Orthodox have not cel-ebrated Israeli civil holidays and have not recited prayers for the safety and well-

---

18   Cf. Friedman; Heilman There is an extensive literature from the perspective of women on the division of labor in the ultra-Orthodox community.

19   Cf. Janet Belcove-Shalin (Ed.) (1995). *New World Hasidism*. Albany: SUNY Press.; Cf. Deborah Feldman (2012). Unorthodox: the Scandalous Rejection of my Hasidic Roots. New York: Si-mon and Schuster.; Cf. Lis Harris (1995). Holy Days: The World of a Hasidic Family. New York: Touchstone.; Cf. Samuel Heilman (1992). *Defenders of the Faith: Inside Ultra-Orthodox Judaism*. New York: Schocken Books.

20   There is an extensive literature from the perspective of women on the division of labor in the ultra-Orthodox community. For example, Judith Rotem (1992). *Distant Sister: the Women I Left Behind*. Philadelphia: Jewish Publication Society.

21   See *Life Apart: Hasidism in America*, Documentary, by Menachem Daum and Oren Rudovsky, New York, 1997.

being of the state. The exempt from military service has been a huge source of contention in a country that has had ongoing conscription since its inception.[22]

Still, the community has been on the growth. In addition to a remarkable demographic growth, since the late 1960s, it received unexpected reinforcements from a post-modernist movement of return to tradition that has brought tens of thousands of young men and women to abandon open liberal societies and join the more conservative ultra-Orthodox.[23] Rejecting much of the modernist worldview, which their grandparents' generation had embraced, the new adherents included artists, soldiers, former Kibbutz members, and children of the veteran Israeli elites and, in America, also academicians and professionals. The growing trend has boosted the morale of the ultra-Orthodox. Here are liberal Jews turning their backs on the freedoms and opportunities embodied in the open, secular society, 'coming back' into the fold. A number of ultra-Orthodox groups and leaders decided to create venues of outreach in order to further enlarge the community's ranks. Their mode of evangelism is based on the understanding that becoming observant and joining ultra-Orthodox life is a long process involving extensive studies. For that purpose, they have created a large number of *yeshivot* for beginners, a novelty in Jewish life.

The growth of the ultra-Orthodox community and the self-understanding of its members, who see themselves as representatives of the true and authentic tradition, has affected the more acculturated Zionist Orthodox. The trend since the 1960s has been towards more rigid observance and greater acceptance of ultra-Orthodox norms. By the 1980s, Zionist Orthodox have attempted to combine both sets of values and standards.[24] The *Hardalim*, ultra-Orthodox Zionists, coupled ultra-Orthodox norms of piety and observance with a messianic nationalist faith. Many in the Settlers movement have promoted this combination.

In the 1980s-2010s, the veteran, almost exclusively *Ashkenazi*, ultra-Orthodox community, was both strengthened and challenged by a large movement of religious revival and return to the roots of *Mizrahi* Jews in Israel. Previously, most Jews from Middle Eastern and North African countries were mildly traditional, with only a minority choosing secular outlooks or adhering to Orthodox norms. The new movement changed that reality and brought tens of thousands of *Mizrahi* Jews to adopt both ultra-Orthodox standards of piety and anti-modernist stands.[25]

---

22 On Israeli liberal resentment of Haredi society, see Shahar Ilan (2001). *Haredin LTD.* Jerusalem: Keter.

23 Cf. Lynn Davidman (1993). *Tradition in a Rootless: Women Turn to Orthodox Judaism.* Berkley: University of California Press.

24 On the background to this trend, see Gideon Aran (1991). Jewish Zionist Fundamentalism: Gush Emunim, the Bloc of the Faithful in Israel. In Martin E. Marty and R. Scott Appleby (Eds.). *Fundamentalisms Observed.* Chicago: Chicago University Press, pp. 62-128.

25 Cf. Nissim Leon (2009). *Gentle Ultra-Orthodoxy: Religious Renewal in Oriental Jewry in Israel.* Jerusalem: Yad Yitzhak Ben-Zvi.

The movement also promoted ethnic pride and the preservation of *Mizrahi* culture and tradition. It created parallel political, educational, rabbinical and welfare institutions similar to those of the veteran ultra-Orthodox community and used its new political power to obtain extensive government support.[26]

The political influence of the ultra-Orthodox has been on the rise in Israel. As a rule, the ultra-Orthodox parties offer the government backing in matters that relate to security, foreign-policy, and the economy, in exchange for allowing them exemption from military service, cultural autonomy and financing for separate educational and housing systems. Ultra-Orthodox parties often became essential members of the coalition, and the budgets allocated for their community's educational and housing projects have grown considerably. Similar developments have taken place on the local level, such as in Jerusalem's municipal politics, where the ultra-Orthodox have successfully demanded, in return for their support, to have their neighborhoods closed to traffic on the Sabbath and holidays. This has affected the character of Jerusalem, where many neighborhoods and schools have become ultra-Orthodox. Outside of Israel, the ultra-Orthodox as a rule do not run for offices but lend their support to those candidates that respect their cultural separatism and educational autonomy. The Zionist Orthodox have also been active on the political front and have promoted an educational network for culturally acculturated, modernist Orthodox Jews.

3.   The Nationalist Zionist Orthodox

Zionist Orthodoxy has come on the scene a short while after the rise of political Zionism. The group represented a minority voice within both Jewish Orthodoxy and Zionism. Its proponents established HaMizrahi, a moderate political party that saw its mission in carving a niche for observant Jews who supported the Zionist agenda. HaPoel Hamizrahi, which combined Labor Zionism with moderate observance, became a larger political party, although the two parties united after the birth of the state of Israel. This Moderate stand on politics and piety ended after the June 1967 war. While many Jews reacted with joy to the Israeli victory, seeing in it a triumph of the Zionist project at large, for many in the Zionist Orthodox camp it signified a messianic development. Already during the war, the chief military rabbi who was known for his accommodating rulings, Shlomo Goren, appeared near the Wailing Wall blowing a *shofar*, ram's horn, as if to announce the beginning of Messianic times. About a year after the war, a group of a few dozen Zionist Orthodox,

---

26   On Mizrahi ultra-Orthodox, see David Lehmann and Batia Siebzehner (2006). *Remaking Israeli Judaism: the challenge of Shas.* New York: Oxford University Press.

headed by Rabbi Moshe Levinger (1935-2015), settled in Hebron, disregarding government regulations. In October 1974, this early attempt turned into a large movement. Thousands marched, and hundreds settled, in newly established posts in what had been the West Bank of Jordan, and for the settlers has become Judea and Samaria.[27] For the Zionist Orthodox enthusiasts, building their homes in these areas embodied a messianic purpose. They were taking steps towards the building of David's Messianic kingdom. The Settlers adopted Rabbi Zvi Yehuda Kook as their spiritual leader and source of inspiration. The son of a chief rabbi and a mystic, Abraham Isaac Hacohen Kook, Zvi Yehuda took his father's teachings a few steps further.[28] The Land of Israel has become a central component and a focal point of his and his disciples' theology.

The Settlers' Movement received an enormous boost with the rise of the Likud to power in 1977, moving from a handful of small caravan towns to nicely built neighborhoods subsidized by government funding. The Zionist Orthodox have mobilized politically to defend their settlements from possible restrictions that the Israeli government might impose and to ensure government support for the enlargement of the settlements project. In spite of the Israeli withdrawal from Gaza, the settlers' community has grown considerably, reaching hundreds of thousands of people. It has created its own subculture, complete with its own dress code, a mixture of countercultural attire and ultra-Orthodox norms, and independent media ventures.

While the settlers' community is devoted to Israel and its sons play a growing role in its military, members of the community have at times taken the law into their hands. In 1983, the Israeli security services discovered cells of underground militants among the Settlers that were stocking arms and ammunition in preparation for a possible clash with the Israeli state and its security forces, in case of an Israeli attempt to withdraw from the occupied territories and evacuate the settlements.[29] There have also been at times incidents of violence directed against Palestinians, allegedly in retaliation against terrorist acts directed against Jews. These have included the destruction of trees, injuring mayors of Palestinian towns, and even incidents that resulted in fatalities. While most settlers have not resorted to underground activities or to sabotage or harassment of Palestinians, the settlers'

27　On the gradual up hazard building of a large infrastructure of settlements, see Gershom Gorenberg (2007). *The Accidental Empire: Israel and the Birth of the Settlements, 1967-1977.* London: Macmillan.

28　Cf. Gideon Aran (1997). The Father, the Son and the Holy Land. In R. Scott Appleby (Ed.). *Spokesmen for the Despised: Fundamentalist Leaders of the Middle East.* Chicago: Chicago University Press, pp. 294-327.

29　Cf. Ehud Sprinzak (1991). *The Ascendance of Israel's Radical Right.* New York: Oxford University Press.; Cf. Robert I. Friedman (1992). *Zealots for Zion: Inside Israel's West Bank Settlement Movement.* New York: Random House.

camp as a whole has stood on the radical side of the Israeli political and ideological spectrum and many have come to see it as a potential obstacle to a peace agreement and to an atmosphere of reconciliation between Arabs and Jews.

4. Preparing to Build the Temple

Of special concern for peace-hopefuls, in Israel and other countries, as well as security services, has been the possibility that Messianic oriented radical Jews or Christians might heart the Muslim mosques on the Temple Mount and bring about a regional doomsday.[30] In order to appreciate this fear, one has to examine the role of the Temple and the Land of Israel in Jewish, as well as Christian and Muslim thought.

The Temple in Jerusalem had been a central institution in Israelite religion, as well as in the Judaism of the Second Temple period. For Jews of that period, the Temple served as the ultimate spiritual point on earth, a place where it was possible for them to atone for their sins and reconcile with God in a definite manner. Pilgrimages to the Temple in Jerusalem were essential rites. The Temple developed into a unifying symbol for a growingly diverse Jewish community around the Mediterranean world.[31] The destruction of the Temple in 70 CE created therefore a serious vacuum in Jewish communal and spiritual life. Instead of a physical temple, rabbinical Judaism put its premium on sacred texts, and promoted a "temple in time," as the weekly Sabbath had become a holy day, similar in sanctity to a holy place. Jews purified themselves in honor of the Sabbath and entered the holy day in the same manner they would enter a holy place, cleaning their bodies, wearing special cloths, preparing festive meals, lighting candles and recite special prayers. Synagogues, "houses of gatherings" in Hebrew, came about during the Second Temple period and developed, after the Temple's destruction, into houses of worship and learning, where Jews prayed and read sacred texts.

Still, Jews prayed to God to gather them back to Zion, rebuild Jerusalem, recreate the Temple and enable them to atone for their sins and reconcile with God. The Temple came to symbolize redemption. Rabbis have spent time on issues relating to the Temple, its measures, sacrificial system, and the alms and donations presented to it. Most rabbinical authorities throughout the Middle Ages and Modern Era have viewed the Temple Mount as being as sacred as it was when the Temple

---

30   Yaakov Ariel (2001). Doomsday in Jerusalem? Christian Messianic Groups and the Rebuilding of the Temple. *Terrorism and Political Violence*, Vol. 13, No. 1. Spring, 1-14.
31   Yaakov Ariel (2016). Tempel. In Dan Diner (Ed.). *Enzyklopädie jüdischer Geschichte und Kultur.* Bd. 6, pp. 62-65.

was standing.[32] The Mishnah, the post-Biblical compilation of lore and law, out-lined the various degrees of sanctity of areas on the Temple Mount and the rituals of purification people needed to perform in order to enter these areas. Jews have been required to purify themselves with the ashes of a Red Heifer before entering the Mount, although there are no longer red heifers to be found. Rabbis have also feared that Jews might step on restricted sacred ground, such as the Holy of Holies, onto which ordinary Jews, and even ordinary priests, are not allowed to enter. Most Jews have accepted the rabbinical ban and saw entrance to the Temple Mount as taboo. However, Jews had not much to say about the manner in which the Temple Mount was governed. Between the destruction of the Temple in 70 CE and 1967, the Temple Mount had been ruled by Pagans, Christians and Muslims. In the seventh and eighth century C.E., the new rulers of the city have turned the mountain into a sacred Muslim site, building a number of mosques and chapels.[33]

In June 1967, when Israel conquered East Jerusalem, including the Temple Mount, the results of the war symbolized to many Israelis an historical victory, the realization of an old dream. However most Israelis did not wish to rebuild the Temple. By this time, the Temple Mount was a Muslim site, administered by a Muslim *Waqf* (religious endowment) and both secular and observant Jews had no interest anymore in building the Temple. The Israeli government proclaimed its wish to maintain the *status quo ante bellum* on the Temple Mount as well as in other Muslim and Christian holy sites. The chief Israeli rabbis of that time, Yitzhak Nissim and Issar Unterman, even issued a declaration that Jews were forbidden to enter the Temple Mount. In 1967, voices, such as that of Shlomo Goren, who wished to establish a synagogue on the Temple Mount, were in the minority. The mood in Israel changed after the war of 1973. Paradoxically, external threats to Israel's territorial gains, whether through war or peace negotiations, have inspired Jewish religious nationalists to take a proactive stand, including their determination to see the Temple rebuilt.[34]

Not all Jewish settlers in the West Bank have been interested in building the Temple in an immediate way. Similarly, not all Jewish Temple Builders are settlers. However, the Temple Builders' Movement has shared a great deal in its theology, ideology, and community with the Settlers' Movement. Since the 1980s, both move-ments have been part of Israel's Radical Right and currently many of the would-be Temple Builders live in settlements.

---

32   Cf. Mishnah, Tractate *Middot*. Measures. Translated by Jacon Neusner (1988). New Haven: Yale University Press, pp. 873-882.

33   On the Temple Mount, see Yitzhak Reiter (2001). *Sovereignty of God and Men: Sanctity and Po-litical Centrality on the Temple Mount*. Jerusalem: Jerusalem Institute.

34   Cf. Motti Inbari (2012). *Messianic Religious Zionism Confronts Israeli Territorial Compromises*. New York: Cambridge University Press.

Groups of Temple-Builders reinterpreted Jewish texts, placing greater emphasize on sacred space than most Jews had done in the Middle Ages and Modern Era. Rejecting the understanding that the building of the Temple should be left for the Messiah to accomplish at the Fullness of Time, radical Zionist Orthodox thinkers have declared the traditional rabbinical ban on entering the Temple Mount to be erroneous and null.

The first organization of Temple-Builders was the Temple Mount and Land of Israel Faithful. Led by Gershon Solomon, a disabled IDF veteran and a lawyer, the Temple Mount Faithful gave voice at its inception, in the 1970s, to a large variety of Jews interested in the building of the Temple. Its periodic attempts to enter the Temple Mount, and organize prayers there, have enjoyed much media coverage. In the 1980s, Rabbi Joel Bin Nun, a leader of the now defunct *Gush Emunim*, the Settlers' major organization in the 1970s, established an institute for the halachic study of the building of the Temple. In a series of publications he pointed to what he considered to be the merits of the Temple and the sacrifices therein, which he believed would help reconcile God and humanity, and would therefore help bring about a messianic age. Other groups that formed during the 1980s-2010s, have included, among others: *Reshit-Yerushaliim*, Jerusalem First, an Academy for Studying Jerusalem and the Temple; *Ha Tnuaa Lekinun ha Mikdash*, the Movement for the Building of the Temple; *Yeshivat Torat HaBayit*, The Temple-Laws Yeshiva; *El Har Adonai*, Unto the Mountain of the Lord; *Ha Tnuaa LeShihrur Har HaBayit*, the Movement for the Liberation of the Temple Mount; and *Yeshivat Ateret Cohanim* The Priest's Crown Yeshiva.[35]

Jewish movements that have strived to build the Temple would not have carried their activities the way they did if it were not for evangelical Christians providing encouragement and assistance. Christian thinkers had traditionally seen the Temple as redundant after Jesus' sacrifice on the Cross and interpreted the destruction of the Temple in 70 CE as resulting from the Jewish unwillingness to acknowledge Jesus' role and mission. The idea that the Jews should go back to Palestine and rebuild Jerusalem and the Temple became predominant among Christian Messianic groups, especially pietist and evangelical Protestants. After the 1967 war, evangelicals with messianic yearnings have come more than before to expect the building of the Temple at the end of the current era, in preparation for the return of the Messiah to earth. In such scenarios, they often expect Antichrist, an imposter of the Messiah, to achieve global power and initiate the building of the Temple. The Temple, or rather its rebuilding, seemed to evangelical Christians to be the one event standing between this era and the next.

In the late 1970s and the 1980s, premillennialist Christians and groups of Orthodox Jews, holding to an expansionist and messianic visions, including the building

---

35   Cf. Motti Inbari (2009). *Jewish Fundamentalists and the Temple Mount*. Albany: SUNY Press.

of the Temple, discovered each other. Such Christians have received reassurance for their messianic faith from Jews who were studying the Temple rituals, and manufactured utensils for sacrificial purposes according to biblical or Talmudic measures. Similarly, Orthodox Jews received reassurances from interest and support, which Christians demonstrated. Initially, Jewish proponents of the building of the Temple did not appreciate the Christian faith more than Christian messianic groups appreciated the intrinsic value of the Jewish faith, but they saw such details as being beside the point. The important thing for them has been the Christian willingness to support their work.[36]

Christian proponents of building the Temple have made efforts to discover the exact site of the Temple. Some have searched for the lost Ark of the Covenant, adding a touch of adventure and mystery to a potentially explosive topic. The search for the "Lost Ark" has inspired a number of novels and a movie based in part on a real life figure. Some premillennialist evangelicals have also searched for the ashes of the Red Heifer, which are necessary, according to Jewish law, in order to allow Jews to enter the Temple Mount, while others have supported Jewish attempts at breeding red heifers or began breeding such heifers on their own.

Pat Robertson, the renowned leader of the 700 Club and a one-time presidential hopeful, offered his support and hospitality to Gershon Solomon. In August 1991, the 700 Club aired an interview with Solomon. Robertson described Solomon's group as struggling to gain a rightful place for Jews on the Temple Mount. "We will never have peace," Robertson declared, "until the Mount of the House of the Lord is restored."[37] Solomon, for his part, described his mission as embodying the promise for a universal redemption. "It's not just a struggle for the Temple Mount, it's a struggle for the . . . redemption of the world," he declared.[38]

Examination of the mutual enchantment between evangelical Christians and Orthodox Jews, such as Robertson and Solomon, shows mutual influences. Solomon, for example, claimed to have divine revelations, not unlike those among evangelical charismatic Christians. Jewish would-be builders of the Temple have also changed their opinion on Christians, impressed by the keen Christian interest and support.[39] Those Christians, they discovered, were more enthusiastic about the prospect of building the Temple than most Jews. The theology and message of people, such as Gershon Solomon, has come to include Christians as important participants in the divine drama of salvation. Resurfacing the traditional Jewish idea that since the days of Noah all of humanity is in covenant with God, Jewish

---

36   Yaakov Ariel (2013). *An Unusual Relationship: Evangelical Christians and Jews*. New York: New York University Press, pp. 198-213.
37   Cf. Robert I. Friedman (1982). *Zealots for Zion*. New York: Random House, pp.144-145.
38   Ib.
39   Cf. Ariel (2013).

radical thinkers of the Settlers Movement are claiming that Christians too have to strive and make an effort towards the advancement of the messianic times.

In assessing the tensions embodied in the struggle for the Temple Mount, one needs to take into consideration also the strong feelings of the local Muslim community and the support and sympathy of Muslims worldwide. An adversarial symbiosis has developed between Muslims and the Jewish and Christian Temple Builders. The agenda of some Jewish and Christian groups that wish to change the status quo on the Temple Mount, has served to fuel and enhance Palestinian territorial claims. Throughout the 1970s-2010s, the Temple Mount, or the Haram al Sharif, became a symbol of national liberation for Palestinian Muslims and their regard for the Mount has become even more pronounced. Sovereignty over the Mount played a prominent part in the peace talks that took place between Palestinians and Israelis in the late 1990s, and Ariel Sharon's visit to the Temple Mount in September 2000 served as a starting point of the Second *Intifada*. Protecting the Temple Mount mosques became a priority for the Israeli security services. Even symbolic attempts to claim the Temple Mount as a Jewish site have had explosive consequences. On *Sukkot*, the Feast of the Tabernacles, October 1990, the Temple Mount Faithful planned to enter the Temple Mount, and this time to lay a corner stone for the future Temple. The police, however, refused to allow them entrance and they left the place. But Muslim worshipers on the Mount felt threatened, and threw rocks at Jewish worshipers in the Wailing Wall. The atmosphere became volatile, as Muslim demonstrators chased the small police unit out of the Mountain, and Israeli anti-riot police stormed the area a short while later. Dozens of demonstrators and police officers were killed or wounded. The possibility that acts inspired by groups holding to messianic hopes would bring about a mini-apocalypse therefore became a concern for those taking interest in the developments in the Middle East. Should the mosques be seriously damaged, all hell will break loose.

Laboring towards the rebuilding the Temple concerns groups of nationalist Orthodox and represents their larger religious nationalist agenda. This is not the case for most members of the ultra-Orthodox communities. The differences between the two camps reached a crescendo during the first months of the Corona epidemic.

5.   Ultra-Orthodox and Nationalist Orthodox in Corona Times

During the first months of the Corona epidemic, the differences between Nationalist 'modern' Orthodoxy, and the more separatist ultra-Orthodox became evident as never before. Both Orthodox streams are committed to preserving Jewish identity and tradition. Both believe in the need to maintain the *Halacha* and observe Jewish law and Jewish rituals. The movements differ, however, in the means to achieve that goal and over their understanding of the place of observant Jews vis a vis the open non-observant, or non-Jewish society. The Corona pandemic sharpened the different paths the two communities have taken, enhancing rift and animosity.

As the Corona pandemic unfolded the Zionist Orthodox, in Israel, America, and other countries, reacted in a manner not much different from non-Orthodox Jews and non-Jews in the communities around them. This was true both in the measures they took in the private sphere as well as the public. The realities of the Corona Pandemic forced almost all Jewish groups to modify their religious rituals.[40] To the ultra-Orthodox, it took longer to realize the scope and danger of the plague and to adapt to the newly introduced rules and regulations of keeping distance, covering faces and avoiding gatherings. Leading rabbis were initially reluctant to permit their followers to follow the Corona prevention guidelines, which meant closing synagogues, or altering modes of prayer. Likewise, yeshivot remained open even as other academies and schools shut their doors. Some rabbis changed their minds and asked community members to comply with the regulations, which many of them did, even if belatedly and reluctantly.

This resulted in particularly high numbers of sick and dying in the ultra-Orthodox communities. It did not help that members of the community have lived in poor and crowded homes and neighborhoods, and that the celebrations of religious rituals, which are important to members of the community, are often marked by physical proximity of multiple participants. Many in the more liberal Jewish communities chastised the ultra-Orthodox. So did the national Orthodox. They pointed a finger at the ultra-Orthodox as betraying the Jewish dictum of putting safety of life above all. Zionist Orthodox clearly cast their vote in the modernist ballot, and felt morally superior to, as well as more sophisticated than the separatist ultra-Orthodox.

Coming to the defense of the ultra-Orthodox, Shaul Magid wrote: "The Haredim are certainly aware of avoiding danger. The question is more about authority – who gets to determine danger and who gets to dictate what activities need to cease in light of it."[41]

Conclusion

The Corona epidemic has highlighted the differences between the Haredim, ultra-Orthodox and the Zionist national Orthodox as never before. Granted, there are

---

40   Cf. Ejewish Philantrophy (2020). Preserving these moments. A call to action for the American Jewish Community. July 24, 2020. See: https://ejewishphilanthropy.com/preserving-these-m oments-a-call-to-action-for-the-american-jewish-community/

41   Shaul Magid (2020). Covid19, Haredi Judaism, and Magical Thinking. *Tablet*. April 30, p. 2.

strong similarities between the worldviews of the ultra-Orthodox and Zionist Orthodox. Both groups relate with owe to the Jewish sacred texts as the foundation of their religious tradition. Both view the biblical narratives as the basis of what they consider the special relationship between God, the people of Israel, and, especially in the case of the Zionist Orthodox, the Land of Israel. Both communities are messianic in their theologies and yearnings, directing their lives towards the arrival of the Messianic times.

However, the two groups have promoted different paths to achieve that goal. National Orthodox have participated in the Zionist endeavor, at first as minor participants. Since 1967, the Zionist Orthodox have become more nationalist and right wing than most other segments of the Jewish population. The ultra-Orthodox have traditionally resented the politically pro-active expansionist Zionist agenda, although they too see themselves as troopers in God's army, struggling, through prayers, studies and righteous lives to bring in the Messianic age. A number of ultra-Orthodox groups, most notably the Hasidic group Chabad, have become engaged in outreach, wishing to bring more people to fulfil the commandments as a means of ushering in the Messianic times.

While in the last decades the Zionist Orthodox have strengthened their standards of daily observance and commitment to studying rabbinical texts, the two communities are far removed from each other in their life choices, lifestyles, and areas of residency. The two streams of Judaism have different sources of authority and relate very differently to the non-Orthodox world. The Zionist Orthodox have embraced Modern science, incorporated liberal education alongside the study of sacred texts, and have allowed women a growing amount of traditional education. While Zionist Orthodox women also cover their hair and body, they study, obtain degrees, and build secular careers. Women of both communities are committed to pro-creation with the aim of enlarging the community and ensure the continuity of the Jewish people. Except that the growth of the number of Zionist Orthodox children has been motivated in no small measure by nationalist concerns over Israel's demographic strength.

The Corona pandemic created a dramatic rift between the Zionist Orthodox and the ultra-Orthodox. The dangers of the disease forced both groups to show their colors and identify as either: a separatist community that has its own norms, sources of authority and priorities; or as a modernist community, part of a larger civic society, abiding by the standards and laws of the land. Already in middle months of 2020, as the Corona epidemic spread globally, it become apparent that the pandemic and its devastating effects highlight the character of the Orthodox communities as well as altered it in some measures.

Only when the plague is over will we be able to assess the full scope of the challenges that the communities have faced and examine the long-range effects of the pandemic to the inner life of the community, as well as to its relationship with the Zionist Orthodox and with non-Orthodox Jews.

Bibliography

Aran, Gideon (1991). Jewish Zionist Fundamentalism: Gush Emunim, the Bloc of the Faithful in Israel. In Martin E. Marty and R. Scott Appleby (Eds.). *Fundamentalisms Observed*. Chicago: Chicago University Press, pp. 62-128.

Aran, Gideon (1997). *The* Father, the Son and the Holy Land. In R. Scott Appleby (Ed.). *Spokesmen for the Despised: Fundamentalist Leaders of the Middle East*. Chicago: Chicago University Press, pp. 294-327.

Ariel, Yaakov (2016). Tempel. In Dan Diner (Ed.). *Enzyklopädie jüdischer Geschichte und Kultur*. Bd. 6, pp. 62-65.

Ariel, Yaakov (2001). 'Doomsday in Jerusalem? Christian Messianic Groups and the Rebuilding of the Temple'. *Terrorism and Political Violence*, Vol. 13, No. 1. Spring, 1-14.

Ariel, Yaakov (2013). *An Unusual Relationship: Evangelical Christians and Jews*. New York: New York University Press. pp. 198-213.

Bacon, Gershon (1996). *The Politics of Tradition: Agudat Yisrael in Poland*. Jerusalem: Magness Press.

Belcove-Shalin, Janet (Ed.) (1995). *New World Hasidism*. Albany: SUNY Press.

Breuer, Mordechai (1992). *Modernity within Tradition*. New York: Columbia University Press.

Daum, Menachem, and Rudovsky, Oren (1997). *Life Apart: Hasidism in America*. Documentary. New York.

Davidman, Lynn (1993). *Tradition in a Rootless: Women Turn to Orthodox Judaism*. Berkley: University of California Press.

Feldman, Deborah (2012). Unorthodox: the Scandalous Rejection of my Hasidic Roots. New York: Simon and Schuster.

Friedman, Menachem (1991). *The Haredi (ultra-Orthodox) Society*. Jerusalem: Jerusalem Institute.

Friedman, Robert I. (1992). *Zealots for Zion: Inside Israel's West Bank Settlement Movement*. New York: Random House.

Friedman, Robert I. (1982). *Zealots for Zion*. New York: Random House.

Gorenberg, Gershom (2007). *The Accidental Empire: Israel and the Birth of the Settlements, 1967-1977*. London: Macmillan.

Harris, Lis (1995). Holy Days: The World of a Hasidic Family. New York: Touchstone.

Heilman, Samuel (1992). *Defenders of the Faith: Inside Ultra-Orthodox Judaism*. New York: Schocken Books.

Heilman, Samuel (2000). *Defenders of the Faith: Inside Ultra-Orthodox Jewry*. Berkley: University of California Press.

Shahar Ilan (2001). *Haredin LTD*. Jerusalem: Keter.

Inbari, Motti (2009). *Jewish Fundamentalists and the Temple Mount*. Albany: SUNY Press.

Inbari, Motti (2012). *Messianic Religious Zionism Confronts Israeli Territorial Compromises*. New York: Cambridge University Press.

Inbari, Motti (2016). *Jewish Radical ultra-Orthodoxy Confronts Modernity*. New York: Cambridge University Press.

Kahana, Maoz (2015). *From the Noda BeYehuda to the Hatam Sofer: Halacha and Thought in Response to the Challenges of the Time*. Jerusalem: Zalman Shazar.

Katz, Jacob (1973). *Out of the Ghetto: the Social Background of Jewish Emancipation*. Syracuse: Syracuse University Press.

Lehmann, David, and Siebzehner, Batia (2006). *Remaking Israeli Judaism: the challenge of Shas*. New York: Oxford University Press.

Leon, Nissim (2009). *Gentle Ultra-Orthodoxy: Religious Renewal in Oriental Jewry in Israel*. Jerusalem: Yad Yitzhak Ben-Zvi.

Magid, Shaul (2020). 'Covid19, Haredi Judaism, and Magical Thinking'. *Tablet*. April 30, p. 2.

Marsden, George (1982). *Fundamentalism and American Culture: the Shaping of Twentieth Century Evangelicalism, 1870-1925*. New York: Oxford University Press.

Mayer, Michael (1995). *Response to Modernity: A History of the Reform Movement in Judaism*. Detroit: Wayne State University Press.

Mishna. Translated by Jacon Neusner (1988). New Haven: Yale University Press.

Ravitzky, Aviezer (1996). *Messianism, Zionism, and Jewish Religious Radicalism*. Chicago: Chicago University Press.

Reiter, Yitzhak (2001). *Sovereignty of God and Men: Sanctity and Political Centrality on the Temple Mount*. Jerusalem: Jerusalem Institute.

Rotem, Judith (1992). *Distant Sister: the Women I Left Behind*. Philadelphia: Jewish Publication Society.

Silber, Michael (1992). The Invention of Ultra-Orthodoxy: the Emergence of a Tradition. In Jack Wertheimer (Ed.). *The Uses of Tradition: Jewish Community in the Modern Era*. New York: Jewish Theological Seminary, pp. 23-82.

Sprinzak, Ehud (1991). *The Ascendance of Israel's Radical Right*. New York: Oxford University Press.

Weber, Timothy (1983). *Living in the Shadow of the Second Coming: American Premillennialism*. Grand Rapids: Zondervan.

Online Open Sources

Ejewish Philantrophy (2020). 'Preserving these moments. A call to action for the American Jewish Community'. July 24, 2020. URL: https://ejewishphilanthrop

y.com/preserving-these-moments-a-call-to-action-for-the-american-jewish-community/

Kashti, Or (2020). *Haaretz*. URL: https://www.haaretz.co.il/news/education/.premium-1.8999355

Pfeffer, Anshel (2020). *Haaretz*. April 28. URL: https://www.haaretz.co.il/health/corona/.premium-MAGAZINE-1.8803930

Netflix (2020). *Unorthodox*. URL: https://www.imdb.com/title/tt9815454/

The Impact of Covid-19 on Orthodox Groups and Believers in Russia

Anastasia V. Mitrofanova

Abstract

This chapter intends to discover how Orthodox groups and believers of different ideological orientations in Russia reacted to the 2020 world health crisis. Its focus lies on the groups and individual believers from the field of Russian Orthodoxy who could be labelled as 'fundamentalists'. Therefore, an analysis of the official ecclesiastical reaction to the pandemic will be provided, that underlines how some contradictory messages from above caused significant numbers of believers to sympathize with the so called "corona-dissidents" within the Church. Under the topic 'dissidents', various other groups apart from the fundamentalists such as the moderate traditionalists, liberals, or individuals who usually follow the mainstream ecclesiastical opinion, can be subsumed.

Furthermore, it could be observed that fundamentalists mostly discuss themes that might be common for all "dissidents", although they are more open towards their criticism in view of the mainstream reactions. They stick to the assumption that both mundane and ecclesiastical leaders have discredited themselves and need to be replaced.

Keywords: Orthodox Christianity, Covid-19, Ecclesiastical Lockdown, Corona-Dissidents, Fundamentalist Networks, Traditionalism, Russian Orthodox Church

1. Introduction

This chapter intends to discover how Orthodox groups and believers of different ideological orientations in Russia reacted to the 2020 world health crisis. It focusses on groups and individuals who are labelled as "fundamentalists", because they believe for instance that the entire socio-political life should be changed in terms of collective religious salvation.[1] Apart from the official position of the Moscow Patriarchate («the patriarchal platform»), Irina Papkova distinguishes three informal political ideologies within the Russian Orthodox Church (ROC): liberal (associated with intra-church movements initiated by late Fr. Aleksandr Men' and Fr. Georgii Kochetkov), traditionalist, and fundamentalist. Traditionalists are more conservative than the patriarchal platform, and, unlike fundamentalists, willing to work constructively with the post-Soviet regime; their position is prevalent among the majority of clergy and active believers.[2] The situation with Covid-19 confirms that it should not be automatically associated with the official position.

There is no strict border between the traditionalist and fundamentalist platforms and sometimes they share each other's ideologies; but the former remain loyal to mundane and ecclesiastical authorities, while the latter are in the opposition to both hierarchies.[3] Fundamentalists are not ultra-traditionalists; paradoxically, they have many things in common with liberals: both platforms show distrust towards the church hierarchy and the mundane authorities, because both groups refuse the current administration of the church and want to expand the role of laity.

According to Papkova, liberals are reformists, while fundamentalists follow invented traditions.[4] In fact, the latter are no less reformist than the former: fundamentalists often appear as the most radical reformists with revolutionary intentions in comparison to the liberals who seem to be more interested in «restoring traditions» in view of an ecclesiastical reform.[5]

Though the ROC's jurisdiction covers many countries, the present chapter concentrates on the discussion of the various positions of believers and groups who are operating on the territory of the Russian Federation. Because of this focus, opinions of the other Orthodox Churches will not be considered. In addition, other opinions don't represent a common position in view of the pandemic, whereas the policy of ROC mostly bases on the decisions of Russian authorities.

---

1   Anastasia V. Mitrofanova (2014). Orthodox Fundamentalism: Intersection of Modernity, Postmodernity and Tradition. In K. Tolstaya (Ed.). *Orthodox Paradoxes: Heterogeneities and Complexities in Contemporary Russian Orthodoxy.* Leiden, Boston: Brill, p. 101.

2   Irina Papkova (2011). *The Orthodox Church and Russian Politics.* New York: Oxford UP and Woodrow Wilson Center Press, pp. 47, 51-53.

3   Some scholars use both terms to characterize social movements like *Sorok Sorokov,* e.g. Roman Lunkin (2017). Dvizhenie «Sorok Sorokov»: pravoslavnyi fundamentalizm vo vrazhdebnom okruzhenii. *Religiya i pravo.* September 18. See: http://www.sclj.ru /news/detail.php?SECTION_ID =484&ELEMENT_ID =7677&fbclid= IwAR12Bz_ Pb81 f SwLtki8NKrpQ8YOsoefMe7jnYiNt3PoDDmem2lHBZJpkO5A

4   Lunkin, 2017, pp. 53, 61.

5   For instance, liberals promote a restored Liturgy of Saint James as a more laity-centered but also the oldest known form of liturgy.

Apart from a loose network of communities and individuals known as «non-commemorating» believers, who e.g. insist on remaining part of the ROC, while refusing to commemorate Patriarch Kirill and/or other bishops liturgically, alternative Orthodox groups in Russia will neither be analysed. Many fundamentalists, although not all of them, are part of this network. It exists no single ecclesiastical community nor a "church" solely for the fundamentalists. Some of the not so radical believers often attend mainstream, "commemorating" communities. Generally speaking, fundamentalists are less interested in the formal relationship between a priest and the hierarchy, but in terms of his decisions in view of sensitive religious-political issues.

The chapter's methodology is based on the analysis of open access materials produced by Orthodox groups and individuals responding to the emerging challenge of the global pandemic. With regard to immediate reactions of people and groups to that topic, video blogs (mostly YouTube-hosted) and social media (Facebook, Telegram, Vkontakte) are extensively examined. Last years' most important speakers issued more videos than texts, although most of them were "talking heads videos". The fact that people present most of their ideas rather visually than verbally can be partly explained by the general popularity of social media that hardly overran traditional blogging. Furthermore, videos are less likely to be monitored and removed from the Internet than texts. With respect to some of the aforementioned points, the author refers to her own observations according to the national lockdown in Russia.

The analysis of the official patriarchal position is based on documents that have been issued by the Patriarch's Office, the Working group for the coordination of the activities of ecclesiastical bodies according the circumstances of the transmission of the infection with the coronavirus, or by separate bishoprics. Further sources are the Patriarch's public speeches and sermons, statements released by Vladimir Legoyda, the Chairman of the Synodal Department for the Church's Relations with Society and Mass Media and official spokesperson for the Church in view of mass media, and Legoyda's official Telegram-account. To demonstrate that the Patriarch's policy of ecclesiastical lockdown has provoked mixed reactions, the author turns to diverse public figures representing positions from total support of the patriarchal platform to critical evaluations but without invectives against ecclesiastical or mundane authorities. Generally speaking, people who distrust official information about the pandemic have become known in Russia as "corona-dissidents", or "corona-sceptics". Conspiracy theories, propagated by some of them, such as the idea that the disease is being caused by 5G wireless technologies, are loaned from Western anti-Covid discourses, because in Russia 5G is not in use so far.[6]

Finally the author analyses various positions within fundamentalist networks by showing a broad spectrum of their opinions. Therefore, she firstly discusses the position of these individuals who balance between traditionalism and fundamentalism such as Andrei Kormoukhin, the leader of *Sorok Sorokov*, a social movement, Schemahegumen Sergii Romanov, the founder and former spiritual father of a convent in the Urals and Sergii (Ruslan) Aliev, a sportsman, philanthropist and entrepreneur from Yekaterinburg. In a second step, the ideas of non-commemorating believers such as Schemahegumen Daniil (Filippov), a spiritual leader of a non-commemorating community that hides in a remote abandoned village and spreads its ideas via YouTube[7] will be discussed. Furthermore, the concept of militant, highly politicized activists such as Andrei Saveliev, the leader of an unregistered party called "Great Russia", as well as the ideas of Colonel Ret. Vladimir Kvachkov, the informal leader of the most radical fundamentalists and Russian nationalists, who developed a specific ideology of "Russian Christian Socialism",[8] are debated. In this context it is noteworthy, that the website "Moscow the Third Rome", owned by Aleksei Dobychin, provides an aggregator of the news from around the world and has become an important source of various opinions.

2.   The Patriarchal Stay-at-home Policy and its vulnerabilities

Ecclesiastical leaders in Russia were aware of the approaching challenges well beforehand: already in the midst of March 2020 divine services were suspended in the ROC's parishes located in Europe.[9] For instance the Diocese of the Russian Orthodox Church in Spain and Portugal discontinued public worships on March 14th,

---

6   Russian corona-dissidents developed this theory quickly: it was reported that at least one mobile mast had been set on fire in the region of North Ossetia. The perpetrators were, most likely, not religiously motivated. Participants of a major anti-lockdown meeting that took place in the same region and was organized by the neo-Communist Vadim Chaldiev were also not religiously motivated.

7   Viktor Shnirelman (2017). *Koleno Danovo. Eskhatologiya i antisemitizm v sovremennoi Rossii.* Moscow: BBI, pp. 523-524.

8   Colonel Kvachkov spent twelve years in detention in total: The first time he was arrested for preparing an assasination on Anatolii Chubais in the year 2005 (vindicated by a jury), the second time he went to prison because of an attempt to initialize an armed revolt in the year 2010, and the third time he was imprisoned for public extremist declarations in the year 2017. Kvachkov was released in early February 2019 because hate speech had been decriminalized and reclassified as minor offence in Russia.

9   Roman Lunkin (2020). Mekhanizmy religioznoi reaktsii na pandemiyu koronavirusa. In *Nauchno-analiticheskii verstnik IE RAN*, No. 2, pp. 104-109.

the Latvian Orthodox Church (autonomous within the ROC) did so on March 15th. At that moment, the number of confirmed coronavirus cases in Russia were officially estimated by only 48; no severe lockdown measures had been discussed so far within Russia.

Nevertheless, some monasteries, such as Sretensky in Moscow, started online video streaming of their divine services. On March 18th, all spiritual schools of the ROC went online, following the example of the secular universities. On March 23rd, the Patriarch's Office established a Working group for the activities of ecclesiastical bodies according the circumstances of the transmission of the infection with the coronavirus under the leadership of the Metropolitan Dionisii (Porubai), Chancellor of the Moscow Patriarchy.

From the very beginning, the official position of the ROC assumed demonstrating its loyalty to the state and its willingness to obey the public health regulations. Potentially it was a source of misunderstandings, because Orthodox Christian rituals and daily practices imply multiple physical contacts between people, as well as between people and sacred objects. Believers usually kiss icons, relics, hands of priests; priests kiss each other in the altar during the Divine Liturgy and in consolidated parish communities existed also the exchange of the "kiss of peace". Church buildings are often overcrowded (especially in big cities) and poorly ventilated. Usually, all of the believers share glasses of water mixed with wine as well as cups for holy water that they drink separately after they have received the communion. In view of the pandemic, the tradition to receive the communion from one chalice and the use of one liturgical spoon, pose a specific threat to the believers. To prevent the Blood of Christ from spilling all lips after Communion are wiped with a single piece of red cloth. Some parishes, well before Covid-19, introduced the practices of using disposable post-communion cups, or wet-wiping icons after each worshiper's kiss. Still, the practice of using shared spoons and clothes with regard to the communion remained inviolable and non-discussible, at least in public.

Coronavirus abruptly changed everything. On March 17th, the Patriarch issued instructions for all parishes and monasteries in Moscow that demanded sterilizing liturgical spoons with ethanol after each communion and the use of disposable paper napkins for wiping lips that must be burned subsequently.[10] This order, later reproduced by most bishops in their dioceses, has led to many troubles that will be discussed in the following.

In early April 2020, special rules were introduced for giving communion to people presumably infected with Covid-19; priests had to wear disposable personal

---

10   Cf. Russkaya Pravoslavnaya Tserkov. (2020). Instruktsiya nastoyatelyam prikhodov i podvorii, igumenam i igumeniyam monastyrei Moskovskoi eparkhii v svyazi s ugrozoi rasprostraneniya koronavirusnoi infektsii. *Russkaya Pravoslavnaya Tserkov. Official web site of the Moscow Patriarchy.* March 17. See: http://www.patriarchia.ru/db/text/5608418.html

protection equipment (PPEs) and the communion was allowed to be given only in the form of the Presanctified Gifts[11]. In addition, the Patriarch announced that penalties would be given to clerics who have not been following these hygienic rules of procedure by the Ecclesiastical court.[12]

In June, when the lockdown in Moscow was close to the end, the Metropolitan Dionicii additionally issued a letter, demanding all priest to wear face masks, also during the confessions.[13]

More troubles for the Church were ahead as the national epidemic situation worsened and state officials were leaning towards introducing the lockdown that was commonly called "self-isolation regime"[14] in Russia.

Due to the fact that Russia is a federation, epidemic situations in its regions varied. Therefore, on April 2nd the President granted additional rights to the heads of federal subjects and enabled them with a right to establish protective measures they might find appropriate in terms of their territories. As a result, the national lockdown was established in March 30th, but in some parts of Russia regional authorities suspended public divine services earlier, for instance in the Republic of Karelia, where it was established on March 27th or in St.-Petersburg where it has been established on March 28th. Local bishops had to make their decisions about ecclesiastical lockdowns depending on their personal relations with regional officials. In some bishoprics public worships continued – either with the permission of regional authorities, e.g. in Novosibirsk oblast, or without it, in Sverdlovsk oblast.[15]

Moscow, the capital city, inhabited by 13 million people and constituting a separate federal subject, was affected increasingly and earlier by Covid-19 than other

---

11   Cf. Russkaya Pravoslavnaya Tserkov (2020). Pravila dlya soversheniya treb na domu i v lecheb-nykh uchrezhdeniyakh pri poseshchenii lyudei, nakhodyashchikhsya v rezhime izolyatsii, svyazannoi s opasnostiyu zarazheniya, ili zarazhennykh koronavirusnoi infektsiei. *Russkaya Pravoslavnaya Tserkov. Official web site of the Moscow Patriarchy.* April 6. See: http://www.patria rchia.ru/db/text/5618000.html

12   Cf. Russkaya Pravoslavnaya Tserkov (2020). Rasporyazhenie Svyateishego Patriarcha Kirilla ob otvetstvennosti za nesoblyudenie ukazanii, napravlennykh na ogranichenie rasprostra-neniya koronavirusnoi infektsii. *Russkaya Pravoslavnaya Tserkov. Official web site of the Moscow Patriarchy.* April 27. See: http://www.patriarchia.ru/db/text/5629099.html

13   Cf. Russkaya Pravoslavnaya Tserkov (2020). Tsirkulyarnoe pismo Mitropolita Voskresenskogo Dionisiya. *Russkaya Pravoslavnaya Tserkov. Official web site of the Moscow Patriarchy.* June 1st. See: http://www.patriarchia.ru/db/text/5645698.html

14   This term was also in use in Great Britain, but its meaning was different; in Russia the whole lockdown became known as self-isolation.

15   The impact of these local ecclesiastical lockdowns, their peculiarities and consequences on the believers are currently the subject of various sociological and ethnographical examina-tion. See, e.g. Irina Kuznetsova (2020). Traditions and Technologies: a Change in the Practice of Orthodox Worship During COVID-Pandemic: The Case of the St. Elias Church of Krasnodar (Russia). Virtual presentation within the 7th LUMEN online conference NASHS. June 25-26. *Editura Lumen.* June 24. See: https://www.youtube.com/watch?v=eHOmzuwSumY

Image 1: *Priest, wearing PPE, gives communion to a sick woman.*

Photo from the public Facebook page of Fr. Vasilii Gelevan. URL:
https://www.facebook.com/padrebasilio/posts/3513566135325185

regions. A city lockdown was established on March 30th and initially implied no public church service restrictions. Nevertheless, on March 29th, the Fourth Sunday of Great Lent, the Patriarch, addressing a small number of worshippers (some of them used face coverings) in the Cathedral of Christ the Saviour. In this context, he emphasises the story of St. Mary of Egypt in order to testify that a believer could be saved without attending churches or public divine services. The Patriarch even compared St. Mary's life with the present situation by pointing out that she went on "full isolation"[16]. The necessity to address the need for believers to stay away from the Church in order to protect themselves, by simultaneously expressing that the believers will receive salvation despite of the receiving of the communion, was extremely challenging the for ROC.

On April 11th, the Chief Sanitary Officer of Moscow ordered to suspend public divine services in the city starting on April 13th – this ban was only lifted only

---

16   Cf. Telekanal Spas (2020). Patriarkh prizval veruiushchikh molitsya doma, sleduya podvigu Marii Egipetskoi. *Telekanal Spas.* March 29. See: https://www.youtube.com/watch?v=8uztpNf Gvco

on June 6th. Thus, Palm Sunday of April 12th, the last Sunday before Easter, became also the last day of unrestricted church attendance for ordinary believers in Moscow. The Patriarch's Office issued a circular letter, signed by the Metropolitan Dionisii (Porubai), and demanding all services from now on to be conducted without parishioners, only in the presence of clergy and needful "co-workers and volunteers"[17]. Above all, the co-workers and volunteers were needed to organize video streams of the altar. Since this moment the parishes of Moscow went online – at least, officially. Bishoprics located in some other federal subjects, e.g., the Republic of Udmurtia, Kemerovo oblast, managed to keep churches open nearly until Easter (April 19th), or even to celebrate Easter with public divine services that had not been formally suspended.

On April 12th – when the number of the infected people in Moscow had reached ten thousand – Patriarch Kirill celebrated the Divine Liturgy in a nearly empty cathedral and once again repeated his call to the believers to stay at home. It was evident that the Patriarch not just took public health concerns seriously, but personally perceived Covid-19 as a severe danger. It was also clear that this year in Moscow, as well as in most of the federal regions, Easter would be celebrated at home.

On April 15th, the Patriarch allowed to bless Paschal foods at home and introduced a special prayer to be accompanied by holy water sprinkling, "if one has it"[18]. This decision contradicted all the previous experiences of believers, including the late Soviet practices, because the Easter blessing of the ritual food such as cakes, eggs and sweetened cottage cheese, was a longstanding tradition observed even by some non-believers, as a popular custom.

Therefore, the Easter Sunday of 2020 was painful for most of the Orthodox in the federal subjects of Russia who have been affected by the lockdown. Worshipers were not allowed to visit the Patriarchal Liturgy at the Cathedral of Christ the Saviour, although the event was, as usual, televised and commented. At some point the commentator mentioned that the Patriarch proceeded "surrounded by hypodeacons"; however, everyone was able to notice that he walked surrounded by empty space that reflected the policy of social distancing.[19] A tiny group of priests

---

17   Cf. Russkaya Pravoslavnaya Tserkov (2020). Tsirkulyarnoe pismo Mitropolita Voskresenskogo Dionisiya. *Russkaya Pravoslavnaya Tserkov. Official web site of the Moscow Patriarchy.* June 1st. See: http://www.patriarchia.ru/db/text/5645698.html Many believers understood the fact that the letter was signed not by the Patriarch himself, but by his First Vicar, as a sign of distress.

18   Cf. Russkaya Pravoslavnaya Tserkov (2020). O blagoslovenii kulichei i paskh v domashnikh usloviyakh. *Russkaya Pravoslavnaya Tserkov. Official web site of the Moscow Patriarchy.* April 14. See: http://www.patriarchia.ru/db/text/5621930.html

19   Cf. NTV (2020). Paskha Khristova. Bogosluzhenie v Khrame Khrista Spasitelya. *NTV.* April 18. See: https://www.youtube.com/watch?v=Himz9wrsUwg

and nuns who have been standing in the huge cathedral, watched only by the Patriarch's bodyguards from the Federal Protective Service, looked as if the Doomsday was approaching. The Ambassador Vladimir Yakunin, who delivers every Easter the Holy Light from Jerusalem to Moscow and hands it over to the Patriarch, stood near the Patriarch and wearing a face mask and blue rubber gloves posed a surrealistic picture. Even people working at Patriarchy-sponsored organizations could not help expressing their distress. For example, Elena Zhosul, a popular broadcaster from the ecclesiastical TV-channel *Spas* (Saviour), shared the indignation against a Paschal service without parishioners on her Facebook page: "That empty church floor was beautifully tiled. We will not forget these tiles for the rest of our lives"[20].

Image 2: *Naked floor of the Cathedral of Christ the Saviour during the 2020 Paschal Liturgy*

Source: Paskha Khristova. Bogosluzhenie v Khrame Khrista Spasitelya. NTV. 18 April 2020. URL: https://www.youtube.com/watch?v=Himz9wrsUwg

The digitalization of the Easter service was shocking but it also engendered some previously unknown opportunities, such as "jumping" from one liturgical stream to another to attend virtually remote churches, dear to one's heart. But even having this in mind, the patriarchal position on church attendance was, indeed, very vulnerable. In the post-Soviet period, the liturgical attendance and Eucharist celebrated at least once per month, became the cornerstone of the missionary philosophy of the Church. Fr. Georgii Breev, one of the most respected clerics in Moscow, said in an interview in the year 2013: "One cannot be a Christian without Eucharist [...] A community, not built around Eucharist, is hardly an ecclesiastical

---

20   Cf. Elena Zhosul (2020). *Facebook*. 18 April. See: https://www.facebook.com/ezhosul

community"[21]. Physical access to churches for everyone was behind an ambitious "Program-200" initiated by Patriarch Kirill in 2010. This program implies building at least two hundreds new "walking distance churches" in the remote districts of Moscow. Vladimir Legoyda explained that they should make attendance easier for "senior parishioners, the disabled, people with health problems, and new mothers"[22]. The same idea of church attendance as a necessity was an argument in favour of the restitution of the church property, nationalized after the revolution, and other projects, such as constructing a magnificent Orthodox complex in Paris.

Not only clerics, but also scholars often considered church attendance as one of the main parameters of religiosity, while what was happening outside the church walls was frequently labelled as vernacular, popular, or folk religion.[23] This way of practicing faith was assumed to be somehow "simpler" than institutionalised religious behaviour.

In contrary to this established vision of what is right and wrong for an Orthodox Christian, Patriarch Kirill suggested rethinking self-isolation as a God's blessing: "this virus has destroyed a sinful human idea of our full mightiness, of our central place in the whole civilization [...] It is really a chance for the human race to change itself in order to regain God's grace"[24]. Some speakers were fully supportive of this patriarchal position. Aleksei Osipov, professor of the Moscow Spiritual Academy and one of the leading secular theologians in Russia, said that the coronavirus is a God-given *epitemia* (Greek: penance), which believers need because they "got used" to receive the communion and therefore lost the awe towards this mystery[25]. The same ideas were articulated by Bishop Pitirim (Tvorogov), rector of the

---

21   Cf. Aleksandra Kuzmicheva & Georgii Breev (2013). Fr. Protoierei Georgii Breev ob anatomii tserkovnoi obshchiny, nastoyashchei druzhbe i glavnom interese v zhizni. December 3. See: https://www.pravmir.ru/protoierej-georgij-breev-ob-anatomii-cerkovnoj-obshhiny-na stoyashhej-druzhbe-i-glavnom-interese-v-zhizni/#ixzz3clJl7kRb ; Fr. Georgii Breev, 83, died from double pneumonia on April 29, 2020.

22   Cf. Vladimir V Legoida (2010). Moskve stroyat tserkvi shagovoi dostupnosti. September 15. See: http://www.patriarchia.ru/db/text/1275696.html

23   Critical reception of this approach may be found in: Yulia Sinelina (2001). O kriteriyakh opredeleniya religioznosti naseleniya. *Sotsiologicheskie issledovaniya*, No. 7, 95-96.; Olga Kazmina (2009). Russkaia Pravoslavnaia Tserkov i novaia religioznaia situatsia v Rossii. Moscow: Izdatelstvo MGU, pp. 130-133; Svetlana Riazanova (2018). Vot lyudi-to tam stoyat, a ty ne mozhesh: poseshchenie tserkvi v sovremennom permskom pravoslavnom soobshchestve. Perm: PGIK, pp. 29-31.

24   Cf. Patriarch Kirill (2020). Slovo Svyateishego Patriarcha Kirilla v den pamayti prepodobnogo Sergiya Radonezhskogo posle Liturgii v Troitse-Sergievoi lavre. *Russkaya Pravoslavnaya Tserkov. Official web site of the Moscow Patriarchy*. July 18. See: http://www.patriarchia.ru/db/t ext/5665266.html

25   Cf. Telekanal Spas (2020). Reaktsiya professora Alekseya Osipova. May 20. See: https://www. youtube.com/watch?v=H1SYxOJCxYM&feature=youtu.be&fbclid=IwAR28wKo-tZ_yZGIIlPP XD4TETJzQzPISV9z1ADPIbM8dRB9PsWTjN-fpy6U

Academy, initially a corona-dissident, who changed his position after his own hospitalization with Covid-inflicted pneumonia. "We have forgotten about living God, having replaced him with the continuous communion" – he wrote in his Telegram-account.[26]

3. From dissidents to reformers: reactions to the ecclesiastical lockdown

For the first time in the post-Soviet history of the ROC, its speakers officially declared that the communion and the church attendance in general were not necessary conditions with regard to the salvation. It was no surprise that many bishops, clerics and lay, normally supportive of the patriarchal platform, openly stated that the ecclesiastical lockdown was, in their eyes, an exaggerated measure. These inner-church related Covid-dissidents embraced people of different ideological orientations, who remained basically loyal to ecclesiastical and mundane authorities, but reserved their right to be sceptical towards these measures. Some of the dissidents did not believe in the pandemic at all, considering it a cloak for a global conspiracy; the majority admitted the existence of the virus, but viewed measures taken against it as redundant. Some limited their objections to verbal polemics; some, despite the prohibition, continued public church services.

Expressing formal loyalty to the patriarchal policy, some bishops and ordinary priests, spoke, in fact, against it. Hieromonk Feodorit Senchukov, medical doctor, openly claimed: "we have not a coronavirus pandemic, but a pandemic of fear"[27]. Just before the ecclesiastical lockdown Daniil (Dorovskikh), Metropolitan of Kurgan and Belozerskoe, said:

> "This thought that we can avoid sickness only hiding in our homes and, vice versa, that it is more likely that we will fall ill after attending the churches is not the thought of the Holy Fathers [...] the coronavirus is the consequence of our sins, God's punishment for our people. It reminds us to trust not in ethanol and other disinfecting solutions, but first of all in God".[28]

---

26   Cf. Episkop Pitirim (2020). Official channel of the rector of the Moscow Spiritual Academy, 24-25 April. See: https://t.me/pitirimtvorogov

27   Cf. Pyotr Selinov (n.d.). Pandemiya strakha. COVID-19 glazami svyashchennika-vracha. Inter-vyu s Feodoritom Senchukovym. *Prikhozhanin*. See: https://prihozhanin.msdm.ru/home/pogo vorit/2733-pandemiya-strakha-covid-19-glazami-svyashchennika-vracha.html

28   Cf. Mikhail Tyurenkov and Daniil Metropolitan (Dorovskikh) (2020). Koronavirus – nakazanie Bozhie nashemu narodu. *Tsargrad TV*. April 7. See: https://tsargrad.tv/articles/mitropolit-dani il-dorovskih-koronavirus-nakazanie-bozhie-nashemu-narodu_246712

Some priests were reported to renounce lockdowns in their dioceses in spite of the perspective to be examined by ecclesiastical courts. Fr. Nikolai Boldyrev from Nizhegorodskaya oblast, where public worship services were suspended since April 15th, refused to close the church and to wipe the liturgical spoon with ethanol, calling the patriarchal recommendations "blasphemous".[29] Fr. Aleksandr Zakharov from Tikhvin diocese issued a video where he said that "never and not for anything" he would take two of the prescribed anti-Covid measures: to sterilize the liturgical spoon with ethanol and to keep church doors closed for worshippers.[30]

A specific form of dissidence was offered by Andrei Kormoukhin, the head of a para-ecclesiastical social movement *Sorok sorokov* (Forty of Forties – a reference to the number of churches in pre-revolutionary Moscow). The organization's ideological position sways from traditionalism to fundamentalism, but in this case Kormoukhin spoke not on behalf of the movement, but as a private citizen. In this capacity he, first of all, expressed his respect and obedience to the patriarchal instructions. Then, Kormoukhin explained that his personal choice is, nevertheless, to go to the church for the Paschal service, even risking not to gain access to it: "Christ my Lord will wait for me on Easter Sunday at the church, not online, or at the TV-set. That is why I will go to the church [...] The church is more of vital necessity for me than a grocery store or a pharmacy"[31].

On April 14th, a couple of days before Easter, Kormoukhin initiated a flash mob consisting of postings from social media, one photo portrayed himself holding a placard that reads: "Christ will help" (with a hashtag).

There were at least two reasons why so many believers, who usually were obedient to the Patriarch, refused to accept his policy in view of the ecclesiastical lockdown.

First of all, the idea to receive the salvation at home, promoted as a strategy against the pandemic, contrasted historical experiences of anti-faith persecutions of the 20th century, when even a simple opportunity to gather in public for the divine service in a church building was priceless. The presence of venerated icons that could have been kept in the same building for centuries, or continuity of clerics and parishioners of this particular church, was even of greater value. Suspending public services, especially Paschal Liturgy, was painful for most believers, because "anti-

---

29   Cf. Volga. MBKh Media. (2020). Eto khula na Boga». Svyashcenniku iz Nizhegorodskoi oblasti zapretili sluzhenie posle otkaza zakryt khram dlya prikhozhan. *Volga. MBKh Media.* April 16. See: https://vk.com/@volgambk.media-eto-hula-na-boga-svyaschenniku-iz-nizhegorodskoi-oblasti-zap

30   Cf. Aleksandr Zakharov (2020). Batyushka Aleksandr o koronaviruse. June 7. See: https://www.youtube.com/watch?v=juYj-vRvhRo

31   Cf. Andrei Kormoukhin (2020). Pochemu ya poidu v khram na Paskhu. April 14. See: https://vk.com/wall209290103_3657

Image 3: *Andrei Kormoukhin's flash mob.*

URL: https://sun1-88.userapi.com/mzbupVvj1Xs_AbiYYO9540WF9E
8rPPlvt-dYSw/W84mc4bJN90.jpg

sanitary" conditions in churches were a noticeable part of Soviet anti-religious propaganda. Stories were invented about microbes found in baptism bowls, or about outbreaks of infectious diseases during pilgrimages[32]. Fr. Vladimir Rozhkov, who served in Orenburg bishopric, recalled how in 1964 a sanitary commission came to the city cathedral: "They took 'smears' from the icons, most venerated and kissed by believers, from the altar crosses, chalices, spoons. They demanded Presanctified

---

32   Cf. Liubov Soskovets (2005). Fenomen sovetskogo antireligioznogo Agitpropa. *Vestnik Tomskogo gosudarstvennogo universiteta*, No. 288, p. 190.; Cf. Daria Makarova (2013). Ateisticheskaya propaganda v SSSR v 1954–1964 godakh (na materialakh Kurskoi oblasti). *Izvestiya Saratovskogo gosuniversiteta. Seriya Istoriya. Mezhdunarodnye otnosheniya* 13, No. 3, p. 36.

Gifts for analysis, but Fr. Aleksandr... refused"[33]. Fr. Vladimir cites sanitary regulations issued by the former bishop: they included disinfecting crosses and liturgical vessels with eau-de-cologne after each use.

Apart from direct references to anti-sanitary conditions in churches, Soviet anti-religious propaganda utilized some clichés, portraying religion (not necessarily Orthodoxy) as "poison", "deadly breath"; "infection"; believers and clergy – as "parasites" (i.e. insects or mice), inflicting "harm"[34]. This discourse is a result of the famous statement coined by Karl Marx that religion is the opium of the people (*Opium des Volkes*), later repeated by Lenin[35]. Soviet clichés about "religious infection" are parodied and summarized by a Russian rock-band "Elysium" that issued in 2018 a composition "Religion is poison" with the following verses, repeating antireligious slogans:

"Protect kids from the claws of priests! [from a 1962 poster]
Faith is harmful, more harmful than wine. [from a 1933 brochure]
Religion is poison. Protect kids! [from a 1930 poster]"[36]

Many corona-dissidents draw parallels between suspending public divine services because of the pandemic and closing churches by the Soviet government in the period of persecutions. The aforementioned Fr. Aleksandr Zakharov stated:

"All this totalitarianism, when someone, somewhere decided for us where we should go, and where not; what we should want and what we shouldn't; how we are allowed to think and how we aren't allowed at all – we have been fed up with it in the Soviet Union"[37].

Andrei Kormoukhin also referred to the «satanic terror» of the early 20th century and reminded that the New Martyrs and Confessors of Russia "were afraid nei-

---

33   Cf. Ahilla (2020). «Sanitarnyi terror»: tserkvi kak «rassadniki epidemicheskikh zabolevanii». Iz knigi protoiereya Vladimira Rozhkova «Zapiski svyashchennika». *Ahilla*. Feburary 27. See: https://ahilla.ru/sanitarnyj-terror-tserkvi-kak-rassadniki-epidemicheskih-zabolevanij/

34   Aleksei Gorbatov (2014). Propaganda i SMI v period khrushchovskoi antireligioznoi kampanii (1954 1964 gg.). *Vestnik Kemerovskogo gosudarstvennogo universiteta* 2, No 3, 157f.; Aleksandr Panchenko (2013). «Religioznye infektsii» i «dukhovnye kaleki»: tema detstva v sovetskoi ateisticheskoi propagande 1960-kh gg. M. Balina (Ed.). *«Ubit Charskuyu...»: paradoksy sovetskoi literatury dlya detei (1920-e – 1930-e gg.)*. St. Petersburg: Aleteiya, pp. 310–329.; Kseniya Kolkunova (2013). Ateisticheskaya propaganda v khudozhestvennoi literature 1950–1960-X gg. *Vestnik PSTGU. Seriya 1: Bogoslovie. Filosofiya*. No. 5, pp. 113-132.

35   In the age of Marx opium was seen as a basically harmless pain-relief; in the 1920s, however, this label associated religion with a dangerous, or even lethal, narcotic drug.

36   The composition may be found at the band's Youtube channel: Elysium (2018). 'Religion is poison.' *YouTube*. See: https://www.youtube.com/watch?v=WPiOCM3orpw

37   Cf. Zakharov (2020).

ther of a virus, nor of the real terrorists killing them for their Christian faith."[38]. Conservative journalist Mikhail Tyurenkov[39], belonging to a community of Old Believers within the jurisdiction of the ROC, reminded the others of the fact that public divine services continued even in the 1930s, in the period of the "godless five year plans"[40], and that the victims of abortion, which is not restricted in Russia, outnumbered the victims of the virus. Encouraging believers to obey the hierarchy, Tyurenkov, nevertheless, wrote:

> "No one can forbid a believer to meet… [Easter] in a church of the Lord. Neither a policeman nor an official or a priest. And if you (yes, I mean you personally) strive to come to church in the Easter night, I cannot imagine who is able to deter a believer"[41].

Official ecclesiastical speakers tried to prevent the tracing of parallels between the Soviet persecutions and the lockdown. Instead, they stressed that believers who strived to be in a church were unsocial and rampant. Vladimir Legoyda declared that comparing contemporary believers, staying comfortably at home, with the New Martyrs would be forged or even "slightly indecent"[42]. Fr. Aleksandr Volkov, the former Head of the Moscow Patriarchate's Press Service, said on his Facebook page that believers who do not follow the regulations should not compare themselves neither with the first Christians in the catacombs nor with those persecuted in the 20th century. Accusing such people of pride and blasphemy, he questioned the purity of their intentions: "Can anyone really say about himself that one actually needs to meet Christ that strongly and that this person cannot wait for a couple of weeks to do so?"[43]. Bishop Pitirim (Tvorogov) emphasized savagery of believers who did not observe sanitary regulations, blaming them for the spread of Covid-19 in his monastery:

---

38   Cf. Kormoukhin (2020).

39   Tyurenkov is not in the opposition either to the ecclesiastical hierarchy nor to mundane authorities; nevertheless, on his Facebook page he writes that «It is not at all embarassing for me, when someone labels me as 'Orthodox fundamentalist'…». See Tyurenkov (2020). *Facebook*. May 25. See: https://www.facebook.com/tyurenkov/posts/3197908793592950).

40   A godless five year plan was announced by the Union of the Militant Godless in 1932 with a purpose to exterminate religion in the Soviet Union by 1937.

41   Cf. Mikhail Tyurenkov (2020). Paskha bez prikhozan": kak perezhit koronavirusnoe ispytanie, *Tsargrad TV*. April 13. See: https://tsargrad.tv/articles/pasha-bez-prihozhan-kak-perezhit-koronavirusnoe-ispytanie_247838?fbclid=IwAR1CdyqLc_BCl5GOHTtBJFciv_ocVWjHEAMPDIe bF3BxoY8jLwJ34ZMIyxc

42   Cf. Legoyda (2020). Neumestno sravnivat situatsiyu v Tserkvi seichas i v nachale 20 veka. April 17. See: https://ria.ru/20200417/1570191862.html

43   Cf. Aleksandr Volkov (2020). O bogosluzhebnoi partizanshchine. *Facebook*. April 5. See: https ://www.facebook.com/permalink.php?story_fbid=3932984456742489&id=100000-929212448

"Holy Monday. Morning. The gates of the Trinity – St. Sergius Lavra[44] are closed. There is an exited mob in front of them, demanding to open the Lavra. The protesters behave very aggressively; they use obscene words. [Vicar] Vladyka Paramon opens the Lavra for the whole Passion Week and Easter. On Good Friday the plague has begun"[45].

The second reason why some believers and priests considered ecclesiastical lockdown harmful was the problem conceptualized by sociologist Ivan Zabaev as "sacral individualism". This concept implies that contemporary believers in Russia see the Church primarily as individual communicating with God, not a community of people.[46]

Many people attend public worships on an individual basis whenever they need them and join no steady ecclesiastical communities. This type of congregation is known as «the temple model», fully acceptable for other faiths, for example Hinduism, but not for Christianity.[47] This absence of a shared parish life has been noticed by many researchers, such as Jeanne Kormina with her concept of "the Orthodox nomads" who "carefully avoid the very chance to become a community"[48]. Aleksandr Agajanian theorizes that an average Orthodox parish consists of an active core of constant attendees, whom local priests mostly know personally, and a scattered periphery consisting of people, who attend the parish from time to time and basically remain anonymous for priests and steady parishioners.[49] Both priests and scholars suggest that lack of solidarity between the believer dates back to the anti-church policies of the past: "the whole life of a parish in the Soviet period was aimed at admitting one, separately attending [...] parishioner. One comes, confesses, takes the communion and leaves – no contacts"[50]. Eventually, the very idea of a «parish community» became suspicious in terms of them probably being

---

44   Lavra is an ancient title of honour for the most respected Orthodox monasteries.

45   Cf. Episkop Pitirim (2020).

46   Ivan Zabaev (2011). "Sakralnyi individualizm" i obshchina v sovremennom russkom pravoslavii ["The sacral individualism" and community in today's Russian Orthodoxy]. In Aleksandr Agajanian and Kathy Rousselet (Eds.). *Prikhod i Obshchina v Sovremennom Pravoslavii*. Moscow: Ves mir, p. 347.

47   R. A. Cnaan and D. W. Curtis (2012). Religious Congregations as Voluntary Associations: An Overview. *Nonprofit and Voluntary Sector Quarterly* 42, No. 1, pp. 16-17.

48   Jeanne Kormina (2012). Nomadicheskoe pravoslavie: o novykh formakh religioznoi zhizni v sovremennoi Rossii. *Ab Imperio*, No. 2, p. 217.

49   Aleksandr Agadjanian (2011). Prikhod i obshchina v russkom pravoslavii: sovremennye protsessy v retrospektive poslednego stoletiya. Aleksandr Agajanian and Kathy Rousselet (Eds.). *Prikhod i obshchina v sovremennom pravoslavii*. Moscow: Ves mir, p. 33.

50   Oksana Golovko and Fr. Fyodor Borodin (2019). «Esli svyashchennik ne umeet druzhit, obshchiny ne poluchitsya». I pochemu inogda v khrame ne gotovy prinyat postoronnikh. *Pravmir*. September 26. See: https://www.pravmir.ru/esli-svyashhennik-ne-umeet-druzhit-ob shhiny-ne-poluchitsya-i-pochemu-inogda-v-hrame-ne-gotovy-prinyat-postoronnih/

a «sect»[51]. This situation is far from the Christian norm, especially in the light of the Patriarch's repeating calls to involve the newcomers into communities.[52]

Vladimir Legoyda renounced this argumentation by saying that believers do not lose the connection with their parishes, and that they continue communicating with priests and practice common prayers from a distance.[53] This position seems overly optimistic, because suspending a church attendance can potentially destroy the existing fragile ties between at least some believers. At the same time, the digitalization of parishes could as well be constitutive for more consolidated communities: people who are involved in new practices, such as studying the Bible on Zoom, get to know each other's names, backgrounds and experiences. Unfortunately, digital communication leaves too many people on the side simply because they are not Internet users, and this is particularly true with regard to senior parishioners.

Apart from Covid-dissidence, there emerged another inner-church reaction in view of the lockdown that is a source of ambivalent potential. Introducing new techniques of the communion provoked a discussion about the possibility of transmitting diseases through sacred objects. This discussion had been long overdue; some believers and even priests did raise the topic of church practices (including the communion) being inconsistent with modern sanitary rules.[54] A standard reaction was that communion bread and wine are safe[55]. Actually, priests answered not the questions, because for Orthodox Christians it is out of the question that an infection could be transmitted via the Blood and Body of Christ; there were, however, material mediators (spoons, clothes, and chalices) to which no attention had been paid until the pandemic began. Discussions about the holy water, icons, and the like were not fierce, because the Church never denied that such objects can transmit infections, and some parishes took measures in order to prevent infections. Latent hygienic concerns became visible when the ecclesiastical hierarchy, by suspending Eucharist nationwide, legitimated them in a way. Unfortunately, the

---

51   Fr. Fyodor Kotrelev (2012). Chto delayet prikhod obshchinoi? Opyt pastyrei i prikhozhan. *Neskuchnyi sad*. January 7. See: http://www.nsad.ru/articles/chto-delaet-prihod-obshhinoj; Agadjanian, 2011, p. 31.

52   Patriarch Kirill (2014). Na prikhodakh dolzhna byt pravilno postavlena rabota po priobshcheniyu k obshchine tekh, kto tolko vkhodit v khram. December 23. See: http://www.patriarchia.ru/db/text/3888293.html

53   Cf. Legoyda (2020). Paskhu prazdnovali i vo vremya chumy – otprazdnuem i seichas. *Ria*. April 4. See: https://ria.ru/20200404/1569577073.html

54   Cf. Sergii Fr Adodin (2017). Mikrobiologiya. *Pravoslavie*. March 15. See: https://pravoslavie.ru/101843.html

55   Cf. Anna Utkina and Evgeniya Nun (Senchikova) (2020). Kak prichashchatsya vo vremya epidemii grippa? *Pravmir*. February 2nd. See: https://www.pravmir.ru/prichashhenie-vo-vremya-epidemii-est-li-risk-1/; Fr. Andrei Efanov (2020). Kak prichashchatsya vo vremya epidemii koronavirusa? *Foma*. March 7. See: https://foma.ru/kak-prichashhatsya-vo-vremya-epidemii.html

Patriarchy has not yet provided any clear answers for the believers that would reconcile the new normality of the pandemic with "if they drink any deadly thing, it shall not hurt them" (*Marcus* 16.18).

In the absence of official clarifications, discussions about liturgical techniques soon took an unexpected turn: streaming liturgies together with social distancing brought into the surface the idea of a digital communion. On May 11th two clerics from the Orthodox Church of Ukraine[56], Dmitrii Vaisburd and Igor Savva, who had to stay at home, provided the communion remotely by using Hangouts, a platform for video-conferences. Lay, also staying in their homes, positioned bread and wine in front of their cameras to be distantly transfigured into the Blood and Body of Christ. Then each of them consumed the Holy Gifts individually.

Explanations given later by Igor Savva show that his reasons were much more profound than providing the communion in emergency. The discussion about sacramental techniques was actually a template of the discussion about the communities as opposed to the individualism of believers. Savva emphasized that off-line Divine Liturgy is attended, but not participated by lay, who observe it distantly, while priests are celebrating in the altar:

> "The main diverge for a real community regarding a solemn Liturgy in a full church and in a videoconference is not based on the use of the Internet, but that in the case of an **real** Liturgy most of the attendees, although faithful and reverent, remain observers of how the sacrament is performed, while in the **online** Liturgy, the assembly, faithful and reverent, becomes a direct part of the sacrament".[57]

Dmitrii Vaisburd added that, in his opinion, iconostasis that divides the altar from the nave of the church "is a much more substantial barrier for full value communication than the Internet"[58].

Some people obviously prefer being a digital community rather than being a collection of atomized church-attendees. Their choice, however, is at odds with the whole Orthodox tradition, and has a potential of undermining the foundations of

---

56   The Orthodox Church of Ukraine splitted from the Ukrainian Orthodox Church (autonomous within the ROC) in 2018; it is at the moment recoginized as an autocephalous Orthodox Church by several other sister-Churches, but not by the ROC (see: Jeanne Kormina and Vlad Naumescu (2020). A new 'Great Schism'? Theopolitics of communion and canonical territory in the Orthodox Church. Anthropology Today 36, No. 1, 7-11).

57   Fr. Igor Savva (2020). Gospod otvechaet na Evkharisticheskuyu molitvu distantsionno na kazhdoi liturgii. *Cerkvarium*. May 16. See: https://cerkvarium.org/ru/spetstemy/tserkov-i-koron avirus/otets-igor-savva-gospod-otvechaet-na-evkharistich eskuyu-molitvu-distantsionno-na-kazhdoj-liturgii

58   Dmitrii Vaisburd (2020). Evkharistiya onlain: predvaritelnye itogi. *Ahilla*. June 10. See: https://ahilla.ru/evharistiya-onlajn-predvaritelnye-itogi/?fbclid=IwAR0XV-E84fQ-pjeW3-MRzG5F74kd8 doZM 25GTZljiQPQXFK2AM_9DyeSKQs8

the Church. Unfortunately, Vaisburd and Savva, the two clerics who are involved in the digital communion case, belonged to a non-canonical (at least, for the ROC) jurisdiction. As a result, the ROC simply refused to continue serious theological discussions on this issue. Vladimir Legoyda made an ironical statement about a liturgical "breakthrough"[59]; Metropolitan Hilarion (Alfeev) compared this distant worship with notorious tele-healers of the early 1990s and said that it "cannot be taken seriously"[60]. Other commentators, instead of discussing the topic of preserving liturgical communities during the lockdown, preferred to discuss how digitalization might assist in getting rid of what they envisioned as "folk" religion.[61]

4. Fundamentalist reactions to the corona-crisis

Generally, fundamentalists share the discourse of the other corona-dissidents, but, apart from being more radical in expressing their vision, they also accentuate things in a slightly different way than the speakers who belong to the other ideological platforms.

Fundamentalists use the concept of "corona-posession" (*koronabesie*) considering the worldwide lockdown and other safety measures as an analogy to being possessed by evil spirits. Most of them do not deny that some epidemic exist, but perceive it as an "ordinary infection" backed with a "disinformation", or as a "psychobiological occupation"[62]. Measures taken by state to ensure social distancing and stay-at-home policies represent the real threat in their eyes. Sergii Aliev labelled Covid-19 as a "hoax" saying that "there is no threat of coronavirus; there is a pandemic of fear created with the help of the mass media"[63]. Fundamentalists do not trust testing, assuming that via tests people get infected.

Suspending public worship was less important for fundamentalists, because many of them do not attend mainstream church services, considering the hierar-

---

59   Cf. Vladimir Legoyda (2020). *Telegram*. May 12. See: https://t.me/vladimirlegoyda
60   Cf. Vesti (2020). Tserkov i mir. Broadcast of 30.05.2020. Ekaterina Gracheva asks questions. *Vesti*. May 30. See: https://vera.vesti.ru/video/show/video_cid/2152528
61   Cf. Novaya gazeta. (2020). Kogda RPTs perestala byt tserkoviyu? Strim s Andreem Kuraevym. *Novaya gazeta*. May 10. See: https://novayagazeta.ru/articles/2020/05/10/85321-kogda-rpts-pe restala-byt-tserkovyu-strim-s-andreem-kuraevym
62   Cf. Andrei Saveliev (2020). Beseda 58. Koronavirus. Sotsialno-ekonomicheskie posledstviya. *Live*. March 24. See: https://www.youtube.com/watch?v=BsWDei9z2o4; Pryamoi efir s Andreem Kormoukhinym. Dvizhenie Sorok Sorokov. *DSS*. April 6. See: https://vk.com/videos-53664310?z=video-53664310_456240982%2Fpl_-53664310_-2; Cf. Vladimir Kvachkov (2020/2). Koronavirus, Trump, biologicheskoe oruzhie, tsifrovoi kartser. *Svobodnaya pressa*. April 29. See: https://www.youtube.com/watch?v=2ni6h-PoS8A
63   Cf. Aliev Sergii (2020). vystupil v zashchitu skhiigumena Sergiya (Romanova). Pervyi mezhdunarodnyi pozitivnyi portal. May 1st. See: https://www.youtube.com/watch?v=oprvAoPaIlI

chy contaminated by heresies. Fundamentalist leaders are commonly lay; clerics openly confessing fundamentalist ideas mostly come to odds with the hierarchy and eventually become suspended, dismissed, or excommunicated. Schemahegumen Daniil (in that time – Fr. Veniamin Filippov) was defrocked as early as in 2008; Schemahegumen Sergii Romanov – in July 2020 as a direct consequence of his video appeals in the period of the lockdown. Nevertheless, fundamentalist media also compared closing churches for public worship with the Soviet policy of state-imposed atheism. In their opinion, the ecclesiastical lockdown was not just distressing the believers, but proved that contemporary Russia, like the Soviet Union, was a godless state.[64]

The Website "Moscow the Third Rome" commented on the news that the church space on the territory of a hospital in Kiev was utilized as an improvised workshop to sew protective overalls:

"We all remember how in the Soviet time the militant godless were closing churches to turn them into granaries, workshops, plants, theatres and the like. Well, those godless, god-fighting times are returning, the only difference is that desecrating the holy takes place not because of the orders of mundane authorities, but with direct blessing from the hierarchy"[65].

Colonel Kvachkov symbolically returned to anti-Church invectives of the Soviet period about the "poison" of mundane authorities by saying that "until we get rid of inner parasites who are ruling us, we will not cope with the other parasites"[66]. According to Aleksei Dobychin, suspending public worships and other lockdown measures proved that mundane authorities "are satanic... and the Church is led by the servants of the antichrist, which are both involved in a symphony with god-fighting authorities in order to deprive people of the sacraments"[67].

Fundamentalist speakers present what they see as satanic measures as a free decision of the ecclesiastical leaders; the latter, thus, become much less victims than perpetrators of the lockdown. They parallel the non-commemorating of today with the non-commemorating believers of the 1920s-1940s, who did not accept

---

64   Cf. Skhiigumen Sergii Romanov (2020/2). Gde vera v chistote – tam net raskola / Sredneuralskii zhenskii monastyr. *Vsevolod Moguchev*. June 19. See: https://www.youtube.com/watch?v=T9NabgOOnNo

65   Cf. Moskva – Tretii Rim (2020). Tsekh v pomeshchenii krama... Kak v starye «dobrye» bezboznye vremena. *Moskva – Tretii Rim*. April 11. See: https://3rm.info/main/79675-ceh-v-pomeschenii-hrama-kak-v-starye-dobrye-bezbozhnye-vremena.html

66   Vladimir Kvachkov (2020/1). Koronavirus operatsiya mirovoi zakulisy Chipirovanie. *Andreyiz1946*. March 25. See: https://www.youtube.com/watch?v=kK8-R_-JrUU

67   Cf. Aleksei Dobychin (2020). Kreml rasprostranyaet koronavirus... Khramy pusty – v metro anshlag. *3rm*. April 17. See: https://3rm.info/main/79754-kreml-nachal-rasprostranenie-koronavirusa-hramy-pusty-v-metro-anshlag-aleksej-dobychin-video.html

Metropolitan Sergii's decision of the year 1927 about loyalty to the Soviet government.[68] Some speakers draw public attention to the aforementioned issue of insufficient solidarity of Orthodox parishes. Andrei Kormoukhin reminded that in most churches worshippers do not live like one big family, and that the suspending of public divine services would inevitably mean further "atomization" of the believer.[69] Andrei Saveliev also suggested that the purpose of a lockdown might be to sow seeds of division and the further destruction of a society.[70]

Fundamentalists do neither interpret the Patriarch's instructions about the wiping of liturgical spoons with ethanol and burning used liturgical cloths in terms of the attempt to suppress the folk forms of religiosity, nor as an invitation to an open discussion about Christian ecclesiology. Unlike some Islamic radicals, fighting against culturally specific rituals, Orthodox fundamentalists do not object vernacular traditions and rites. The attempt to examine these reasons, would lead far be beyond the scope of this chapter; the author suggests that both fundamentalists and traditionalists envision vernacular rituals as representing the authentic Orthodox tradition.[71] New types of the communion pose a proof of the hierarchy's apostasy for the fundamentalists and would therefore fulfil their deepest fears. "How can one be infected through the [liturgical] spoon from Christ; is not this assumption itself the *real* blasphemy against the Holy Ghost?" – Fr. Sergii (Romanov) asks rhetorically, referring to *Matthew*, 12.31.[72] Actually, here fundamentalists are more consistent than official speakers, emphasizing that not only the Blood and Body of Christ, but also their mediators (spoons and chalices) cannot be contagious.

Unprecedented measures taken by authorities in Moscow and some other big cities, such as the introduction of digital passes containing QR-codes for all people intending to leave their homes by car or public transport, except for work, or instant blocking of city transportation passes for all people older than 65, confirmed the long expected fears of the fundamentalists. For many decades they struggled against all forms of control over individuals and families: from mandatory vaccina-

---

68   Cf. Dvizhenie nepominaushchikh (2020). V podderzhku skhiig. Sergiya. Ch. 2. Obrashchenie k russkomu narodu. *Dvizhenie nepominaushchikh. Analitika sobytii.* July 28. See: https://www. youtube.com/watch?v=Pq]__-liL4A&list=PL8i7s8Nj2FNNwoFmB4tvdHcl]6U4RD4fG&index=1

69   Cf. Pryamoi efir s Andreem Kormoukhinym. Dvizhenie Sorok Sorokov. *DSS.* April 6. See: http s://vk.com/videos-53664310?z=video-53664310_456240982%2Fpl_-53664310_-2

70   Cf. Saveliev (2020).

71   The author's field research shows that fundamentalists are mostly neophytes, born in average Soviet families; their first encounter with Orthodoxy in most cases happened via senior relatives living in villages.

72   Skhiigumen Sergii Romanov (2020/1). Pandemiya neveriya. Ne propoved Srednii Put. May 26. See: https://www.youtube.com/watch?v=KySJRYBFe-8

tion to the introduction of machine-readable identity cards.[73] Fundamentalists see these innovations in the light of the apocalypse. Schemahegumen Daniil (Filippov) declared that passes with QR-codes contained 666 (Number of the Beast) and were nothing but "a mark in their right hand or in their forehead" (*Rev.* 13.16); he also referred to some prophesies of the 18th century about "cards" without people would not be allowed to travel.[74] The same was the fundamentalist's understanding of the government's demands to prefer electronic money instead of cash for sanitary reasons (some web-stores discontinued all payment opportunities except plastic cards) and assessed this measurements as a sign for the apocalpyse: «and that no man might buy or sell, save he that had the mark» (*Rev.* 13.17). Fundamentalists suggested that public health concerns were just a pretext for a total digitalization of humanity to subjugate it then to the power of antichrist:

> "there is no pandemic, but there are deliberately made up data everywhere in the world; under this cloak they try to organize the world's electronic concentration camp that will have to be headed by the world ruler, the antichrist"[75]; "the pandemic needs to digitalize all people in the world, it is not that digitalization helps to avoid the pandemic"[76].

It was important that lockdown in Russia became known as «self-isolation», because this approach implies a voluntary subjugation to the antichrist: Fr. Daniil (Filippov) compared those who obeyed the regulations with Judas, tacitly referring to "Satan entered into him" (*John*, 13.27).[77]

Speakers more traditionalist or rather conservative than the fundamentalists, such as Andrei Kormoukhin, stressed that they were "not against technologies", but opposed (mis)using them to control people's behaviour.[78] Kormoukhin, never-

---

73   See: Kathy Rousselet (2015). Religiya i sovremennye tekhnologii, ili protivorechivoe mirovozzrenie pravoslavnykh khristian. In J. Kormina, A. Panchenko and S. Shtyrkov (Eds.). Izobretenie religii: desekuliarizatsiia v postsovetskom kontekste. St. Petersburg: Izdatelstvo Evropeiskogo Universiteta, pp. 46-62.

74   Cf. Dvizhenie nepominaushchikh (2020). Predatelstvo Khrista i tshifrovye propuska. Chast 1. *Dvizhenie nepominaushchikh. Analitika sobytii.* April 17. See: https://www.youtube.com/watch?v=rT55Au3w6gs&list=PL8i7s8Nj2FNNwoFmB4tvdHclJ6U4RD4fG&index=6

75   Cf. Dvizhenie nepominaushchikh (2020). Predatelstvo Khrista i tshifrovye propuska. Chast 2. *Dvizhenie nepominaushchikh. Analitika sobytii.* April 17. See: https://www.youtube.com/watch?v=xf5ZQC-kRAw&list=PL8i7s8Nj2FNNwoFmB4tvdHclJ6U4RD4fG&index=5

76   Cf. Dvizhenie nepominaushchikh (2020). Predatelstvo Khrista i tshifrovye propuska. Chast 2. *Dvizhenie nepominaushchikh. Analitika sobytii.* April 17. See: https://www.youtube.com/watch?v=xf5ZQC-kRAw&list=PL8i7s8Nj2FNNwoFmB4tvdHclJ6U4RD4fG&index=5

77   Ib.

78   Cf. VKontakte (2020). Pryamoi efir s Andreem Kormoukhinym. Dvizhenie Sorok Sorokov. *VKontakte.* April 8. See: https://vk.com/videos-53664310?z=video-53664310_456240982%2Fpl_-53664310_-2

Image 4: *Colonel Ret. Vladimir Kvachkov with Schemahegumen Sergii (Romanov).*

URL: https://sun9-44.userapi.com/JEurilNfXohk7dekiDUXSg-CaE5 sD1dSum8CvRw/ewwXDFzeUGg.jpg.

theless, agreed that the digitalization and the subsequent "dehumanization" paved the way to the coming of the antichrist.[79] It is worth noting that the fundamentalists in Russia generally are keen in utilizing new technologies.[80] Even those who formally withdrew themselves from the world demonstrate a perfect knowledge of the latest mundane developments; they obviously watch TV and use the Internet, moreover, most of their propaganda is done on the web.

---

79   Pryamoi efir s Andreem Kormoukhinym. Dvizhenie Sorok Sorokov. DSS. April 8. See: https:// vk.com/videos-53664310?z=video-53664310_456240999%2Fpl_-53664310_-2

80   Mitrofanova, 2014, p. 97f.

Many fundamentalists speak about the pandemic using an overly "scientific" language; this can partly be explained by the fact that they were often educated in spheres like engineering and technologies.[81] This is one example of that behaviour:

"The vaccine will contain nanocomponents-chips based on "smart dust" working principle, to be activated by external electromagnetic radiation. At any moment this radiation can be turned on with the help of mobile masts, and people will rave or die en masse"[82].

As soon as the authorities announced that Covid-inflicted restrictions would be lifted only after inventing a vaccine, fundamentalists resided to picturing vaccination as another step to the universal antichristian dictatorship: they claimed that vaccine injections would be used to introduce microchips, or "liquid chips" into people's bodies.[83] "Moscow the Third Rome" warned in an editorial article that

"as we used to say, the coronavirus is a worldwide act of sabotage conducted by the new world government of the antichrist [...] the vaccine will become that very lethal agent in the body of every vaccinated person, using every moment it can to control an individual physically and mentally, or even kill him/her"[84].

Some fundamentalist speakers, mostly those who withdrew into closed communities, envisioned the lockdown, vaccination and subsequent "chipping" as clear signs that the great tribulation is nigh (*Matthew*, 24.21-22) and expected to be universally hated and even killed.[85] Fr. Daniil (Filippov) said: "it is strange, of course, but we have probably reached the times described in the [book of] Revelation"[86].

---

81 Andrei Saveliev graduated in Physics; Aleksei Dobychin - in Computing; Andrei Kormukhin was initially a student of Physics and Math; See: Anastasia V. Mitrofanova (2008). Natsionalizm i paranauka. In Marlene Laruelle (Ed.). *Russkii natsionalizm. Sotsialnyi i kulturnyi kontekst.* Moscow: NLO, pp. 87-104.

82 Cf. Moskva – Tretii Rim (2020). Antikhrista gotovyat k prezentatsii miru... V Britanii predlozhili dlya borby s Covid-19 sozdat mirovoe pravitelstvo. *Moskva – Tretii Rim.* March 28. See: https://3rm.info/main/79516-antihrista-gotovjat-k-prezentacii-miru-v-britanii-predlozhili-dlja-borby-covid-19-sozdat-mirovoe-pravitelstvo.html

83 Cf. Saveliev (2020).; Cf. Kvachkov (2020/2).

84 Cf. Moskva – Tretii Rim (2020). Antikhrista gotovyat k prezentatsii miru... V Britanii predlozhili dlya borby s Covid-19 sozdat mirovoe pravitelstvo. *Moskva – Tretii Rim.* March 28. See: https://3rm.info/main/79516-antihrista-gotovjat-k-prezentacii-miru-v-britanii-predlozhili-dlja-borby-covid-19-sozdat-mirovoe-pravitelstvo.html

85 Cf. Moskva – Tretii Rim (2020). Tserkov ne dolzhna podchinyatsya gosudarstvu... O zaprete na bogosluzheniya v svyazi s koronovirusom. *Moskva – Tretii Rim.* March 15. See: https://3rm.info/main/79374-cerkov-ne-dolzhna-podchinjatsja-gosudarstvu-o-zaprete-na-bogosluzhenija-v-svjazi-s-koronavirusom.html

86 Cf. Dvizhenie nepominaushchikh (2020). Predatelstvo Khrista i tshifrovye propuska. Chast 1. *Dvizhenie nepominaushchikh. Analitika sobytii.* April 17. See: https://www.youtube.com/watch?v=rT55Au3w6gs&list=PL8i7s8Nj2FNNwoFmB4tvdHcIJ6U4RD4fG&index=6

Alternatively, people, involved into socio-political activism are less pessimistic; they described the worldwide lockdown more in geopolitical terms as a "special operation" against Russia, or "command and stuff exercises of those who rule the world behind the scenes to gain full control over humanity"[87]. Analogies between World War II and the corona-crisis are common. Fr. Sergii (Romanov) stated that vaccination and chipping would in the perspective lead to the world "fascist regime"[88]. More direct connection was offered by Fr. Daniil (Filippov), who suggested that the lockdown was imposed (presumably, by the clandestine world government) "first, to occupy the resources of the other side and to feed its own people [...] then to provide a sort of reason for living; this is how the Germans did during the second world war"[89]. These dangers, although staged by satanic forces, were still located in the earthly domain and can be fought back.

Apart from Easter, the lockdown in Russia did not let the people celebrate properly the Victory Day (May 9th), that was usually celebrated in an unique place as a national holiday equally important for the state and for many families whose ancestors either fell on battlefields, or returned to their homes as decorated heroes. Suspending the public V-day celebrations and introducing virtual fests instead of it, could be be easily understood in terms of no-victory, or "defeat" and has led fundamentalists to comparing the generation of war heroes with the contemporary generation of cowards ready to do everything for the sake of their individual health.[90]

Sergii Aliev has sponsored the printing and placement of 250 posters throughout Yekaterinburg in the night before Victory Day, reading:

"June 22nd 1941! Our grandfathers left their homes to die without fear for the sake of grandchildren! May 9th, 2020 – Day of the Great Victory! Grandchildren are sitting at home, afraid of "cow virus" [wordplay in Russian: *korona – korova*, cow] and worried about their lives".

Explaining his action, Aliev renounced virtual celebration as "betrayal" and emphasized that he wanted not just to congratulate veterans, but also to say excuses.[91]

---

87   Cf. Kvachkov (2020/1).

88   Cf. Sergii Romanov (2020).

89   Cf. Dvizhenie nepominaushchikh (2020). V podderzhku skhiig. Sergiya. Ch. 2. Obrashchenie k russkomu narodu. *Dvizhenie nepominaushchikh. Analitika sobytii.* July 28. See:https://www.youtube.com/watch?v=PqJ__-liL4A&list=PL8i7s8Nj2FNNwo FmB4tv-dHclJ6U4RD 4fG&index=1

90   Cf. Saveliev (2020).

91   Cf. Pervyi mezhdunarodnyi pozitivnyi portal (2020). Dorogie veterany: Prostite nas! Ispravimsya! S Dnem Pobedy! 9 maya 2020 g. *Pervyi mezhdunarodnyi pozitivnyi portal.* May 8. See: https://www.youtube.com/watch?v=mc3eJA6pD1c

Image 5: *Aliev, with his son, friends and supporters congratulates war veterans in the evening of May 8th and asks them for forgiveness.*

URL: https://www.youtube.com/watch?v=mc3eJA6pD1c

Aliev and those who joined his well wishes also promised to do right, which shows how emotionally powerful events such as the V-Day are. They lead not just for to unpleasant comparisons to war heroes, but might also be misused as a source of strength in view of the pandemic. Some fundamentalists envision the world crisis as a breeding ground for some radical changes that would result in Russia's transformation into an Orthodox monarchy.[92] «I am very happy that all this occurs... It has become clear that the present state is a structure fully alien to us [...] it is anti-Orthodox, it is anti-Muslim», Colonel Kvachkov said[93]. "Let us prepare for the moment when we have to take Russia into our hands [...] let us pray, God will give another tsar to us", Aleksei Dobychin concluded optimistically.[94]

In order to avoid legal consequences, fundamentalists are evasive in specifying how exactly this change may happen. "We are not revolutionaries, we cannot seize power by force, we have no right to do so, it is the way of Satanists", Kormoukhin

---

92   More about monarchy as a fundamentalist political project can be found in Tatiana Chumakova (2013). Predstavlenie o tsarskoi vlasti v srede sovremennykh pravoslavnykh marginalov. *Vestnik SPBGU.* Seriia 6, No. 3, 61-65.; Maija Turunen (2007). Orthodox monarchism in Russia: is religion important in the present-day construction of national identity? *Religion, State and Society 35,* No. 4, 319-334.

93   Cf. Kvachkov (2020/2).

94   Cf. Dobychin (2020).

said.[95] Kvachkov recommended his followers to appeal to God, because "now such infernal, satanic forces [...] act against Russians and the other indigenous peoples of Russia that we will not cope without appealing to the light, the heavenly forces"[96]. The most radical measures were offered by Andrei Saveliev in view of a sabotage of the self-isolation and the vaccination.[97] Fr. Sergii (Romanov) even called the Russian President Vladimir Putin and the Patriarch Kirill to hand over their power to him and promised to restore the order in Russia in three days.[98] Unfortunately, he provided no plans how he expected to achieve it.

Conclusion

The pandemic of Covid-19 has brought both challenges and opportunities for the Russian Orthodox Church; the balance between the two remains so far unclear. The pandemic caused no specific challenges for the Orthodox communities in Russia, but exacerbated and visualized many longstanding and previously suppressed problems. These problems came to be of equal importance for all political platforms within the Church, including people who are usually absolutely loyal towards the ecclesiastical leaders, and in view of laity and clergy.

The author was able to identify several themes which were important for the Orthodox public in the period of the lockdown:

a) Insufficient solidarity in parishes, "sacral individualism" of believers and the prevalence of non-parish forms of communication, including political groupings (e.g. fundamentalist networks).

b) Deep distrust towards the hierarchy as a mutual element of all political platforms; even loyal members of the Church remain supportive of the Patriarch personally, but not with regard to the bishops. Liberals and fundamentalists are the last groups that trust both, the ecclesiastical and the mundane authorities.

c) A fragmentary vision of faith practices, a lack of a common understanding in terms of changeable and unchangeable religious practices and the difference

---

95   Cf. VKontakte (2020). Pryamoi efir s Andreem Kormoukhinym. Dvizhenie Sorok Sorokov. *VKontakte.* April 6. See: https://vk.com/videos-53664310?z=video-53664310_456240982%2Fpl_ -53664310_-2

96   Cf. Kvachkov (2020/2).

97   Cf. Saveliev Andrei (2020). Vot vsyo i proyasnilos. Zamysel koronavyrusei oboznachilsya v detalyakh. *YouTube.* May 21. See: https://www.youtube.com/watch?v=CW3IPdsdjfk

98   Cf. Skhiigumen Sergii Romanov (2020/3). Komu prinadlezhit vlast v Rossii? Predlozhenie dlya prezidenta Vladimira Putina. July 12. See: https://www.youtube.com/watch?v =_eydP556eu4&feature=youtu.be&fbclid=IwAR1Tb38j6PXJ25X_dG-Z76sW4Ax F5URVpfKXypdRo_d4fOHSQkJVjy2Bt4U

between "vernacular" and "genuine" ecclesiastical tradition. In sum, disagreements about religious practices led to further decreases of solidarity and the emergence of antagonistic groups within the Church.

Fundamentalists, similar to the other inner-church ideological groups, did not raise new issues, but continued discussing sensitive longstanding problems in their own religious-political language, hastily adjusted to the new situation of the pandemic. What makes them specific is their combined critique on both the hierarchy and mundane authorities, represented by the Patriarch and the President of Russia respectively. At the same time, fundamentalist speakers carefully avoid direct political statements, at least in public, and it remains unclear how they intend to achieve a political and ecclesiastical "regime change".

Bibliography

Agadjanian, Aleksand (2011). Prikhod i obshchina v russkom pravoslavii: sovremennye protsessy v retrospektive poslednego stoletiya [Parish and community in Russian Orthodoxy: contemporary processes in the retrospective of the last century]. Aleksandr Agadzhanian and Kathy Rousselet (Eds.) *Prikhod i obshchina v sovremennom pravoslavii*. Moscow: Ves mir, pp. 15-36.

Chumakova, Tatiana (2013). Predstavlenie o tsarskoi vlasti v srede sovremennykh pravoslavnykh marginalov [The image of tsar's power in the milieu of the contemporary marginal Orthodox]. *Vestnik SPBGU*. Seriya 6, No. 3, 61-65.

Cnaan, R. A., and Curtis, D.W. (2012). Religious Congregations as Voluntary Associations: An Overview. *Nonprofit and Voluntary Sector Quarterly* 42, No. 1. 7-33.

Gorbatov, Aleksei (2014). Propaganda i SMI v period khrushchovskoi antireligioznoi kampanii (1954 1964 gg.) [Propaganda and mass media in the period of Khrushchev's anti-religious campaign]. *Vestnik Kemerovskogo gosudarstvennogo universiteta* 2, No 3, 157-160.

Kazmina, Olga (2009). *Russkaia Pravoslavnaia Tserkov i novaia religioznaia situatsia v Rossii* [The Russian Orthodox Church and the New Religious Situation in Russia]. Moscow: Izdatelstvo MGU.

Kolkunova, Kseniya (2013). Ateisticheskaya propaganda v khudozhestvennoi literature 1950–1960-kh gg. [Atheistic propaganda in the belletristic literature of the 1950s-1940s]. *Vestnik PSTGU*. Seriya 1: Bogoslovie. Filosofiya. No. 5, 113-132.

Kormina, Jeanne and Naumescu, Vlad (2020). A new 'Great Schism'? Theopolitics of communion and canonical territory in the Orthodox Church. *Anthropology Today* 36, No. 1, 7-11.

Kormina, Jeanne (2012). Nomadicheskoe pravoslavie: o novykh formakh religioznoi zhizni v sovremennoi Rossii [Nomadic Orthodoxy: on the new forms of religious life in contemporary Russia]. *Ab Imperio*, No. 2, 195-227.

Kuznetsova, Irina (2020). Traditions and Technologies: a Change in the Practice of Orthodox Worship During COVID-Pandemic: The Case of the St. Elias Church of Krasnodar (Russia). Virtual presentation within the 7th LUMEN online conference NASHS 2020. June 25-26. *Editura Lumen.* June 24. URL: https://www.youtube.com/watch?v=eHOmzuwSumY

Lunkin, Roman (2017). Dvizhenie «Sorok Sorokov»: pravoslavnyi fundamentalizm vo vrazhdebnom okruzhenii [Sorok Sorokov movement: Orthodox fundamentalism in hostile environment]. *Religiya i pravo,* September 18. URL: http://www.sclj.ru/news/detail.php?SECTION_ID =484&ELEMENT_ID =7677&fbclid= IwAR12Bz_ Pb81 f SwLtki8NKrpQ8YOsoefMe7jnYiNt3PoDDmem2lHBZJpkO5A

Lunkin, Roman (2020). Mekhanizmy religioznoi reaktsii na pandemiyu koronavirusa [Mechanisms of religious reaction to the coronavirus pandemic]. *Nauchno-analiticheskii verstnik IE RAN,* No. 2, 104-109.

Makarova, Daria (2013). Ateisticheskaya propaganda v SSSR v 1954–1964 godakh (na materialakh Kurskoi oblasti) [Atheistic propaganda in the USSR in 1954–1964 (the case of Kursk oblast)]. *Izvestiya Saratovskogo gosuniversiteta. Seriya Istoriya. Mezhdunarodnye otnosheniya* 13, No. 3, 33-39.

Mitrofanova, Anastasia V. (2008). Natsionalizm i paranauka [Nationalism and parascience]. In Marlene Laruelle (Ed.). *Russkii natsionalizm. Sotsialnyi i kulturnyi kontekst.* Moscow: NLO, pp. 87-104.

Mitrofanova, Anastasia V. (2014). Orthodox Fundamentalism: Intersection of Modernity, Postmodernity and Tradition. In K. Tolstaya (Ed.). *Orthodox Paradoxes: Heterogeneities and Comple21ties in Contemporary Russian Orthodoxy.* Leiden, Boston: Brill, pp. 93-104.

Panchenko, Aleksandr: «Religioznye infektsii» i «dukhovnye kaleki»: tema detstva v sovetskoi ateisticheskoi propagande 1960-kh gg. ["Religious infections" and "spiritual creeps": the topic of childhood in the Soviet atheistic propaganda of the 1960s] In M. Balina (Ed.). *«Ubit Charskuyu...»: paradoksy sovetskoi literatury dlya detei (1920-e – 1930-e gg.).* St. Petersburg: Aleteiya, 2013, pp. 310–329.

Papkova, Irina (2011). *The Orthodox Church and Russian Politics.* New York: Oxford University Press and Woodrow Wilson Center Press.

Riazanova, Svetlana (2018). *"Vot lyudi-to tam stoyat, a ty ne mozhesh": poseshchenie tserkvi v sovremennom permskov pravoslavnom soobshchestve* ["Look, people are standing there, and you can not": church attendance in contemporary Orthodox community of Perm]. Perm: PGIK.

Rousselet, Kathy (2015). Religia i sovremennye tekhnologii, ili protivorechivoe mirovozzrenie pravoslavnykh khristian [Religion and contemporary technologies, or Contradictory Weltanschauung of Orthodox Christians]. In J. Kormina, A. Panchenko and S. Shtyrkov (Eds.) *Izobretenie religii: desekuliarizatsiia v postsovetskom kontekste.* S.Petersburg: Izdatelstvo Evropeiskogo Universiteta, pp. 46-62.

Shnirelman, Viktor (2017). *"Koleno Danovo". Eskhatologiya i antisemitizm v sovremennoi Rossii* ["The Tribe of Dan". Eschatology and anti-Semitism in contemporary Russia]. Moscow: BBI.

Sinelina, Yulia (2001). O kriteriyakh opredeleniya religioznosti naseleniya [On the criteria of measuring people's religiosity]. *Sotsiologicheskie issledovaniya*, No. 7, 89-96.

Soskovets, Liubov (2005). Fenomen sovetskogo antireligioznogo Agitpropa [The phenomenon of Soviet anti-religious Agitprop]. *Vestnik Tomskogo gosudarstvennogo universiteta*, No. 288, 189-199.

Turunen, Maija (2007). Orthodox monarchism in Russia: is religion important in the present-day construction of national identity? *Religion, State and Society* 35, No. 4, 319-334.

Zabaev, Ivan (2011). "Sakralnyi individualizm" i obshchina v sovremennom russkom pravoslavii ["The sacral individualism" and community in today's Russian Orthodoxy]. In Aleksandr Agadzhanian and Kathy Rousselet (Eds.). *Prikhod i Obshchina v Sovremennom Pravoslavii*. Moscow: Ves mir, pp. 341–54.

Online Open Sources

Adodin, Sergii Fr. (2017). Mikrobiologiya. *Pravoslavie*. March 15. URL: https://pravoslavie.ru/101843.html

Dobychin, Aleksei (2020). Kreml rasprostranyaet koronavirus... Khramy pusty – v metro anshlag. *Moskva – Tretii Rim*. 17 April. URL: https://3rm.info/main/79754-kreml-nachal-rasprostranenie-koronavirusa-hramy-pusty-v-metro-anshlag-aleksej-dobychin-video.html

Dvizhenie nepominaushchikh (2020). Predatelstvo Khrista i tshifrovye propuska. Chast 1. *Dvizhenie nepominaushchikh. Analitika sobytii*. April 17. URL: https://www.youtube.com/watch?v=rT55Au3w6gs&list=PL8i7s8Nj2FNNwoFmB4tvdHcIJ6U4RD4fG&index=6

Dvizhenie nepominaushchikh (2020). Predatelstvo Khrista i tshifrovye propuska. Chast 2. *Dvizhenie nepominaushchikh. Analitika sobytii*. April 17. URL: https://www.youtube.com/watch?v=xf5ZQC-kRAw&list=PL8i7s8Nj2FNNwoFmB4tvdHcIJ6U4RD4fG&index=5

Dvizhenie nepominaushchikh (2020). V podderzhku skhiig. Sergiya. Ch. 2. Obrashchenie k russkomu narodu. *Dvizhenie nepominaushchikh. Analitika sobytii*. July 28. URL: https://www.youtube.com/watch?v=PqJ__-IiL4A&list=PL8i7s8Nj2FNNwo FmB4tvdHcIJ6U4RD4fG&index=1

Efanov, Andrei, Fr. (2020). Kak prichashchatsya vo vremya epidemii koronavirusa? *Foma*. March 7. URL: https://foma.ru/kak-prichashhatsya-vo-vremya-epidemii.html

Golovko, Oksana and Borodin, Fyodor, Fr. (2019). «Esli svyashchennik ne umeet druzhit, obshchiny ne poluchitsya». I pochemu inogda v khrame ne gotovy prinyat postoronnikh. *Pravmir*. September 26. URL: https://www.pravmir.ru/ esli-svyashhennik-ne-umeet-druzhit-obshhiny-ne-poluchitsya-i-pochemu-inogda-v-hrame-ne-gotovy-prinyat-postoronnih/

Kirill, Patriarch (2014). Na prikhodakh dolzhna byt pravilno postavlena rabota po priobshcheniyu k obshchine tekh, kto tolko vkhodit v khram. *Russkaya Pravoslavnaya Tserkov. Official web site of the Moscow Patriarchy*. December 23. URL: http:// www.patriarchia.ru/db/text/3888293.html

Kirill, Patriarch (2020). Slovo Svyateishego Patriarcha Kirilla v den pamayti prepodobnogo Sergiya Radonezhskogo posle Liturgii v Troitse-Sergievoi lavre. *Russkaya Pravoslavnaya Tserkov. Official web site of the Moscow Patriarchy*. July 18. URL: http://www.patriarchia.ru/db/text/5665266.html

Kormoukhin, Andrei (2020). Pochemu ya poidu v khram na Paskhu. *VKontakte*. April 14. URL: https://vk.com/wall209290103_3657

Kotrelev, Fyodor, Fr. (2012). Chto delayet prikhod obshchinoi? Opyt pastyrei i prikhozhan. *Neskuchnyi sad*. January 7. URL: http://www.nsad.ru/articles/chto-delaet-prihod-obshhinoj

Kvachkov, Vladimir (2020/1). Koronavirus operatsiya mirovoi zakulisy Chipirovanie. *Andreyiz1946*. March 25. URL: https://www.youtube.com/ watch?v=kK8-R_-JrUU

Kvachkov, Vladimir (2020/2). Koronavirus, Trump, biologicheskoe oruzhie, tsifrovoi kartser. *Svobodnaya pressa* April 29. URL: https://www.youtube.com/ watch?v=2ni6h-PoS8A

Kuzmicheva, Aleksandra and Breev, Georgii, Fr. (2013). Protoierei Georgii Breev ob anatomii tserkovnoi obshchiny, nastoyashchei druzhbe i glavnom interese v zhizni. *Pravmir*. December 3. URL: https://www.pravmir.ru/protoierej-georg ij-breev-ob-anatomii-cerkovnoj-obshhiny-nastoyashhej-druzhbe-i-glavnom-interese-v-zhizni/#ixzz3clJI7kRb

Legoyda, Vladimir (2020). Paskhu prazdnovali i vo vremya chumy – otprazdnuem i seichas. *RIA*. April 4. URL: https://ria.ru/20200404/1569577073.html

Legoyda, Vladimir (2020). *Telegram*. May 12. URL: https://t.me/vladimirlegoyda

Legoida, Vladimir (2020). V Moskve stroyat tserkvi shagovoi dostupnosti. *Russkaya Pravoslavnaya Tserkov. Official web site of the Moscow Patriarchy*. September 15. URL: http://www.patriarchia.ru/db/text/1275696.html

Moskva – Tretii Rim (2020). Tserkov ne dolzhna podchinyatsya gosudarstvu... O zaprete na bogosluzheniya v svyazi s koronovirusom. *Moskva – Tretii Rim*. March 15. URL: https://3rm.info/main/79374-cerkov-ne-dolzhna-podchinjatsja-gosud arstvu-o-zaprete-na-bogosluzhenija-v-svjazi-s-koronavirusom.html

Moskva Tretii Rim (2020). Antikhrista gotovyat k prezentatsii miru... V Britanii predlozhili dlya borby s Covid-19 sozdat mirovoe pravitelstvo. *Moskva–Tretii*

Rim. March 28. URL: https://3rm.info/main/79516-antihrista-gotovjat-k-prezentacii-miru-v-britanii-predlozhili-dlja-borby-covid-19-sozdat-mirovoe-pravitelstvo.html

Moskva – Tretii Rim (2020). Tsekh v pomeshchenii krama... Kak v starye «dobrye» bezboznye vremena. *Moskva–Tretii Rim.* April 11. URL: https://3rm.info/main/79675-ceh-v-pomeschenii-hrama-kak-v-starye-dobrye-bezbozhnye-vremena.html

Novaya gazeta. (2020). Kogda RPTs perestala byt tserkoviyu? Strim s Andreem Kuraevym. May 10. URL: https://novayagazeta.ru/articles/2020/05/10/85321-kogda-rpts-perestala-byt-tserkovyu-strim-s-andreem-kuraevym

NTV (2020). Paskha Khristova. Bogosluzhenie v Khrame Khrista Spasitelya. April 18. URL: https://www.youtube.com/watch?v=Himz9wrsUwg

Pervyi mezhdunarodnyi pozitivnyi portal (2020). Dorogie veterany: Prostite nas! Ispravimsya! S Dnem Pobedy! 9 maya 2020 g. *Pervyi mezhdunarodnyi pozitivnyi portal.* May 8. URL: https://www.youtube.com/watch?v=mc3eJA6pD1c

Pitirim. Bishop (2020). Episkop Pitirim. Official channel of the rector of the Moscow Spiritual Academy. *Telegram.* April 24-25. URL: https://t.me/pitirimtvorogov

RIA (2020). Legoyda: neumestno sravnivat situatsiyu v Tserkvi seichas i v nachale 20 veka. April 17. URL: https://ria.ru/20200417/1570191862.html

Rozhkov, Vladimir, Fr. (2020). Sanitarnyi terror»: tserkvi kak «rassadniki epidemicheskikh zabolevanii». Iz knigi protoiereya Vladimira Rozhkova «Zapiski svyashchennika». *Ahilla.* Feburary 27. URL: https://ahilla.ru/sanitarnyj-terror-tserkvi-kak-rassadniki-epidemicheskih-zabolevanij/

Russkaya Pravoslavnaya Tserkov. (2020). Instruktsiya nastoyatelyam prikhodov i podvorii, igumenam i igumeniyam monastyrei Moskovskoi eparkhii v svyazi s ugrozoi rasprostraneniya koronavirusnoi infektsii. *Russkaya Pravoslavnaya Tserkov. Official web site of the Moscow Patriarchy.* March 17. URL: http://www.patriarchia.ru/db/text/5608418.html

Russkaya Pravoslavnaya Tserkov (2020). Pravila dlya soversheniya treb na domu i v lechebnykh uchrezhdeniyakh pri poseshchenii lyudei, nakhodyashchikhsya v rezhime izolyatsii, svyazannoi s opasnostiyu zarazheniya, ili zarazhennykh koronavirusnoi infeksiei. *Russkaya Pravoslavnaya Tserkov. Official web site of the Moscow Patriarchy.* April 6. URL: http://www.patriarchia.ru/db/text/5618000.html

Russkaya Pravoslavnaya Tserkov (2020). Tsirkulyarnoe pismo Mitropolita Voskresenskogo Dionisiya. *Russkaya Pravoslavnaya Tserkov. Official web site of the Moscow Patriarchy.* April 11. URL: http://www.patriarchia.ru/db/text/5620438.html

Russkaya Pravoslavnaya Tserkov (2020). O blagoslovenii kulichei i paskh v domashnikh usloviyakh. *Russkaya Pravoslavnaya Tserkov. Official web site of the Moscow Patriarchy.* April 14. URL: http://www.patriarchia.ru/db/text/5621930.html

Russkaya Pravoslavnaya Tserkov (2020). Rasporyazhenie Svyateishego Patriarcha Kirilla ob otvetstvennosti za nesoblyudenie ukazanii, napravlennykh na ogranichenie rasprostraneniya koronavirusnoi infektsii. *Russkaya Pravoslavnaya Tserkov. Official web site of the Moscow Patriarchy*. April 27. URL: http://www.patri archia.ru/db/text/5629099.html

Russkaya Pravoslavnaya Tserkov (2020). Tsirkulyarnoe pismo Mitropolita Voskresenskogo Dionisiya. *Russkaya Pravoslavnaya Tserkov. Official web site of the Moscow Patriarchy*. June 1st. URL: http://www.patriarchia.ru/db/text/5645698.html

Saveliev, Andrei (2020). Beseda 58. Koronavirus. Sotsialno-ekonomicheskie posledstviya. Live. March 24. URL: https://www.youtube.com/watch?v=BsWDei9z204

Saveliev Andrei (2020). Vot vsyo i proyasnilos. Zamysel koronavyrusei oboznachilsya v detalyakh. YouTube. May 21. URL: https://www.youtube.com/watch?v=CW3IPdsdjfk

Savva, Igor, Fr. (2020). Gospod otvechaet na Evkharisticheskuyu molitvu distantsionno na kazhdoi liturgii. *Cerkvarium*. May 16. URL: https://cerkvarium.org/ru/spetstemy/tserkov-i-koronavirus/otets-igor-savva-gospod-otvechaet-na-evkharisticheskuyu-molitvu-distantsionno-na-kazhdoj-liturgii

Selinov, Pyotr (n.d.). Pandemiya strakha. COVID-19 glazami svyashchennika-vracha. Intervyu s Feodoritom Senchukovym. *Prikhozhanin*. URL: https://prihozhanin.msdm.ru/home/pogovorit/2733-pandemiya-strakha-covid-19-glazami-svyashchennika-vracha.html

Sergii, Aliev (2020). vystupil v zashchitu skhiigumena Sergiya (Romanova). Pervyi mezhdunarodnyi pozitivnyi portal. May 1st. URL: https://www.youtube.com/watch?v=oprvAoPaIII

Sergii (Romanov), Skhiigumen (2020/1). Pandemiya neveriya. Ne propoved Srednii Put. May 26. URL: https://www.youtube.com/watch?v=KySJRYBFe-8

Sergii (Romanov), Skhiigumen (2020/2). Gde vera v chistote–tam net raskola. Sredneuralskii zhenskii monastyr. *Vsevolod Moguchev*. 19 June 2020. URL: https://www.youtube.com/watch?v=T9NabgOOnNo

Sergii (Romanov), Skhiigumen (2020/3). Komu prinadlezhit vlast v Rossii? Predlozhenie dlya prezidenta Vladimira Putina. *Vsevolod Moguchev*. July 12. URL: https://www.youtube.com/watch?v=_eydP556eu4&feature=youtube&fbclid=IwAR1Tb38j6PXJ25X_dG-Z76sW4AxF5URVpfKXypdR0_d4fOHSQkJVjy2Bt4U

Telekanal Spas (2020). Patriarkh prizval veruiushchikh molitsya doma, sleduya podvigu Marii Egipetskoi. *Telekanal Spas*. March 29. URL: https://www.youtube.com/watch?v=8uztpNfGvco

Telekanal Spas (2020). Reaktsiya professora Alekseya Osipova. *Telekanal Spas*. May 20. URL:https://www.youtube.com/watch?v=H1SYxOJCxYM&feature=youtu.be&fbclid=IwAR28wK0-tZ_yZGlIlPPXD4TETJzQzPISV 9z1AD-PIbM8dRB9PsWTjN-fpy6U

Tyurenkov, Mikhail and Metropolitan Daniil (Dorovskikh) (2020). Koronavirus – nakazanie Bozhie nashemu narodu. *Tsargrad TV*. April 7. URL: https://tsar grad.tv/articles/mitropolit-daniil-dorovskih-koronavirus-nakazanie-bozhie-nashemu-narodu_246712

Tyurenkov, Mikhail (2020). "Paskha bez prikhozan": kak perezhit koronavirusnoe ispytanie. *Tsargrad* TV. April 13. URL: https://tsargrad.tv/articles/pasha-bez-prihozhan-kak-perezhit-koronavirusnoe-ispytanie_247838?fbclid=IwAR1CdyqLc_BCl5GOHTtBJFciv_ocVWjHEAMPDlebF3BxoY8jLwJ34ZMIyxc

Tyurenkov, Mikhail (2020). *Facebook*. May 25. URL: https://www.facebook.com/tyu renkov/posts/3197908793592950

Utkina, Anna and Nun Evgeniya (Senchukova) (2016). Kak prichashchatsya vo vremya epidemii grippa? *Pravmir*. February 2nd. URL: https://www.pravmir.ru/pr ichashhenie-vo-vremya-epidemii-est-li-risk-1/

Vaisburd, Dmitrii (2020). Evkharistiya onlain: predvaritelnye itogi. *Ahilla*. June 10. URL: https://ahilla.ru/evharistiya-onlajn-predvaritelnye-itogi/?fbclid=IwAR0X V-E84fQ-pjeW3MRzG5F74kd8doZM25GTZljiQPQXFK2AM_9DyeSKQs8

Vesti (2020). Tserkov i mir. Broadcast of 30.05.2020. Ekaterina Gracheva asks questions. *Vesti*. May 30. URL: https://vera.vesti.ru/video/show/video_cid/2152528

VKontakte (2020). Pryamoi efir s Andreem Kormoukhinym. Dvizhenie Sorok Sorokov. *VKontakte*. April 6. URL: https://vk.com/videos-53664310?z=video-53664310_456240982%2Fpl_-53664310_-2

VKontakte (2020). Pryamoi efir s Andreem Kormoukhinym. Dvizhenie Sorok Sorokov. *VKontakte*. April 8. URL: https://vk.com/videos-53664310?z=video-53664310_456240999%2Fpl_-53664310_-2

Volga. MBKh Media. (2020). Eto khula na Boga». Svyashcenniku iz Nizhegorodskoi oblasti zapretili sluzhenie posle otkaza zakryt khram dlya prikhozhan. *Volga. MBKh Media*. April 16. URL: https://vk.com/@volgambk.media-eto-hula-na-boga-svyaschenniku-iz-nizhegorodskoi-oblasti-zap

Volkov, Aleksandr (2020). O bogosluzhebnoi partizanshchine. *Facebook*. April 5. URL:https://www.facebook.com/permalink.php?story_fbid=39329844567424 89&id=100000929212448

Volkov, Vladimir (2020). O bogosluzhebnoi partizanshchine. *Facebook*. April 5. URL: https://www.facebook.com/permalink.php?story_fbid=393298445674248 9&id=100000929212448

Zakharov, Aleksandr (2020). Batyushka Aleksandr o koronaviruse. *YouTube*. June 7. URL: https://www.youtube.com/watch?v=juYj-vRvhR0

Zhosul, Elena (2020). Facebook. April 18. URL: https://www.facebook.com/ezhosul

Towards a Covid-Jihad – Millennialism in the field of Jihadism

Nina Käsehage

Abstract

Since the appearance of Covid-19, various jihadist voices from the environment of the former Islamic State (IS) emerged and invoked their previous combat fellows to resume the battle towards the 'disbelievers'. Self-appointed religious authorities claim to possess the interpretational sovereignty regarding the 'divine signs' visualized by the pandemic: the 'just punishment' for those who have not been true believers.

The narrative of the final battle between the 'good' and the 'evil' indicates a well-known tradition in the field of millennialism. Against the background of a transnational health crisis, this motive is currently revitalized and interlinked by IS affiliated groups and individuals with the fear of some Muslims regarding the end time. With this strategy, IS tries to fuel hatred and violence towards European societies and regain fame again.

Specific vulnerable groups such as (hopeless) former Foreign Terrorist Fighters (FTFs) and female inhabitants of detention camps in Syria as well as their children are the main targets of the IS narratives concerning Covid-19. According to their inner assessment, they seem to have nothing to 'lose' in this live but to gain a lot more in the afterlife. Therefore, a discussion of the elements of religious fundamentalism, especially in view of its millennialist and apocalyptic elements, is supposed to visualize possible points of reference regarding a deconstruction of the jihadist misuse of the pandemic. This approach could be helpful in terms of a change of perspective for those who are (still) addicted to the violence promoting ideology of IS.

Keywords: Covid-Jihad, IS, Jihadism, Millennialism, Pandemic, Psychological Warfare, Religious Fundamentalism

1. Introduction

In 2009, Andreas Armborst stated: "While religious fundamentalism in general isn't necessarily related to violent or even terrorist activism this is the case with jihadism."[1] Armborst's statement indicated the increasing trend to equate religious fundamentalism with violence or terrorism and in addition with Islamic extremism since 9/11. Although voices occurred that considered the rise of the pandemic as a possible opportunity to weakening terrorism in a larger amount[2], this chapter aims to examine the narratives of actors and groups related to jihadist movements such as the Islamic State (IS) or Al Qaeda (AQ) with regard to the pandemic. With the help of various examples from the field of jihadism, this chapter aims to illustrate how Covid-19 will be misused for new recruitments and the motivation of the present adherents in view of the possible resurrection of jihadist movements that rendered meaningless.

It starts with a short description of basic elements of Islamic fundamentalism as an expression of an *Abrahamic Fundamentalism* and its relation to violent activism. Beside groups as for instance the Liberation Tigers of Tamil Eelam, jihadist groups affiliated to AQ and IS as well as former FTFs, can be labelled as millennialist groups with regard to their "apocalyptic interpretation of reality".[3] According to Abdul Basit, the pandemic "feeds into the apocalyptic, end-of-time narratives of ISIS".[4] The aforementioned groups use the vulnerability of both, societies and states in terms of the pandemic, for the mobilization of their adherents in terms of Covid-19 that is religiously interpreted as a divine plague for sinners, who are – beside the disbelievers – those Muslims who have joined a 'Western' life-style and follow national laws as well as values in Western countries.[5]

The pandemic sows the seeds for fundamentalist tendencies within the field of violent Islamist extremism. The number of new opportunities for adapting or expanding jihadist activities in certain ways, including violent acts, increased since

---

1   Andreas Armborst (2009). A Profile of Religious Fundamentalism and Terrorist Activism. *Defence Against Terrorism Review* Vol. 2, No. 1. Spring, p. 51.

2   Cf. Dylan Nicholson (2020). 'COVID-19 an opportunity for terrorists or a threat to their existence'. *Defence Connect*. April 29. See: https://www.defenceconnect.com.au/key-enablers/5995-global-terror-and-covid-19

3   G. A. Almond, R. Scott Appleby and Emmanuel Sivan (2003) (Eds.). *Strong Religion. The Rise of Fundamentalism around the World*. Chicago; London: The University of Chicago Press, p. 104.

4   Abdul Basit (2020). 'The COVID-19 Pandemic: An Opportunity for Terrorist Groups?' *Counter Terrorist Trends and Analyses* 12, 3, 8.

5   Cf. MEMRI (2020/1). 'The way forward - A word of advice on the coronavirus pandemic'. In Al-Qaeda Central: *COVID-19 Is Divine Punishment For Sins Of Mankind; Muslims Must Repent, West Must Embrace Islam*. March 31. See: https://www.memri.org/reports/al-qaeda-central-covid-19-divine-punishment-sins-mankind-muslims-must-repent-west-must

the rise of Covid-19. In certain circumstances the fear for the 'invisible' divine punishment could even act as a motivation for action. This development will be discussed in a second step with regard to *major forms of jihadist interpretations regarding the pandemic* in the field of jihadist movements, with a specific regard to IS.

This discussion is followed by a reflection of the future socio-political consequences *in the age of pandemic* that might shape the terrorism landscape in both the short and long term.

2. Elements of religious fundamentalism in the field of Jihadism

With regard to Almond et al. "nine characteristics of fundamentalism, five ideological and four organizational characteristics of fundamentalism" [6] can be identified:

"Ideological characteristics:
  Reactivity to the Marginalized of Religion
  Selectivity
  Moral Manichaeism
  Absolutism and Inerrancy and
  Millenialism and Messianism.

Organizational characteristics:
  Elect, Chosen Membership
  Sharp Boundaries
  Authoritarian Organization and
  Behavioural Requirements." [7]

By discussing elements of religious fundamentalism, for instance with regard to IS affiliated groups and actors, some of the typical patterns of behaviour of these jihadists are described, that could be predictive for their future performance concerning Covid-19 and the further development of the pandemic. [8]

---

6   Almond et al., 2003, pp. 93; 90-115.
7   Ib., pp. 93-98. Due to the fact that only some of these characteristics will be part of this chapter, not all of them are discussed in detail.
8   Although the discussion of the origins and development of (religious) fundamentalism could be debated at a larger amount, this chapter concentrates on a short discussion of this topic, mostly based on the research of Almond, Appleby and Sivan (2003).

2.1 Selected religious knowledge

According to Almond et al., religious leaders play a major role in terms of establishing and modelling fundamentalist movements.[9] Based on their privileged role within the jihadist community, self-declared 'preachers' with an affiliation for violence, legitimate individually selected Islamic sacred text passages from the Qur'an and the Ahādīth to identify Covid-19 as a 'divine punishment' for those believers who failed in fulfilling their (daily) religious duties and declare the virus as a wake-up sign for those, who still satisfy Allah's laws appropriately[10]. The latter ones should therefore join the fight against the *mushrikūn* (polytheists).[11] The use of the term 'Covid-Jihad'[12], a mixture of the classical interpretation of the concept of militant jihad, interlinked with the virus Covid-19, shall underline the need for each believer to follow Allah's will to divide the 'good' from the 'evil' and to establish a pure religiosity that could be practiced in a 'perfect' Islamic environment: the caliphate. The victims on the side of the Muslim fighters who might themselves die as a consequence of the pandemic are sacrificed as martyrs who gave their lives for the right Islamic cause and are guaranteed a place in Ǧanna (paradise).

The selection of religious knowledge by self-declared religious authorities follows the patterns of religious fundamentalism where some individuals pretend to be the 'true' interpreters of God's own will in order to gain the sovereignty towards religious sources. "A given religious leader inclined to extremism thereby nurtures the characteristic traits and elements of fundamentalism within the sector(s) of the religious community over which he exercises authority."[13]

2.2 The religious field and the religious capital

According to Bourdieu, the *religious field* is defined by interactions between laypersons and religious actors such as prophets and structured by the consumers and producers of spiritual goods. The producer's side provides a set of specialists who

---

9   Almond et al., 2003, p. 118.

10   For instance groups such as "the Taliban reflect the situation by issuing a statement that the Coronavirus is the result of divine wrath and that the "threat" must be faced with measures in accordance with Islamic teachings, such as praying and consulting the Qur'ān." In: Carmelo Galindo (2020). COVID-19, Jihadism and Biological Weapons. *Islamic Theology of Counter Terrorism (ITCT)*, p. 2.

11   Cf. Real Instituto el cano (2020). 'Crisis del coronavirus. La pandemia segun los yihadistas'. See: https://blog.realinstitutoelcano.org/crisis-del-coronavirus-la-pandemia-segun-los-yihadistas/

12   Cf. *Corona Jihad* in: Shewta Desai and Amarnath Amarasingam (2020). COVID-19, Misinformation and Anti-Muslim Violence in India. ISD (Ed.). *Strong Cities*. London; Washington DC, Beirut, Tokio, pp. 1-34.

13   Almond et al., 2003, p. 119.

are very competitive to each other because they are struggling about the accumulation of *religious capital*, which can be observed e.g. with regard to AQ and IS in terms of the 'right' interpretation of Allah's will (concerning the pandemic and beyond). Bourdieu defines *religious capital* as a product of this enhanced religious work in order to secure the continued existence of the *religious capital*.[14] On the side of communication, the laypersons are separated from the production as well as from the administration of spiritual goods[15], but must follow the imposed *religious habitus*.[16] As a consequence, a tension of power between the religious specialists and the laypersons can be observed. The specialists determine which kind of performances will be valued. Their own way of living is concerned as valuable for the society. That's why the *symbolic capital* provides a form of exercise of power that is imagined as (religiously) legitimized and considers the support and the acknowledgment by its adherents as a logical consequence of the superior position of the religious specialists in the *religious field*.[17] With respect to this assumption, the *charismatic leaders* of IS affiliated groups don't question their own religious authority.

2.3 Apocalyptic and millenialist expectations

Instead of looking for possibilities to make use of Covid-19 with regard to their group, some jihadist actors are inspired by the pandemic's effects such as *death* that much that they are likely to interpret it as the 'purge' of the world. Among those who link the rise of the pandemic with their apocalyptic or millenialist expectations towards the world, two groups can be identified:

> "those who believe that they must merely passively prepare for the end and that no other actions on their part are necessary, as well as [those] who believe that when the time is right they must act to facilitate or even initiate their version of Armageddon in order to secure salvation."[18]

The second type of actors could consider Covid-19 as an omen for the forecasted end time or as a sign of Allah's anger towards humanity: "The pandemic, which is evocative of [...] divine punishments, might then act as a catalyst for these groups

---

14   Pierre Bourdieu (2001). *Meditationen. Zur Kritik der scholastischen Vernunft*. Frankfurt a.M.: Suhrkamp, pp. 80; 320.

15   Bourdieu, 2001, pp. 56-57.,78; 304-305.

16   Ib., pp. 77-78, 318.

17   Ib., pp. 66-67; 310.; Cf. Pierre Bourdieu (1993). *Sozialer Sinn. Kritik der theoretischen Vernunft*. Frankfurt a. M.: Suhrkamp, pp. 205-221; Cf. Pierre Bourdieu (1998). *Praktische Vernunft. Zur Theorie des Handelns*. Frankfurt a. M.: Suhrkamp, pp. 173-176.; Cf. David Swartz (1996). Bridging the Study of Culture and Religion: Pierre Bourdieu's Political Economy of Symbolic Power. *Sociology of Religion* Vol. 57, No. 1, 77.

18   Gary Ackerman and Hayley Peterson (2020). Terrorism and COVID-19: Actual and Potential Impacts. *Perspectives on Terrorism* Vol. 14, iss. 3, June, 63.

to initiate whatever long-term plans they have been hatching, some of which might include violence against the public."[19]

3.   Major forms of jihadist interpretations regarding the pandemic

While the numbers of the victims of Covid-19 around the world increased, various jihadist interpretations concerning the reasons for the origin and the targets of the pandemic arose. The following two major IS narratives could be framed in view of Covid-19 and will be discussed in this chapter:

a) Covid-19 as a divine punishment for disbelievers and
b) The Impact of Covid-19 on IS Detention Camps.

Beside the major narrative, Covid-19 is partly described as a 'Western' construction to threat Muslims and conquer the increase of Islam[20]. Various Sunni jihadists have "claimed that Covid-19 is a plot by Islam's enemies".[21] According to *Abū Shekau*, one of the leaders of the IS-affiliated group Boko Haram, 'true' believer won't get infected with the virus. Therefore exists no need to combat the pandemic, but to see the virus as a governmental strategy against Islam.[22]

3.1   Covid-19 as a divine punishment for disbelievers

With regard to the lockdown and the social distancing, people are becoming more and more mistrustful towards their environment and their periods of internet use

---

19   Ackerman & Peterson, 2020, 63.
20   This topic is also used in return such as in India where "Hindu nationalist groups began to see the virus not as an entity spreading organically throughout India, but as a sinister plot by Indian Muslims to purposefully infect the population." In: Desai & Amarasingam, 2020, p. 2.
21   Ackerman & Peterson, 2020, p. 61.
22   Cf. John Campbell (2020). Boko Haram's Shekau Labels Anti-COVID-19 Measures an Attack on Islam in Nigeria. *Council on Foreign Relations.* April 17. See: https://www.cfr.org/blog/boko-hara ms-shekau-labels-anti-covid-19-measures-attack-islam-nigeria ; Cf. Hesham Shehab (2020). 'Islamist hate preacher warns Muslims to arm themselves amid coronavirus threats'. *JNS.* April 27. See: https://www.jns.org/opinion/islamist-hate-preacher-warns-muslims-to-arm-the mselves-amid-coronavirus-threats/

increased.[23] This provides a perfect breeding ground for jihadist online-recruitment with regard to people at risk for radicalization.[24]

According to Williams, a movement contains the following elements: a mutual ideology, recognized leadership, shared resources and operational coordination.[25] With regard to the concerned movements, it can be stated that this definition is applicable on IS affiliated movements, because they share the same jihadist ideology, followed at first *Abū Bakr al-Baghdadi* as their 'Khalif Ibrahim' and his successor at a later time, use the same selected religious and technical sources to exchange and have been (or still are) part of the caliphate's organizational structure.

With respect to the elements of religious fundamentalism, the search for *selectivity* symbolizes the wish to find a reliable peer group, in a world that seems to be cynical very often.[26] This search corresponds with a change in behaviour, when the new adherent of a religious fundamentalist group has found his new reference persons: this new peer group will present the rules of conduct that are of 'divine origin' to the new member, for instance related to food custodies, clothes and in view of contact to former friends. Usually, this behavioural change would be recognized by family, friends and neighbours of the radicalized individual. In times of the lockdown, this behavioural change will probably not be observed by the former social environment, because of the social distancing. The boundaries "between the saved and sinful in behaviour as well as in doctrine"[27] will be clearly defined by the 'new' family. Instead of the former societal contacts of the 'new-born' believer, the religious sources and explanations will become the new guideline for the convert. Though, nobody from the former social environment will be able to question the new religious messages, the convert might be at risk for a violent radicalization. According to the Metropolitan Police, "some terrorist groups have adapted their methods and messaging to the new environment, including using the coronavirus crisis."[28] The more time a vulnerable individual spends online, the more he or she might be at risk for adopting the jihadist truth about the 'real' origin of the pandemic as a 'divine punishment' for disbelievers and could be manipulated in terms of terrorist attacks.

---

23   Cf. Gordon Corera (2020). 'Coronavirus: Police warn of lockdown radicalisation threat'. *BBC*. June 10. See: https://www.bbc.com/news/uk-52997441, accessed on June 17, 2020.

24   Cf. Randy Borum (2004). *Psychology of Terrorism*. Tampa: University of South Florida.; Cf. David Ciampi (2005). Developmental and motivational factors of transnational terrorists. *Forensic Examiner* 14 (3), 29-34.

25   Cf. Rhys H. Williams (1994). Movement Dynamics and Social Challenge: Transforming Fundamentalist Ideology and Organization. In Martin E. Marty and R. Scott Appleby (Eds.). *Accounting for Fundamentalisms: The Dynamic Character of Movements*. Chicago, pp. 785-825.

26   Almond et al., 2003, p. 102.

27   Ib.

28   Cf. Corera (2020).

3.1.1 Online recruitment leading to offline actions

Online and offline recruitment efforts of jihadist groups are strengthened *in the age of pandemic*[29], such as through IS's creation of Covid-19 related hashtags that lead users to their propaganda sites.[30] The Hashtag#COVID19 of the new IS spokesman *Abū Hamza al-Qurashi* provides his speech *And the Disbelievers Will Know who Gets the Good End.* It contains *Abū Hamza's* framing of the pandemic "as God's justice against the West for their attacks against the so-called caliphate and the killing of Muslims."[31] In addition, he claims the will of IS to continue the fighting and calls the Doha peace agreement "a "cover" to strengthen an alliance between the "apostate" Taliban and "Crusaders" to fight ISIS in Afghanistan."[32] Covid-19 is described as a measure of the local "tyrant" governments to pretend public "health and safety" while putting "hundreds of thousands of Muslims in their prisons" where they are "tormented."[33] The online content of *Abū Hamza* functions as a mental instruction for jihadist recruits with regard to their individual renunciation of 'the' West that could lead to violent acts against it as a last resort.

According to Bourdieu, *Abū Hamza* possesses the *symbolic capital* within the *religious field* (of IS adherents) and expects the laypersons to follow his interpretation of God's will in view of the pandemic. Therefore, his current religious legitimacy be understood as a status quo of the religious balance of power and the result of former battles in relation to the monopol with regard to the legitimate practice of religious force, or better religious authority.[34]

3.1.2 Using the vulnerability of Western individuals at risk for radicalization

Beside the conflicts abroad, the hashtags and propaganda sites are focussing on Western populations that have been affected by the lockdown and are most vulnerable for radicalization because of "perceived personal losses, frustrations and

---

29   Cf. General Secretariat of the Council (2020). *Council Conclusions on EU External Action on Preventing and Countering Terrorism and Violent Extremism.* In Council of the European Union (Ed.). June 16. No. prev. doc.: 8742/20 + COR 1, pp. 1-16.; Cf. Edith Lederer (2020). 'UN chief: Extremists using COVID-19 to recruit online youths'. *AP News.* April 27. See: https://apnews.com/a6cf967c03f7ff00e170949a9eaeb11a

30   Cf. Annelies Pauwels (2020). 'How Europe's terrorists take advantage of the pandemic'. *EU Observer.* April 29. See: https://euobserver.com/opinion/148173

31   See Rita Katz (2020). Hashtag#ISIS. *SITE Intelligence Group.* May 29. See: https://www.linkedin.com/feed/, accessed on May 30, 2020.

32   Ib.

33   Ib.

34   Pierre Bourdieu (2000). Eine Interpretation der Religion nach Max Weber. In Pierre Bourdieu (Ed.). *Das religiöse Feld. Texte zur Ökonomie des Heilsgeschehens.* Konstanz: UVK, p. 25.

reminders of death, all of which can be associated with the pandemic."[35] They offer messages that Allah's rage towards the disbelievers can only be interrupted by following the path of 'pure' Islam. Therefore, jihadist groups such as AQ[36] and IS who consider the pandemic as a punishment towards the evil, personalized by apostates, atheists and crusaders, "have used their communication channels to send action guidelines to their followers to offer a doctrinal response to the current situation and [...] indications for the mobility of their assets and not be detected by security forces."[37] AQ has encouraged adherents to convert to Islam during the lockdown and to stay at home in a recent online publication.[38]

Another target of IS supporters are the security forces. IS affiliated groups and networks are calling their followers for spreading the virus among them.[39]

According to Juan Zarate, a senior fellow at the *Combating Terrorism Center* in West Point,

"The severity and extreme disruption of a novel coronavirus will likely spur the imagination of the most creative and dangerous groups and individuals to reconsider bioterrorist attacks. [...] With the world now reeling simply from a novel coronavirus with a relatively low lethality rate, some extreme terrorist groups and rogue scientists willing to venture into apocalyptic fields might see this moment as a catalyst for exploring again the possibilities of bioterrorism. The Islamic State and al-Qa`ida have already touted the destructive effects of the virus on the West, and white supremacist groups have called for their adherents to use the virus in spray bottles to infect specific targets."[40]

3.1.3   New types of terrorism and the threat of bioterrorist attacks

Lockdowns and social distancing measures will prevent various terrorist acts in terms of logistical aspects such as "the movement of operatives within and across borders, the acquisition of vehicles, weapons and equipment."[41] Therefore, the or-

---

35   Ackerman & Peterson, 2020, p. 61.
36   Cf. MEMRI (2020/1).
37   Galindo, 2020, p. 2.
38   Cf. Julie Coleman (2020). The Impact of Coronavirus on Terrorism in the Sahel. *International Centre for Counter-Terrorism*. April 16. See: https://icct.nl/publication/the-impact-of-coronaviru s-on-terrorism-in-the-sahel/
39   Cf. Kyler Ong and Nur Aziemah Azman (2020). 'Distinguishing Between the Extreme Far-right and IS's Calls to Exploit COVID-19'. *Counter Terrorist Trends and Analyses* 12, 18-21.
40   Paul Cruickshank and Don Rassler (2020). A View from the CT Foxhole: A Virtual Roundtable on COVID-19 and Counterterrorism with Audrey Kurth Cronin, Lieutenant General (Ret.) Michael Nagata, Magnus Ranstorp, Ali Soufan, and Juan Zarate. *CTC Sentinel* Vol. 13, iss. 6. June, p.4.
41   Ackerman & Peterson, 2020, 60.

ganization of attacks will be modified, e.g. with regard to a growing number of lone wolf attacks as could be seen in the case of a jihadist who stabbed seven people in Romans-sur-Isère in April 2020.[42]

With respect to EUROPOL's *EU Terrorism Situation and Trend report 2019 (TE-SAT 2019)* "online discussions of planning Chemical, Biological, Radioactive or other Nuclear (CBRN) attacks increased in 2018."[43] The intensions to use such materials with regard to an attack were mainly expressed by jihadists in closed forums. In July and August 2018, the IS-linked group al-Abd Al-Faqir Media (AF Media) launched a campaign titled *"Bio-Terror via Telegram* promoting the use of biological weapons."[44]

The use of chemical and biological weapons of mass destruction, such as the biological toxins abrin and ricin, that have been characterized as "the nuclear weapons of the poor", because they are accessible by any individual or group with terrorist intentions, could be observed in the sarin attack of the millennialist group *Aum Shinrikyo* on the Tokyo subway in 1995.[45] Three years before this attack, the group has tried to collect samples of the Ebola virus in Zaire.[46]

According to Galindo, the Islamic State made use of chemical weapons in recent years: "From 2014 to 2017, a total of 76 chemical weapons (chlorine and sulphur mustard) attacks occurred in Iraq and Syria."[47]

Several cases of IS-affiliated individuals who tried to make use of CBRN ingredients for terrorist attacks in European cities occurred in 2018. The following three ones are just an example of this development within the European Jihadist milieu:

"In May, a man with Egyptian heritage was arrested in Paris "on suspicion of preparing a terrorist attack" with ricin.[48]

In June, a terrorist plot by a Tunisian citizen using ricin was prevented in Cologne.[49]

---

42   Cf. Francesco Marone (2020). Terrorism and Counterterrorism in a Time of Pandemic. *Italian Institute for International Political Studies.* May 15. See: https://www.ispionline.it/en/pubblicazi one/terrorism-and-counterterrorism-time-pandemic-26165.

43   EUROPOL (2020). *European Union Terrorism Situation and Trend report 2019 (TE-SAT).* Brussels, p. 20.

44   Ib.

45   Galindo, 2020, p. 2.; Cf. Robert Lifton (1999) *Destroying the World to Save It: Aum Shinrikyo, Apocalyptic Violence, and the New Global Terrorism.* New York: Metropolitan Books.; Cf. Senate Government Affairs Permanent Subcommittee on Investigations (Minority Staff) (1995). *Hearings on Global Proliferation of Weapons of Mass Destruction: A Case Study on the Aum Shinrikyo.* October 31.

46   Cf. David Kaplan (2000). Aum Shinrikyo (1995). In Jonathan Tucker (Ed.) *Toxic Terror: Assessing Terrorist Use of Chemical and Biological Weapons.* Cambridge, Massachusetts: MIT Press.

47   Galindo, 2020, pp. 2-3.

48   EUROPOL, 2020, p. 19.

49   Ib.

In November, a Lebanese individual was arrested for the preparation of a chemical-biological plot in Sardinia that was linked with another attack in Lebanon."[50]

According to Nicholas J. Rasmussen, the former director of the *National Center for Counter-Terrorism* (NCCT), this bio-terrorism warfare practiced by IS adherents can be seen as a result of

"the conflict in Iraq and Syria [that] has been [...] a gaming laboratory for ISIS and other extremist organizations to participate in efforts to refine their ability to use chemicals, toxins [and] other materials that would have a chemical or toxic effect on the battlefield."[51]

Therefore, the CBRN attacks by former IS fighters and groups as well as individuals who are affiliated to IS will probably replace the conventional terrorist attacks within Europe in the future.[52]

The risk assessment concerning these new terror methods[53] depends on various factors such as "technical experience, availability of materials, delivery capacity"[54] and of course on the effectiveness of the measures of the prevention of violent extremism (PVE) regarding both returnees and vulnerable individuals 'at home' who are at risk for violent Islamic radicalization.

A particular challenge in terms of the pandemic and the related lockdown is

"the isolation from others and alienation from normal social intercourse itself [that] means that there is a lower chance that behaviors associated with radicalization will be noticed by others who might otherwise be able to intervene."[55]

As a consequence of the possible threat of CBRN attacks by violent Islamic extremists, national catastrophe plans – with regard to a Covid-19 linked bio-warfare caused by jihadists – have to be developed immediately at this stage for enabling for instance European countries to be prepared for this worst case scenario as possible targets.[56]

---

50   Ib.

51   Nicholas Rasmussen in January 2018, cited from Galindo, 2020, p. 3.

52   Cf. European Institute for Counter Terrorism and Conflict Prevention (2020).; Cf. Gary Ackerman & Kevin Moran (2005). Bioterrorism and Threat Assessment. Paper #22. *Weapons of Mass Destruction Commission*. Stockholm, pp. 1-18. See: http://docshare01.docshare.tips/files/2791/27919768.pdf ; Cf. Cheryl Loeb (2009). Jihadists and Biological and Toxin Weapons. In Gary Ackerman and Jeremy Tamsett (Eds.). *Jihadists and Weapons of Mass Destruction*. Boca Raton, Florida: CRC Press.

53   Cf. Jessica Stern (1999). *The Ultimate Terrorists*. Cambridge, MA: Harvard University Press.

54   Galindo, 2020, p. 4.

55   Ackerman & Peterson, 2020, p. 62.

56   Cf. Richard Pilch (2020). 'How to keep the new coronavirus from being used as a terrorist weapon'. *Bulletin of the Atomic Scientists*. March 27. See: https://thebulletin.org/2020/03/how-to-keep-the-new-coronavirus-from-being-used-as-a-terrorist-weap-on/# ; Cf. Law and Crime

4.   The Impact of Covid-19 on IS Detention[57] Camps

Since the decline of IS, its members have tried to flew the former occupied territories in Syria and other regions but were caught by Kurdish groups such as the *Syrian Democratic Forces (SDF)*. According to Savage, the *SDF* has installed several detention camps for former IS fighters in Ain Issa, Hasaka and Kobani.[58] The information about the number of the detainees, vary widely and were quantified by Savage "on approximately 9,000 Syrian or Iraqi men, and 2,000 men from 50 other countries"[59] in the year 2019.

The *SDF* is responsible for the hygienic measures against Covid-19 within the detention camps and prisons. They call for more international support because adequate resources and infrastructure are needed in a greater extent.[60]

The longer the former IS members will be imprisoned the more realistic seems their will to organize breakouts.[61] This assumption correspondents with the fear of an outbreak of Covid-19 within the camps and its use for terrorist recruitment by the media centers of IS in view of possible attacks in Western cities on the so called disbelievers. Accordingly, several riot attempts within prisons and detention camps have been reported so far.[62]

(2020). 'DOJ Just Warned That Intentional Spread of COVID-19 Could Be Terrorism - What It Means'. March 26. See: https://lawandcrime.com/covid-19-pandemic/doj-just-warned-that-intentional-spread-of-covid-19-could-be-terrorism-what-it-means

57   The use of the terms 'detention camp' as well as word the 'imprisoned' applied on individuals that might not be 'guilty' in terms of criminal offences in the name of the former Islamic State such as children of (former) IS affiliated individuals, is difficult from an academic perspective. Therefore, it is not used in its common understanding but as a reference to the publications on that topic. Similar difficulties appeared in terms of the use of the word 'prison' in this context. A comparable discussion on this issue can be found by Audrey Alexander (2020/1). The Security Threat COVID-19 Poses to the Northern Syria Detention Camps Holding Islamic State Members. *CTC Sentinel* Vol. 13, iss. 6. June, p.16.

58   Cf. Charlie Savage (2020/1). 'The Kurds' Prisons and Detention Camps for ISIS Members, Explained'. *New York Times*. October 22nd. See: https://www.nytimes.com/2019/10/22/world/middleeast/the-kurds-prisons-and-detention-camps-for-isis-members-explained.html

59   Savage cited from Alexander, 2020/1, p. 16.

60   Cf. Ibrahim and Christou Kajjo (2019). 'Virus Fears Spread at Camps for ISIS Families in Syria's North East'. *Report of the Independent International Commission of Inquiry on the Syrian Arab Republic*. United Nations Human Rights Council. September.

61   Cf. Lead Inspector General Report to the United States Congress (2020). *Operation Inherent Resolve*, January 1, 2020 - March 31, 2020'. May 13, pp. 57-59.; Cf. John Dunford and Brandon Wallace (2019). 'ISIS Prepares for Breakout in Prisons and Camps'. *Institute for the Study of War*. September 23rd. See: https://www.understandingwar.org/background/isis-prepares-for-breakout-in-prisons-and-camps

62   Cf. Rojava Information Center (2020/1). 'Coronavirus crisis in North and East Syria: 22 April Update'. April 22nd. See: https://rojavainformationcenter.com/2020/04/coronavirus-crisis-in-north-and-east-syria-22-april-update / Cf. John Dunford and Jennifer Cafarella (2019). 'ISIS's

With respect to the examinations of Alexander, both the risks of riots as well as breakouts remain high. As a consequence,

> "the SDF adapts its security presence within detention facilities to mitigate the spread of COVID-19 [...because if] an outbreak occurs in the facilities and significantly affects security forces and other administrators in detention sites, further reductions in staffing or substitutions with personnel who have less experience managing camps or prisons, could further amplify these risks".[63]

4.1 The influence of IS narratives on Covid-19 on female detainees

According to the estimate of Arafat, "approximately 11,000 foreign women and children of ISIS militants from about 54 countries are held in a separate part of the camp known as the ISIS Foreigners' Section."[64]

Foreign female IS adherents have organized their own court as well as they have installed their own religious police in comparison to the female religious police units such as the *Al-Khanssa Brigade* of the former Islamic State. The religious court of IS related detainees set penalties for 'irreligious' behavior, "including killing Iraqi refugees and Syrian IDPs on the other side of the camp [and] even killing children when they disobey orders of the ISIS council."[65]

IS's weekly magazine *Al-Naba* published an article dealing with the Islamic principles to protect believers in view of Covid-19 in March 2020.[66] In comparison to the first three generations of followers of the Islamic prophet Muḥammad, the Ṣaḥāba, quotes from Ahādīth, e.g. *Abū Huraira*, were taken that distributed to their individual hygienic in order to avoid sickness. According to some IS related propaganda groups on *Facebook* or *Twitter*, the virus was supposed to be sent by Allah. Therefore, it was said that those believers who put their trust in Allah and pray for support would be protected from illness by his shelter.

Although the IS guideline towards the pandemic that had been published in *Al-Naba* never referred to other organizations such as the *World Health Organization*

Opportunity in Northern Syria's Detention Facilities and Camps'. *Institute for the Study of War.* May 13. See: https://www.understandingwar.org/background/isiss-opportunity-in-northern-syria

63   Alexander, 2020/1, p. 19.

64   Cf. Hisham Arafat (2020). 'Remittances for ISIS women in northeast Syria's al-Hawl camp trigger imminent resurgence of the jihadist group'. *North Press Agency.* May 31st. See: https://npasyria.com/en/blog.php?id_blog=2695&sub_blog=4%20&name_blog=Remittances%20for%20ISIS%20women%20in%20northeast%20Syria%E2%80%99s%20al-Hawl%20camp%20trigger%20imminent%20resurgence%20of%20the%20jihadist%20group

65   Cf. Ib.

66   Cf. توجيهات شرعية للتعامل مع الأوبئة, Al-Naba, 225.

(WHO) as sources in view of health security, they provided WHO's and other organization's hygienic requirements, e.g. the cover of the mouth in view of avoiding and spreading infections and the necessity for saving and covering water and food. IS used the expertise of the organizations and nations whom they generally marked as 'disbelievers' with regard to the prevention of the disease, while simultaneously referring to Allah and the Ahādīth as the origins of their preventive recommendations.[67]

Messages on *Telegram* included videos of female IS adherents who are located in refugee camps, such as Al-Hawl in Syria, and said that they will not be infected with Covid-19 because *Abū Bakr al-Baghdadi* would guide them and their 'true' Islamic religious practice would save them from falling ill. In addition, they claimed that Muslims, who would die of Covid-19, would be 'unmasked' as disbelievers.[68] In their opinion, Covid-19 was sent above from Allah to serve as his soldier in a war against the so called 'infidels'.[69]

Predominately female[70] detainees from Turkey[71] and Western countries receive a lot of financial support from their relatives outside the camps.[72] In 2019, five female IS adherents tried to bribe security guards with $2,000 per person to get them out of the camp, but were discovered before they could reach Idlib province.[73] The detained women financed specific attacks on the camp's security personnel with the help of the money transfers.[74] When *Abū Bakr al-Baghdadi* died, the new caliph

---

67   Sigalit Maor-Hirsh (2020). ISIS in the Age of COVID-19 - From Islamizing the Pandemic to Implementing the Jihadist Strategy. *International Institute for Counterterrorism* (ICT). April, pp. 2-3.

68   Cf. MEMRI (2020/2). 'ISIS Women at Hawl Refugee Camp: Coronoavirus does not infect true Muslims; Only Infidels and Oppressors Die of the Virus.' April 9. See: https://www.memri.org /tv/isis-women-at-hawl-refugee-camp-coronavirus-does-not-infect-true-muslims

69   Cf. Al-Naba, 227.

70   Cf. Aymenn Jawad Al-Tamimi (2019). 'Free the Female Prisoners: A Campaign to Free Women Held in SDF Camps'. *Aymenn Jawad Al-Tamimi blog*. October 15. See: https://www. aymenn-jawad.org/free-the-female- prisoners-a-campaign-to-free

71   Cf. Aaron Zelin (2019/1). 'Turkish Woman Promotes Fundraising Effort for Widows of 'Martyrs,' Children, Prisoners in Turkey and in Al-Hol Camp in Syria.' *MEMRI*. January 28.

72   Cf. James Longman (2020). 'Caliphate Wives share their stories year after ISIS defeat: Reporter's Notebook'. *ABC News*. February 19. See: https://www.abcnews.go/International/ caliphate-wives-share-stories-year-isis-defeat-reporter/story?id=69055474 ; Cf. Richard Hall (2019/1). 'ISIS Suspects in Syrian camp raise thousand through online crowdfunding campaign'. *Independent*. July 25. See: https://www.independent.co/uk/news/world/middle-east/isi s-syria-camp-hol-paypal-telegram-online-crowdfunding-a9021006.html

73   Cf. Arafat (2020).

74   Cf. Ib.; Cf. Richard Hall (2019/2). 'Tunnels, knives and riots: This Syrian camp holding thousands of ISIS wives is at a breaking point'. *Independent*. December 9. See: https:// www.independent.co/uk/news/world/middle-east/isis-wives-al-hol-camp-syria-islamic-state-terror-uk-a9236221.html

called for the death of anyone cooperating with camp authorities. As a consequence of several knives attacks by Russian and Turkish female IS members on security guards within the main market of the camp in 2019, the camp authorities established a separate market for the IS foreign section where a money transfer is only possible once a month.[75]

Especially during the rise of the pandemic the online activities of (foreign) females and children increased. On the one hand, the reasons for this increased internet use could be seen as a result of the fear of families that their detained relatives could fall ill with Covid-19. On the other hand, this could be a sign for the attempt of some detainees to use the weakened administrative situation of the camp concerning the pandemic for breakouts.[76]

The use of the vulnerability and the bad conditions of the imprisoned IS supporters[77] in detention camps and prisons led by for instance the Kurdish forces[78], was used in the form of a psychological warfare of IS towards its own adherents.[79] The jihadist movement manipulated the women, men and children[80] who have already been weakened by their individual fears for the future[81], loneliness and bad physical as well as psychological conditions, in terms of the pandemic as a 'divine punishment' for those who might have quit the 'true' faith and tried to mobilize their last will to survive in view of a fight towards the disbelievers.[82] This strategy was also used by Joseph Goebbels, minister of propaganda during the Nazi-regime, to mobilize the masses with his 'Sportpalast'-speech on February 18, 1943[83]. The victory of the Anti-IS alliances towards IS territories – associated with the loss of IS

---

75 Cf. Arafat (2020).
76 Cf. Audrey Alexander (2020/2). 'Help for Sisters': A Look at Crowdfunding Campaigns with Potential Links to Terrorist and Criminal Networks'. *Global Network on Extremism and Technology*. June 11. See: https//www.gnet-research.org/2020/06/11/help-for-sisters-a-look-at-crowdfunding-campaigns-with-potential-links-to-terrorist-and-criminal-networks/ Cf. Gina Vale (2019). 'Women in Islamic State: From Caliphate to Camps'. *International Centre for Counter-Terrorism*. October, p. 6.; Cf. Dunford & Wallace (2019).
77 Cf. Eric Schmitt (2020). 'Virus Fears Spread at Camps for ISIS Families in Syria's North East'. *International Crisis Group*. April 7.
78 Cf. Charlie Savage (2020/1).
79 Cf. Asia-Pacific Foundation (2020). 'APF Analysis: The Coronavirus (COVID-19) Impact on the ISIS Detention Camps in Syria'. April 27.
80 Cf. Myriam Francois and Azeem Ibrahim (2020).'The Children of ISIS Detainees: Europe's Dilemma'. *Center for Global Policy*. June 18. See: https://www.foreignpolicy.com
81 Cf. Charlie Savage (2020/2). 'What is going to happen to us? Inside ISIS Prison Children ask their Fate. *New York Times*. October 23rd. See: https://www.nytimes.com/2019/10/23/world/middleeast/what-is-going-to-happen-to-us-inside-isis-prison-children-ask-their-fate.html
82 Cf. Asia-Pacific Foundation (2020).
83 Uwe Backes (2006). *Eine Wort- und Begriffsgeschichte von der Antike bis zur Gegenwart*. Here: Extrembegriffe in der politischen Sprache deutscher Idiokratien. Göttingen: Vandenhoeck & Ruprecht, p. 174.

affiliated relatives by the camp inhabitants – could probably support the IS strategy of mobilizing the 'imprisoned' for a 'Covid-Jihad' towards the disbelievers.[84]

At the same time, it is a successful recruitment strategy in terms of new adherents with regard to IS objectives who live abroad, e.g. in Europe. The wish of the new recruits to solidarize with the detained 'brothers and sisters', the so called 'true believers', could be used for virus-attacks within Europe in the name of detention camps such as Al-Hawl.[85]

4.2   Training the next generation of IS

According to various reports, IS related women are training their children as 'cubs of the caliphate' within the detention camp.[86] The next generation of IS is forced "to slaughter chicken and goats first as practice to behead humans and become suicide bombers"[87] at a later time.[88] If they were not allowed to leave the camp, they should be able to fight within and – in the end – die for God's sake.[89]

As a consequence of various defeated attempts to escape the camps, some of the female IS detainees believe that it is their 'fate' to stay in the camp and follow God's plan to help the Islamic State rise again from the camps.[90] The emergence of the pandemic is graded as a divine sign to hold out the multiple bad circumstances in detention.

The religious education of the imprisoned children follows the same patterns: the kids have been told that "they will go to paradise"[91], if they would stay in the camps and suffer everything in silence. Another narrative of these lessons are the remembrance of Islamic ancestors who "fought against 'kuffār' (infidels) bravely in the last 1,400 years"[92] –they represent the role models especially for the young boys whose fathers have died on the battlefield or are still missing.

---

84   Cf. Politico (2020). 'US military fears ISIS resurgence coronavirus Pandemic'. April 2nd. See: https://www.politico.com/news/2020/04/02/us-military-fears-isis-resurgance-coronaviru s-pandemic-162046
85   Cf. Rojava Information Center (2020/2). 'Briefing: Coronavirus risks and preventative measures in Hol camp'. May 21st. See: https://rojavainformationcenter.com/2020/05/briefing-coro navirus-risks-and-preventative- measures-in-hol-camp/
86   Cf. Arafat (2020).
87   Cf. Ib.
88   Cf. Joseph Hincks (2020). 'With the World Busy Fighting COVID-19, Could ISIS Mount a Resurgence?' *Time*, April 29. See: https://time.com/5828630/isis-coronavirus/
89   Cf. Aaron Zelin (2019/2). 'Wilayat al-Hawl: 'Remaining' and Incubating the Next Islamic State Generation'. *Washington Institute*. October. See: https://www.washingtoninstitute.org/policy-analysis/view/wilayat-al-hawl-remaining-and-incubating-the-next-islamic-state-generation
90   Cf. Arafat (2020).
91   Cf. Ib.
92   Ib.

Religion functions in this specific situation as a broker between the desperate former IS members who are beached at a camp – often far away from their original home countries and left behind with broken dreams of a 'perfect live' in the caliphate – and the jihadist recruiters who are trying to reactivate their 'belief' in Allah and its secular representative, the caliph of the Islamic State (although its regional existence has passed away, its digital presence is unbroken).

According to Almond et al., "fundamentalist movements tend to have an "elect", a chosen, divinely called membership, described variously as "the faithful", "the remnant", "the last outpost", the "Covenant keepers", those who "bear witness", who "walk with the Lord"[93] and so on. Applied on the situation of the detained women and their children, the only escape of their hopeless situation is to believe that they are the faithful remainders and will finally be saved by Allah or rather the 'new born' IS, whenever it will rise again; maybe with the help of their own children. Therefore, they truly believe in the narrative of the chosen members of God, obey under authoritarian organizational rules and structures of the former IS that are represented by IS camp courts and the religious police and distance themselves from other groups or 'false' believers.[94] If they would quit these belief systems they would lose their footings and probably break down.[95]

4.3   Various roles regarding the symbolic capital of female detainees

With regard to the IS messages of *Al Naba* concerning the pandemic, the female detainees interpreted the content in view of the religious leader *Abū Hamza al-Qurashi*. In relation to their own teaching of religious education or better religious knowledge with regard to the children, the control of the IS court and the religious police within the detention camps, they possess the *symbolic capital* themselves. This is an exercise of power that is obviously not seen as such but in reality a legitimized demand of recognition.[96]

With respect to Riesebrodt, the typology of religious fundamentalism includes two forms: the *escapism* and the *world domination*.[97] While *escapism* offers two forms, the *symbolic segregation* (*subculture*) and the *aerial segregation* (*community*), the *world domination* provides four possibilities:

---

93   Almond et al., 2003, p. 97.
94   Cf.Ib., pp. 97-98.
95   In view of this development, it might be helpful to increase the number of polyglot psychologists within the camps.
96   Bourdieu, 2001, pp. 66-67; 310.
97   Martin Riesebrodt (1990). *Fundamentalismus als patriachalische Protestbewegung, Amerikanische Protestanten (1910-1928) und iranische Schiiten (1961-1979) im Vergleich.* Tübingen, p. 23.

a) "A religious movement
b) A social protest-/movement
c) A secret society and
d) A party."[98]

Whereas IS could be defined as religious movement that strives to obtain the *world domination* with the support of its adherents, the female detainees who have unsuccessfully tried to *escape* the camps in *reality*, abandoned their plans and *escaped symbolically* within the camps by remaining among their religious peer group, the other female IS members. In addition, the security guards *segregated* them *aerially* in the IS foreign section in order to protect others in terms of their (religious) influence and violence and to keep an eye on their activities. In this sense, the female IS detainees support IS's wish regarding the *world domination* paradoxically through *escapism*.

Conclusion

Undoubtedly, *the age of pandemic* has just begun and the rise of Covid-19 is the first sign for other lethal virus to come. Religious fundamentalists have used pandemics, plagues and natural disasters at all times, because it is part of their religious self-conception and manichaeist world view that mankind is divided in 'good' and 'evil', believers and disbelievers. Based on their religious understanding, after a period of blossoming, the world must perish in order to raise again, renewed and 'purified' from transgressions and unbelief.

In view of this present chapter and its discussion of the IS related groups and actors, we could speak about one form of the so called *Abrahamic Fundamentalism*. The common heritage of the Abrahamic religions Judaism, Christianity and Islam and their share of specific religious elements such as the belief in one God make some of their members most likely to 'defend' these specific religious doctrines towards worshippers of other religions or new religious movements.[99] Obviously, this anthology shows that other types of religious fundamentalism (might) exist as well. But the search for a strong leadership and the heartfelt wish to belong to a chosen community of 'true' believers are responsible for the following of the path of the Islamic State by some Muslims who are most vulnerable for its fundamentalist religious narratives. As we have seen before, beside religious motives exist certainly other reasons for IS adherents – regardless of their gender – to follow the jihadist pathway such as a search for love, a thirst of adventure, a lack of individual

---

98   Riesebrodt, 1990, p. 23.
99   Almond et al., 2003, pp. 105-106.

and professional perspectives, an individual disposition towards narcissism and sadism[100] and the like, that could not be discussed in this chapter.

The chapter *Towards a Covid-Jihad – Millennialism in the field of Jihadism* can therefore only be seen as a snapshot with regard to the further misuse of (the) pandemic(s) by jihadist movements such as IS or AQ in the short term. As indicated, the increased attempts of the use of biological weapons for terrorist attacks by jihadist groups and actors seems to mark just the beginning of an era of bio-warfare that will be fought by various fundamentalist and extremist groups in the upcoming years.

Religious fundamentalism is no new phenomenon, but its use of modern technology in order to restore old times and preferred lifestyles will nevertheless pose a challenge for the world community – today and tomorrow. The misuse of Islam and the misuse of a pandemic, both visualized in the term 'Covid-Jihad' by some misguided actors who are glorifying violence instead of peace, should clearly underline their 'true' intentions towards the believers who are still belonging to their ideology.

In addition, it is now up to all of us, to deconstruct apocalyptic and millennialist narratives of jihadist movements such as IS for the sake of all mankind. It must be demonstrated towards IS adherents – in and outside the detention camps – that a decision for *life* is much more valuable than a decision for *death*.

According to the statement of Michelle Obama during the 2020 US Election Campaign:

"Going high is the only thing that works! Because when we go low, when we use the same tactics of degrading and de-humanizing others, we just become part of the ugly noise that's drowning out everything else."[101]

With regard to the attempt of IS and other jihadist movements to misuse the pandemic for a 'Covid-Jihad' by othering and de-humanizing possible enemies, we

---

100 Narcissism as well as sadism can certainly not diagnosed by remote diagnosis, but need to be determined by experts such as psychologists. In context of a possible interlinking between mental disorders and an increased interest or rather participation in violent extremism or in view of religious fundamentalism, some recent publications are mentioned in the following that deal with these research areas as well as topics: Cf. Franziska Wolf (2020). *The relationship between narcissism and sadism: is general, grandiose and vulnerable trait narcissism differentially related to self-reported and state-level sadism?* Master-Thesis. University of Maastricht. July 12.; Cf. Makkonen et al. (2020). Fear-triggering effects of terrorism threats: Cross-country comparison in a terrorism news scenario experiment. *Personality and Individual Differences* 161, Article 109992.; Cf. Johann Brink (2015). Crime and Mental Health. *Encyclopedia of Forensic and Legal Medicine.* 2nd ed. December, pp. 1-13.

101 Cf. Michelle Obama (2020). 'Full Speech At The 2020 DNC'. *NBC News.* August 17. See: https://www.youtube.com/watchv=VZwfEWpG_wA , accessed on August 22nd, 2020.

should join the aforementioned statement and go high in view of our P/CVE[102] strategies and narratives. The only reasonable way to meet these religious fundamentalists is to explain Covid-19 with the help of rational numbers and arguments presented by virologists who don't care about the religion of their patients.

Bibliography

Ackerman, Gary, and Peterson, Hayley (2020). Terrorism and COVID-19: Actual and Potential Impacts. *Perspectives on Terrorism* Vol. 14, iss. 3, June, 59-73.

Alexander, Audrey (2020/1). The Security Threat COVID-19 Poses to the Northern Syria Detention Camps Holding Islamic State Members. *CTC Sentinel* Vol. 13, iss. 6., June, 16-25.

Almond, Gabriel A.; Appleby, R. Scott, and Sivan, Emmanuel (2003) (Eds.). *Strong Religion. The Rise of Fundamentalism around the World.* Chicago; London: The University of Chicago Press.

Armborst, Andreas (2009). A Profile of Religious Fundamentalism and Terrorist Activism. *Defence Against Terrorism Review* Vol. 2, No. 1. Spring, pp. 51-71.

Asia-Pacific Foundation (2020). 'APF Analysis: The Coronavirus (COVID-19) Impact on the ISIS Detention Camps in Syria'. April 27.

Backes, Uwe (2006). *Eine Wort- und Begriffsgeschichte von der Antike bis zur Gegenwart.* Göttingen: Vandenhoeck & Ruprecht.

Basit, Abdul (2020). 'The COVID-19 Pandemic: An Opportunity for Terrorist Groups?' *Counter Terrorist Trends and Analyses* 12, 3, 7-12.

Borum, Randy (2004). *Psychology of Terrorism.* Tampa: University of South Florida.

Bourdieu, Pierre (2001). *Meditationen. Zur Kritik der scholastischen Vernunft.* Frankfurt a.M.: Suhrkamp.

Bourdieu, Pierre (2000). Eine Interpretation der Religion nach Max Weber. In Pierre Bourdieu (Ed.). *Das religiöse Feld. Texte zur Ökonomie des Heilsgeschehens.* Konstanz: UVK, pp. 11-37.

Bourdieu, Pierre (1993). *Sozialer Sinn. Kritik der theoretischen Vernunft.* Frankfurt a. M.: Suhrkamp.

Bourdieu, Pierre (1998). *Praktische Vernunft. Zur Theorie des Handelns.* Frankfurt a. M.: Suhrkamp.

Brink, Johann (2015). Crime and Mental Health. *Encyclopedia of Forensic and Legal Medicine.* 2nd ed. December, pp. 1-13.

Ciampi, David (2005). Developmental and motivational factors of transnational terrorists. *Forensic Examiner* 14 (3), 29-34.

Cruickshank, Paul, and Rassler, Don (2020). A View from the CT Foxhole: A Virtual Roundtable on COVID-19 and Counterterrorism with Audrey Kurth Cronin,

Lieutenant General (Ret) Michael Nagata, Magnus Ranstorp, Ali Soufan, and Juan Zarate. *CTC Sentinel* Vol. 13, iss. 6. June, 1-15.

Desai, Shewta, and Amarasingam, Amarnath (2020). COVID-19, Misinformation and Anti-Muslim Violence in India. ISD (Ed.). *Strong Cities*. London; Washington DC, Beirut, Tokio, pp. 1-34.

EUROPOL (2020) *European Union Terrorism Situation and Trend report 2019 (TE-SAT)*, Brussels, pp. 1-98.

Galindo, Carmelo (2020). 'COVID-19, Jihadism and Biological Weapons'. *Islamic Theology of Counter Terrorism (ICTC)*, pp. 1-4.

General Secretariat of the Council (2020). *Council Conclusions on EU External Action on Preventing and Countering Terrorism and Violent Extremism*. In Council of the European Union (Ed.). June 16. No. prev. doc.: 8742/20 + COR 1, pp. 1-16.

Kaplan, David (2000). Aum Shinrikyo (1995). In Jonathan Tucker (Ed.) *Toxic Terror: Assessing Terrorist Use of Chemical and Biological Weapons*. Cambridge, Massachusetts: MIT Press.

Kajjo, Ibrahim and Christou (2019). 'Virus Fears Spread at Camps for ISIS Families in Syria's North East'. *Report of the Independent International Commission of Inquiry on the Syrian Arab Republic*. United Nations Human Rights Council. September.

Lead Inspector General Report to the United States Congress (2020). *Operation Inherent Resolve*, January 1, 2020–March 31, 2020. May 13.

Loeb, Cheryl (2009). Jihadists and Biological and Toxin Weapons. In Gary Ackerman and Jeremy Tamsett (Eds.). *Jihadists and Weapons of Mass Destruction*. Boca Raton, Florida: CRC Press.

Lifton, Robert (2000). *Destroying the World to Save It: Aum Shinrikyo, Apocalyptic Violence, and the New Global Terrorism*. New York: Metropolitan Books.

Makkonen, Anna; Oksane, Atte; Kushner Gadarian, Shana, et al. (2020). Fear-triggering effects of terrorism threats: Cross-country comparison in a terrorism news scenario experiment. *Personality and Individual Differences* 161, Article 109992. July.

Maor-Hirsh, Sigalit (2020). ISIS in the Age of COVID-19–From Islamizing the Pandemic to Implementing the Jihadist Strategy. *International Institute for Counterterrorism (ICT)*. April, pp. 1-8.

Ong, Kyler, and Azman, Nur Aziemah (2020). 'Distinguishing Between the Extreme Far-right and IS's Calls to Exploit COVID-19'. *Counter Terrorist Trends and Analyses* 12, 18-21.

Riesebrodt, Martin (1990). *Fundamentalismus als patriachalische Protestbewegung, Amerikanische Protestanten (1910-1928) und iranische Schiiten (1961-1979) im Vergleich.* Tübingen.

Senate Government Affairs Permanent Subcommittee on Investigations (Minority Staff) (1995). *Hearings on Global Proliferation of Weapons of Mass Destruction: A Case Study on the Aum Shinrikyo.* October 31.

Stern, Jessica (1999). *The Ultimate Terrorists*. Cambridge, MA: Harvard University Press.

Swartz David (1996). Bridging the Study of Culture and Religion: Pierre Bourdieu's Political Economy of Symbolic Power. *Sociology of Religion* Vol. 57, No. 1, 71-85.

Williams, Rhys H. (1994). Movement Dynamics and Social Challenge: Transforming Fundamentalist Ideology and Organization. In Martin E. Marty and R. Scott Appleby (Eds.). *Accounting for Fundamentalisms: The Dynamic Character of Movements.* Chicago, pp. 785-825.

Wolf, Franziska (2020). *The relationship between narcissism and sadism: is general, grandiose and vulnerable trait narcissism differentially related to self-reported and state-level sadism?* Master Thesis. University of Maastricht. July 12.

Online Open Sources

Ackerman, Gary, and Moran, Kevin (2005). Bioterrorism and Threat Assessment. Paper #22. *Weapons of Mass Destruction Commission.* Stockholm, pp. 1-18. URL: http://docshare01.docshare.tips/ files/2791/27919768.pdf

Alexander, Audrey (2020/2).'Help for Sisters': A Look at Crowdfunding Campaigns with Potential Links to Terrorist and Criminal Networks'. *Global Network on Extremism and Technology.* June 11. URL: https//www.gnet-research.org/2020/06/11/help-for-sisters-a-look-at-crowdfunding-campaigns-with-potential-links-to-terrorist-and-criminal-networks/

Al Naba, 225, توجهات شرعية للتعامل مع الأوبئة

Al Naba, 227.

Al-Tamimi, Aymenn Jawad (2019). 'Free the Female Prisoners: A Campaign to Free Women Held in SDF Camps'. *Aymenn Jawad Al-Tamimi blog.* October 15. URL: h ttps://www. aymennjawad.org/free-the-female-prisoners-a-campaign-to-free

Arafat, Hisham (2020). 'Remittances for ISIS women in northeast Syria's al-Hawl camp trigger imminent resurgence of the jihadist group'. North Press Agency. May 31st. URL: https://npasyria.com/en/blog.php?id_blog=2695&sub_blog=4%20&name_blog=Remittances%20for%20ISIS%20women%20in%20northeast%20Syria%E2%80%99s%20al-Hawl%20camp%20trigger%20imminent%20resurgence%20of%20the%20jihadist%20group

Campbell, John (2020). 'Boko Haram's Shekau Labels Anti-COVID-19 Measures an Attack on Islam in Nigeria'. *Council on Foreign Relations.* April 17. URL: https://www.cfr.org/blog/boko-harams-shekau-labels-anti-covid-19-measures-attack-islam-nigeria

Coleman, Julie (2020). 'The Impact of Coronavirus on Terrorism in the Sahel'. *International Centre for Counter-Terrorism.* April 16. URL: https://icct.nl/publication/the-impact-of-coronavirus-on-terrorism-in-the-sahel/

Dunford, John, and Cafarella, Jennifer (2019). 'ISIS's Opportunity in Northern Syria's Detention Facilities and Camps'. *Institute for the Study of War*. May 13. URL: https://www.understandingwar.org/background/isiss-opportunity-in-n orthern-syria

Dunford, John, and Wallace, Brandon (2019). 'ISIS Prepares for Breakout in Prisons and Camps'. *Institute for the Study of War*. September 23rd. URL: https://www.understandingwar.org/background/isis-prepares-for-brea kout-in-prisons-and-camps

European Institute for Counter Terrorism and Conflict Prevention (2020). 'COVID-19: Is Bioterrorism on the Rise Now?' URL: https://www.eictp.eu/en/covid-19-is-bioterrorism-on-the-rise-now/

Francois, Myriam, and Ibrahim, Azeem (2020). 'The Children of ISIS Detainees: Europe's Dilemma'. *Center for Global Policy*. June 18. URL: https://www.foreignp olicy.com

Gordon Corera (2020). 'Coronavirus: Police warn of lockdown radicalisation threat'. *BBC*. June 10. URL: https://www.bbc.com/news/uk-52997441, accessed on June 17, 2020.

Hall, Richard (2019/1). 'ISIS Suspects in Syrian camp raise thousand through online crowdfunding campaign'. *Independent*. July 25. URL: https://www.indep endent.co/uk/news/world/middle-east/isis-syria-camp-hol-paypal-telegram-online-crowdfunding-a9021006.html

Hall, Richard (2019/2). 'Tunnels, knives and riots: This Syrian camp holding thousands of ISIS wives is at a breaking point'. *Independent*. December 9. URL: https://www.independent.co/uk/news/world/middle-east/isis-wives-a l-hol-camp-syria-islamic-state-terror-uk-a9236221.html

Hincks, Joseph (2020). 'With the World Busy Fighting COVID-19, Could ISIS Mount a Resurgence'? *Time*, April 29. URL: https://time.com/5828630/isis-coronavirus/

Katz, Rita (2020). Hashtag#ISIS. *SITE Intelligence Group*. May 29. URL: https://www. linkedin.com/feed/, accessed on May 30, 2020.

Law and crime (2020). 'DOJ Just Warned That Intentional Spread of COVID-19 Could Be Terrorism – What It Means'. March 26. URL: https://lawandcrime.c om/covid-19-pandemic/doj-just-warned-that-intentional-spread-of-covid-19-could-be-terrorism-what-it-means

Lederer, Edith (2020). 'UN chief: Extremists using COVID-19 to recruit online youths'. *AP News*. April 27. URL: https://apnews.com/a6cf967c03f7ff00e170949 a9eaeb11a

Longman, James (2020). 'Caliphate Wives share their stories year after ISIS defeat: Reporter's Notebook'. *ABC News*. February 19. URL: https://www. abcnews.go/International/caliphate-wives-share-stories-year-isis-defeat-reporter/story?id=69055474

Marone, F. (2020). Terrorism and Counterterrorism in a Time of Pandemic. *Italian Institute for International Political Studies*. May 15. URL: https://www.ispionline.it /en/pubblicazione/terrorism-and-counterterrorism-time-pandemic-26165.

MEMRI (2020/1). 'The way forward–A word of advice on the coronavirus pandemic'. In Al-Qaeda Central: *COVID-19 Is Divine Punishment For Sins Of Mankind; Muslims Must Repent, West Must Embrace Islam*. March 31. URL: https://www.memri.org/reports/al-qaeda-central-covid-19-divine-punis hment-sins-mankind-muslims-must-repent-west-must

MEMRI (2020/2). 'ISIS Women at Hawl Refugee Camp: Coronoavirus does not infect true Muslims; Only Infidels and Oppressors Die of the Virus.' April 9. URL: https://www.memri.org/tv/isis-women-at-hawl-refugee-camp-coronavi rus-does-not-infect-true-muslims

Meyer, Birgit (2020). *Religious matters*. 'Dossier Corona'. *Religious Matters in an Entangled World*. April 21. URL: https://religiousmatters.nl/dossier-corona/, accessed on May 16, 2020.

Obama, Michelle (2020). 'Full Speech At The 2020 DNC'. *NBC News*. August 17. URL: https://www.youtube.com/watchv=VZwfEWpG_wA , accessed on August 22nd, 2020.

Nicholson, Dylan (2020). 'COVID-19 an opportunity for terrorists or a threat to their existence'. *Defence Connect*. April 29. URL: https://www.defenceconnect. com.au/key-enablers/5995-global-terror-and-covid-19

Pauwels, Annelies (2020). 'How Europe's terrorists take advantage of the pandemic'. *EU Observer*. April 29. URL: https://euobserver.com/opinion/148173

Pilch, Richard (2020). 'How to keep the new coronavirus from being used as a terrorist weapon'. *Bulletin of the Atomic Scientists*. March 27. URL: https://thebul letin.org/2020/03/how-to-keep-the-new-coronavirus-from-being-used-as-a-terrorist-weap-on/#

Politico (2020). 'U.S. military fears ISIS resurgence coronavirus Pandemic'. April 2nd. URL: https://www.politico.com/news/2020/04/02/us-military-fears-isis-r esurgance-coronavirus-pandemic-162046

Real Instituto el cano (2020). 'Crisis del coronavirus. La pandemia segun los yihadi-stas'. URL: https://blog.realinstitutoelcano.org/crisis-del-coronavirus-la-pand emia-segun-los-yihadistas/

Rojava Information Center (2020/1). 'Coronavirus crisis in North and East Syria: 22 April Update'. April 22nd. URL: https://rojavainformationcenter.com/2020/04/ coronavirus-crisis-in-north-and-east-syria- 22-april-update /

Rojava Information Center (2020/2). 'Briefing: Coronavirus risks and preventative measures in Hol camp'. May 21st. URL: https://rojavainformationcenter.com/2 020/05/briefing-coronavirus-risks-and-preventative-measures-in-hol-camp/

Savage, Charlie (2019/1). 'The Kurds' Prisons and Detention Camps for ISIS Members, Explained'. *New York Times*. October 22nd. URL: https://www.nytimes.

com/2019/10/22/world/middleeast/the-kurds-prisons-and-detention-camps-for-isis-members-explained.html

Savage, Charlie (2019/2). 'What is going to happen to us? Inside ISIS Prison Children ask their Fate'. *New York Times*. October 23rd. URL: https://www.nytimes.com/2019/10/23/world/middleeast/what-is-going-to-happen-to-us-inside-isis-prison-children-ask-their-fate.html

Schmitt, Eric (2020). 'Virus Fears Spread at Camps for ISIS Families in Syria's North East'. *International Crisis Group*. April 7.

Shehab, Hesham (2020). 'Islamist hate preacher warns Muslims to arm themselves amid coronavirus threats'. *JNS*. April 27. URL: https://www.jns.org/opinion/islamist-hate-preacher-warns-muslims-to-arm-themselves-amid-coronavirus-threats/

Zelin, Aaron (2019/1). 'Turkish Woman Promotes Fundraising Effort for Widows of 'Martyrs,' Children, Prisoners in Turkey and in Al-Hol Camp in Syria.' *MEMRI*. January 28.

Zelin, Aaron (2019/2). 'Wilayat al-Hawl: 'Remaining' and Incubating the Next Islamic State Generation'. *Washington Institute*. October. URL: https://www.washingtoninstitute.org/policy-analysis/view/wilayat-al-hawl-remaining-and-incubating-the-next-islamic-state-generation

How Central Asian Salafi-Jihadi Groups are Exploiting the Covid-19 Pandemic: New Opportunities and Challenges

Uran Botobekov

Abstract

The global coronavirus pandemic crisis not only poses serious additional risks, challenges and threats to the security of the modern world, but also creates new opportunities and prospects for the global Salafi-Jihadi-Movement. This report seeks to analyze the actions of both Central Asian Salafi-Jihadi groups' view of Covid-19 and its original parent organizations such as the Taliban, al Qaeda and Hayat Tahrir al-Sham during the coronavirus crisis. The reason for this is the small and fragmented Uighur and Uzbek Islamist extremist groups from Chinese Xinjiang region and post-Soviet Central Asia are affiliated precisely with these major players of the Sunni jihadist world, such as ISIS and al Qaeda, which are their military patron and ideological banner.

Keywords: Covid-19, Sunni Islam, Salafism, Global Jihadism, Central Asia, Taliban, Terrorism and Counter-Terrorism, Hayat Tahrir al-Sham

1. Introduction

The Covid-19 outbreak has negatively impacted not only the global economy and financial markets, but has also exacerbated the threat of transnational terrorist organizations, such as ISIS and al Qaeda. Indeed, amid the global panic and socio-economic shock caused around the world by the SARS-CoV-2 virus, the Sunni Salafi-Jihadi Movement has tried to extract the maximum dividends from this global threat. The critical situation, accompanied by loss of life, a sharp decline in income, rising unemployment and decimation of trade, has created fertile ground for the activation of radical Islamist organizations around the world.

In early 2020, when the coronavirus hit China's Wuhan hard, Central Asian Salafi-Jihadi groups pioneered the use of Covid-19 as a propaganda tool, presenting the virus as "divine punishment to the Beijing communist regime for persecuting Uighur Muslims." It was the Uighur jihadists of the Turkestan Islamist Party (TIP) who gave the new virus the ominous name "invisible warriors of Allah", which later began to be widely used by other terrorist groups in the Middle East and Southeast Asia.

This briefing paper seeks to identify and analyze how Covid-19 has influenced the strategic goals and tactics of Salafi-Jihadi groups in Afghanistan, the five former post-Soviet republics of Central Asia, and the Middle East. With the rise of extremist religious movements all over the world in this pandemic era, describing the particular role that Central Asian Salafist communities are playing in the region is of fundamental importance.

The ultimate aim of this research is to create an accurate picture – utilizing a combination of different sources – of how Islamist terrorist and extremist groups are exploiting various coronavirus cracks in society. Focusing on the Central Asian Salafi-Jihadi movement's views to Covid-19, this report also seeks to analyze the actions of its original parent organizations such as the Taliban, al Qaeda and Hayat Tahrir al-Sham (HTS) during the coronavirus crisis, because the small and fragmented Uighur and Uzbek Islamists extremist groups from Chinese Xinjiang region and post-Soviet Central Asia are affiliated precisely with these major players of the Sunni jihadist world, who are their military patron and ideological banner.

The global coronavirus pandemic crisis not only created serious additional risks, challenges and threats to the security of the modern world, but also created new opportunities and prospects for Salafi-Jihadi militant groups. Since the problem of Covid-19 entered the forefront of world politics in 2020, it seems to have temporarily overshadowed the threat of Islamist extremism. Meanwhile, this threat has not disappeared and retains its destructive potential.

In accordance with the purpose of this paper, we will analyze in more detail the initial reaction to the coronavirus pandemic, its adaptation and its use by the leading Salafi militant groups for conducting global jihad. However, the harsh reality is that after Covid-19 hit Chinese Wuhan hard, it also hit hard the Sunni extremist organizations located in Afghanistan, Syria and Iraq in April-May 2020. After that happened, their initial enthusiastic position, in which they framed the pandemic as "Divine Retribution" and "warriors of Allah", turned into a defensive posture. They took the same protection measures against the spread Covid-19, which were developed by "Kafir (infidels) nations" and the World Health Organization (WHO), and recommended to their jihadists to abide them.

Today, all across the world, the non-state entities from hard-liner terrorist groups to relatively moderate Salafi rebel movements, who control certain territories, are taking steps to respond to the Covid-19 pandemic. However, the perception and capitalization of the coronavirus pandemic by the Salafi-Jihadi groups differed from each other.

For example, while al Qaeda and ISIS used the coronavirus pandemic crisis to increase its own combat capacity, recruit new followers and to carry out new terror attacks, the Taliban and HTS were more concerned about the health of the population in the controlled territories. According to the UN Security Council[1], at present the Taliban have an available fighting force of 55,000-85,000 jihadists and contests 50-60 percent of Afghan territory with 21 districts under full Taliban control. The office of the United Nations High Commissioner for Refugees[2] (UNHCR) estimates that there are currently over four million civilians in the north-western Syrian province of Idlib, controlled by jihadists of the most powerful Islamist militant group HTS, former al Qaeda's branch in Syria. Therefore, it is not surprising to observe that the Taliban in its controlled Afghan territory and HTS through the local Salvation Government (SG) in parts of northern Idlib and western Aleppo actually tried to cope with the consequences of the pandemic[3], in fact, fulfilling the role of a quasi-state.

2.   The root of the Central Asian Salafi Jihadism

Salafi Jihadism has become a serious problem in Central Asia that encompasses five former Soviet republics – Uzbekistan, Kazakhstan, Kyrgyzstan, Tajikistan, and Turkmenistan – collectively known as the "Five Stans", as well as Afghanistan and western China. Central Asia, which for 3,000 years was a place of revival of many religions such as Zoroastrianism, Buddhism, Shamanism, Manichaeism, Nestorian Christianity and Judaism, and where the great Sunni Islamic scholars as al-Bukhari, al-Ghazali, and Ahmed Yesevi lived, has become today a target for militant Salafi-Jihadist ideology.

---

1   Cf. UN Security Council. (2020). 'Letter from the Chair of the Security Council Committee Established Pursuant to Resolution 1988 (2011) Addressed to the President of the Security Council.' May 19, 2020. See: https://www.undocs.org/S/2020/415.

2   Cf. UNHCR (2020). 'UN High Commissioner for Refugees Appeals for Safety for Civilians Trapped in Idlib.' UNHCR. February 20. See: https://www.unhcr.org/news/press/2020/2/5e4e51d04/un-high-commissioner-refugees-appeals-safety-civilians-trapped-idlib.html.

3   Muriel Asseburg, Aziz Hamidreza, Dalay Galip and Moritz Pieper (2020). 'The Covid-19 Pandemic and Conflict Dynamics in Syria. Neither a Turning Point Nor an Overall Determinant'. Stiftung Wissenschaft und Politik. The German Institute for International and Security Affairs. Berlin. May 21st, p.8. See: https://www.swp-berlin.org/10.18449/2020C21/

In Central Asia, the focus of Islamic revival and of Jihadists groups has been the Ferghana Valley[4], a densely populated and ethnically mainly Uzbek territory divided politically between Uzbekistan, Kyrgyzstan and Tajikistan. The valley has traditionally been a center of Islamic fervor, and was the area where Salafists first established a presence. The mass poverty of the population, the drop in the level of education after the collapse of the Soviet Union, the corrupt and authoritarian rule of political regimes, and the repressive methods of law enforcement have played a role in the radicalization of Islamic groups in Central Asia.

In the early 1990s, the first armed jihadist groups in the region appeared in response to harsh persecution by the authoritarian regimes of communist China and of Karimov's regime in Uzbekistan. In that period, many members of the Islamic Movement of Uzbekistan (IMU) and China's Uyghurs of the East Turkestan Islamic Movement[5] (now Turkestan Islamic Party – TIP) who adhered to the Salafist ideology, moved to neighboring Afghanistan and fought under the wing of the Taliban. The combination of repressive governments and economic deprivation in Central Asia, particularly China, Uzbekistan, and Tajikistan, served as an incubator of Salafi Jihadism. After 9/11, Central Asia's jihadists, who are members of IMU and TIP, were the mainstay of Al Qaeda's defense in southern Waziristan as well as participants in the fight against the armies of Afghanistan, Pakistan and NATO.

Central Asian jihadist groups are supporters of Takfirizm, a kind of religious extremism that accuses other Muslims of disbelief or apostasy. This ideology became the banner of the caliphate and led to jihad against other Muslims and open disobedience against the authorities. These practices are part of the legacy of the Takfirist instructions and ideas that emerged from the al Qaida environment.

Many of Central Asia's Islamists have been infected with the "virus" of the Salafi ideology from Arab preachers and local theologians who were educated in Saudi Arabia, Syria and Egypt. After the link into al-Qaeda and the Taliban, they laid an accusation of unbelief (takfir) against the rulers of the "Stans". They refused to recognize official state institutions and declared jihad against the armed forces of their respective countries.

In response, the governments of the "Stans" and China have suppressed, and continue to suppress, the activities of more than twenty Islamic groups that are recognized by the court as extremist or terrorist organizations, because they constitute a danger to the state's constitutional order. In particular, the activities of the

---

4   Cf. Radio Free Europe/Radio Liberty. (2015). 'Islamic State Militants Target Ferghana Valley'. March 5. See: https://www.rferl.org/a/islamic-state-ferghana-valley-kyrgyzstan-tajikistan-uzb ekistan/26883693.html.

5   Colin Clarke and Paul Rexton Kan (2017). 'Uighur Foreign Fighters: An Underexamined Jihadist Challenge.' *The International Centre for Counter-Terrorism - The Hague (ICCT)*. November 15, p. 18. See: https://doi.org/10.19165/2017.2.05.

following Islamic groups have been suppressed[6]: The Islamic Movement of Eastern Turkestan, Katibat Imam al Bukhari (KIB), TIP, Katibat al Tawhid wal Jihad (KTJ), IMU, Islamic Jihad Union (IJU), Jaishul Mahdi, Jund-Al-Khalifa, Ansarullah, Ğannat Oshiklari (Fans of Paradise), and others.

The second wave of the outflow of Central Asian Islamists abroad occurred after the start of the Syrian civil war. After the Syrian civil war broke out in 2011 and ISIS emerged as a competing alternative to al-Qaeda three years later, thousands of Central Asian jihadists who had streamed into Syria had to decide between al Qaeda and ISIS.

Some jihadists of IMU and Jund-Al-Khalifa shifted to Syria and joined ISIS[7]. Central Asians, and especially the migrant workers from Russia, who traveled to Syria, independent of any of the main Salafi-Jihadi groups after 2014 tended to join al-Baghdadi's Caliphate. Uyghur's TIP, Uzbek's KTJ and KIB became enmeshed with al Qaeda in Syria and maintained loyalty to the Taliban[8].

After joining al Qaeda, the Taliban and ISIS, the ideological base of Central Asian militants broadened and was affected by the more-global agenda of transnational Salafi-jihadi networks. Today, the goal of these religious groups from Central Asia has greatly expanded so that now their goal is to develop a world-wide caliphate. They have become an integral part of world-wide terrorism and jihadism. Thus, Central Asian Islamists have expanded their influence and militant activities to the Middle East. Over the past two decades, the locus of Central Asian radicals has moved from the Fergana Valley through Afghanistan into the tribal badlands of Pakistan and toward Syria.

As the experience of combating religious extremism has shown, it is small Islamic terrorist groups associated with ISIS or al Qaeda, such as the Central Asian jihadists that, due to the difficulty to triangulate on them, can pose the greatest danger to global stability. Indeed, Central Asian Salafi-Jihadi groups pose a significant threat to the security of not only the "Five Stans" but to the security of the EU and the U.S. Over the past decade, they have carried out more than ten high-profile

---

6   Cf. Kabar News Agency. (2018). 'List of Officially Banned Extremist and Terrorist Organizations in Kyrgyzstan'. December 26. See: http://en.kabar.kg/news/list-of-officially-banned-extremist-and-terrorist-organizations-in-kyrgyzstan/.

7   USAID (2015). 'Central Asian Involvement in the Conflict in Syria and Iraq: Drivers and Responses'. *United States Agency for International Development*. ed., Noah Tucker, Arlington. May 4. See: https://2012-2017.usaid.gov/sites/default/files/documents/1866/CVE_CentralAsiansSyriaIraq.pdf., p. 31.

8   Uran Botobekov (2018). 'Central Asian Jihadists under Al Qaeda's & Taliban's Strategic Ties.' *Modern Diplomacy*, August 23rd. See: https://moderndiplomacy.eu/2018/08/23/central-asian-jihadists-under-al-qaedas-talibans-strategic-ties/.

terrorist attacks in New York[9], St. Petersburg[10], Istanbul[11], Stockholm[12], and even tried to assassinate US President Barack Obama[13].

3.   Turkestan Islamic Party: Covid-19 is the Divine Punishment of China

Uighur militants TIP were one of the first Central Asian Salafi-Jihadi groups to respond to the coronavirus outbreak in the city of Wuhan, where, according to Chinese authorities[14], 3,869 people died, and a curfew was imposed in the city. Their early reaction was related to the fact that China's Xinjiang is the historical homeland of more than 12 million Uighurs, the Turkic-speaking Muslim ethnic group, who are subjected to constant religious persecution by the Chinese Communist Party (CCP)[15].

According to Human Rights Watch (HRW)[16], the Chinese government has detained more than a million Uighur Muslims in so-called "political re-education" camps. Their religious, linguistic, and cultural differences are deemed evidence of disloyalty to the CCP.

---

9   Cf. Corey Kilgannon and Joseph Goldstein (2017). 'Sayfullo Saipov, the Suspect in the New York Terror Attack, and His Past.' *The New York Times*. October 31. See: https://www.nytimes.com/2017/10/31/nyregion/sayfullo-saipov-manhattan-truck-attack.html.

10   Cf. Ivan Nechepurenko and Neil MacFarquhar (2017). 'St. Petersburg Bomber Said to Be Man From Kyrgyzstan; Death Toll Rises'. *The New York Times*. April 4. See: https://www.nytimes.com/2017/04/04/world/europe/st-petersburg-russia-explosion-suspect.html.

11   Cf. Hürriyet Daily News (n. d.). 'Turkish Police Identify Reina Attacker as Abdulkadir Masharipov - Turkey News'. See: https://www.hurriyetdailynews.com/turkish-police-identify -reina-attacker-as-abdulkadir-masharipov-108266, accessed on August 6, 2020.

12   Cf. New Europe (2017). 'Rahmat Akilov Confesses to Stockholm Attack.' *Blog*. April 11. See: https://www.neweurope.eu/article/rahmat-akilov-confesses-stockholm-attack/.

13   Cf. Federal Bureau of Investigation (FBI) (2012). Uzbek National Sentenced to Nearly 16 Years in Prison for Threatening to Kill the President and Providing Material Support to Terrorism. *Federal Bureau of Investigation*. July 13. See: https://www.fbi.gov/birmingham/press-releases/2012/uzbek-national-sentenced-to-nearly-16-years-in-prison-for-threatening-to-kill-the-president-and-providing-material-support-to-terrorism.

14   Cf. Xinhuanet (2020). 'Full Text of Wuhan's Notification on Revising Numbers of Confirmed COVID-19 Cases, Deaths.' *Xinhua News Agency*. April 17. See: http://www.xinhuanet.com/english/2020-04/17/c_138984653.htm.

15   Cf. Elanor Albert, Beina Xu, and Lindsey Maizland. (2020). The Chinese Communist Party. In *Council on Foreign Relations*. June 9. See: https://www.cfr.org/backgrounder/chinese-communist-party.

16   Cf. Maya Wang, (2020). 'More Evidence of China's Horrific Abuses in Xinjiang'. *Human Rights Watch*. February 20, See: https://www.hrw.org/news/2020/02/20/more-evidence-chinas-horrific-Abū ses-xinjiang.

Ironically, only the US is the ardent[17] and consistent defender of the religious[18] and cultural rights of the Uighurs, while many Muslim nations remain silent. Prioritizing their economic ties and strategic relationships with China, many Central Asian, Middle Eastern and Arab governments have defended China's repression of Uighur[19] and other Muslim minorities in the Xinjiang region, instead of defending their rights.

Uighur's TIP refers to the region as East Turkestan and wages jihad for the liberation of it from China. The Chinese government has come to characterize any expression of Islam in Xinjiang as extremist, a reaction to past independence movements. Beijing has blamed TIP for domestic terrorist attacks and occasional outbursts of violence. The government also fears that thousands of Uighur jihadists of TIP could return from Syria and Afghanistan to China and spark violence.

On February 29, 2020, the TIP's Media Center "Islam Awazi" published a video that was titled "The Perspective of the Mujahedeen Regarding the Corona Outbreak in China."[20]

According to the TIP's video, Covid-19 is the divine punishment for China's brutal persecution of Uighur Muslims, banning Islam and the result of their committing to Haram (anything that is prohibited by the Quran, for example, eating pork, drinking alcohol, having sex outside of marriage).

TIP's media product is accompanied by video clips of sick people in China, of natural disasters, and of Chinese people eating and preparing various animals for consumption. The narrator said that Chinese people are the most impure of all people because they eat every impurity and do not show mercy to humans or animals. He further continued that due to the deadly outbreak the Chinese people are experiencing sleeplessness and continual fear. A Uighur TV news anchor concluded that it is due to the coronavirus, which the Chinese communists do not know how to treat and for which they cannot find a cure.

---

17   Cf. Congress. Government (2020). 'Uyghur Human Rights Policy Act. 2020.' *The Library of the U.S. Congress*. June 17. See: https://www.congress.gov/116/plaws/publ145/PLAW-116publ145.pdf.

18   Cf. U.S. Department of State. (2019). 'U.S. Department of State Imposes Visa Restrictions on Chinese Officials for Repression in Xinjiang'. October 8, 2019. See: https://www.state.gov/u-s-department-of-state-imposes-visa-restrictions-on-chinese-officials-for-repression-in-xinjiang/.

19   Cf. Human Rights Watch. (2013). 'Joint Letter to the President of the United Nations Human Rights Council.' *Human Rights Watch*. July 12, 2019. See: https://www.hrw.org/sites/default/files/supporting_resources/190712_joint_counterstatement_xinjiang.pdf.

20   Cf. MEMRI TV. (2020). 'Turkestan Islamic Party: Covid-19 Is a Divine Punishment for China's Treatment of Uyghurs and the Result of Eating Meats Prohibited by the Quran - Warning: Graphic.' *MEMRI*. March 1st. See: https://www.memri.org/tv/turkestan-islamic-party-perspective-mujahideen-coronavirus-china.

Then he inquired who will save you from the dark recesses of land and sea, when you call upon Him in humility and silent terror? The narrator answers himself that all affairs are in the hands of Allah the most exalted, and He is able to punish those that go against His command, at any time He wills, however He wills. The TIP's media output reiterates that this small virus Covid-19 is a Divine Punishment, which transformed the commercial, very populous China's Wuhan, in which 11 million people reside, into a ghost city.

The narrator recalled that the source of the coronavirus was a marine animal market in Wuhan, where many different kinds of birds and land animals were sold, that have been prohibited in the Qur'an. Then the Uighur Media Center directed its anger at the Chinese, calling them the most impure and dirty among the peoples of the world, for they eat every impurity and filth, and they do not show mercy to either human or animal.

"Islam Awazi" expressed the firm belief of the Uighur Mujahedeen (Holy warriors who engage in jihad for their Muslim beliefs) that the coronavirus is a punishment from Allah for the oppression and persecution that the Chinese Kafirs have committed and continue to commit against the Uighur Muslims. Then the Surah Al-Anfal of the Quran appeared on the screen: "Remember how the Unbelievers plotted against thee, to keep thee in bonds, or slay thee, or get thee out (of thy home). They plot and plan, and Allah too plans; but the best of planners is Allah."

Then Jihadi's media output raised the most painful problem of Uighur Muslims about China's occupation of the Eastern Turkistan, which has long been transformed by TIP's ideological doctrine. The narrator said: "The atheist communist nation of China has occupied Eastern Turkistan since 1949, and exercised against the Muslims the worst kinds of oppression, tyranny, and torture, and they ignored that these Muslims have a Lord who is able to avenge them at any time He wishes, and today we witness the punishment of Allah with this virus. Allah the Exalted, the owner of Sovereignty, and He is the supporter of the weak, and thus we ask Him the Exalted, to make this outbreak a reason for the destruction of the atheist Chinese, and to preserve all Muslims around the globe, especially our people in Eastern Turkistan."

The "Islam Awazi" Media Center mocked the president of communist China, who recently boasted that nobody can stand in the face of his country and its superior development. According to Uighur Mujahedeen's conclusion, Allah the Most Exalted by sending a small deadly virus has progressively lead China toward destruction in this world and the next. Now his (Xi Jinping) situation is like all other tyrants, who are mired in sin, and Allah Almighty has quickly sent them his punishment, the narrator concluded.

TIP's Media Center described in detail "the atrocities of the Chinese infidels" against Uighur Muslims. "Tyrannical atheistic China made apparent their enmity towards Allah and His Messenger and the believers, destroyed the mosques and changed them to places of dancing, vices and insolence, they trampled upon the Qur'an and burned them, they transgressed upon the honor and raped the women, and made permissible the impermissible. They killed the scholars and the preachers that teach the people their religion, and tortured our Muslim Uighur brothers with the worst kinds of torture, oppression, and subjugation. They separated the sons from their fathers, they did not have mercy upon the young and did not respect the elders, not a single woman was safe from their tyranny, tyranny and their torture, they removed the Hijabs (Muslim women's head-coverings) from the pure Muslim women, and their prisons were filled with Muslims under the false name of (re-education camps) thinking that they will be able to hide this reality from the world and from the Muslims outside China. But the entire world, especially the Muslims, know that these centers are prisons in which the Muslims are forced to become atheist communists. Thus, the revenge from Allah for His servants came against these criminals, and He sent upon them the deadly coronavirus and thus became isolated from the world, as if they are imprisoned."

The TIP's media output noted that "Allah the Just punished the criminal Chinese regime" for removing the khimar (part of hijab) from Muslim women. He compared the Chinese authorities' directive obliging everyone to wear a medical mask with the khimar. "This is their reward from Allah for them for removing the khimar from our Muslim sisters, and thus Allah forced them to wear the khimar both men and women", Islam Awazi stated.

"This outbreak is just a warning for the Chinese government, so that they may repent from their actions and stop their oppression and tyranny against the Muslims. If they do not refrain, then the punishment from Allah on the Day of Judgment is deserved, and the punishment of Allah is severe", stated in the statement.

In conclusion, TIP perceived the coronavirus as God's assistance for the oppressed Uighur people, who could not defend themselves from the hostility of the Chinese oppressors and criminals. The statement ends with a request to "Allah the Exalted to destroy the oppressors with this virus and to save the Muslims from their oppression and hostility by His causes."

Thus, TIP, as usual, focused entirely on the anti-Chinese topic in its statement on Covid-19. And this is no coincidence.

First of all, the strategic goal of Uighur militants of TIP is to establish their own independent state in East Turkestan, which will be ruled by Sharia law. Indeed, over the past decade, Uighur nationalists have launched several terror attacks at a local government office, train station, and open-air market, as well as Tiananmen Square in Beijing. Nearly two hundred people were killed during Uighur protests against state-incentivized Han Chinese migration in the region and widespread economic and cultural discrimination in Xinjiang's capital, Urumqi, in 2009.

Second, the anti-Chinese doctrine forms the basis of the Salafi-Jihadi and nationalist ideology of TIP. Abdul Haq al-Turkistani[21], the emir of the TIP, regularly makes anti-Chinese statements that usually receive public support from al Qaeda[22] and other globally active jihadist terror groups. He has always harshly criticized China's repressive policies, disguised under the political slogan of fighting "the three evils" – separatism, religious extremism, and international terrorism.

Third, the coronavirus outbreak in China, from where Uighur jihadists were forced to flee by Beijing's bloody repression, caused their natural gloating reactions. Therefore, they maintain a doctrinal line about an "invisible soldier of Allah" who killed thousands upon thousands of Chinese unbelievers. TIP is convinced that God punishes the Chinese kafirs, who persist in defying his authority. Uighur Jihadi group's ideologues have argued that the Chinese repression of Uighur Muslims and its anti-Islamic policies sparked the "wrath of God" which has become the "nightmare of the crusaders".

When TIP claims Covid-19 to be "God's punishment", it does not speak in its own name, but utilizes the Quran's Surah Al-Buruj [85:12], in order to demonstrate the timeless dimension of the prophetic message. The literal translation is therefore: "The onslaught of your Lord is severe." According to the ideological doctrine of Jihadi-Salafism, the keys to all today's problems lie in the roots of "the pious predecessors", since Islam is eternal. What was revealed yesterday remains valid today. The Salafi-Jihad draws its inspiration from primary sources during the time of the "Righteous Ancestors" when the Messenger of Allah and his Companions waged a perennial jihad. That is why, when TIP claims "God's punishment" of the Chinese infidels, it returns to the primary sources of the Quran over and over again.

As is well known, the Uighur jihadists of TIP, Sunni Muslims of Turkic descent from China's northwest province of Xinjiang, have become a prominent cog in the constellation of globally active jihadist terror groups since the 1990s. The organization is a part of al Qaeda's network and is located in the Middle East and Southeast Asia. Some of the TIP members are continuing the "holy jihad" in Afghanistan under the command of the Taliban to restore the Islamic Emirate of Afghanistan to power. A second group of Uighur jihadists, the TIP, are fighting with the former al Qaeda umbrella group Hayat Tahrir al-Sham in Syria.

The Turkestan Islamic Party is adept at using Beijing's heavy hand to recruit new followers and raise money from Uighur entrepreneurs in Turkey and Central

---

21   Thomas Joscelyn, and Caleb Weiss (2019). 'Turkistan Islamic Party Head Decries Chinese Occupation.' | *FDD's Long War Journal*. March 19. See: https://www.longwarjournal.org/archives/2019/03/turkistan-islamic-party-head-decries-chinese-occupation.php.

22   Thomas Joscelyn (2019). 'Al Qaeda Declares Solidarity with Turkistan Islamic Party in the Face of Chinese Oppression'. *FDD's Long War Journal*. April 17. See: https://www.longwarjournal.org/archives/2019/04/al-qaeda-declares-solidarity-with-turkistan-islamic-party-in-the-face-of-chinese-oppression.php.

Asia under the slogan "participate in holy Jihad with your property." Abdul Haq himself, the number one Uighur jihadist, continues to constantly emphasize his allegiance to both the al Qaeda's emir Ayman al-Zawahiri[23] and the Taliban's top leader Haibatullah Akhundzada. In 2009, the U.S. Treasury Department designated the TIP's leader Abdul Haq as a terrorist[24], noting that he had been a member of al-Qaeda's elite Shura Council since 2005 and described Abdul Haq's TIP as a part of al-Qaeda's "support network."

The TIP's anti-Chinese Covid-19 statement was supported by Abd Al-Razzaq Al-Mahdi, a prominent Syrian Jihadi cleric known for his constant ideological backing of the Uighur Jihadists. On January 23, 2020, he issued a fatwa permitting Muslims to celebrate the spread of the coronavirus in China, and further permitting Muslims to pray to Allah to annihilate the people of China. The fatwa[25], which was posted on the "Fatwas from the Land of Sham" on his Telegram channel, states that "We should express our joy and pray for their [the Chinese] annihilation. They have declared resounding war and they killed, slaughtered, imprisoned, and oppressed the Uighurs and non-Uighur Muslims. They are the enemies of Allah and are Buddhists and communists."

The anti-Chinese coronavirus rhetoric and protection of the Uighur Muslims in Xinjiang was also touched upon by the famous Saudi Arabian Salafi cleric Abdallah al-Muhaysini who has close relations with the Turkistan Islamic Party. On January 26, 2020, the pivotal ideologist of the Syrian jihad published a post on his Telegram channel accusing China of "exporting" the coronavirus to Xinjiang, the motherland of the Uighurs. In the post, al-Muhaysini wrote: "China's criminal policy was aimed at exporting the coronavirus to East Turkestan (Xinjiang Uighur Autonomous Region of China) by canceling all flights to and from the city of Wuhan except the ones heading to East Turkestan. As usual, Communist China, will not waste any opportunity to annihilate the Muslim nation of Uyghurs." It should be noted that the US Treasury Department identified Abdullah al-Muhaisini[26] as a senior al-Qaeda member in Syria and choked off his access to the international financial system in November 2016.

---

23   Cf. Thomas Joscelyn (2020). 'How China's Repressive Policies Could Fuel the Jihad'. *Foundation for Defense of Democracies.* April 29. See: https://www.fdd.org/analysis/2020/04/29/how-chinas-repressive-policies-could-fuel-the-jihad/.

24   Cf. U.S. Department of Treasury (2009). 'Treasury Targets Leader of Group Tied to Al Qaida.' April 20. See: https://www.treasury.gov/press-center/press-releases/Pages/tg92.aspx.

25   Cf. Christine Douglass-Williams (2020). 'Muslim Cleric's Fatwa Permits Muslims to Celebrate Coronavirus Spread and Pray for 'Annihilation' of Chinese People'. *Jihad Watch.* February 1st See: https://www.jihadwatch.org/2020/02/muslim-clerics-fatwa-permits-muslims-to-celeb rate-coronavirus-spread-and-pray-for-annihilation-of-chinese-people.

26   Cf. U.S. Department of the Treasury's Office (2016). 'Treasury Designates Key Al-Nusrah Front Leaders.' *The U.S. Department of the Treasury's Office of Foreign Assets Control.* October 11. See: https://www.treasury.gov/press-center/press-releases/Pages/jl0605.aspx.

4.   The Taliban and Covid-19

The Taliban, which is the "godfather" of the Uighur militants' TIP and Uzbek Salafi-Jihadi groups KTJ, KIB, IJU and IMU, have capitalized on the Coronavirus factor to strengthen their political and military potential. The first reports on Covid-19 in China came precisely at a time when the Taliban and the United States signed peaceful cooperation, which allows the insurgent group to legitimize itself as an independent political force in the future and free itself from the UN, US and EU sanctions.

As we noted at the beginning of our article, the Taliban's response to the spread of the coronavirus has been a stark contrast from other global terrorist groups such as ISIS and al Qaeda, who have called Covid-19 "divine retribution" and have used the opportunity to intensify new attacks and intimidate the "kafir's world". The Taliban have long sought to establish that they are a more effective administration than the current Afghan government, and, as a result, they are using the pandemic to further this goal.

The Afghan Ministry of Public Health has predicted[27] that at its peak, coronavirus may infect 25 million and kill 110,000 Afghans, which is more than the number of civilian deaths the 19-year-long conflict has caused. There have been 36,829 confirmed cases of the virus in Afghanistan, and approximately 1,294 deaths at the end of July 2020, according to the Johns Hopkins University[28], which added that cases were expected to increase.

Regarding Covid-19, the main difference between the Taliban and other transnational terrorist groups ISIS and al Qaeda is that it actually controls more than 50 percent of the country's territory, which forces them to take care of the health of the population living there.

On March 18, 2020, the Taliban official website, "Voice of Jihad", published a "Statement concerning the fight against coronavirus"[29], which combines their religious views on the virus with practical recommendations to combat it at home. The Taliban's religious views on the virus have been in tune with their long-term strategic partner al Qaeda. As previously, both groups this time have also pursued a 'hearts-and-minds' strategy to win over ordinary Muslims aimed at further penetrating the local audience.

For example, the Taliban believe that

---

27   Cf. Nathan Paul Southern, Mehrad Ezzatullah, and Lindsey Kennedy (2020). 'In Afghanistan, the Coronavirus Could Be Deadlier Than War.' *Foreign Policy*. Blog. April 17. See: https://foreignpolicy.com/2020/04/17/in-afghanistan-coronavirus-could-be-deadlier-than-war/.

28   Cf. Johns Hopkins Coronavirus Resource Center (2020/2.). 'Afghanistan'. August 6. See: https://coronavirus.jhu.edu/region/afghanistan, accessed on August 6, 2020.

29   Cf. Official website of Islamic Emirate of Afghanistan (2020/a). 'Statement of Islamic Emirate concerning fight against corona virus.' March 3rd. See: http://alemarahenglish.net/?p=33722

«Coronavirus is a disease ordained by the Almighty Allah which has perhaps been sent by Allah (SwT) because of the disobedience and sins of mankind or other reasons. Our Muslim nation must consider this disease a decree of Allah (SwT) and deal with it in accordance with the teachings of the Holy Prophet (PBUH). As per the directives of scholars – people should recite effective prayers and astaghfar (seeking forgiveness) frequently, increase the reading of the Holy Quran, give in alms and charity and turn to Allah (SwT) in repentance for their past sins».[30]

However, at the end of the statement, the Taliban embarked on the first practical measures to combat the coronavirus. Specifically, they offered three medical proposals:

"- The safety guidelines issued by health organizations, doctors and other health experts must be observed and all safety precautions followed to the best of one's abilities."
- International relief, health and humanitarian organizations should execute their obligation of sending necessary equipment, medicine and aid to areas under our control and we shall lay the groundwork for their secure travel.
- Our brotherly businessmen – in line with their Islamic and humanitarian responsibility – must also support their fellow people in this time of crisis. They must refrain from unlawful profit, price hikes and hoarding and instead show affinity towards the people."[31]

However, thereafter the Taliban gradually moved away from a religious assessment of the coronavirus to pragmatic measures to combat it. They regularly published coronavirus disease advice for the public, quarantine guidelines, and ways to prevent the infection. Pictures of their militants, medical staff, and local authorities wearing protective masks have been widely circulated on their website[32] and on Twitter. The Taliban's seemingly pragmatic steps to combat Covid-19, combined with religious motives, could help them gain the support of local conservative Afghan society.

Since April 2020, on the website Voice of Jihad, the Taliban have been actively reporting on the activity of their officials of the Health Commission (an alternative body of the Ministry of Public Health of Afghan Government) to prevent and

---

30   Cf. Ib.
31   Cf. Ib.
32   Cf. Official website of Islamic Emirate of Afghanistan (2020/c). 'Photo report of public awareness meeting about Corona virus epidemic in Logar'. March 29. See: http://alemarahenglish.net/?p=34066

spread of coronavirus epidemic in their controlled regions[33]. "The Islamic Emirate via its Health Commission assures all international health organizations and WHO of its readiness to cooperate and coordinate with them in combating the coronavirus," Taliban spokesman Suhail Shaheen said on Twitter[34]. Thus, they have clearly grasped the dangers posed by the coronavirus pandemic sweeping the rest of the world.

On April 2, the Taliban announced a cease-fire in all areas under their control hit by the coronavirus and launched campaigns to raise awareness about the dangers of the virus. At some critical points, they sent suspected cases to local government hospitals. Thus, amid the escalating coronavirus spread, Taliban's Health Commission for the first time began to cooperate with government and international institutions, including WHO. Covid-19 has positively changed the Taliban's attitude towards international medical organizations, as they have historically targeted healthcare workers of WHO, Red Cross and others by claiming to be agents of the West.

This has given cause for cautious optimism to the United States Institute of Peace that the Covid-19 crisis could lead to the start of long-awaited[35] peace process between the Afghan government and the Taliban. But the slow progress on prisoner releases[36], which is envisaged in the US-Taliban peace agreement[37], has pushed the war parties even further apart. A key point of this deal aimed at ending the 19-year-long war was that 5,000 Taliban prisoners would be released by March 10, 2020. Less than 400 Taliban prisoners had been freed as of May 3.

From the early days of the coronavirus, the Taliban began sounding the alarm for their 40,000 jihadist prisoners in Afghan government jails (In our opinion, the

---

33   Cf. Official website of Islamic Emirate of Afghanistan (2020/d). 'Essential awareness materials for Prevention of corona virus disease distributed in Badghis'. March 29. See: http://alemara henglish.net/?p=34058

34   Cf. Suhail Shaheen (2020.). '(1/2) The Islamic Emirate via Its Health Commission Assures All International Health Organizations and WHO of Its Readiness to Cooperate and Coordinate with Them in Combatting the Corona Virus.' See: https://twitter.com/suhailshaheen1/status/1239594471576256512, accessed August 6, 2020.

35   Cf. Belquis Ahmadi and Palwasha L. Kakar (2020.). 'Coronavirus in Afghanistan: An Opportunity to Build Trust with the Taliban'? *United States Institute of Peace*. April 16. See: https://www.usip.org/publications/2020/04/coronavirus-afghanistan-opportunity-build-trust-taliban, accessed on August 6, 2020.

36   Cf. Al Jazeera (2020). 'Taliban Set to Release 20 Afghan Government Prisoners'. April 12. See: https://www.aljazeera.com/news/2020/04/taliban-set-release-20-afghan-government-p risoners-200412085539496.html.

37   Cf. State Government (2020). 'Agreement for Bringing Peace to Afghanistan between the Islamic Emirate of Afghanistan Which Is Not Recognized by the United States as a State and Is Known as the Taliban and the United States of America'. February 29. See: https://www.state.gov/wp-content/uploads/2020/02/Agreement-For-Bringing-Peace-to-Afghanistan-02.29.20.pdf.

Taliban claims for 40,000 prisoners are overstated). In a statement[38] on 15 March, they urged "international health organizations" to look into their health situation, accused the Afghan government of not taking sufficient measures to ensure their wellbeing. The Taliban described government prisons as "overcrowded and lacking basic health and sanitary facilities, and facing a most serious threat". The statement ends with the threat that "in the event of a catastrophic tragedy with forty thousand detainees all responsibility shall fall squarely on the shoulders of the KAbū l administration and its foreign backers".

In another statement published on April 29, 2020[39], the Taliban accused the Afghan government of "wielding the Covid-19 disease as a weapon of war" against "innocent prisoners" in Afghan jails, thereby seeking to derail the peace agreement. According to them, "the coronavirus is raging in Kabul administration jails and there were identified 46 cases of the disease among prisoners". This time the Taliban directly blamed the United States for the spread of coronavirus in jails "because if it had shown urgency in the implementation of the agreement, we could have made major progress in all facets including the release of prisoners and detainees would have been saved from this danger of Covid-19". They promised to take cruel revenge for every coronavirus death and advised their "prisoners to show reliance upon Allah, have patience and follow health precautions to the best of their abilities".

Another aspect of the Taliban's efforts to combat Covid-19 has been organizing of seminars and meetings in its controlled territories to educate people on how to use gloves and masks, wash hands with soap, and practice social distancing. To achieve their objectives, they have spread public health information through a very active social media campaign, counteracting a flood of misinformation about Covid-19 on popular networks such as Facebook and WhatsApp. On their Telegram channels, Central Asian jihadists in Afghanistan have widely disseminated videos of the Taliban's spokesman Zabihullah Mujahid[40] of how the Taliban are successfully managing the pandemic response.

The Taliban's Health Commission has distributed medical equipment, including surgical masks and protective gloves, and also brochures listing health precau-

---

38   Cf. Official website of Islamic Emirate of Afghanistan (2020/b). 'Statement by Prisoners Commission concerning spread of corona virus in prisons'. March 15. See: http://alemarahenglish. net/?p=33682

39   Cf. Official website of Islamic Emirate of Afghanistan (2020/e). 'Statement of Islamic Emirate regarding dire situation of prisoners in KAbū l administration jails'. April 29. See: http://alem arahenglish.net/?p=34603

40   Cf. Official Twitter Account of the Spokesman of Islamic Emirate of Afghanistan, Zabihullah Mujahid (2020/1). 'The Islamic Emirate of Afghanistan Health Commission carried out campaign against Covid-19 in Maidan Wardak province'. *Twitter.* March 30. See: https://twitter. com/Zabehulah_M33/status/1244574450990841856?lang=en

tions. All these processes were accompanied by a wide information campaign. Images and videos of Health Commission workers wearing white gowns and masks distributing[41] soap and surgical masks to local residents were widely shared on WhatsApp and Telegram groups. Thus, the factor of Covid-19 has gradually begun to make changes in the Taliban's Islamist ideology in regard to once-forbidden items such as film and photography.

To combat the spread of Covid-19, the Taliban has set up quarantine centers to isolate those suspected of carrying the virus and testing residents coming from other provinces. As is well known, they have long been very effective at setting standards for public conduct (layeha)[42] and enforcing them, with often brutal methods. The layeha – a set of "rules" for the Taliban – helped them take action to combat the pandemic, spreading direction on how to act through religious sermons. During the peak of the coronavirus spread in May, they cancelled public events and instructed people to pray at home instead of visiting mosques.

Taliban's Covid-19 response[43] has shown that its shadow administration is less corrupt, more responsive and is better aligned with local conservative values than that of the Afghan government. As a result, the Taliban's shadowy conservative and authoritarian government with parallel constitutional apparatuses has tried to use its coronavirus approach to project itself as a responsible and credible actor. Observers noted the pandemic may end up giving the Taliban a moment of glory, both within Afghanistan and internationally. Remarkably, the U.S. State Department has also acknowledged[44] the Taliban has done an effective job handling the pandemic.

In May-June 2020, in the midst of the fight against the Covid-19 pandemic, the Taliban unexpectedly faced challenges that had a negative impact on their morale. Rumors surfaced that the Taliban leader, Mullah Haibatullah Akhunzada had allegedly died of coronavirus, while his deputy, Sirajuddin Haqqani was seriously ill

---

41   Cf. Ruchi Kumar (2020). 'Taliban Launches Campaign to Help Afghanistan Fight Coronavirus'. *Al Jazeera*. August 14. See: https://www.aljazeera.com/news/2020/04/taliban-launches-campaign-afghanistan-fight-coronavirus-200406055113 086.html.

42   Cf. Phil Halton (2018). *The Taliban Layeha*. December 26. See: https://philhalton.com/2018/12/26/taliban-layeha/.

43   Cf. Thomas Ruttig (2020). 'Covid-19 in Afghanistan (1): No large outbreak yet in the country'. *Afghanistan Analysts Network*. March 27. See: https://www.afghanistan-analysts.org/en/reports/economy-development-environment/no-large-outbreak-yet-the-coronavirus-situation-in-afghanistan/.

44   Cf. State_SCA on Twitter (2020.). 'We Join the Afghan Ministry of Public Health in Welcoming the Taliban's Efforts to Raise Awareness against #COVID19 and Their Offer of Safe Passage to Health Workers & International Organizations Working to Prevent the Spread of the Virus. ACW Https://T.Co/ETyUlo8ZWy'. *Twitter*. April 10. See: https://twitter.com/State_SCA/status/1248731243287662593, accessed August 6, 2020.

in a Pakistani military hospital. On June 1, Foreign Policy magazine[45], adding fuel to the fire, reported that the Taliban emir had contracted Covid-19 and died while receiving medical treatment abroad.

Taliban spokesman Zabihullah Mujahid on June 2 denied that Mullah Akhundzada or any other senior leaders had contracted the disease or had died. In a tweet[46], Mujahid accused Foreign Policy of spreading "propaganda" and said Mullah Akhundzada was well and "busy with his daily activities." While the Taliban have denied that their leader has dead, it is important to note that they have a history of concealing the death of prominent emirs, including the deaths of the founding leader Mullah Omar and Jalaluddin Haqqani, the top leader of the Haqqani network. These deceptions created serious schisms within the group in the past. However, it is unclear how these rumors will impact the Taliban's efforts to curb the spread of coronavirus.

But despite fighting Covid-19, the Taliban haven't ceased their attacks during the pandemic, blaming KAbū l for forcing their hand. Indeed, it is ironic that, while the coronavirus has ground much of life to a halt in this war-torn country, the civil war continues to devour more and more victims. In the practical realm, the Taliban have been responding to the coronavirus while continuing to wage "holy jihad" against the government.

Throughout 2020, Afghanistan, one of the poorest countries in Central Asia, is experiencing the double burden of the ongoing civil war and the Covid-19 epidemic. The warring sides, chiefly the Afghan government and Taliban, have appeared to be unshaken when thousands and thousands of ordinary citizens caught the coronavirus infection and died quietly. The Covid-19 epidemic has failed to dent their mutual deep distrust.

5. ISIS, Al Qaeda, HTS and Central Asian Jihadi Groups: Common Perspectives on Covid-19

"Global players of Sunni Jihadism" such as ISIS and al-Qaeda, as well as its affiliated fragmentary Central Asian extremist groups have much in common in their views of the Covid-19 outbreak, which indicates that they are adept at exploiting confusion and chaos to further their ideological goals. Their views on the coronavirus pandemic boil down to trying to create more propaganda, lure more recruits and

---

45   Cf. Mirwais Khan and Lynne O'Donnell (2020). 'Leader of Afghan Taliban Said to Be Gravely Ill With the Coronavirus'. *Foreign Policy*. Blog. June 1st. See: https://foreignpolicy.com/2020/06/01/afghan-taliban-coronavirus-pandemic-akhunzada/.

46   Cf. Official Twitter Account of the Spokesman of Islamic Emirate of Afghanistan, Zabihullah Mujahid (2020/2). *Twitter*. June 2$^{nd.}$. See: https://twitter.com/Zabehulah_M33/status/1267703509681651714.

plot new attacks. Despite the tactical differences in the use of the Covid-19 pandemic, the strategic vision of all these Sunni extremist groups is the same: they agree that the virus is a punishment from God.

5.1   ISIS view on the coronavirus

ISIS has followed the coronavirus outbreak since its early detection in Wuhan in February 2019, regularly including updates in the news briefs section of the al-Naba weekly newsletter. In one of its first reports of the virus on 'al-Naba' on February 5, 2020[47], ISIS lauded the spread of the deadly coronavirus. "A new virus spreads death and terror in China," al-Naba reports, adding that "communist China is panicking after a new virus has spread".

The Islamic State has adapted speedily to the deepening Covid-19 crisis within a small-time frame and managed to turn the plight of the pandemic into an opportunity. ISIS issued medical guidelines for its jihadists in the following article on March 12, 2020, entitled "Islamic guidance on dealing with Epidemics" in the 225th issue of 'al Naba'[48]. The guidelines included realistic prevention methods and ways of avoiding the disease," which included instructions such as covering the mouth when yawning and sneezing, washing hands, and avoiding entering or exiting an area where infections are found.

Also in the next editorial, published on March 19, 2020, in the 226th issue of 'al Naba'[49], the Islamic State considered this pandemic the worst nightmare of the Crusader. ISIS ideologues called for utilizing the rest of the world's preoccupation in their favor, orchestrating new attacks and freeing its jihadist prisoners.

In one of its most recent editorials, published on May 28, 2020, in 'Al Naba'[50], the Islamic State tried, again and again, to energize fighters and followers to instigate bolder attacks again and again. "We advise you to be harsh upon the disbeliever enemies of God," Abū Hamza al Qurashi, the ISIS spokesman. "Address them with

---

47   Cf. MEMRI (2020/1). 'ISIS Article Describes Coronavirus as Allah's 'Epidemic' Visited On Chinese 'Unbelievers', Disagrees With Those Calling It Allah's Punishment For China's Persecution Of Muslims.' *The MEMRI Jihad and Terrorism Threat Monitor*. February 7. See: https://www.memri.org/jttm/isis-article-describes-coronavirus-allahs-epidemic-visited-c hinese-unbelievers-disagrees-those.

48   Cf. Aymenn Jawad Al-Tamimi (2020/1). 'Islamic State Advice on Coronavirus Pandemic.' March 12. See: http://www.aymennjawad.org/2020/03/islamic-state-advice-on-coronavirus-pandemi c.

49   Cf. Aymenn Jawad Al-Tamimi (2020/b). 'Coronavirus and Official Islamic State Output: An Analysis'. April 15. See: http://www.aymennjawad.org/24046/coronavirus-and-official-islamic -state-output.

50   Cf. Aymenn Jawad Al-Tamimi (2020/2). 'New Speech by the Islamic State's Official Spokesman: Translation and Analysis.' June 1st. See: http://www.aymennjawad.org/2020/06 /new-speech-by-the-islamic-state-official.

sharp swords and ignite the expeditions and do not stop the raids. And do not let a day pass for the apostates and their Crusader masters without disturbing their life. Ambush them on the roads, burn their convoys with IEDs, destroy their checkpoints and barracks." And ISIS jihadists heard their leader's call and took advantage of the reduced pressure from the coalition. In April, ISIS launched 151 attacks[51] in Syria and Iraq, up 50 percent from the previous month. In May, it claimed 193 attacks.

Ideologues of ISIS, al Qaeda, Taliban and HTS, as well as Central Asian Salafi-Jihadi terror groups have successfully promoted an explanation for the virus in line with their apocalyptic narratives. For example, according to ISIS, the pandemic is God's punishment for anyone who goes against their interpretation of the Prophet and his teachings. The organization crystallized this idea in issue 220 of its al Naba newspaper[52], which contains Quran Surah Al-Buruj 85:12: "Indeed, the vengeance of your Lord is severe."

5.2   Al-Qaeda's view on the coronavirus

Like the Islamic State, al Qaeda discusses Covid-19 and its global impact quite intensively. While both agree that the coronavirus is a punishment from God, they have different approaches in their tactics of its exploitation. If ISIS has taken a totalitarian view of the pandemic, asking its supporters to step up their violent attacks on infidels, al Qaeda has opted for the milder route of exploiting Covid-19. Unlike its counterpart ISIS, al Qaeda rhetoric has not called on its followers to carry out terrorist operations during this period.

Instead of a violent approach, Ayman al Zawahiri's organization used softer religious rhetoric aimed at gaining broad sympathy of Muslims in adopting a message of communal support. In its numerous statements, al Qaeda called upon businessmen to donate to the organization, its followers and invited Western citizens to convert to Islam by studying the holy Quran during the quarantine.

Of the numerous messages on Covid-19, we analyzed al Qaeda's main statement titled in "The Way Forward – A word of Advice on the Coronavirus Pandemic"[53], which was published on March 31, 2020, in its Central's media outlet, the Al-Sahab Foundation.

51   Cf. Andrew Hanna (2020). 'ISIS Offensive Exploits Pandemic.' *Wilson Center.* June 8. See: http s://www.wilsoncenter.org/article/isis-offensive-exploits-pandemic.

52   Cf. Aymenn Jawad Al-Tamimi (2020/b).

53   Cf. MEMRI (2020/2). 'Al-Qaeda Central: COVID-19 Is Divine Punishment For Sins Of Mankind; Muslims Must Repent, West Must Embrace Islam'. *The MEMRI Jihad and Terrorism Threat Monitor.* April 1st. See: https://www.memri.org/reports/al-qaeda-central-covid-19-divine-punishme nt-sins-mankind-muslims-must-repent-west-must.

The document stresses that it is forbidden to flee infected areas, stating that "The Prophet issued strict orders that anyone who finds himself in an area infected by a viral disease must not leave that area or travel to any other region, town, or village, lest the infection spread to new localities. The Prophet taught us that the one who patiently remains in his locality when a viral disease spreads, his reward will equal that of a martyr because of his choice to preserve and protect human life and prosperity in other localities."

Further al Qaeda addresses the West and the US, accusing it of waging war against Islam and of angering God through the widespread practice of usury. It exhorts non-Muslims to use the time in quarantine to study and embrace Islam, and castigates Western governments, which it says devote vital resources to warfare and the spread of atheism instead of to healthcare and welfare services. An "invisible soldier of Allah" has supposedly exposed the inherent weakness of the West's materialistic ways, says al Qaeda.

Al Qaeda praises Covid-19, God's invisible soldier: "O' people of the Western World! You have seen with your own eyes the power and might of Allah exhibited in this weak, invisible soldier. This is a God-gifted opportunity for you to reflect on the wisdom hidden in the havoc wrecked by a weak intruder. Your governments and armies are helpless, utterly confused in the face of this weak creature. Allah, the Creator, has revealed the brittleness and vulnerability of your material strength. It is now clear for all to see that it was but a deception that could not stand the test of the smallest soldier of God on the face of the earth. The very technological advancement and globalization that man took immense pride in has become his undoing. Today, if someone sneezes in China, those in New York suffer from its consequences."

According to this transnational terrorist group, Covid-19 is a punishment from the Lord of the Worlds for the injustice and oppression committed against Muslims. At the same time, Al Qaeda recognizes the role of hygiene during the coronavirus crisis, and connects this, again, with the Islamic religion. "Islam is a hygiene-oriented Religion. It lays great stress on principles of prevention so as to protect one from all forms of disease. This it implements through a system of personal hygiene that takes the form of a regular routine that is repeated several times throughout the day", claims al Qaeda.

Al Qaeda ends his message to "Crusaders, Zionists and apostates" with the following wishes: "The fear and panic that has struck you is a good omen for us, and we ask Allah to demonstrate His powers in your suffering and hasten your doom."

Al Qaeda's statement has become a kind of guide and ideological instruction for Uighur and Uzbek jihadists supporting its religious views on Covid-19. This is especially true for TIP, KIB and KTJ in their numerous online propaganda messages, in which they used fragments and thoughts from al Qaeda's document.

5.3   HTS' Islamic view on the Covid-19 pandemic

Hayat Tahrir al-Sham, the most powerful jihadist group in the last province held by rebels in Syria, has two different approaches to Covid-19. Its first approach was developed by prominent HTS ideologues and other Salafi-Jihadi thinkers, who viewed the coronavirus pandemic from a religious point of view. This approach is close to al Qaeda's position and aims to glorify the global and exclusive role of Islam throughout the world.

HTS's second approach to the Covid-19 crisis is related to the practical policies that it is promoting to combat the coronavirus in its controlled territory. Although HTS continues to pursue a jihadist agenda, it formally split from al Qaeda in 2016, prompting harsh criticism from al Qaeda leader Ayman al-Zawahiri and defections by al Qaeda loyalists.

While the HTS-backed Salvation-Government worked closely with the local population to combat Covid-19, prominent HTS ideologies were leading a religious discourse on the coronavirus online. On March 28, the Ebaa newsletter[54], HTS' propaganda mouthpiece, published an editorial outlining the group's religious vision for Covid-19. HTS claimed that the virus had been sent by God to kill disbelievers who "shed the blood of Muslims all over the world." It also told followers "not to be preoccupied with tracking the news and reports" of the virus. The HTS ideologists assure that "a virus, which only seen by the microscopes, was sent by Almighty God to destroy modern Nimrods, who have tyrannized and killed thousands of Muslims." HTS once again taunted Iran, "which has killed Syrians for 10 years and is now stretching out its hand to the International Monetary Fund to borrow money to fight the coronavirus." At the end of its message, HTS asked its followers to rely only on God, not to worry about the coronavirus or exaggerate its matter, but rather to be concerned about the relationship with the Lord Almighty.

On March 17, 2020, a well-known Salafi cleric Abdullah al-Muhaysini[55], a former controversial HTS ideologue, has opposed the closure of mosques due to the coronavirus. He recalled that the West looks at the coronavirus through a materialist perspective only. "And in our religion, the solution to any problem (including coronavirus) lies in prayer, then prayer, then prayer," he wrote. He has close relations with Uighur's Turkistan Islamic Party. It is known that he regularly visited Central Asian jihadist's ribat (front line) before important battles and performed dua (prayer) for them, inspiring them to the "holy jihad."

---

54   Cf. Al-Tamimi (2020/a). 'Jihadist Perspectives on Coronavirus Pandemic': Primary Sources.' March 25. See: http://www.aymennjawad.org/2020/03/jihadist-perspectives-on-coronavirus-p andemic.

55   Cf. Ib.

Al-Zubair al-Ghazi, one of the HTS faithful ideologues[56], praised Muslims of al-Sham because, despite the Covid-19 threat and Russian aerial bombardments, all mosques were crowded with His followers. "In their prayers, Muslims in Al-Sham ask Allah Almighty to rid them of human viruses, Russians, Rafidi (the derogatory term applied by the Sunnis to describe Shia's Iran) and Nusayra (Alawites), and to protect them from coronavirus," he wrote in his post on 20 March 2020.

Abū Mariya al-Qahtani, the notorious ideologue of the Syrian Jihad, tweeted on 24 March 2020, where he noted that the coronavirus is a dangerous epidemic, but even worse when people rebel against God. "We need sincere repentance as Muslim societies because materialism has drowned the minds and distracted them. The coronavirus has come to make clear that this materialism and practical development are impotent before the grandeur of the Creator in Whose hands are the keys to everything", said al-Qahtani.

On March 23, 2020, al-Idrissi, HTS' Islamic scholar, wrote: "Because of the coronavirus, the earth today is less sinful and full of the hope for God's mercy and an answer to prayer." Thus, in his short message, he unequivocally made it clear that the coronavirus was sent by Allah himself so that through its suffering unbelievers could turn to religion and worship Him, the only Creator of the world.

Dr. Mudhir al-Weis[57], another spiritual mentor of HTS, believes Covid-19 has provided an opportunity for people to return to their religious origins. As he wrote on 22 March 2020, "Coronavirus has not only exposed the weakness of the bodies of modern humans but also it has exposed the weakness of the new systems and revealed their defects and clarified the hidden element of the deceit of this transitory materialist civilization." Like other ideologues of HTS, al-Weis also believes that people can find their salvation in Allah Almighty.

Abū Muḥammad al-Maqdisi[58], an ideological mastermind of Uighur militants, a Jihadi cleric in Sham, on March 23, 2020, on his Telegram channel, listed several benefits of the coronavirus. In his opinion, Covid-19 has helped people return to their Lord, strengthened their dependency on Him, covered the faces of women and isolated people from Taghut (idols or demons who worship another God). "And among the benefits of coronavirus is that those who praised West civilization yesterday, today have resulted in advice to beware of Italy, France, Britain and China," he writes. According to him, the coronavirus helped "the West clean up its dirt, because they started gargling and washing their hands four times a day, while a Muslim praying repeats it five times a day. In conclusion, he advised: "So do not curse coronavirus and be patient, and be hopeful. Perhaps God will bring us more benefits and blessings and glad tidings from it." Abū Muḥammad al-Maqdisi is

---

56   Cf. Aymenn Jawad Al-Tamimi (2020/a).
57   Cf. Ib.
58   Cf. Ib.

also known for being an ideological opponent of ISIS and a supporter of the Al Qaeda-lined Central Asian Salafi-Jihadi groups TIP and KTJ. The Combating Terrorism Center of the US Military Academy[59] concluded that Maqdisi "is the most influential living Jihadi Theorist" and that "by all measures, Maqdisi is the key contemporary ideologue in the Jihadi intellectual universe".

5.4 HTS's Salvation Government and fight against Covid-19 in Northwest Syria

As we noted at the beginning of the paper, in north-western Syria's province of Idlib, under the HTS' military leadership Uighur jihadists of TIP, Uzbek groups KTJ and KIB are waging "holy jihad" against the Bashar al-Assad's regime. Therefore, the Central-Asian Salafi-Jihadi Movement's coronavirus policy in Sham is in many respects harmonious and identical with the HTS.

Given that HTS controls the last stronghold of the Syrian opposition in Sham, its tactics and strategy for combating Covid-19 are in many ways similar to the Taliban, which also control more than 50 percent of Afghan soil. In order to analyze the coronavirus policy of HTS and its-affiliated Central Asian Salafi-Jihadi groups, it was necessary to benchmark and analyze their social media messages in Arabic, Russian, Uzbek, Tajik, Kyrgyz, Uyghur and Turkish. Due to the fact that TIP, KTJ and KIB have branches in Afghanistan and Syria, their messages on social media are sometimes inconsistent. In addition, during their long stay in Syria and Afghanistan, many Uzbek jihadists abandoned the use of Russian, preferring Arabic and Pashtun instead of it.

The Covid-19 pandemic is testing the authority and antivirus capabilities of Hayat Tahrir al-Sham, the most powerful jihadist group in Syria, which has ruled Idlib province since 2016 with Sharia law. HTS, which backs the local Salvation Government (SG) in the last rebel-held enclave in northwest Syria, took first preventive measures in early March to deal with the consequences of the pandemic since there are more than 4 million people living under its control. Almost half of the population has been displaced from other parts of the country and more than two-thirds depend on humanitarian assistance.

The epidemiological and humanitarian situation in the region was further complicated by the Assad regime, Russian, Iranian, and Shia militia's offensive[60] to return the Idlib governorate to regime control in March-June 2020. In particular, the

---

59 Cf. William McCants and Jarret Brachman (2006). 'Militant Ideology Atlas. Executive Report'. *Combating Terrorism Center, U.S. Military Academy*. November, p. 22. See: https://www.ctc.usma.edu/wp-content/uploads/2012/04/Atlas-ExecutiveReport.pdf.

60 Cf. Fabrice Balanche (2020). 'Idlib May Become the Next Gaza Strip'. *Washington Institute*. March 26. See: https://www.washingtoninstitute.org/policy-analysis/view/idlib-may-become-the-next-gaza-strip.

regime's and Russian air attacks destroyed 70 percent of the local health/medical infrastructure, and conditions in "Greater Idlib" became extremely poor, especially in displaced informal camps (IDP) in Idlib. Many IDPs are simply living rough out in the open. Thus, the coronavirus pandemic exacerbated an already highly precarious humanitarian situation in northern Idlib and western Aleppo mixing ailments and injuries caused by the war and the dire consequences of coronavirus.

Despite these challenges, the HTS' Salvation Government began taking preventive measures in early March. The Ebaa news agency[61], an HTS-linked media outlet, has systematically reported on SG's disease prevention efforts in Idlib. SG authorities created an emergency response committee[62] on March 23 to coordinate across the whole administration, chaired by Abdullah al-Shawi on behalf of the SG president. In early April, the SG set up medical control centers[63] at the Bab al-Hawa border crossing with Turkey to check returnees or deportees from Turkey. Suspected virus carriers have been quarantined for 14 days at this medical control center, so as not to spread the virus from Turkey. According to the Ebaa news agency, 200 to 300 people were quarantined daily in this center in April-May. Also, the SG opened quarantine centers and isolation tents in Sarmada, Jisr al-Shughour, and Kafr Karmin for suspected virus carriers until they could get proper testing.

The SG's Ministry of Health on March 17 provided guidance for those in its territory on preventative measures to deal with the virus based on international medical understandings of it. This was both an online and real-world campaign to get the message out. Indeed, the HTS' Salvation Government held a number of awareness campaigns and conducted preventative measures to prepare those in its territory for the potential outbreak of the virus.

The Syrian American Medical Society (SAMS) Foundation opened the first hospital "Ziraat"[64] specializing in the treatment and isolation of coronavirus patients in Idlib on 9 June. This greatly facilitated the work of SG's medical facilities in HTS-controlled areas. Prior to that, the opposition forces in northwestern Syria had only one coronavirus PCR kit in the epidemiological monitoring laboratory in Idlib.

---

61   Cf. Ebaa News Agency (2020/1). 'مكتب شؤون المرأة يقيم ندوة تعريفية بمرض كورونا والوقاية منه. شبكة إباء الإخبارية'. Blog. July 22. See: https://ebaa.news/news/news-details/2020/07/70173/.

62   Cf. Aaron Y. Zelin (2020). 'The Jihadi-Backed Salvation Government and Covid-19 in Northwest Syria'. *Washington Institute*. May 15. See: https://www.washingtoninstitute.org/policy-analysis/view/the-jihadi-backed-salvation-government-and-covid-19-in-northwest-syria.

63   Cf. Obaida Al Nabwani (2020). 'Salvation Government Establishes Center in Idlib to Quarantine Syrians Who Return from Turkey'. *SMART News Agency*. April 28. See: https://smartnews-agency.com/en/wires/2020-04-28-salvation-government-establishes-center-in-idlib-to-quarantin.

64   Cf. Enab Baladi (2020/2). 'Idlib Opens First Hospital to Fight COVID-19'. June 18. See: https://english.enabbaladi.net/archives/2020/06/idlib-opens-first-hospital-to-fight-covid-19/.

Indeed, the HTS-backed SG has implemented an extensive effort of measures to prevent coronavirus, so that Covid-19 has hit Idlib less than Damascus. In particular, local officials sterilized schools, mosques, government buildings and other infrastructure. Especially the SG's Minister of Health Dr. Ayman Jibis regularly appeared in local media and explained coronavirus and its preventive measures. The Women Affairs Bureau of the Culture Directorate[65] under the Salvation Government organized nursing courses and workshops to explain Covid-19 prevention measures in Idlib.

Local entrepreneurs opened a factory for making[66] masks for the local population, supported by the SG. The local Salvation Government officials organized press conferences, passed out guidance notices to local passersby and to drivers. They also hung up banners, released an informational video and a series of essays explaining coronavirus and preventive measures. Despite its difficult economic state, the Salvation Government, through its Department of Humanitarian Affairs, has launched a campaign 'To protect our people from coronavirus' and has distributed face masks, hand sanitizer and medicine to Idlib refugee camps.

However, some of HTS's anti-coronavirus measures have been challenged by the rival Turkish-backed Syrian Interim Government (SIG) and its Jaish al-Watani[67] (the Syrian National Army). Also, the HTS-affiliated Salvation Government's order to close mosques, shops and street markets was largely ignored. Videos from Idlib show that jihadists of Huras ad-Din, al Qaeda's official branch in Syria, openly demonstrated their defiance against closing mosques. Central Asian jihadists posted videos on Telegram that they continued to attend and conduct sermons at their mosques. Indeed, all mosques in Greater Idlib remained full during Ramadan prayers with people standing shoulder to shoulder.

Sheikhs and imams publicly defied the order in the name of Sharia law and several ex-HTS commanders and jihadi leaders challenged the group's authority and their religious legitimacy[68]. The coronavirus crisis has shown that HTS cannot rely solely on brutal means to impose social preventive measures. Sometimes, not

---

65   Cf. Ebaa News Agency (2020/2). 'إحصائيات صادمة للإصابات كورونا في مناطق ميليشيات الأسد ومبالغ خيالية مقابل الكشف عن المرض.' 2020. شبكة إباء. Blog. July 23rd. See: https://ebaa.news/news/news-details/2020/07/70183/.

66   Cf. Reuters (2020). 'Syrians Sew Masks as Idlib Prepares for Coronavirus'. YouTube. April 1st. See: https://www.youtube.com/watch?v=k84aBoVKE2k.

67   Cf. Fehim Tastekin (2019). 'Who Are Turkish-Backed Forces in Latest Syria Incursion'? Al-Monitor. October 13. See: https://www.al-monitor.com/pulse/originals/2019/10/turkey-syria-k urds-militias-in-operation-peace-spring.html.

68   Cf. Enab Baladi (2020/1). 'Coronavirus and Sharia law: Divide over closure of mosques and ban of Friday prayers in Idlib'. Enab Baladi, Syrian media organization. April 16. See: https://english.enabbaladi.net/archives/2020/04/coronavirus-and-sharia-law-divide-ove r-closure-of-mosques-and-ban-of-friday-prayers-in-idlib/#ixzz6KO7Bvoym.

only tough rivals such as al Qaeda's Huras ad-Din resisted SG's orders, but HTS-affiliated Uzbek and Uighur jihadists also openly defied it.

Due to ideological differences, the well-known Uzbek jihadist Abū Saloh, along with his 50 militants, left the HTS and joined al Qaeda, for which he was arrested by HTS[69]. Extreme coercion could jeopardize the legitimacy the group enjoys among Central Asian Muhajireen (foreign fighters) and undermine its ability to control them. Therefore, HTS began resorting to a limited use of force that however proved insufficient to produce the kind of outcomes needed to effectively wage jihad during the pandemic.

As early as mid-February, there were rumors circulating in Central Asian Salafi-Jihadi groups' social media that the coronavirus arrived in Syria via Iran and its Shia militia proxies, since Iran was the first major vector of the disease in the Middle East.

Particularly, KTJ and TIP on its Telegram channels reported in detail and regularly information on the coronavirus crisis in Iran, providing photos of the funerals of those who died from the Covid-19 pandemic. They made no secret of their pleasure that Covid-19 had severely hit and continued to mow down the military and religious leadership of Iran's Islamic revolutionaries.

Uzbek and Uighur Sunni Jihadi groups attempted to weave Iran's and Bashar al-Asad's regime's failures to control the virus into their own propaganda narratives. They openly gloated over the Iranian losses and prayed to Allah to destroy even more the enemies of the Muslim Ummah – the Russian military, Tehran's proxy Shia militias and "Bashar al-Assad's bandits".

The HTS' Ebaa news Agency[70] and Central Asia jihadists Telegram channels mocked that the number of coronavirus cases in the Bashar al-Assad's army and among Shia militia forces is very high, and that the regime was hiding it. They gleefully described the extremely critical coronavirus situation in the Syrian government-controlled territories, calling it "Shocking Crown casualties among Assad's army."

The Uzbek jihadists wrote that the Syrian government army soldiers, fearing of being infected Covid-19, do not want to jointly fight the Shia fighters Kataib al-Imam al-Hussein, Quwat al-Ridha, and Liwa Fatemiyoun. According to KTJ, many Iranian-backed fighters were quarantined near the frontlines in Idlib and Aleppo. Uzbek jihadists on the hidden Telegram channels joked about not taking prisoner

---

69   Cf. Uran Botobekov (2020). 'Top Uzbek Jihadist Leader Suffers for Loyalty to Al Qaeda'. *Modern Diplomacy.* July 20. See: https://moderndiplomacy.eu/2020/07/10/top-uzbek-jihadist-leader-s uffers-for-loyalty-to-al-qaeda/

70   Cf. Ebaa News Agency (2020/2). إحصائيات صادمة للإصابات كورونا في مناطق ميليشيات الأسد ومبالغ خيالية مقابل الكشف عن المرض". شبكة إباء 2020. *Blog.* The Ebaa News Agency. July 23. See: https://ebaa.news/news/news-details /2020/07/70183/.

Shia militia member, saying, it is better to kill them on the spot so that the coronavirus infection does not penetrate into Greater Idlib. According to Abū Mariya al Qahtani, an HTS commander, "the heavy Iranian and foreign Shia militia presence has corrupted the religion of the people and their earthly life." Thus, HTS and Central Asian Salafi-Jihadi groups have come out in a united front, blaming predominantly Shiite Iran and its proxy militias in the Middle East for infecting Greater Idlib.

Despite rumors that the coronavirus entered Syria back in mid-February through Iranian and foreign Shia militia, Syrian health minister Nizar Yazigi acknowledged the country's first official case of coronavirus[71] on state television only on March 22. Since then, the coronavirus pandemic has severely hit the Syrian population living in government-controlled territories. On August 6, 2020, according to Johns Hopkins University[72], 944 coronavirus cases were officially registered in Syria, including 48 deaths in regime-held areas.

Indeed, when compared across the country, prior to July 2020, the coronavirus situation in Greater Idlib was more favorable than the Bashar al-Assad's regime-held territories. The first Covid-19 case was confirmed in HTS-controlled Idlib province on July 9[73]. The head of the World Health Organization (WHO)'s office in Turkey's southeastern Gaziantep, Mahmoud Daher, said the patient was a male Syrian doctor in his 30s who had been working in a hospital in the town of Bab al-Hawa on the Syrian-Turkish border. The registration of the first case of Covid-19 in Idlib Governorate raised the anticipated concerns of HTS, its Salvation Government and the Central Asian Salafi-Jihadi groups.

Because, during the two-year-long offensive of the Syrian-Russian military alliance critical civilian infrastructure was repeatedly attacked across Idlib, including hospitals and healthcare centers[74]. Many of the displaced are now living in camps in northern Idlib and along the Turkish border, where most barely have access to basic necessities, including health care, water, and food, making social distancing and basic hygiene almost impossible.

---

71   Cf. Khaled Al-Khateb (2020). 'Coronavirus in Syria: A Catastrophe in the Making.' *Al-Monitor*. March 27. See: https://www.al-monitor.com/pulse/originals/2020/03/syria-coronavirus-who-pandemic-denial-cases-detention-camps.html.

72   Cf. Johns Hopkins Coronavirus Resource Center (2020/1.). 'Syria - COVID New Cases, Deaths, Testing Data'. August 6. See: https://coronavirus.jhu.edu/region/syria, accessed on August 6, 2020

73   Cf. AFP, French Press Agency (2020). 'Syria's Idlib Announces First Case of Coronavirus.' *Daily Sabah*. July 9. See: https://www.dailysabah.com/politics/syrias-idlib-announces-first-case-of-coronavirus/news.

74   Cf. Physicians for Human Rights (2020). 'Medical Personnel Are Targeted in Syria.' *Blog*. Accessed on August 6. See: http://phr.org/our-work/resources/medical-personnel-are-targeted-in-syria/.

5.5   Uzbek jihadists view on the coronavirus

On March 16, 2020, Ahluddin Navqotiy, an ardent ideologue of the Uzbek extremist group Katibat Tawhid wal Jihad, posted a video on Telegram channel, entitled "Allah Almighty supports his faithful followers." In the Jummah Khutbah (Friday Sermon), he said that "today Allah Almighty is destroying China and Iran through an invisible virus. The economy of these infidels is collapsing in front of our eyes. They are stranded and cannot find a cure for the coronavirus. This is God's punishment for their sins! Kafirs are powerless before the invisible warriors of the Lord. Therefore, we must vigorously continue our holy jihad." Ahluddin Navqotiy's description of Covid-19 is closely aligned with al Qaeda's religious propaganda on the concept of "soldier of Alla".

On July 14, 2020, the Uzbek group KTJ posted on its Telegram channel a message entitled "Coronavirus is like the plague" and a short quote from famous Islamic scholar Muḥammad al-Bukhari's Hadith collection 'Sahih'. KTJ claims that Islamic guidelines on epidemics, going back to the time of the Prophet Muḥammad, can help them cope with Covid-19. "If you hear of an outbreak of plague in a land, do not enter it; if the plague breaks out in a place while you are in it, do not leave that place," according to Sahih al-Bukhari. According to the Uzbek Jihadi group, the outbreak is a threat to all jihadists, and Hadith of al-Bukhari recommends how to minimize its spread and encouraging people to avoid it.

Abū Yusuf Muhojir, the famous leader of the Uzbek group Katibat Imam al Bukhari, on his Telegram channel often praised the exceptional role of the coronavirus as a "soldier of Allah". On March 28, 2020, he posted that "if yesterday the Shia Shaitans killed the Sunni Muslims of Sham, today the smallest and invisible soldier of Allah is destroying them in Iran itself. You are the fairest and most protective of the innocent, o Allah."

The KIB top leader also appealed to Western infidel regimes, where school students are prohibited from wearing the hijab. "Yesterday these infidels forbade Muslim women to wear hijab. However, today, when the invisible soldier of Allah Almighty came to their land, they are not saved even by the mask, which they have to wear instead of the hijab. Because Allah punishes them for their sins before Islam", said he. Further, the Uzbek jihadist concluded that "Almighty Allah has revealed the brittleness and vulnerability of the West's material strength. It is now clear for all to see that it was but a deception that could not stand the test of the smallest soldier of Allah on the face of the earth."

Abū Yusuf Muhojir's statement proved once again the basic commonality of the Central Asian Salafi-Jihadi groups and their parent organizations – al Qaeda, the Taliban and HTS. Uighur militants of TIP and Uzbek terrorists of KTJ and KIB accepted and reflected the view the Al-Qaeda leadership that the Covid-19 pandemic as an "invisible soldier of Allah", sent to weaken the enemies of Islam and punish the disbelievers. Thus, the coronavirus pandemic has provided an additional platform and an excellent opportunity for Central Asian terrorist groups to articulate and disseminate their violent Salafi-Jihadi ideologies.

Conclusion

In conclusion, it should be noted that the Covid-19 pandemic offers the Central Asian Salafi-Jihadi movement and its parent organizations such as al Qaeda, the Taliban and Hayat Tahrir al-Sham new opportunities. This study underlines that the Salafi-Jihadi movements from across the political spectrum have been fully exploiting coronavirus opportunities. These events open up political space for jihadist organizations to advance their operational goals and re-declare their extremist ideology.

Review of their online statements in multiple languages disclosed that Central-Asian Salafi-Jihadi groups have capitalized on the coronavirus factor for their ideological purposes in three ways:

a) The Taliban are exploiting Covid-19 to once again demonstrate their advantages over the Afghan government and pressure it to release their prisoners from Afghan prisons. The Taliban aim to withdraw the United States-led foreign forces from Afghanistan and rebuild their Islamic Emirate. At the same time, they want to rule the country alone, without sharing power with anyone. Therefore, they are not sincere in conducting peace negotiations with the current Afghan government of Ashraf Ghani, considering it to be a US puppy.

b) Central Asian militants of TIP, KIB, KTJ and IJU conducting jihad alongside the main insurgent group in Afghanistan fully support the Taliban's coronavirus ideology. They regularly report in Uzbek and Tajik on successful Taliban attacks on the "corrupt Kabū l administration's troops." The Uzbek KIB's website "Galaba Shabodasi" on Telegram has become a successful conductor of the Taliban ideology in Central Asia.

c) Uighur jihadists of the Turkestan Islamic Party exploited Covid-19 as "divine punishment" against the government of communist China for its brutal repression against the ethnic Muslim Uighur minority. Additionally, the extremist group taps on such individuals' sentiments, as it indirectly puts the blame for the virus on China's "impure" dietary practices, capitalizing on growing anti-Chinese sentiments around the world. TIP understands very well that such derogatory nicknames as "Wuhan virus" or "China virus" raise negative sentiments in many people. And Uighur extremists are trying to bring grist to someone's mill with these nicknames

d) Uzbek jihadists of KTJ and KIB in Syria directed their "coronavirus anger" against the "criminal regime" of Bashar al-Assad and his main "terrorist sponsors", Putin's Russia and "chief Shia Shaitan (evil)" Khamenei's Iran." They have widely shared the Dua (prayer) on social networks that Allah Almighty will severely punish these three political crime regimes "for the destruction of peaceful Sunni Muslims in Syria." Also, Uzbek, Tajik and Kyrgyz extremists on Telegram channel published their prayers for Covid-19 to punish Central Asian "Taghut" (idols) states. The essence of their wishes is that the virus helps the release of Muslims from prisons.

An analysis of the reaction of Central Asian extremist movements to Covid-19 revealed that they sought to exploit the coronavirus crisis to reinforce their violent ideologies in two ways. Firstly, at the beginning of the coronavirus pandemic, when it spread to non-Muslim China, Western Europe and the United States, they portrayed the virus as "divine retribution against infidels and crusaders" for waging a war against Islam with an ecstatic note.

Secondly, however, when the pandemic began to spread to Muslim-majority areas, particularly those controlled by the Salafi-Jihadi groups, they put forward a conspiracy theory about its origins, blaming the West, Chinese and Zionist enemies who have united against Islam.

Either way, violent Salafi-Jihadi groups claiming to fight for Islam in Central Asia and the Middle East will continue to use the virus outbreak to recruit and radicalize militants and justify their narratives of hate, division, and enmity. We have already seen examples of this from al Qaeda, the Taliban, HTS and its Central Asian subsidiaries TIP, KIB and KTJ in their coronavirus messaging.

Strategically, the Taliban and HTS increased their efforts to exploit the humanitarian situation created by the widespread coronavirus outbreak. Our studies have found that both rebel groups sought to deliver governance services in their controlled territories such as health and infrastructure to recruit members and build credibility with sympathizers even in normal times.

However, after the coronavirus outbreak, they are now trying to control the activities of Western international humanitarian organizations. For example, the Taliban recently announced[75] that all private companies and aid organizations operating in Afghanistan must register with them. Last year, the Taliban briefly banned the International Committee of the Red Cross and the World Health Organization from operating in the country and accused them of conducting activities against Islam. The Afghan government said the Taliban was making desperate attempts to assert control over government functions during the coronavirus outbreak.

---

75   Cf. Abdul Qadir Sediqi (2020). 'Taliban Push to Control Private Companies, Aid Agencies in Afghanistan.' *Reuters*. July 27. See: https://www.reuters.com/article/us-afghanistan-taliban-id USKCN24S197.

Currently during this coronavirus outbreak, the Taliban and HTS have increased service provision in their controlled areas, while the weak Afghan government and the Syrian regime of Bashar al-Assad are failing in medical, water, and food provisions, in order to build popular support for their cause and proto-states. Thus, both jihadist groups were able to display their pragmatic streak in their dealings during the coronavirus pandemic and reap political dividends at the international level. To some extent, the Taliban and HTS have managed to turn themselves into a more proficient responder to the Covid-19 challenges than the Afghan and Syrian governments.

The fight against this crisis has even more clearly revealed the authoritarian and overly tough management style of the Taliban and HTS, which are trying to impose a conservative form of Islamic rule in their controlled area. Both jihadi groups are using this pandemic to portray themselves as the only military and religious-political force in the region, caring for the health of Muslims in "Islamic territories". Accordingly, Central Asian Uighur and Uzbek Salafi-Jihadi groups actively praised the efforts of their "parent organizations" to combat Covid-19. But in parallel with this, TIP, KTJ and KIB, at the same time, tried to adhere to the messaging of al Qaeda on Covid-19.

In conclusion, it is clear that Covid-19 has established itself as a phenomenon of the greatest importance that has managed to inspire Islamist extremist groups around the globe to new goals. The post-soviet Central Asian five governments already face a tall task in responding to Covid-19, but they should remain hyper vigilant of the now greater threat posed by Islamists extremist groups. After gaining strong energy through Covid-19, violent extremism and terrorism, associated with Salafi-Takfiri ideologies, could have huge implications and effects on the security of the world in the medium and long term.

Images:

Image 1: *Abdul Aziz Uzbeki, the amir of Katibat al Tawhid wal Jihad*

Image posted by Katibat al Tawhid wal Jihad on its *Telegram* channel, May 25, 2019.

Image 2: *Abū Yusuf Muhojir, the amir of Katibat Imam al Bukhar*

Image posted by Katibat Imam al Bukhari on its *Telegram* channel, February 2018.

Image 3: *Ahluddin Navqotiy, the new imam of Katibat al Tawhid wal Jihad, during the Jummah Khutbah tells the Uzbek jihadists about the "invisible soldiers of God"*

Screenshot from the video of Katibat al Tawhid wal Jihad, March 16, 2020, *Telegram* channel.

Image 4: *Taliban doctors distribute masks and drugs for Covid-19*

Official website of Islamic Emirate of Afghanistan (2020/d). 'Essential awareness materials for Prevention of corona virus disease distributed in Badghis'. March 29, 2020. See: http://alemarahenglish.net/?p=34058

Image 5: *The Turkestan Islamic Party's Media Center "Islam Awazi" promoted Covid-19 as "God's punishment" for China*

Screenshot from the video of the Turkestan Islamic Party's Media Center "Islam Awazi", February 29, 2020.

Image 6: *Turkestan Islamic Party believes that Coronavirus is a soldier of God*

Joscelyn, Thomas (2019). 'Turkistan Islamic Party musters large force for battles in Syria.' | *FDD's Long War Journal*. June 29. URL: https://www.longwarjournal.org/archives/2019/06/turkistan-islamic-party-musters-large-force-for-battles-in-syria.php

Bibliography

Ahmadi, Belquis, and Kakar, Palwasha L. (2020). 'Coronavirus in Afghanistan: An Opportunity to Build Trust with the Taliban'? *United States Institute of Peace*. April 16. URL: https://www.usip.org/publications/2020/04/coronavirus-afghanistan -opportunity-build-trust-taliban, accessed August 6, 2020.

Albert, Eleano; Xu, Beina, and Maizland, Lindsey (2020). 'The Chinese Communist Party'. *Council on Foreign Relations*. June 9, 2020. URL: https://www.cfr.org/bac kgrounder/chinese-communist-party

Al Nabwani, Obaida. (2020). 'Salvation Government Establishes Center in Idlib to Quarantine Syrians Who Return from Turkey'. *SMART News Agency*. April 28. URL: https://smartnews-agency.com/en/wires/2020-04-28-salvation-governm ent-establishes-center-in-idlib-to-quarantin.

Asseburg, Muriel; Hamidreza, Aziz; Galip, Dalay, and Pieper, Moritz (2020). 'The Covid-19 Pandemic and Conflict Dynamics in Syria. Neither a Turning Point Nor an Overall Determinant'. *Stiftung Wissenschaft und Politik. The German Institute for International and Security Affairs*. Berlin. May 21st. URL: https://www.swp-berlin.org/10.18449/2020C21/

Balanche, Fabrice (2020). 'Idlib May Become the Next Gaza Strip'. *Washington Institute*. March 26. URL: https://www.washingtoninstitute.org/policy-analysis/ view/idlib-may-become-the-next-gaza-strip.

Botobekov, Uran (2018). 'Central Asian Jihadists under Al Qaeda's & Taliban's Strategic Ties.' *Modern Diplomacy*. August 23. URL: https://moderndiplomacy.eu/2018 /08/23/central-asian-jihadists-under-al-qaedas-talibans-strategic-ties/.

Uran Botobekov, Uran (2020). 'Top Uzbek Jihadist Leader Suffers for Loyalty to Al Qaeda'. *Modern Diplomacy*. July 20. URL: https://moderndiplomacy.eu/2020/07/ 10/top-uzbek-jihadist-leader-suffers-for-loyalty-to-al-qaeda/

Clarke, Colin, and Kan, Paul Rexton (2017). 'Uighur Foreign Fighters: An Under-examined Jihadist Challenge.' *The International Centre for Counter-Terrorism – The Hague* (ICCT). November 15. URL: https://doi.org/10.19165/2017.2.05.

Congress Government (2020). 'Uyghur Human Rights Policy Act. 2020.' *The Library of the U.S. Congress*. June 17. URL: https://www.congress.gov/116/plaws/publ145/ PLAW-116publ145.pdf.

Douglass-Williams, Christine (2020). 'Muslim Cleric's Fatwa Permits Muslims to Celebrate Coronavirus Spread and Pray for 'Annihilation' of Chinese People'. *Jihad Watch*. February 1st. URL: https://www.jihadwatch.org/2020/02/muslim-clerics-fatwa-permits-muslims-to-celebrate-coronavirus-spread-and-pray-for-annihilation-of-chinese-people.

Federal Bureau of Investigation (FBI) (2012). 'Uzbek National Sentenced to Nearly 16 Years in Prison for Threatening to Kill the President and Providing Material

Support to Terrorism'. July 13. URL: https://www.fbi.gov/birmingham/press-releases/2012/uzbek-national-sentenced-to-nearly

Hanna, Andrew (2020). 'ISIS Offensive Exploits Pandemic'. *Wilson Center*. June 8. URL: https://www.wilsoncenter.org/article/isis-offensive-exploits-pandemic.

Islamic Emirate of Afghanistan (2020/a). 'Statement of Islamic Emirate concerning fight against corona virus.' March 3rd. URL: http://alemarahenglish.net/?p=33722

Islamic Emirate of Afghanistan (2020/b). 'Statement by Prisoners Commission concerning spread of corona virus in prisons.' March 15. URL: http://alemarahenglish.net/?p=33682

Islamic Emirate of Afghanistan (2020/c). 'Photo report of public awareness meeting about Corona virus epidemic in Logar.' March 29. URL: http://alemarahenglish.net/?p=34058

Islamic Emirate of Afghanistan (2020/d). 'Essential awareness materials for Prevention of corona virus disease distributed in Badghis'. March 29. URL: http://alemarahenglish.net/?p=34058

Islamic Emirate of Afghanistan (2020/d). 'Statement of Islamic Emirate regarding dire situation of prisoners in Kabul administration jails'. April 29. URL: http://alemarahenglish.net/?p=34603

Johns Hopkins Coronavirus Resource Center (2020/1). 'Syria – COVID New Cases, Deaths, Testing Data.' August 6. URL: https://coronavirus.jhu.edu/region/syria, accessed on August 6, 2020.

Johns Hopkins Coronavirus Resource Center (2020/2). 'Afghanistan'. August 6. URL: https://coronavirus.jhu.edu/region/afghanistan, accessed on August 6, 2020.

Joscelyn, Thomas, and Weiss, Caleb (2019). 'Turkistan Islamic Party Head Decries Chinese Occupation'. *FDD's Long War Journal*. March 19. URL: https://www.longwarjournal.org/archives/2019/03/turkistan-islamic-party-head-decries-chinese-occupation.php.

Joscelyn, Thomas (2019). 'Al Qaeda Declares Solidarity with Turkistan Islamic Party in the Face of Chinese Oppression.' *FDD's Long War Journal*. April 17. URL: https://www.longwarjournal.org/archives/2019/04/al-qaeda-declares-solidarity-with-turkistan-islamic-party-in-the-face-of-chinese-oppression.php.

Joscelyn, Thomas (2020). 'How China's Repressive Policies Could Fuel the Jihad'. *Foundation for Defense of Democracies*. April 29. URL: https://www.fdd.org/analysis/2020/04/29/how-chinas-repressive-policies-could-fuel-the-jihad/.

Physicians for Human Rights (n.d.). 'Medical Personnel Are Targeted in Syria.' *Blog*. Accessed on August 6, 2020. URL: http://phr.org/our-work/resources/medical-personnel-are-targeted-in-syria/.

Kabar News Agency (2018). 'List of Officially Banned Extremist and Terrorist Organizations in Kyrgyzstan'. December 26. URL: http://en.kabar.kg/news/list-of-officially-banned-extremist-and-terrorist-organizations-in-kyrgyzstan/.

Khan, Mirwais and O'Donnell, Lynne (2020). 'Leader of Afghan Taliban Said to Be Gravely Ill With the Coronavirus'. *Foreign Policy*. Blog. June 1st. URL: https://forei gnpolicy.com/2020/06/01/afghan-taliban-coronavirus-pandemic-akhunzada/.

McCants, William, and Brachman, Jarret (2006). 'Militant Ideology Atlas. Executive Report'. *Combating Terrorism Center. U.S. Military Academy*. November. URL: https://www.ctc.usma.edu/wp-content/uploads/2012/04/Atlas-Executive Report.pdf.

Ruttig, Thomas (2020). 'Covid-19 in Afghanistan (1): No large outbreak yet in the country'. *Afghanistan Analysts Network*. March 27. URL: https://www. afghanistan-analysts.org/en/reports/economy-development-environment/no-large-outbreak-yet-the-coronavirus-situation-in-afghanistan/.

UNHCR (2020). 'UN High Commissioner for Refugees Appeals for Safety for Civilians Trapped in Idlib'. *UNHCR*. February 20. URL: https://www.unhcr. org/news/press/2020/2/5e4e51d04/un-high-commissioner-refugees-appeals-safety-civilians-trapped-idlib.html.

UN Security Council. (2020). 'Letter from the Chair of the Security Council Committee Established Pursuant to Resolution 1988 (2011) Addressed to the President of the Security Council.' May 19. URL: https://www.undocs.org/S/2020/ 415.

USAID (2015). 'Central Asian Involvement in the Conflict in Syria and Iraq: Drivers and Responses'. *United States Agency for International Development*. ed., Noah Tucker, Arlington. May 4. URL: https://2012-2017. usaid.gov/sites/default/files/documents/1866/CVE_CentralAsiansSyriaIraq.pdf.

US Department of State. (2019). 'U.S. Department of State Imposes Visa Restrictions on Chinese Officials for Repression in Xinjiang'. October 8. URL: https://www.state.gov/u-s-department-of-state-imposes-visa-restrictio ns-on-chinese-officials-for-repression-in-xinjiang/.

U.S. Department of Treasury (2009). 'Treasury Targets Leader of Group Tied to Al Qaida.' April 20. URL: https://www.treasury.gov/press-center/press-releases/ Pages/tg92.aspx.

U.S. Department of the Treasury's Office (2016). 'Treasury Designates Key Al-Nusrah Front Leaders'. *The U.S. Department of the Treasury's Office of Foreign Assets Control*. October 11. URL: https://www.treasury.gov/press-center/press-release s/Pages/jl0605.aspx.

Shaheen, Suhail (n.d.). '(1/2) The Islamic Emirate via Its Health Commission Assures All International Health Organizations and WHO of Its Readiness to Cooperate and Coordinate with Them in Combatting the Corona Virus.' URL: ht tps://twitter.com/suhailshaheen1/status/1239594471576256512, accessed August 6, 2020.

State Government (2020). 'Agreement for Bringing Peace to Afghanistan between the Islamic Emirate of Afghanistan Which Is Not Recognized by the United

States as a State and Is Known as the Taliban and the United States of America'. February 29. URL: https://www.state.gov/wp-content/uploads/2020/02/Agree ment-For-Bringing-Peace-to-Afghanistan-02.29.20.pdf.

State_SCA (2020). 'We Join the Afghan Ministry of Public Health in Welcoming the Taliban's Efforts to Raise Awareness against #COVID19 and Their Offer of Safe Passage to Health Workers & International Organizations Working to Prevent the Spread of the Virus. AGW Https://T.Co/ETyUlo8ZWy'. *Twitter*. April 10. URL: https://twitter.com/State_SCA/status/1248731243287662593, accessed August 6, 2020.

Southern, Nathan Paul, Ezzatullah, Mehrad, and Kennedy, Lindsey (2020). 'In Afghanistan, the Coronavirus Could Be Deadlier Than War'. *Foreign Policy*. April 17. URL: https://foreignpolicy.com/2020/04/17/in-afghanistan-coronavirus-co uld-be-deadlier-than-war/.

Wang, Maya. (2020). 'More Evidence of China's Horrific Abuses in Xinjiang'. *Human Rights Watch*. February 20. URL: https://www.hrw.org/news/2020/02/20/more-evidence-chinas-horrific-Abū ses-xinjiang.

Zelin, Aaron Y. (2020). 'The Jihadi-Backed Salvation Government and Covid-19 in Northwest Syria'. *Washington Institute*. May 15. URL: https://www.washington institute.org/policy-analysis/view/the-jihadi-backed-salvation-government-and-covid-19-in-northwest-syria.

Online Open Sources

Al Jazeera (2020). 'Taliban Set to Release 20 Afghan Government Prisoners.' April 12. URL: https://www.aljazeera.com/news/2020/04/taliban-set-release-20-afg han-government-prisoners-200412085539496.html.

AFP. French Press Agency (2020). 'Syria's Idlib Announces First Case of Coron-avirus.' *Daily Sabah*. July 9. URL: https://www.dailysabah.com/politics/syrias-idlib-announces-first-case-of-coronavirus/ news.

Al-Khateb, Khaled (2020). 'Coronavirus in Syria: A Catastrophe in the Making.' *Al-Monitor*. March 27. URL: https://www.al-monitor.com/pulse/originals/2020/03 /syria-coronavirus-who-pandemic-denial-cases-detention-camps.html.

Al-Tamimi (2020/a). 'Jihadist Perspectives on Coronavirus Pandemic: Primary Sources'. March 25. URL: http://www.aymennjawad.org/2020/03/jihadist-per spectives-on-coronavirus-pandemic.

At-Tamimi, Aymenn Jawad (2020/b). 'Coronavirus and Official Islamic State Out-put: An Analysis'. April 15. URL: http://www.aymennjawad.org/24046/coronavi rus-and-official-islamic-state-output.

Al-Tamimi, Aymenn Jawad (2020/1). 'Islamic State Advice on Coronavirus Pandemic.' March 12. URL: http://www.aymennjawad.org/2020/03/islamic-state-advice-on-coronavirus-pandemic.

Al-Tamimi, Aymenn Jawad (2020/2). 'New Speech by the Islamic State's Official Spokesman: Translation and Analysis'. June 1st. URL: http://www.aymennjaw ad.org/2020/06/new-speech-by-the-islamic-state-official.

Baladi, Enab (2020/1). 'Coronavirus and Sharia law: Divide over closure of mosques and ban of Friday prayers in Idlib'. April 16. URL: https://english.enabbaladi. net/archives/2020/04/coronavirus-and-sharia-law-divide-over-closure-of-mosques-and-ban-of-friday-prayers-in-idlib/#ixzz6KO7Bvoym.

Baladi, Enab (2020/2). 'Idlib Opens First Hospital to Fight COVID-19'. June 18. URL: https://english.enabbaladi.net/archives/2020/06/idlib-opens-first-hospit al-to-fight-covid-19/.

Ebaa News Agency (2020/1). 'مكتب شؤون المرأة يقيم ندوة تعريفية بمرض كورونا والوقاية منه." شبكة إباء الإخبارية.'. Blog. July 22. URL: https://eb aa.news/news/news-details/2020/07/70173/.

Ebaa News Agency (2020/2). 'إحصائيات صادمة للإصابات كورونا في مناطق ميليشيات الأسد ومغالبها خيالية مقابل الكشف عن المرض." شبكة. 2020 إباء الإخبارية '. Blog. July 23. URL: https://ebaa.news/news/news-details/202 0/07/70183/.

Halton, Phil (2018). 'The Taliban Layeha'. December 26. URL: https://philhalton.co m/2018/12/26/taliban-layeha/.

HRW (2013). 'Joint Letter to the President of the United Nations Human Rights Council'. July 12. URL: https://www.hrw.org/sites/default/files/supporting_ resources/190712_joint_ counterstatement_xinjiang.pdf.

Hürriyet Daily News (2017). 'Turkish Police Identify Reina Attacker as Abdulkadir Masharipov – Turkey News'. January 8. URL: https://www.hurriyetdailynews.c om/turkish-police-identify-reina-attacker-as-abdulkadir-masharipov-108266, accessed on August 6, 2020.

Kilgannon, Corey, and Goldstein, Joseph (2017). 'Sayfullo Saipov, the Suspect in the New York Terror Attack, and His Past'. The New York Times. October 31. URL: https://www.nytimes.com/2017/10/31/nyregion/sayfullo-saipov-manhatt an-truck-attack.html.

Kumar, Ruchi (2020). 'Taliban Launches Campaign to Help Afghanistan Fight Coronavirus'. Al Jazeera. August 14. URL: https://www.aljazeera.com/news/2020/04/ taliban-launches-campaign-afghanistan-fight-coronavirus-200406055113 086.html.

MEMRI (2020/1). 'ISIS Article Describes Coronavirus as Allah's 'Epidemic' Visited On Chinese 'Unbelievers', Disagrees With Those Calling It Allah's Punishment For China's Persecution Of Muslims.' February 7. URL: https://www.memri.

org/jttm/isis-article-describes-coronavirus-allahs-epidemic-visited-chinese-unbelievers-disagrees-those.

MEMRI (2020/2). 'Al-Qaeda Central: COVID-19 Is Divine Punishment For Sins Of Mankind; Muslims Must Repent, West Must Embrace Islam'. April 1st. URL: https://www.memri.org/reports/al-qaeda-central-covid-19-divine-punishment-sins-mankind-muslims-must-repent-west-must.

MEMRI TV. (2020). 'Turkestan Islamic Party: Covid-19 Is a Divine Punishment for China's Treatment of Uyghurs and the Result of Eating Meats Prohibited by the Quran – Warning: Graphic.' March 1st. URL: https://www.memri.org/tv/turkestan-islamic-party-perspective-mujahideen-coronavirus-china.

Mujahid, Zabihullah (2020/1). 'The Islamic Emirate of Afghanistan Health Commission carried out campaign against Covid-19 in Maidan Wardak province'. Twitter. March 30. URL: https://twitter.com/Zabehulah_M33/status/1244574450990841856?lang=en

Mujahid, Zabihullah (2020/2). Official Twitter Account of the Spokesman of Islamic Emirate of Afghanistan. Twitter. June 2. URL: https://twitter.com/Zabehulah_M33/status/1267703509681651714.

Nechepurenko, Ivan, and MacFarquhar, Neil (2017). 'St. Petersburg Bomber Said to Be Man From Kyrgyzstan; Death Toll Rises.' The New York Times. April 4. URL: https://www.nytimes.com/2017/04/04/world/europe/st-petersburg-russia-explosion-suspect.html.

New Europe (2017). 'Rahmat Akilov Confesses to Stockholm Attack.' Blog. April 11. URL: https://www.neweurope.eu/article/rahmat-akilov-confesses-stockholm-attack/.

Radio Free Europe/Radio Liberty (2015). 'Islamic State Militants Target Ferghana Valley'. March 5. URL: https://www.rferl.org/a/islamic-state-ferghana-valley-kyrgyzstan-tajikistan-uzbekistan/26883693.html.

Reuters (2020). 'Syrians Sew Masks as Idlib Prepares for Coronavirus'. YouTube. April 1st. URL: https://www.youtube.com/watch?v=k84aB0VKE2k.

Sediqi, Abdul Qadir (2020). 'Taliban Push to Control Private Companies, Aid Agencies in Afghanistan.' Reuters. July 27. URL: https://www.reuters.com/article/us-afghanistan-taliban-idUSKCN24S197.

Tastekin, Fehim. 2019). 'Who Are Turkish-Backed Forces in Latest Syria Incursion'? Al-Monitor. October 13. URL: https://www.al-monitor.com/pulse/originals/2019/10/turkey-syria-kurds-militias-in-operation-peace-spring.html.

Xinhuan Net (2020). 'Full Text of Wuhan's Notification on Revising Numbers of Confirmed COVID-19 Cases, Deaths'. Xinhua News Agency. April 17. URL: http://www.xinhuanet.com/english/2020-04/17/c_138984653.htm.

Islamic Fundamentalism Framing Politics in Mali: From the Middle Ages to the Age of Pandemic

Olga Torres Díaz

Abstract

This chapter aims to traverse the centuries-long path of the mutualistic relationship between political power and Islam represented by two fundamentalist tendencies clearly discernible in Mali until today, deeming that as fundamentalist is the call to return to an Arabised Islamic orthodoxy that cyclically reappears in the country as the reputed syncretism of the popular Islam that is considered characteristic of the area.

Under this assumption, revisiting certain milestones in this historical coalescence could foster the comprehension of current movements – personified by imams and preachers such as Muḥammad Dicko and Sheikh Madani Haïdara – now that the emergence of the Wahhabi trend has begun to compete again with the prevalent traditional Malian Islam in modulating the orientation of the government.

Keywords: Islamic Fundamentalism, Category Formation, Religion and Politics, Mali

1. Introduction

"[...] On the opposite bank of the Nile is another great kingdom, stretching a distance of more than eight days' marching, the king of which has the title of Daw.[1] The inhabitants of this region use arrows when fighting. Beyond this country lies another called Malal, the king of which is known as al-musulmani. He is thus

---

1 Ancient Roman geographers such as Pliny thought that the river Niger was the western part of the Nile, as did Arab geographers later. The true course of the Niger was not established until the XIXth century by Westerners.

called because his country became afflicted with drought one year following an-other; the inhabitants prayed for rain, sacrificing cattle till they had exterminated almost all of them, but the drought and the misery only increased. The king had as his guest a Muslim who used to read the Quran and was acquainted with the Sunna. To this man the king complained of the calamities that assailed him and his people. The man said: "O King, if you believed in God (who is exalted) and testified that He is One, and testified as to the prophetic mission of Muḥammad (God bless him and give him peace) and if you accepted all the religious laws of Islam, I would pray for your deliverance from your plight and that God's mercy would envelop all the people of your country and that your enemies and adver-saries might envy you on that account." Thus, he continued to press the king until the latter accepted Islam and became a sincere Muslim. The man made him re-cite from the Quran some easy passages and taught him religious obligations and practices which no one may be excused from knowing. Then the Muslim made him wait till the eve of the following Friday when he ordered him to purify him-self by a complete ablution and clothed him in a cotton garment which he had. The two of them came out towards a mound of earth, and there the Muslim stood praying while the king, standing at his right side, imitated him. Thus, they prayed for a part of the night, the Muslim reciting invocations and the king saying "Amen." The dawn had just started to break when God caused Abū ndant rain to descend upon them. So, the king ordered the idols to be broken and expelled the sorcer-ers from his country. He and his descendants after him as well as his nobles were sincerely attached to Islam, while the common people of his kingdom remained polytheists. Since then their rulers have been given the title of al-musulmani."[2]

In the XIth century, Cordovan Abū 'Ubayd al-Bakrī, one of the most notable histo-rians and geographers in Muslim Spain, recorded this account of the conversion to Islam of an early Malinke king in his *Kitāb al-masālik wa'l-mamālik* (Book of High-ways and of Kingdoms).[3] Al- Bakrī's long quotation serves as a starting point and reference for some of the fundamental axes that this chapter will address and that constitute the essential characteristics that are still noticeable in current Malian Is-lam. It involves establishing the seed of a Muslim millennium in Mali – the bench-mark for the sequence to be developed until the present-day; provides a hint to one of the seminal and still present marks of Islam in the country: its attachment to po-litical power; as well as the assertion and tolerance of common people's pre-Islamic traditional beliefs and customs.

---

2   Nehemiah Levtzion and J. F. P. Hopkins (Eds.) (1981). *Corpus of Early Arabic Sources for West African History*. Cambridge, p. 83.
3   Malinke and also Maninka, Mandinka, Mandingo or Manding. Malinke will be used in this text unless direct quotations refer to them otherwise.

Three centuries later, in the XIVth, illustrious Moroccan scholar and explorer Ibn Baṭṭūṭa attested again the coalescence of power, Islam, and commoners' engrained and previous customs. He witnessed the celebration of the Muslim festivities of '*īd al-fiṭr* and '*īd al-aḍḥā* in Mali during the period of Mansa Sulayman (r. 1341-1360), calling attention to their peculiarities, when not lamenting their "vile practices".[4] The presence of the king before both Muslims and non-Muslims on occasion of these celebrations exalted his support to Islam while preachers reinforced the alliance between kingship and the new religion by exhorting people's loyalty to the ruler. Even when Islam was becoming the imperial cult, Muslim festivals had to encompass pre-Islamic traditional rituals as observed by commoners, not all of them converts – at this stage Islam was still a faith of ruling and trading families – but strengthening and upholding the legitimacy of the king.

Ibn Baṭṭūṭa regarded the reciting of the poets, the nudity of young girls in public, or *dyāli* renditions as the "vile practices" previously referred to.[5] Having asked about all these practices, he quotes "I have been told that this was an old custom, which had been current among them before Islam, and they persisted in it."[6] And also noted that although chiefs and nobility appeared to be more islamised, they still cleaved to traditional set of mores.

A third Arab account on medieval Mali was issued by Ibn Khaldūn's famous work *Kitāb al-'ibar*, in the late XIVth century, providing a precise list of Mali kings until his time and emphasising who of them had performed *ḥājj*, the pilgrimage to Mecca.[7] Though brief, Ibn Khaldūn's summary of events in West Africa mentions that the oppressive Soso people were subdued by the Muslim people of Mali, acclaiming Mārī Jāṭa – King Sundiata Keïta, who will be referred to in the next section – as a great leader.

Al-Bakrī's excerpt quoted at the beginning accounted not only the assumption of Islam as an official cult in what would be the germ of the Mali empire but, and very explicitly stated – "He and his descendants after him as well as his nobles were sincerely attached to Islam, while the common people of his kingdom remained polytheists"[8] – the inaugural moment of a characteristic phenomenon of religiosity

---

4   '*īd al-fiṭr* marks the end of the fasting month of Ramadan. '*īd al-aḍḥā* commemorates Abraham's (Ibrahim) sacrifice. Both are celebrated worldwide by Muslims,'*īd al-aḍḥā* the holiest one.

5   Ibn Baṭṭūṭa's *dyāli* (sing. *dyulā*), poets, refer to the later so-called *griots*, hereditary lineages of bards and historians in West Africa. They have preserved genealogies, oral traditions and historical accounts, while also composing laudatory songs.

6   Cited from Ibn Baṭṭūṭa: *Tuḥfat al-nuẓẓār fī gharā'ib al-amṣār wa-'ajā'ib al-asfār*.In Charles Defremery and Beniamino Sanguinetti (Eds.). Paris 1922, p. 414.

7   Cited from Ibn Khaldūn: *Kitāb Tārīkh al-Duwal al-Islāmiyya bil-Maghrib min Kitāb al-'ibar*. In William De Slane (Ed.). Paris 1847, pp. 264-268.

8   Levtzion and Hopkins, 1981, p. 83.

in the area: the distinction between the imported and the purely local beliefs of the country. The fact that with the passing of the centuries they have amalgamated to a certain extent, alternating between periods of peaceful cohabitation and others of open confrontation, has not concealed a basic distinction between what is foreign and what is indigenous, what is revolutionary – in the sense of bringing a major change – and what is traditional.

Both tendencies have vindicated their differences and the validity of their essential values, although both could be categorised, in my opinion, into a broad conception of religious fundamentalism if we attend to the various definitions of fundamentalism. Because the meaning of fundamental is an essential notion here, and also pivotal in the orientation of this article, it must be taken in four of its senses: 'primary', thus serving as an original or generating source; 'radical', relating to essential structure; 'deep-rooted', belonging to innate or ingrained characteristics; and, finally, adhering to fundamentalism, that is, the strict and literal cleaving to a set of basic principles.

Following these senses, as fundamentalist is the call to Arabised Islamic orthodoxy that cyclically reappears in Mali as the assumed syncretism of the popular Islam – the *Islam Noir* that was so dear to and coined by French colonialism, which affiliated to Sufi orders and pre-Islamic beliefs and rituals – that is considered characteristic of the area.[9] One is a textual and Arabic fundamentalism while the other is an oral and vernacular fundamentalism, but both remain attached to what is settled as original and essential in their respective realms. One has been associated, historically as at present, to educated and Arabised minority elites; the other to the less favoured majority of common people. One continues to denounce today the same "vile practices" that had already scandalized Ibn Baṭṭūṭa; the other highlights the "ill intentions" of those who cross the bounds of the purely religious to reach out to social, political and economic control.

Al-Bakrī's, Ibn Baṭṭūṭa's, and Ibn Khaldūn's medieval accounts already disclosed stalwart survivance of traditional beliefs and customs beneath the layers of Islam whilst presenting the origins of the mutualistic relationship that political power and religious authority have held until today in Mali. Therefore, revisiting certain milestones in this historical path seems adequate and useful to present examples of interaction – alternating periods of fluency/adherence and tension/defiance – between Malian empires and political entities, and the manifold manifestations

---

9   A purportedly corrupt form of Islam as a result of blending traditional African beliefs with the "real Islam" from North Africa and the Middle East, and a much-contested notion among scholars within the area. Cf. Vincent Monteil (1964). *L'Islam Noir*. Paris.; Amadou Bâ (1972). *Aspects De La Civilisation Africaine (Personne, Culture, Religion)*. Paris.; Mafakha Touré (1990-1991). *Critique historique d'un concept : l'islam noir. Mémoire de maîtrise, Université Cheikh Anta Diop*. Dakar.

of Islam for centuries. Neglecting these factual precedents undeniably hampers the comprehension of current movements – represented by imams and preachers such as Muḥammad Dicko and Sheikh Madani Haïdara – when the emergence of the Wahhabi/Salafi tendencies began to compete again with the prevalent traditional Malian Islam in modulating the orientation of the government, as well as of society itself, in matters as relevant as the role of women, the jihadist threat or, very recently, the response to the challenges of the Covid-19 pandemic.

2. Two visions of Islam and power in the Malian empires of the Middle Ages: Al-Hājj Salīm Suwārī and Abd al-Karīm al-Maghīlī, Mansa Mūsā and Askia al-Hājj Muhammad.

The late XIIth century witnessed the collapse of the formerly powerful Ghana Empire, fragmented into smaller and competing states, among which the Kaniaga kingdom of the Soso people led by Sumanguru Kanté was prominent. Malinke prince Sundiata Keïta confronted and defeated him in the Battle of Kirina (c. 1230/1235), in the Kulikoro region, after having reunited a sort of coalition of several other kingdoms. Date, battle, and Sundiata Keïta himself are altogether generally accepted as the origin of the Mali Empire, because this initial coalition evolved into a federation of Malinke clans (also including Soninke, Fula, and Songhai groups) under his sole rule. In 1236 the emerging empire was consolidated by enacting what is considered one of the first constitutions in history: the Manden Charter, or Kurukan Fuga after the toponym, near present-day Kangaba, where according to oral tradition of *griots* or *djelis* (Ibn Baṭṭūṭa's *dyulā* in Arabic) it was presented.

Preserved and transmitted by this oral tradition for centuries and by several Malinke peoples in the area, it was almost lost and forgotten until compilation efforts were made during a meeting of *griots* in Guinea in 1998. The Manden Charter – inscribed in 2009 on the Representative List of the Intangible Cultural Heritage of Humanity kept by UNESCO – was finally fixed to include 44 articles divided into four sections: social organisation, goods, safeguard of nature, and final provisions.[10] Subsumed in the first section, article 3 is especially relevant for the subsequent development of politics in Mali until today and, therefore, for the purpose of

---

10   Cf. UNESCO (2009). *Representative List of the Intangible Cultural Heritage of Humanity. The Manden Charter.*; cf. Clyde Ledbetter (2016). Human Rights Studies as a Sub-Field of Africology. In Molefi Asante and Clyde Ledbetter (Eds.). *Contemporary Critical Thought in Africology and Africana Studies.* Lanham, p. 141.; cf. Centre d'Études Linguistiques et Historiques par la Tradition Orale (CELHTO) (2008). *La Charte de Kurukan Fuga. Aux sources d'une pensée politique en Afrique.* Paris.

this essay: "The five clans of *marabouts* are our teachers and our educators in Islam. Everyone has to hold them in respect and consideration."[11]

The original *Manding mori kanda lolou* (literally, the five *marabouts* protectors of the Malinke) belonged to the Touré, Diané, Koma, Cissé, and Béréte clans[12] and inaugurated the close relationship between Muslim scholars and preachers – sanctioned by the constitutional foundation of the empire – and political power represented by the Keïta clan. Nominated by article 8 "as the reigning family upon the empire", the Keïtas always claimed descent of Bilali Bunama from Mecca and, according to Levitzon, they "may refer to Bilāl ibn Rabāḥ, the first companion of the Prophet and the first *mu'adhdhin* (the man who calls for the prayer) in Islam."[13] West African dynasties traditionally traced their ancestors back to Muslim hagiography and usually connected to white figures, while, in the case of the Keïtas, it was a black one, as to emphasise its differentiation and specificity among them. Though nominally Muslim, Sundiata and his immediate successors in the dynasty were supported by a non-Muslim population through his fulfilment of traditional pre-Islamic religious functions associated with rulers in the area. However, their Islamic attachment and knowledge was founded on the advice of the above-mentioned *marabouts* and, therefore, mediated and influenced by the localisms of the area as well as lacking direct contact with the fundamental sources. This situation would experience a significant milestone at the beginning of the XIVth century that resulted in the consolidation of the empire and its Islamic outlines, as well as placed it, both figuratively and literally, on the map of the world at the time. Mūsā I of Mali (r. *ca.* 1312-1332), known as Kankan Mūsā or Mansa Mūsā, set forth from Niani, the imperial capital, in 1324 on his two-years pilgrimage to Mecca, astonishing the world with his piety and riches and making the king and kingdom of Mali known from Arabia to Europe.

This fame was vividly sketched in 1375 when the Majorcan Jewish cartographer Abraham Cresques drew in his Catalan Atlas – considered the most detailed representation of the world as it was known at that time – the realms of the empire and

---

11   *Marabouts* are, still now, the holders of the knowledge of the Qur'an and are responsible for being educators and masters in the teaching of the new religion which was Islam. Often considered holy men and mystics, they were pivotal as preachers calling for the formation of Sufi fraternities in Northern and Western Africa, as will be seen later.

12   Following Robert Pageard (1961). Soundiata Keïta et la tradition orale : A propos du livre de Djibril Tamsir NIANE : Soundjata ou l'Epopée Mandingue, *Présence Africaine* 36, 63. They would be the clans maraboutiques Bérété, Ture, Fofana, Cissé-Haidara and Saganogo following Andreas Massing (2012). Imams of Gonja. The Kamaghate and the Transmission of Islam to the Volta Basin. *Cahiers d'Études africaines* 51, 57-101.

13   Nehemiah Levitzon (1980). *Ancient Ghana and Mali*. New York, p. 55. Also, cf. David Conrad (1985). Islam in the Oral Traditions of Mali: Bilali and Surakata. *Journal of African History* 26, 33-49.

its powerful ruler.[14] Cresques depicted Mansa Mūsā seated on a throne, holding an orb and a sceptre, and wearing a crown, all of them of gold. The king is outwardly black, a fact emphasised by the evident white Tuareg merchant he is receiving and also mentioned in the legend in Catalan above his left shoulder: *"Aquest senyor negre es appellat Musse Melly, senyor dels negres de Gineva. Aquest rey es lo pus riche e'l pus noble senyor de tota esta partida per l'abondancia de l'or, lo quai se recull en la suua terra"* (This black lord is called Musse Melly, lord of the blacks of Guinea. This king is the richest and most noble lord of all this region because of the Abū ndance of gold which is gathered in his land).

Image 1: *Abraham Cresques. Atlas de cartes marines*

Abraham Cresques (1375) Atlas de cartes marines, dit [Atlas Catalan]. The image inserted is the lower part of the fifth and sixth sections. URL: https://gallica.bnf.fr/ark:/12148/btv1b55002481n.image

The return of Mansa Mūsā from Mecca and his contact with the original sources, resulted in a determined impulse in the Islamisation of the state as the ruler brought with him scholars, bureaucrats, and architects who defined the political and even aesthetic contours of the empire. Among them was the Granada poet and architect Abū Isḥāq al-Sāḥilī, who is credited with building the Djinguereber, or Great Mosque, and the Sankoré mosque, which made Timbuktu a centre for the teaching of Qur'anic exegesis or *tafsīr* together with other religious sciences.[15] However, Mansa Mūsā concentrated more in upraising scholarship and

---

14   Abraham Cresques (1375). *Atlas de cartes marines*, dit [Atlas Catalan], BnF. The image inserted is the lower part of the fifth and sixth sections. See: https://gallica.bnf.fr/ark:/12148/btv1b550 02481n.image

15   John Hunwick (1990). An Andalusian in Mali. A contribution to the biography of Abū Isḥāq al-Sāḥilī, c. 1290-1346. *Paideuma* 36, 59-66.

creating a bustling academic corps that could help the spread of Islam than in enforcing it for non-Muslims or obliterating syncretism.

This stance would conform with one of the oldest and most widespread trends of Islam in the Middle Ages in the area: the tolerant and respectful school of thought founded by al-Ḥājj Salīm Suwārī, a Muslim scholar and ideologue born in Massina, Mali.[16] Suwārī advocated that according to the purest principles of Islam unbelief was the fruit of ignorance and that, as a result of God's will, some would remain unaware of it longer than others. His quietist and peaceful elaboration refused proselytism and "represent a scrupulous disavowal of political and military coercion in religious matters and the repudiation of secular political office for professional cleric".[17] Furthermore, Suwārī's prescriptions exhorted Muslims to set an example to non-believers following a way of life according with the *Sunna* that would attract them to Islam.[18] His Mālikī school foundations also fostered trade between Muslims and non-Muslims and therefore supported the extensive social and commercial interfaith activity that the empire held in the area and that Mansa Mūsā epitomises.[19] But this religious and political approach concerning non-believers was soon to be defied and substituted by the first of many irruptions of orthodoxy in both realms, with the new trend represented by 'Abd al-Karīm al-Maghīlī and king Askia Muḥammad, after the collapse of the Mali empire following civil wars and the rise of the Songhay's in the 1460s.

Originating as a small kingdom on the eastern side of the curve of the river Niger c. 1000, it expanded significantly during Sunni 'Alī's reign (c. 1464-1492) conquering principal Mali empire trading and cultural cities. In 1468 Muslim leaders of Timbuktu requested his assistance in forcing out the Tuaregs, who had seized it when Mali rulers' control weakened. He accomplished this enterprise, but only to immediately sack Timbuktu and annihilate many of its inhabitants, a fact that would validate his cruel reputation as stated by al-Sa'di's account *Tārīkh al-Sūdān*: "[...] he was a tyrant, a miscreant, an aggressor, a despot (*mutasalliṭ*), and a butcher who killed so many human beings that only God Most High could count them. He tyrannized the scholars and holymen (sic), killing them, insulting them, and hu-

---

16   Dates of his lifespan have not been fixed and vary between late XIIIth and late XVth centuries.

17   Lamin Sanneh (1997). *The Crown and the Turban: Muslims and West African Pluralism*. New York, p. 37.

18   Ivor Wilks (2000). The Juula and the Expansion of Islam into the Forest. In Nehemiah Levitzon and Randall Pouwels (Eds.). *The History of Islam in Africa*. Oxford, p. 98.

19   On the concept of *darūra* in Mālikī legal school regarding trade, cf. Armando Torres Fauaz (2006). Hacia el Dar al-Harb: Perspectiva legal-histórica de la emigración musulmana. In Zidane Zéraoui and Roberto Marín Guzmán (Eds.). *Árabes y Musulmanes en Europa. Historia y procesos migratorios*. San José, p. 193.

miliating them."[20] His detachment from religious questions and Muslim scholars or advisors was stressed centuries after as well by Triminghan:

> "Ali had no use for Islam, the religion of urban communities. Its learned men constituted a state within a state and were critical of rulers for lukewarmness in Islam and indulgence in pagan rites. Confident in his own power, 'Ali did not need their support and refused to compromise with a religion which involved paying allegiance to a law higher than himself."[21]

A resolute and directly connected response to Sunni 'Alī's policies concerning religious matters would appear shortly after with his successor Askia Muḥammad (r. ca. 1492-1529), who also embodied a reaction to what could be called the Suwārī-Mūsā's political and religious binomial even if not coetaneous. Askia Muḥammad became emperor of Songhay when he challenged the authority of 'Alī's son, Abū Bakr or Bakari, after having compelled him to embrace Islam, which he refused. A convinced Muslim, the new emperor was invested *khalīfa* (deputy) by the *sharīf* of Mecca, Ḥusnī Mawlāya al-'Abbas, during his pilgrimage between 1496 and 1498, as accounted by both *Tārīkh al-Fattāsh* and *Tārīkh al-Sūdān* (known together as the Timbuktu Chronicles and written in the XVIIth century).[22] Also, replacing Sunni 'Alī's lineage and legitimate ruling was considered in both accounts the result of confronting Askia's true Islam with the indulgent beliefs attributed to Sunni 'Alī, a notion recovered by Triaud's reference to the accession of Askia Muḥammad as "the triumph of the Muslim party".[23] Askia himself attributed pagan practices to Sunni 'Alī, linking them to his mother's origins, in his discussions with 'Abd al-Karīm al-Maghīlī, his fundamental and fundamentalist counsellor and the one responsible for many of his endeavours.[24]

Al-Maghīlī personifies the first attempt to redirect what he held as the degradation and defilement of pure Islam as a result of former tolerance and acquiescence to pre-Islamic local customs, consequently opposing both Suwārī's doctrine and precedent rulers' governance. He was neither a Malian, nor a black nor an indigenous language speaker, but a white Berber scholar and Arabic speaker from Tlemcen in present-day Algeria, and thus, an outlander in all senses. His radical and controversial views had already been considered undesirable in Tuat, a region in central Algeria where he called for the destruction of synagogues and exhorted

---

20   John Hunwick (2003). *Timbuktu & the Songhay Empire. Al-Sa'di's Tārīkh al-sūdān down to 1613 and other Contemporary Documents*. Leiden, p. 91.

21   John Triminghan (1962). *A History of Islam in West Africa*. London, p. 94.

22   Cf. Omer El-Nagar (1969). *West Africa and the Muslim Pilgrimage: An Historical Study with Special Reference to the Nineteenth Century*. PhD Thesis, SOAS. London, p. 9.

23   Jean-Louis Triaud (1973). *Islam et sociétés soudanaises au Moyen Age*. Paris, p. 155.

24   John Hunwick (1985/1). Shari'a in Songhay: the replies of al-Maghīlī to the questions of Askia al-Ḥājj Muḥammad. *Studia Islamica* 61, 163-171.

to the strict segregation of non-believers, causing a social discontent that forced him to leave, and in Fez, Morocco, where Islamic jurists made the sultan send him into exile.[25] Fleeing to the south, he finally arrived in the Songhay empire, where he found a haven and fertile ground for his doctrines in Askia's court, a comforting environment for the elaboration of his religious reformism around the idea of the *mujaddid* or renovator of Islam. Together with the emperor, he campaigned against syncretism, innovation and former practices associated with animism, introducing the innovative argument that waging *jihād* – a notion that has not been implemented before in Mali – against those labelled as unbelievers was not only legitimate but obligatory to Muslims. This lawful and corrective *jihād* was sustained in three basic differences with Sunni stances: "[...] al-Maghīlī's doctrine of takfir which declares fellow Muslims as 'unbelievers' on account of their deeds; his sanction of fighting and killing other Muslims as jihad; and his legitimization of jihad against Muslim rulers because of 'oppression'".[26]

The already cited work compiling his replies to the questions of Askia Muḥammad and his most influential treatise – *Tāj ad-dīn fīmā yajibu 'alā al-mulūk* (The Crown of Religion Concerning the Obligation of Kings) – exerted an essential influence not only on the political, military, and religious procedures at that time, but on all following "movements of Islamic renovation in the XIXth century."[27] Movements that constitute a second milestone on the historical path of this article and that, perhaps paradoxically if attending to the general attribution of quietism to their doctrine, were led by Sufis in all of West Africa.

3.   The paradox of 'quietists in motion'? From the Dina of Massina and the Tukulor empire to the French colonisation

In the following centuries, the territorial and political homogeneity achieved by the Songhai empire would turn into the mosaic of diverse spheres – geographical, ethnic, and religious constructions intertwined or overlapped – that is still perceptible today. Different ethnic groups and diverse interpretations of Islam began to settle in well-defined areas with a smattering of denominations and names taking centre stage and whose influence would undoubtedly shape the future of the country. Tuaregs, Bambaras, Fulanis; *Qādiriyya* and *Tijāniyya* Sufi orders (*ṭarīqa*, pl. *ṭarīqāt-ṭuruq*); Seku Amadu and al-Ḥājj 'Umar Tal; Massina, Ségou, or Kaarta began

---

25   John Hunwick (1985/2). Al-Maghīlī and the Jews of Tuwāt. The Demise of a Community. *Studia Islamica* 61, 155-183.

26   John Azumah (2014). *The Legacy of Arab-Islam in Africa. A Quest for Inter-religious Dialogue.* London, p. 123.

27   Habeeb Akande (2014). *Eclairer l'Obscurité. Les Noirs et Les Nord-Africains selon L'Islam.* London, p. 121.

to acquire specific profiles and to leave an indelible mark on the configuration of what would finally be Mali.

By the end of the XVIth century, a Moroccan army crossed the Sahara, defeated the Songhai empire, dismantled its hegemony, and exiled or executed Islamic scholars – who were perceived as a political threat – in Gao, Djenne, and Timbuktu, the latter becoming the capital of the new arrived Pashas.[28] In 1737, Moroccan Pashas were substituted by the Tuaregs, also coming from the north, who imposed their control on the curve of the river Niger and also made of Timbuktu the symbolic representation of their prevalence.

In the early XVIIth century, two new powerful and native Bambara kingdoms emerged: one around Ségou, between the rivers Senegal and Niger; the other around Kaarta, in the middle of Niger. The Bambaras had been part of the Mali empire but, as they had firmly resisted Islam, dissociated from Mansa Mūsā searching for a safe haven for their traditional animist religion and named themselves Bannama (those who refused submission). Kaarta would fall in 1854 and Ségou in 1862, both conquered by the Tukulor empire of al-Ḥajj 'Umar Tal, committed to his *jihād* against unbelief, which he also decidedly conducted towards the Muslim Fulanis, thus providing the first African example of a state being dismantled by coreligionists sharing the same culture.[29]

The Fulanis, who had originally come from Futa Toro, in Senegal, to establish themselves at Massina, in the Mopti region, had also revolted against the Bambaras in 1818. Despite being a minority ethnic group, the Fulanis, under the leadership of Seku Amadu, expanded from south to north at the expense of the Bambaras – whose anti-Muslim warlords resisted the occupation for around forty years – founding the *Qādiriyya* oriented Dina of Massina before being obliterated by al-Ḥājj 'Umar Tal, the most prominent propagator of the *Tijāniyya* order in Mali, in 1862 as well.

The Dina of Massina-*Qādiriyya* and Tukulor empire-*Tijāniyya* binomials not only defined the XIXth century in Mali but clearly conformed some of the imprints that, together with Tuaregs, Bambaras, colonialism and the last arrival of Wahhabism, have been conditioning the events in the country for the last decades. Therefore, a brief recapitulation on these two movements and Islamic states could certainly be of help for a more accurate understanding of current dynamics.

Though Sufism – a quietist and mystical Islamic belief and practice with several stages of growth led by a spiritual guide, whose adherents usually group in fraternal orders or *ṭarīqāt* – had begun to spread in the area around the XVth century, "this

---

28   For Islamic scholars and Timbuktu through History, cf. Elias Saad (2010). *Social history of Timbuktu: the role of Muslim scholars and notables 1400-1900.* Cambridge.

29   For the sequence and impact of this process, cf. Nehemiah Levitzon (1994). *Islam in West Africa: Religion, Society and Politics to 1800.* London.

Sufism was only the fact of individuals, did not carry a brotherhood etiquette and did not unfold substantially."[30] During the following two centuries, several accounts written in Arabic referred to certain figures in the area as "saints" and "sages" using purely Sufi terms and attributes. A distinct example can be found in famous al-Sa'adi's $Tārīkh\ al-Sūdān$ when, describing an imam in Timbuktu, he utilises words imbued with mysticism such as: $qu\underline{t}b\ kāmil$ (the perfect man that has reached the highest degree of the path), '$ārif$ (the knower of God, who has been given Divine Knowledge), $mukāshafāt$ (spiritual disclosures), or abdāl (the changed ones within Sufi hierarchy).[31] However, Triaud maintains that there is no reliable source confirming organised Sufi structures before the XVIII[th]century in West Africa, as he also refuses the rampant simplification – so widely propagated – of an Islam Noir purportedly attached to these brotherhoods.[32]

The XIXth century witnessed the vigorous flourishing of Sufism in West Africa, but with a noteworthy characteristic that differentiated it from the slow spread of Islam itself in the area: although it was at first a minority and elite current, it soon reached all layers of society and contributed undeniably to the Islamisation of the area. This success has been explained by the convergence between Sufism and the ancestral religion in many of their features: the isolation for ritual activities, adherents funding these activities and people in need, a discernible guide or master and a hierarchy, the passing from one stage to the next, the ritual ceremonies including music and dance, etc. These confluences would have fascinated the Malian population, paving the way to a more natural assumption of Sufism, which did not discredit previous customs and rituals as regular Islam had done since its arrival.[33]

In the first decades of the XIX[th]century, Fulani Muslim leader Seku Amadu embraced the $Qādiriyya$ principles that would have been introduced in Mali by Askia Muḥammad's counselor al-Maghīlī.[34] Seku's $\underline{t}arīqa$ is credited to be the first one established in Mali and was undoubtedly influenced by al-Maghīlī's extremist views concerning $jihād$, as well as, and very remarkably too, by his spiritual and political master Usmān Dan Fodio, highest $Qādiriyya$ authority in neighbouring Nigeria and the artificer of the triumphant Sokoto Caliphate, the glorious example of an Islamic state to be emulated.[35] Seku Amadu's efforts towards the creation of his

---

30   Hamadou Boly (2013). *Le soufisme au Mali du XIXème siècle à nos jours: religion, politique et société.* Strasbourg, p. 36.

31   'Abd al-Raḥmān Al-Sa'adi' (1964). *Tārīkh al-Sūdān.* Paris, pp. 20-23.

32   Cf. Triaud, Jean-Louis (1996). L'Afrique occidentale et centrale. In Alexander Popovic and Cille Veinstein (Eds.). *Les voies d'Allah. Les ordres mystiques dans le monde musulman des origines à aujourd'hui.* Paris, p. 418.

33   Boly, 2013, pp. 41-43.

34   Cf. Alphonse Couilly (1952). *L'Islam dans l'Afrique Occidentale Française.* Paris, p. 12.

35   Cf. Seyni Moumouni (2008). *Vie et œuvre du Cheik Uthmân Dan Fodio, 1754-1817: de l'Islam au soufisme.* Paris.

own Islamic state were endorsed by Dan Fodio, even confirming the legitimacy of his holy war against disbelievers – other Fulani and Bambara chiefs he considered pagans. The Dina of Massina (in Fulbe, *dina* means 'religion', from the Arabic *dīn*: religion, custom and judgment), as he named his state, expanded from its original location in Massina to reach Djenné – where he destroyed the great mosque claiming it offended pure Islamic views – and Timbuktu in the north. Founded in 1818, with Hamdallahi as the new capital, this Fulani empire and theocratic state – where *Sharī'a* was enforced and applied severely – left an indelible mark on the social imaginary by establishing governmental institutions, nationalising the economy, and forcing the sedentarisation of the nomadic herders. A Great Council composed of forty *marabouts* was responsible for executive and legislative power, supervising all measures and procedures were in accordance with Islamic law. In addition to the administrative and legal support of the *marabouts*, Seku Amadu was also backed by the most prominent *'ulamā'* – the learned of Islam, those versed in the Muslim sciences – of the *Qādiriyya* order in the region. *Marabouts* and *'ulamā'* therefore became the two essential pillars that supported the legitimacy of his endeavour and that, at the same time and perhaps not unintentionally, connected it with the 'fundamental' currents rooted in the people.

As time passed, however, rigorism and intolerance towards non-Muslims ended up irritating even certain of this *'ulamā'*, who reminded Seku Amadu that tolerance and peace were the main features of Sufism in general and *Qādiriyya* in particular. Among these scholars, spiritual leader al-Bakkay for instance urged him to maintain good relations with non-Muslim Bambaras and stop addressing letters with rigorous measures and interpretations of the law.[36] In any case, religious rigorism and bigotry, mainly focused on fighting pagan Bambaras, should not obscure the Dina of Massina's undeniable merits during the Seku Amadu period: an utterly structured state with egalitarian connotations, social protection systems, and a robust economy. All these achievements were obliterated in 1862 when Tukulor military leader and *Tijāniyya* adept al-Ḥājj 'Umar Tal directed his *jihād* against Massina.[37]

'Umar Tal was initiated into the *Tijāniyya* in his native Futa Toro in Senegal and later travelled to Mecca, where he studied for three years and was appointed deputy of the order in the *Bilād al-Sudān* with the command of "sweeping the countries".[38] Despite his efforts when he returned to Senegal, he failed in seizing animist realms in his homeland, thereupon successfully transferring the attempts and adepts of his Tukulor empire towards the Bambara kingdoms of Kaarta and Ségou between 1852

---

36   Cf. Amadou Bâ and Jaques Daget (1995). *L'Empire peul du Macina (1818-1853)*. Paris, p. 277.
37   For this episode, cf. David Robinson (1985). *The Holy War of Umar Tall. The Western Sudan in the Mid-Nineteenth Century*. Oxford.
38   Bâ and Daget, 1995, p. 239.

and 1861. Until the conquering of 'pagan' Ségou, 'Umar Tal's movements seemed to be congruous with the notion of an alleged licit *jihād* against non-believers, but this lawfulness would undoubtedly be questioned by his following step: the destruction of the Dina of Massina, a Fulani Muslim state also impregnated by Sufism. Though the episode remains obscure, this fratricide and incomprehensible war has been given manifold explanations usually stressing personal rivalry and religious reasons. Personal rivalry is still today remembered in traditional accounts in Senegal and Mali, although very differently: while in his homeland his figure encompasses a lionhearted aura, Malians recall him as a sanguinary invader, covetous of the flourishing and independent Massina.[39] Religious reasons would link the different mystical allegiance, and Massina's resistance to adhere to *Tijāniyya*, with 'Umar Tal's justification "in looking down on them as well as even attacking Hamdallahi".[40]

The Tukulor empire was unquestionably characterised by theocracy and 'Umar Tal's conviction of being divinely guided in his primary mission: the complete Islamisation of the area, banishing all remaining traces of unorthodoxy as understood by the *Tijāniyya*. But a third and relevant cause has also been pointed out when accentuating the strictly political causes of this new example of 'quietism in motion'. Sanankoua remarks that it was 'Umar Tal's broad vision and consciousness – in opposition to the more secluded and encapsulated vision of the Dina of Massina – of the danger of French colonial progress from the coast that led his aim to build a vast and viable conglomerate suitable to resist European pressure.[41] He was certainly aware of this menace after having been compelled to sign a covenant with General Louis Faidherber, governor of French Senegal, recognising the river Senegal as the boundary between his empire and this French territory. 'Umar Tal's fears of French expansion were not unfounded and the Tukulor empire fell about thirty years after his death, as the colonial power viewed it as the main obstacle to its accession to the Niger valley.[42] Beginning in 1883 with a series of military campaigns that would lead to the capture of Bamako, Ségou was conquered in 1893 and Timbuktu in 1894. By the end of the century, French Sudan became part of French West Africa – Afrique Occidentale Française (AOF) – a federation of territories that also included present-day Senegal, Mauritania, Guinea, Benin, Niger, Côte d'Ivoire, and Burkina Faso.

---

39   Cf. Olga Torres Díaz (2020). Islamism and Women in the Sahel: Roots and Evolutions. In Klaus Hock and Nina Käsehage (Eds.). *'Militant Islam' vs. 'Islamic Militancy'? Religion, Violence, Category Formation and Applied Research. Contested Fields in the Discourse of Scholarship*. Zürich, p. 202.

40   Patrick Ryan (2000). The Mystical Theology of Tijānī Sufism and Its Social Significance in West Africa. *Journal of Religion in Africa* 30, N° 2, 216.

41   Cf. Bintou Sanankoua (1990). *Un empire peul au XIXᵉ siècle : la Diina du Maasina*. Paris.

42   Cf. Yves Saint-Martin (1967). *L'Empire toucouleur et la France. Un demi-siècle de relations diplomatiques (1846-1893)*. Dakar.

French colonial irruption in the area implied not only a territorial invasion, but the encounter with an absolute otherness and the appearance of a new actor who would join pre-existing ones. And if colonial power always involved, in one way or another, the domination of a physical space, the appropriation of its resources, and the influence over the local people's mentality, in the case of France the concept of mission civilisatrice had to be added to all the rest.[43] This notion would connote the essence of French achievements, including secular republican values and the fervour for modernising and casting out the evils of ignorance and superstitions in the rural areas of metropolitan France as well as in its colonies. Secularism and the eradication of superstitions constituted two of the main features of France's impact in all of West Africa, challenging the popular understanding of both traditional political exercise and customary beliefs. Therefore, fearing a revivification of these traditional movements in the area, the French determinedly contended with concealing any missionary or armed initiative during their colonial dominion, and even more so with any intrusion of religion in the political realm.

Unquestionably, sixty-seven years of French colonial presence enacting secular republican values constituted a decisive turn in the restructuring of the hitherto intimate blending of political power and religious influence. Whether to adhere to or to challenge this change of events, local and previous actors could not avoid being impacted and taking a stance regarding the new reality. French law on the separation of church and state in 1905 immediately reached the African colonies, also introducing a new dichotomy to tack on the pre-existing ones: religious actors cooperating with colonial power – after the creation of the *Service des affaires musulmanes* – or rejecting any form of interference. The Muslim Affairs Service exerted close control over, for instance, issues concerning the fasting month of Ramadan or the organisation of the yearly pilgrimage to Mecca. However, managing this second question with the intention of gaining popularity among the Muslim community had an unexpected collateral effect in the years to come: together with a rapid spread of Islam among those who had traditionally not been Muslims, the strengthening of Wahhabi reformism – represented by the *ahl al-Sunna* movement – trends in response to Sufi 'whimsicalness'.[44]

---

43   Cf. Alice Conklin (1997). *A Mission to Civilize. The Republican Idea of Empire in France and West Africa, 1895-1930*. Stanford.

44   For these questions, cf. Carsten Hock (1960). *Fliegen die Seelen der Heiligen: Muslimische Reform und staatliche Autorität in der Republik Mali seit 1960*. Berlin; cf. Julia Leininger (2013). *Religiöse Akteure in Demokratisierungsprozessen. Konstruktiv, destruktiv und obstruktiv*. Wiesbaden.

4.   XXth – XXIst centuries. From Independence to the Age of Pandemic

Whereas Wahhabi ideas had been introduced in the country by the 1920s, it was after independence that their adherents began to compete with *marabouts* for closeness to the new post-colonial nationalist governments. Wahhabi's main focus was to reform education, to spread the teaching of Arabic, and, on the whole, to return to an orthopraxy of Islam strictly rooted in the Qur'an and the Sunna.

Concurrently, another phenomenon that had also begun under the colonial domination and that would become crucial in the future of the country finally bourgeoned: the popularisation of Muslim preachers' public sermons outside the mosques, addressing Muslims and non-Muslims, that "[...] became one of the principal means for facilitating the spread of Islam and for the standardization of Islamic practice, with implications for public piety in Mali."[45]

Modibo Keïta, first president of independent Mali, was also the first modern ruler to be compelled to juggle his Muslim origin with his secularist political convictions, as well as to deal with the emergent trends represented by both Wahhabis and Muslim preachers. Born at the beginning of the XXth century in by then French Sudan, he was the co-founder of the socialist inclined Sudanese Union (US) party in 1945, later merging with the anticolonial African Democratic Rally (RDA) to form the US-RDA. Under this coalition, he first had a seat in the territorial assembly in 1948 and later was a deputy in the French National Assembly from 1956 to 1958. Claiming Sudan's autonomy within the French Community and aiming to create a West African federation – that solely resulted in an ephemeral Mali Federation that he presided over, composed of Senegal and Sudan in 1959 – Keïta's party finally proclaimed the independent Republic of Mali in 1960.

Keïta's ruling was based on Marxist ideology, which, together with his French education in the principles of *laïcité*, resulted in an official discourse pushing Islam aside by stating that religion was a private issue and banning Islamic associations.[46] Many of these associations originated after the arrival of returnees from Saudi Arabia after graduating from their religious institutions and often took the form of Islamic nongovernmental organisations providing finance for schools and grants for different projects, as well as distributing Salafi oriented literature.[47]

As in many other countries in the area, post-colonial governments in Mali were characterised by instability and the periodic intrusion of the military seizing con-

---

45   Benjamin Soares (2004). Islam and public piety in Mali. In Armando Salvatore and Dale Eickelman (Eds.). *Public Islam and the common good*. Leiden, p. 210.

46   For Keïta's ideological discourse, cf. Francis Snyder (1967). The Political Thought of Modibo Keita. *Journal of Modern African Studies* 5, N° 1, 79-106.

47   Cf. John Hunwick (1997). Sub-Saharan Africa and the Wider World of Islam: Historical and Contemporary Perspectives. In David Westerlund and Eva Evers Rosander (Eds.). *African Islam and Islam in Africa: Encounters between Sufis and Islamists*. London, pp. 28-54.

trol after *coup d'états*. In Mali, the sequence included Keïta being deposed by Lt. Moussa Traoré in a military coup in 1968, also deposed by Col. Amadou Toumani Touré in 1991, followed by an interim rule to develop a democratic state, which finally led to a new constitution and the first democratic multiparty elections won by Alpha Oumar Konaré in 1992. Democratic elections, even when customarily surrounded in the country by recurrent accusations of fraud, also led Amadou Toumari Touré again to the presidency between 2002 and 2012, when his inability to deal with the Tuareg rebellion in the north catalysed Malian army discontent that resulted in a new *coup d'état*. After a transitional period, new presidential elections were won by Ibrakim Boubacar Keïta in 2013, still in office after having revalidated his mandate in 2018.[48]

Whether they were democratically elected or came to power after military interventions, all Malian presidents have had to face the difficult balance between restricting interference by religious actors and resorting to their incontestable popular support to strengthen their legitimacy. These religious actors presented a wide range of interpretations of Islam, but among them, the aforementioned Wahhabi-Salafi inspired *ahl al-Sunna* and traditional Muslim preachers and *marabouts* cannot be disregarded for the comprehension of present-day Mali intertwinement of politics and Islam.

Wahhabi *ahl al-Sunna* grew and expanded in the 1970s when president Traoré's tolerance towards Islamic organisations counterbalanced the determined marginalisation they had experienced under Keïta's administration. This tolerance had a relevant effect on education, developing Islamic madrasas and the teaching of Arabic, and public presence, opening new mosques as well as broadcasting religious programmes.[49] Together with the reedition of a new wave of fundamentalist reformism, another pertinent outcome has perhaps not been sufficiently pointed out: the Arabisation of certain intellectual and educated layers of the population to distinguish themselves from previous ill-influenced Frenchification as well as from lower classes. In any case, both prior Frenchification and later Arabisation share the common trait of establishing an edge between 'cultivated' elites and common people that has always been a historical characteristic in the area and is still tangible today. Furthermore, even though this Arabisation aspires to spread to other collectives and social classes – through the expansion of its religious schools – its elitist origin cannot be neglected, nor can the fact that it is associated with a certain disdain towards the popular customs of the non-Arabised.

---

48   The list would be completed by the interim presidency of Amadou Sanogo (21 days in 2012) and Dioncounda Traoré (17 months) during the transition between the last military coup and the presidential elections in 2013.

49   Between 1968 and 1983 the number of mosques rose from 77 to 203 in Bamako alone. Cf. Louis Brenner (2001). *Controlling Knowledge: Religion, Power and Schooling in a West Africa Muslim Society*. London, p. 197.

Malian reformers labelled as Wahhabis censure, for instance, the wide range of social roles carried out by *griots* connecting them with social castes and endogamous lineages as well as, in a very similar way Ibn Baṭṭūṭa had done in the XIVth century, consider their performances and rituals immoral.[50] These sorts of appreciations revitalise and actualise the polarisation and the conflict between traditional orthodox Islam and traditional Sufi or popular Islam that has been shaping politics in Mali from the Middle Ages until now.

Two trends that have conspicuous representatives in Mahmoud Dicko and Sheikh Madani Haïdara, whose different visions – regarding the status of women, the response to ethnic schism or terrorist threats, not to be exhaustive – have been playing a substantial role in contemporary Mali, even now in the Age of Pandemic. They are the central figures of this renewed competition which, since the 1990s, the two main tendencies vying for social and spiritual hegemony maintain not only in Mali but in most neighbouring countries. On the one hand, there are the defenders of a Wahhabi-inspired, neo-reformist literalistic Islam with elitist overtones and, on the other, those who claim to embody the popular Islam of the illiterate and the marginalised.

Ousmane Madani Haïdara, a central figure of Malian Islam, was born in 1955 in a village near Ségou, son to a father affiliated with the *Tijāniyya* Sufi order and reluctant to the irruption of Sunni reformism or Wahhabism. His profound Islamic convictions and Qur'anic education led him to devote his life to religious endeavours as a preacher and a *marabout*. Beginning in Côte d'Ivoire in the 1970s, in 1981 he returned to Mopti, in his homeland, where his preaching and activities, critical towards power and establishment, were prohibited by the authorities in 1983 for the first time. He reappeared in Bamako in 1984 and, for the following years, his preaching found a favourable environment in the weakening of the movements linked to *ahl al-Sunna*, which were beginning to be considered too radical and backward in different milieus. Though educated in the *Tijāniyya*, he "[...] developed an idiosyncratic approach to Islam in Mali, blending notions of reform, Sufi principles of organisation, and a doctrine of Malian cultural authenticity critical of Arabism' of Salafis."[51] His hybridism, his iconoclasm, and the crudeness of some of his expressions earned him a second ban in 1989 after having stated, for instance, that "prayer was not Islam" and with Wahhabis assembled around the Malian Association for the Unity and Progress of Islam (AMUPI) accusing him of *bid'a*, heretical innovation.[52] This sentence illustrated his stance against praying as a sort of super-

---

50 For the roles of *griots*, cf. Francesco Zappa (2009). Popularizing Islamic Knowledge through Oral Epic: A Malian Bard in a Media Age. *Die Welt des Islams 49*, N° 3/4, 391.

51 Rahmane Idrissa (2017). *The Politics of Islam in the Sahel: Between Persuasion and Violence*. London, p. 178.

52 AMUPI was founded in 1980 under the auspices of President Traoré. Reuniting Muslims under a unique religious association reproduced the single-party UDPM (Union Démocratique

ficial compliance with social standards, which he attributed to Wahhabi influence in the public sphere, as well as against "the notion of being "Muslim by birth" (*silamèden*). In his opinion, if prayer is one of the pillars of Islam and an obligation for every Muslim, it is not enough to exonerate one from living according to the Qur'ān and *shariah*."[53]

In the following years, clashes between his views and those of the Wahhabis only increased, stressing their different approaches to society and politics. Differences crystallised in 1991, when Haïdara founded the social Islamic movement Ansar Dine and the Wahhabis aimed at participating in the first democratic elections in the country as religious parties, which they were denied.[54] This date also marked a patent division between the secular populism represented by Haïdara – mainly backed by lower classes who felt themselves supported and endorsed after decades of official post-colonial carelessness – and the purported elitism of those involved in manifest political ambitions even when religiously originated.

Following this division, and at the other end of the fundamentalist spectrum in Mali, would be Mahmoud Dicko, whose education and evolution sharply contrast with those of Haïdara in a new reissue of historical religious dichotomies and personalities.

Mahmoud Dicko was also born in the mid-1950s near Timbuktu, to a family of notables, and was originally a teacher of Arabic until ideologically joining the aforementioned trend represented by the latecomer *'ulamā'*, educated in and inspired by Saudi Islamic institutions and responsible for what has been termed "the politicisation of purity."[55] Imam of the reformist mosque of Badalabougou in Bamako, he has always rejected to be labelled as a Wahhabi although this has always been his adscription according to the general perception in the country, which also clearly distinguishes him from Haïdara's positions.[56]

---

du Peuple Malien), both of which were devoted to overseeing potential dissensions and conflicts.

53   Gilles Holder (2012). Chérif Ousmane Madani Haidara and the Islamic Movement Ansar Dine: A Popular Malian Reformism in Search of Autonomy. *Cahiers d'Études Africaines* 206-207, N° 2, 394.

54   Haïdara's movement is by no means to be confused with the terrorist group operating in northern Mali Ansar Dine or Ansar al-Din, led by Iyad ag-Ghaly and whose first action took place in 2012. In March 2017, terrorist organisations Ansar Dine, Saharan branch of al-Qaeda in the Islamic Maghreb, Macina Liberation Front, and al-Murabitun merged in what resulted in Jama'a Nusrat ul-Islam wa al-Muslimin - now the official branch of al-Qaeda in Mali - under ag-Ghaly's leadership.

55   Cf. Terje Østebø (2015). African Salafism: Religious Purity and the Politicization of Purity. *Islamic Africa* 6, N° 1/2, 1-29.

56   Cf. Ahmed Chanfi (2015). *West African 'ulamā' and Salafism in Mecca and Medina: Jawāb al-Ifrīqī - The Response of the African.* Leiden, p. 193.

Paradoxically, their confronted views with respect to the rights of women or the attitude towards jihadist groups, for example, were both sheltered by the High Islamic Council of Mali (HCIM) – also founded by the government in 2002 – in order to oversee the increasing activities and impact of religious actors in Mali. Mahmoud Dicko presided over it between 2008-2019 while Haïdara was its vice-president until he himself became elected president in April 2019. From this position, Dicko firmly opposed a new family code, promoted by President Amadou Toumani Touré in 2009 which would have improved women's rights, claiming that it was against Islam and Malian traditions, a campaign that made him come to higher prominence. In 2012, his political profile was bolstered when he conducted direct negotiations with the jihadist groups that had taken control of large swathes of territory in the north of the country – in the wake of a previous nationalistic Tuareg rebellion in the area – , this time overtly undertaking the place of the government itself although presenting himself as an 'Islamic' mediator. Haïdara, who rejected any kind of leniency towards those who had challenged a legitimate government and destroyed Timbuktu's heritage, accused him of sharing many of their views. Dicko responded that these groups were also Malians and Muslims whose stances could not be marginalised and that "in order not to alienate the Islamists, he did not issue any public statement in condemnation of the mausoleums' destruction."[57]

In a last step in his incessant meddling in almost all domains of the country's life – and now openly challenging the government of President Ibrahim Boubacar Keïta (often referred to as IBK), who came to power thanks in part to his support in 2013 – Dicko has found in the confluence of three extraordinary factors a new battlefield for his fundamentalism.

5.   Mahmoud Dicko's fundamentalism and the perfect storm in the Age of Pandemic

The confluent occurrence of parliamentary elections, Ramadan, and Covid-19 in the first half of 2020 – together with the permanent hazard of jihadist terrorism – has paved the way to an extraordinary opportunity for Mahmoud Dicko to establish a new milestone in the interaction of religious fundamentalism and politics in Mali. As has been the case since the days of the Mali empire in the Middle Ages, the threats of the Age of Pandemic have once again highlighted the politicisation of religious currents and their tendency to influence and modulate governmental action. Once again as well, political power has not been able to disregard the enor-

---

57   Rosa De Jorio (2016). *Cultural Heritage in Mali in the Neoliberal Era*. Chicago, p. 130.

mous capacity, whether it be overt or covert, they have to leverage people to their goals.

While explicitly non-Wahhabi and politically less involved leader Sheikh Madani Haïdara remains far more representative of majority Malian Islam and is critical of the alleged Arabism and politicisation of Wahhabism, his social influence is certainly being challenged by Mahmoud Dicko's growing and determined participation in the public arena in recent years. The examples of these interferences have been multiplying since his intervention in the aforementioned question of women's rights in 2009 or the conflict in the north of the country in 2012. In November 2015, answering a question after a jihadist terrorist attack that resulted in 20 victims at hotel Radisson Blu in Bamako, Dicko explained that the wrath of God was linked to the presence of homosexuals and bars in the country and that "We must learn the lessons from the attacks in Paris, like in Bamako, in Tunis or elsewhere in the world [...] God is angry. Men have provoked God."[58] In 2018, his activism opposing a proposed sexual education textbook for adolescents – including a chapter on sexual orientation that Dicko considered promoting homosexuality – also made the government withdraw it.[59] Finally, shortly after leaving the presidency of HCIM – after all a device of the establishment where at least a certain degree of containment was expected – in September 2019 he launched the Coordination of Movements, Associations, and Sympathisers (CMAS), a much more suitable vehicle to display a political role without restraint.

But while the examples of his activities have been multiplying over the last decade, since March 2020 they have acquired unusual speed and have been occurring parallel to the following chronological sequence of events in the country.

At the beginning of that month, neighbouring countries such as Senegal, Côte d'Ivoire, and Burkina Faso had already confirmed the presence of Covid-19 in their territories and its menacing expansion in view of their precarious health systems. Meanwhile, the Malian government remained astoundingly silent on the matter, raising all kinds of suspicions that linked this silence with the imminence of the first round of parliamentary elections, scheduled for March 29.

By midmonth, the government announced the closing of schools and public spaces as well as the prohibition of gatherings of more than 50 persons and also recommended the closure of mosques. Concurrently, Sheikh Madani Haïdara appealed to the necessity of collective prayer to invoke divine protection against the coronavirus and, in a very different approach, Mahmoud Dicko warned the Malian

---

58   Laure Broulard (2015). *Mali : l'imam Mahmoud Dicko voit dans le terrorisme «une punition divine» et crée la polémique*. December 2. See: https://www.jeuneafrique.com/283688/societe/mali-lim am-mahmoud-dicko-voit-terrorisme-punition-divine-cree-polemique/

59   Andrew Lebovich (2019). *Sacred Struggles: How Islam Shapes Politics in Mali*. November 1, p. 11. See: https://ecfr.eu/publication/secular_stagnation_malis_relationship_religion/

authorities that the elections of March 29 and April 19 could not be maintained while, at the same time, asking the imams to close the mosques to limit the spread of the virus in the country.

On March 25, the Malian government reported the first two confirmed cases, attributing them to nationals returned from France, and a nationwide curfew was finally decreed on March 26 as a necessary measure to combat the expansion of Covid-19. Significantly, however, the closure of places of worship was left to the discretion of religious authorities, a fact that resulted in almost all of them remaining open.

On March 25 as well, Mali's main opposition leader, Soumaïla Cisse, was taken hostage by suspected jihadists while campaigning in the restive Timbuktu region. The opposition then denounced the irregularity of holding elections in which one of the most prominent figures challenging the government was absent.

Turnout in the first round of the parliamentary election, on March 29, plummeted to 35.73 percent of the 7.6 million registered voters and was less than 13 percent in Bamako. Some of the results were later overturned by the country's constitutional court in a decision that was perceived to benefit Keïta's party. In the second round, on April 19, the national percentage fell even further, reaching only 23 percent. The government attributed these figures to the combination of the terrorist threat and Covid-19.[60]

Ramadan began on April 23 and ended on May 23. During the holy month, the mosques – especially that of imam Dicko – were crowded with worshipers despite an April 15 document issued by the World Health Organisation, titled "Balancing Ramadan Practices and Personal Safety", which stated that the cancellation of social and religious gatherings should be seriously considered. Such a decision, according to Dicko was all the more difficult to make when it was known that Malian mosques "do not only have a religious function, but also a social one" and that many indigent people live thanks to these places while benefiting from Muslim solidarity.[61]

On May 10, Prime Minister Boubou Cisse announced the lifting of the curfew in view of the limited success this measure had had in reducing population movements and gatherings – given its coincidence with Ramadan and the lack of support received from the religious authorities – and the obligation to wear masks.

By the end of May, Mahmoud Dicko amassed all these previous events – the concealment of data on the pandemic, the manipulation of the elections, the kid-

---

60   For turnouts in both rounds, cf. France24 (2020/1). *Mali election run off tarnished by intimidation and allegations of vote rigging.* April 20. See: https://www.france24.com/en/20200420-mali-election-runoff-tarnished-by-intimidation-and-allegations-of-vote-rigging

61   Paul Lorgerie (2020). Au Mali, les mosquées resteront ouvertes pendant le mois du ramadán. *Le Monde.* April 24. See : https ://www.lemonde.fr/afrique/article/2020/04/24/au-mali-les-mosquees-resteront-ouvertes-pendant-le-mois-du-ramadan_6037711_3212.html

napping of the opposition leader by jihadist elements, the interference in religious matters, the intervention of the constitutional court, and even the recommendations of the World Health Organisation – together with the terrorist threat, poverty, and the lack of an encouraging horizon for the youth, in an indistinguishable and nuanced assemblage, which he considered an irrefutable proof of the government's corruption and inability to deal with the country's problems, and in which he found a fertile ground for a new and definitive step forward.

On Friday June 5, even with the threat of Covid-19 exacerbated, Mahmoud Dicko was able to gather more than 20,000 people in a demonstration calling for the resignation of President Ibrahim Boubacar Keïta.[62] The June 5 Movement-Rally of Patriotic Forces (M5-RFP), so named after this first protest, brought together a heterogeneous coalition of politicians, anti-corruption activists, different figures from civil society, and religious organisations in a newly formed opposition alliance. Among its numerous elements, however, three main clusters should be outlined in this multifarious constellation: the Front for Safeguarding Democracy (FSD), composed by around thirty opposition parties and created after IBK's re-election in 2018; *Espoir Mali Koura* (EMK), Hope for a New Mali in English, a civil society movement led by filmmaker and former Minister of Culture Cheick Oumar Sissoko; and Mahmoud Dicko's CMAS. The fact that the most visible representative of an alliance that includes multifold political parties and civil movements is a rigorous imam, although not unexpected, is indeed revealing.

Only two weeks later, on Friday 19, a second mass demonstration took place with Dicko leading prayers during the rally and calling again for civil disobedience until President Keïta steps down. Since then, disturbances, rallies, expressions of discontent, and clashes with the security forces have increased, with violence rising to previously unknown levels in Bamako.

On July 10, after gathering at the mosque of imam Dicko, demonstrators attacked the parliament and plundered the national television station, while security forces targeted the headquarters of CMAS.[63] Unrest continued and at least 11 people died and nearly 150 were injured in a period of a week, forcing President Keïta to accept the mediation of ECOWAS (Economic Community of West African States) and even propose a new government of consensus. Dicko called on his followers to show restraint and calm but, at the same time, rejected any negotiations and declared that the struggle would continue until the president's resignation, which he

---

62 Cf. Tiemoko Diallo (2020). Malians rally against President Keita, demand his resignation. *Reuters*. July 5. See: https://de.reuters.com/article/mali-politics-protests-idAFL8N2DI4N T

63 Cf. Al Jazeera (2020). *Mali PM promises from open government mass protests*. July 11. See: https://www.aljazeera.com/news/2020/07/mali-pm-promises-form-open-government-mass-protests-200711174204324.html

considered the only creditable solution to eradicate the endemic corruption that was bringing the country to its knees.[64,65]

Conclusions

Corruption, injustice, and deviation from the values and principles of Islam have historically been the recurring arguments used by fundamentalist religious reformism to endorse and legitimate its claims and actions. Therefore, Dicko using the word 'corruption' to summarise the state of the country may not be accidental, as he is just one of the latest exponents of a long tradition that has been manifesting itself in Mali for a millennium with the accommodations that each age and situation have required. His ideological discourse therefore aspires to be ingrained in a historical continuum abundant with noble antecedents that are now being revived and whose unquestionable purity of intentions cannot be contested.

Mahmoud Dicko's discourse and activities suggest being directed to cover the entire spectrum of whatever affiliations and sensibilities could be present in Mali and which have been reviewed in this chapter. Thus, depending on the circumstances and occasions, he seems to embody the traditional *marabout*, the Islamic *'ālim*, the pro-government political activist, the Wahhabi reformer, or the insurgent. Also, his continuous assertion that he is not a politician does not conceal his volition to shape the country's political future by intervening in every possible realm according to his own inclinations.

This Wahhabi fundamentalism without weapons represented by Dicko may seem more tolerable in its outward manifestations for the Western observer, but it might also be associated with certain menaces that make it perhaps even more hazardous for the stability of the country in the long run than the jihadist one. This is so because in this fundamentalism two seemingly opposite forces, centrifugal and centripetal, are being manoeuvred simultaneously and manifestly as the area of its influence expands, leading to a more than convenient result: the proscription and virtual annihilation of any dissent or contention and the strengthening of its monolithic conception by the increase in the numbers of its followers.

The centrifugal force expels outward those who do not strictly and without fissures share the only interpretation of Islam that this fundamentalism considers legitimate and sanctioned by original purity. A thorough ideological, rather than

---

64   Cf. France24 (2020/2). *Mali protest leader calls for calm after demonstrations turn deadly.* July 12. See: https://www.france24.com/en/20200712-mali-protest-leader-calls-for-calm-after-demonstrations-turn-deadly

65   This article was closed before the end of July 2020. Therefore, not only the future but also the immediate evolution of events remains unknown at this turbulent moment.

just religious, purge of any deviation is thus put into practice based on the arrogation of the capacity to issue or deny a sort of righteousness certificate to any possible response to its hegemony. This meticulous purge commonly evolves towards an impoverishment of the country's social, political, and religious ecosystem, as well as to the monopolisation and standardisation of the public space.

The centripetal force, on the other hand, has an extraordinary capacity to attract all those unattended collectives and social layers – deeming themselves neglected or victims of some kind of discrimination by the government, be it ethnic, economic, social, or political – to the bosom of the movement. The promise that the justice, probity, egalitarianism, and brotherly spirit of purest Islam houses the solution to all these imbalances has an enormous convening power in times of despair, affliction, deprivation, or external threats. It already had it by the times of drought and the conversion of King *al-musulmani* to Islam, as in the account by al-Bakrī in the XIthcentury with which this historical quest began, and it still has it now, when Covid-19 and the rest of the concurrent menaces impel the population to embrace the orthodox refuge that Dicko offers.

Religious revival and an increasing presence of fundamentalist Islam in public spheres are frequently perceived in Mali as a modern utterance of this Wahhabi influence, whose leaders continuously criticise what they hold as the undesirable loss of moral values and Islamic virtues in the country, as well as a resurgence of the dichotomy between Arab Islam and Sufi-impregnated popular Islam.

But the infiltration of this Wahhabi fundamentalist doctrine that is taking place not only in Mali but in other countries of the Sahel and the Gulf of Guinea shares, in my view, obvious similarities and parallelisms with the emergence of Islam itself in the area centuries ago. The penetration of Islam originated in the upper and educated classes before reaching most of the population; took place in an initially soft manner, without resorting to apparent pressure or explicit violence, cohabiting with other trends at a first moment for then gradually replacing previous beliefs and customs; and finally led to a thorough reconfiguration of the exercise of politics and the model of the state. Identifying all those same traits and stages in the Wahhabi infiltration of recent years does not seem to be especially difficult and might also lead to a new reconfiguration, definitively blurring nominal secularism in order to evolve towards a fundamentalist Islamic Republic of Mali.

Radicals, extremists, Salafis, Wahhabis, traditionalists, or any other religious denominations and labels often imposed from abroad – and admitting all sorts of combinations and hyphenations – would certainly feel more identified with and represented by such a new republic. They all hold themselves fundamentalists in the most honourable of its definitions and if they have to name themselves, they are simply Sunni Muslims: emanating from the original sources, attached to them, apprehensive about innovation or deviation based on political, narrowly nationalistic, or cultural reasons.

In this sense, this chapter has deliberately omitted to refer to the diverse terrorist groups that have been operating in Mali for decades now, because their actions and agenda, even when having a mighty impact on the politics of the country, could hardly be framed within Islamic fundamentalism in the way the notion has been used in this article.

The external tendency to hastily associate fundamentalism with groups often categorised under the extensive mark of jihadist has neglected, if not tortuously entangled, the other denotation of 'radical': of or relating to the origin, thus fundamental. The result of this inattentiveness is the evident hazard of confusing Islamic terrorist extremism and Wahhabi fundamentalism, considering them a unique or interchangeable notion and judging both of their adherents in the same way. But, on the other hand, establishing a precipitate differentiation between them, based on the unawareness of the true principles and goals of both currents and on a Manichean attribution of greater or lesser righteousness depending on their actions, is not a minor challenge. This is because these groups often trespass the boundaries between them and because the non-violent activities of Wahhabism are directed towards a project of longer scope and could be much more dangerous in the long term, even if these activities are not so outrageous nor promote international coalitions to counter them in the area.

That this enduring project has been identified and that its attainability concerns very specific social classes was subtly attested by a manifesto titled "Call for a Mali to Be Reconstructed". Published online on July 20 and signed by a group of intellectuals, senior executives, and business leaders, it endorsed the denunciation – initiated by popular protests – of the deep crisis that the country was facing. The text emphasised, in a certainly significant and illuminating detail that Dicko could have subscribed to, that these multiple demands had their origin in two inescapable and constant features: pervasive and impudent corruption and, closely connected to it, intolerable injustice.

However, almost as a colophon, and when praising the qualities that ought to distinguish a future leader, the emphasis was made on respect, very significantly also, respect for the secularism of the state, which "seems to us to be a precious asset, which has often preserved the unity of the Malian nation and must therefore be carefully safeguarded."[66] An asset that is now perceived as endangered, whose preciousness has been deemed necessary to highlight, whose safeguard is being questioned, and whose future appears to be surrounded by incertitude.

---

66   Cf. Maliweb (2020). *Appel pour un Mali à reconstruire : Quatre jours de l'Histoire du Mali.* July 20. See: https://www.maliweb.net/contributions/appel-pour-un-mali-a-reconstruire-quatre-jours -de-lhistoire-du-mali-2886466.html /

Bibliography

Akande, Habeeb (2014). *Eclairer l'Obscurité: Les Noirs et Les Nord-Africains selon L'Islam*. London.

Al-Sa'adi', 'Abd al-Raḥmān (1964). *Tārīkh al-Sūdān*. Paris.

Al-'Umarī (1927). *Masālik al-abṣār fī mamālik al-amṣār*. In Maurice Gaudefroy-Demombynes (Ed.). Paris.

Azumah, John (2014). *The Legacy of Arab-Islam in Africa: A Quest for Inter-religious Dialogue*. London.

Bâ, Amadou (1972). *Aspects De La Civilisation Africaine (Personne, Culture, Religion)*. Paris.

Bâ, Amadou, and Daget, Jacques (1995). *L'Empire peul du Macina (1818-1853)*. Paris.

Boly, Hamadou (2013). *Le soufisme au Mali du XIXéme siècle à nos jours: religion, politique et société*. Strasbourg.

Brenner, Louis (2001). *Controlling Knowledge: Religion, Power and Schooling in a West Africa Muslim Society*. London.

Centre d'Études Linguistiques et Historiques par la Tradition Orale (CELHTO) (2008). *La Charte de Kurukan Fuga. Aux sources d'une pensée politique en Afrique*. Paris.

Chanfi, Ahmed (2015). *West African 'ulamā' and Salafism in Mecca and Medina: Jawāb al-Ifrīqī – The Response of the African*. Leiden.

Conklin, Alice (1997). *A Mission to Civilize. The Republican Idea of Empire in France and West Africa, 1895-1930*. Stanford.

Conrad, David (1985). Islam in the Oral Traditions of Mali: Bilali and Surakata. *Journal of African History* 26, 33-49.

De Jorio, Rosa (2003). Narratives of the Nation and Democracy in Mali. A View from Modibo Keita's Memorial. *Cahiers d'Études africaines* 172, 827-855.

De Jorio, Rosa (2016). *Cultural Heritage in Mali in the Neoliberal Era*. Chicago.

El-Nagar, Omer (1969). *West Africa and the Muslim Pilgrimage: An Historical Study with Special Reference to the Nineteenth Century*. PhD Thesis, SOAS. London.

Gouilly, Alphonse (1952). *L'Islam dans l'Afrique Occidentale Française*. Paris.

Hock, Carsten (1999). *Fliegen die Seelen der Heiligen: Muslimische Reform und staatliche Autorität in der Republik Mali seit 1960*. Berlin.

Holder, Gilles (2012). Chérif Ousmane Madani Haidara and the Islamic Movement Ansar Dine: A Popular Malian Reformism in Search of Autonomy. *Cahiers d'Études Africaines* 206-207, N° 2, 389-425.

Hunwick, John (1964). *Timbuktu & the Songhay Empire. Al-Sa'di's Tar'īkh al-sūdān down to 1613 and other Contemporary Documents*. Leiden.

Hunwick, John (1985/1). Al-Maghīlī and the Jews of Tuwāt: The Demise of a Community. *Studia Islamica* 61, 155-183.

Hunwick, John (1985/2). *Sharī'a in Songhay: the replies of al-Maghīlī to the questions of Askia al-Ḥājj Muḥammad*. London.

Hunwick, John (1990). An Andalusian in Mali. A contribution to the biography of Abū Isḥāq al-Sāḥilī, c. 1290–1346. *Paideuma* 36, 59-66.

Hunwick, John (1997). Sub-Saharan Africa and the Wider World of Islam: Historical and Contemporary Perspectives. In David Westerlund and Eva Evers Rosander (Eds.). *African Islam and Islam in Africa: Encounters between Sufis and Islamists*. London, pp. 28-54.

Hunwick, John (2003). *Timbuktu & the Songhay Empire. Al-Sa'di's Tārīkh al-sūdān down to 1613 and other Contemporary Documents*. Leiden.

Ibn Baṭṭūṭa: Tuḥfat al-nuẓẓār fī gharā'ib al-amṣār wa-'ajā'ib al-asfār. In Charles Defremery and Beniamino Sanguinetti (Eds.). Paris 1922.

Ibn Khaldun: Kitāb Tārīkh al-Duwal al-Islāmiyya bil-Maghrib min Kitāb al-'ibar. In William De Slane (Ed.). Paris 1847.

Idrissa, Rahmane (2017). *The Politics of Islam in the Sahel: Between Persuasion and Violence*. London.

Imperato, Pascal, and Imperato, Gavin (2008). *Historical Dictionary of Mali*. Lanham.

Ledbetter, Clyde (2016). Human Rights Studies as a Sub-Field of Africology. In Molefi Asante and Clyde Ledbetter (Eds.). *Contemporary Critical Thought in Africology and Africana Studies*. Lanham, pp. 135-164.

Leininger, Julia (2013). *Religiöse Akteure in Demokratisierungsprozessen. Konstruktiv, destruktiv und obstruktiv*. Wiesbaden.

Levitzon, Nehemiah (1980). *Ancient Ghana and Mali*. New York.

Levitzon, Nehemiah (1994). *Islam in West Africa: Religion, Society and Politics to 1800*. London.

Levtzion, Nehemiah, and Hopkins, J. F. P. (Eds.) (1981). *Corpus of Early Arabic Sources for West African History*. Cambridge.

Magassa, Hamidou (2006). Islam und Demokratie in Westafrika: Der Fall Mali. In Michael Bröning and Holger Weiss (Eds.). *Politischer Islam in Westafrika. Eine Bestandsaufnahme*. Münster, pp. 116-121.

Massing, Andreas (2012). Imams of Gonja. The Kamaghate and the Transmission of Islam to the Volta Basin. *Cahiers d'Études africaines* 51, 57-101.

Mbaye, Ravane (1982). L'Islam noir en Afrique. *Tiers-Monde* 23, N° 92, 831-838.

Monteil, Vincent (1964). *L'Islam noir*. Paris.

Moumouni, Seyni (2008). *Vie et œuvre du Cheik Uthmân Dan Fodio, 1754-1817: de l'Islam au soufisme*. Paris.

Nievas Bullejos, David (2014). Islam y Política en Mali. *Cadernos de Estudos Africanos* 28, 13-35.

Østebø, Terje (2015). African Salafism: Religious Purity and the Politicization of Purity. *Islamic Africa* 6, N° 1/2, 1-29.

Pageard, Robert (1961). Soundiata Keita et la tradition orale: A propos du livre de Djibril Tamsir NIANE: Soundjata ou l'Epopée Mandingue. *Présence Africaine* 36, 51-70.

Robinson, David (1985). *The Holy War of Umar Tall. The Western Sudan in the Mid-Nineteenth Century.* Oxford.

Ryan, Patrick (2000). The Mystical Theology of Tijānī Sufism and Its Social Significance in West Africa. *Journal of Religion in Africa* 30, N° 2, 208-224.

Saad, Elias (2010). *Social history of Timbuktu: the role of Muslim scholars and notables 1400-1900.* Cambridge.

Saint-Martin, Yves (1967). *L'Empire toucouleur et la France. Un demi-siècle de relations diplomatiques (1846-1893).* Dakar.

Sanankoua, Bintou (1990). *Un empire peul au XIXᵉ siècle: la Diina du Maasina.* Paris.

Sanneh, Lamin (1997). *The Crown and the Turban: Muslims and West African Pluralism.* New York.

Snyder, Francis (1967). The Political Thought of Modibo Keita. *Journal of Modern African Studies* 5, N° 1, 79-106.

Soares, Benjamin (2004). Islam and public piety in Mali. In Armando Salvatore and Dale Eickelman (Eds.). *Public Islam and the common good.* Leiden, pp. 205-226.

Torres Díaz, Olga (2020). Islamism and Women in the Sahel: Roots and Evolutions. In Klaus Hock and Nina Käsehage (Eds.). *'Militant Islam' vs. 'Islamic Militancy'? Religion, Violence, Category Formation and Applied Research. Contested Fields in the Discourse of Scholarship.* Zürich, pp. 195-216.

Torres Fauaz, Armando (2006). Hacia el Dar al-Harb: Perspectiva legal-histórica de la emigración musulmana. In Zidane Zéraoui and Roberto Marín Guzmán (Eds.). *Árabes y Musulmanes en Europa. Historia y procesos migratorios.* San José, pp. 181-196.

Touré, Mafakha (1990-1991). *Critique historique d'un concept: l'islam noir. Mémoire de maîtrise, Université Cheikh Anta Diop.* Dakar.

Triaud, Jean-Louis (1973). *Islam et sociétés soudanaises au Moyen Age: étude historique.* Paris.

Triaud, Jean-Louis (1996). L'Afrique occidentale et centrale. In Alexander Popovic and Gille Veinstein (Eds.). *Les voies d'Allah. Les ordres mystiques dans le monde musulman des origines à aujourd'hui.* Paris, pp. 417-427.

Triminghan, John (1962). *A History of Islam in West Africa.* London.

Wilks, Ivor (2000). The Juula and the Expansion of Islam into the Forest. In Nehemiah Levitzon and Randall Pouwels (Eds.). *The History of Islam in Africa.* Oxford, pp. 93-115.

Zappa, Francesco (2009). Popularizing Islamic Knowledge through Oral Epic: A Malian Bard in a Media Age. *Die Welt des Islams* 49, N° 3/4, 367-397.

Online Open Sources

Al Jazeera (2020). *Mali PM promises from open government mass protests*. July 11. URL: https://www.aljazeera.com/news/2020/07/mali-pm-promises-form-open-government-mass-protests-200711174204324.html

Broulard, Laure (2015). *Mali: l'imam Mahmoud Dicko voit dans le terrorisme «une punition divine» et crée la polémique*. December 2. URL: https://www.jeuneafrique.com/283688/societe/mali-limam-mahmoud-dicko-voit-terrorisme-punition-divine-cree-polemique/

Cresques, Abraham (1375). *Atlas de cartes marines, dit [Atlas Catalan]. Gallica database from the Bibliothèque nationale de France*. URL: https://gallica.bnf.fr/ark:/12148/bt v1b55002481n.image

Diallo, Tiemoko (2020). Malians rally against President Keita, demand his resignation. *Reuters*. July 5. URL: https://de.reuters.com/article/mali-politics-protests-idAFL8N2DI4NT

France24 (2020/1). *Mali election run off tarnished by intimidation and allegations of vote rigging*. April 20. URL: https://www.france24.com/en/20200420-mali-election-runoff-tarnished-by-intimidation-and-allegations-of-vote-rigging

France24 (2020/2). *Mali protest leader calls for calm after demonstrations turn deadly*. July 12. URL: https://www.france24.com/en/20200712-mali-protest-leader-calls-for-calm-after-demonstrations-turn-deadly

Lebovich, Andrew (2019). *Sacred Struggles: How Islam Shapes Politics in Mali*. November 1. URL: https://ecfr.eu/publication/secular_stagnation_malis_relationship_religion/

Lorgerie, Paul (2020). Au Mali, les mosquées resteront ouvertes pendant le mois du ramadán. *Le Monde*. April 24. URL: https://www.lemonde.fr/afrique/article/2020/04/24/au-mali-les-mosquees-resteront-ouvertes-pendant-le-mois-du-ramadan_6037711_3212.html

Maliweb (2020). *Appel pour un Mali à reconstruire: Quatre jours de l'Histoire du Mali*. July 20. URL: https://www.maliweb.net/contributions/appel-pour-un-mali-a-reconstruire-quatre-jours-de-lhistoire-du-mali-2886466.html

Skelton, Rose (2012). Sufism and Salafism, Mali's deep religious divide. *The Africa Report*. URL: https://www.theafricareport.com/6247/sufism-and-salafism-malis-deep-religious-divide/

UNESCO (2009). *Representative List of the Intangible Cultural Heritage of Humanity. The Manden Charter*. URL: https://ich.unesco.org/en/RL/manden-charter-proclaimed-in-kurukan-fuga-00290

Global Virus, International Lamas: Tibetan Religious Leaders in the Face of the Covid-19 Crisis

Miguel Álvarez Ortega

Abstract

This paper aims at analyzing how the Covid-19 (2020) crisis has been treated by leading Tibetan teachers in the global media. First, an introduction to Buddhist notions related to sickness both at the individual and collective levels is provided, followed by a detailed account of the public pronouncements up to early August 2020 of the leading teachers of the main schools of Tibetan Buddhism. The paper tries to show how Tibetan Buddhists' response is characterized by an appeal to an external compliance with the authorities, and an internal plural interpretation that reflects a common tension between a symbolic and a transcendental construal of religious categories. It also attempts to provide interpretative keys for the lack of a successful fundamentalist or millennialist reaction while pointing to the particular suitability of Buddhism to accommodate to the crisis.

Keywords: Covid-19 crisis, pandemic, Tibetan Buddhism, millennialism, esotericism

1. Introduction

In December 2019, several cases of severe pneumonia of unknown etiology were reported in Wuhan, China. A month later, the World Health Organization (WHO) declared that the subsequent outbreak constituted a Public Health Emergency of International Concern, and on March 11, 2020, it declared the novel coronavirus (Covid-19) a global pandemic.[1]

The extent, virulence, and quick propagation of the virus have caused a global crisis obliging states around the world to take drastic measures typically involving

---

1 Domenico Cucinotta and Maurizio Vanelli (2020). WHO Declares COVID-19 a Pandemic. *Acta Bio Medica 91*, N° 1, 157f.

the closing of borders, obligatory use of masks and social distancing, limitations in free circulation, curfews, and quarantines or lockdowns, among others.

A phenomenon of this magnitude has an undeniable impact on the lives of citizens at all levels and questions their belief systems. It is, therefore, interesting to analyze how different religious traditions and groups have reacted towards the crisis and its management, in terms of interpretation and advised reaction according to their own soteriological project, *Weltanschauung*, and set of practices. In particular, this paper attempts to analyze how the Covid-19 crisis has been treated by leading Tibetan teachers in the global media.

With such a purpose, an introduction to Buddhist notions related to sickness both at the individual and collective levels is provided (section 2), followed by a detailed account of the public pronouncements up to early August, 2020 of the leading teachers of the main schools of Tibetan Buddhism (section 3). In this regard, I have opted for a prolixity of literal references at the risk of rendering the text dense and at times repetitive, so that the reader may form his or her own opinion before the data with as little interference as possible. In the concluding section (4) I shall try and argue that Tibetan Buddhists' response is characterized by an appeal to an external compliance with the authorities, and an internal plural interpretation that reflects a common tension between a symbolic and a transcendental construal of religious categories. I shall also attempt to provide interpretative keys for the lack of a successful fundamentalist or millennialist reaction, while pointing to the particular suitability of Buddhism to accommodate to the crisis.

2.   Buddhism and Pandemics: The Internal Conceptual Frame

Leaving aside pop-culture references, for most Western readers Buddhism is not part of their cultural or religious upbringing, unlike Christianity. This means that, for those who are neither practitioners nor specialized scholars, the core notions and soteriological project that characterize Buddhism as a religion and thereby activate before a crisis may need some clarification. Attempting to keep the track of the discourse on the problem of the virus, I herein include a brief summary of the role that sickness as a type of suffering represents, and the particular social connotations presented by a pandemic within Buddhist sources.

2.1   Individual Concepts: Suffering, Disease, and Healing

Arguably one of the most popular instances of the centrality of sickness within Buddhist traditions is the narration of what is known as the Buddha's "four sights," a post-canonical recreation of Prince Siddharta's encountering with worldly afflictions.[2] Secluded in his palace by his father to protect him from exposure to suffering and prevent him from pursing an ascetic life, the tale recounts how one day the prince decided to explore the city in disguise to discover the "real world." He is thus first acquainted with an old man (first sight); and then, as in the phrasing of the *Buddhacarita*, the second sight took place:

> "41. 'Yonder man with a swollen belly, his whole frame shaking as he pants, his arms and shoulders hanging loose, his body all pale and thin, uttering plaintively the word "mother," when he embraces a stranger, — who, pray, is this?'
> 42. Then his charioteer answered, 'Gentle Sir, it is a very great affliction called sickness, that has grown up, caused by the inflammation of the (three) humours, which has made even this strong man no longer master of himself.'
> 43. Then the prince again addressed him, looking upon the man compassionately, 'Is this evil peculiar to him or are all beings alike threatened by sickness?'
> 44. Then the charioteer answered, 'O prince, this evil is common to all; thus pressed round by diseases men run to pleasure, though racked with pain.[3] "

A later excursion exposes him to a dead body (third sight); and finally, he finds inspiration in an encounter with an ascetic (fourth sight).

The tetrad constituted by birth, ageing, sickness, and death, not only appears in such literary accounts, but plays a decisive role in the characterization and understanding of the central Buddhist concept par excellence, suffering.[4] In the context of the explanation of the core of the Buddhist doctrine, the so-called Four Noble Truths (the Truths of suffering, its origin, its cessation, and the path), sickness is repeatedly stated as a clear example of the Truth of Suffering. In the *Dhammacakkappavattana Sutta*, traditionally regarded as the first sermon of the Buddha, it is asserted that:

> "Suffering, as a noble truth, is this: Birth is suffering, ageing is suffering, **sickness** is suffering, death is suffering, sorrow and lamentation, pain, grief and despair are suffering; association with the loathed is suffering, dissociation from the loved is suffering, not to get what one wants is suffering — in short, suffering is the five

---

2   According to Heinz Bechert, although the story "definitely does not belong to the earliest traditions of the life of the historical Buddha" (...) "it became a constituent of all biographies of the Buddha at an early date", originating in a "legendary biography of a former buddha that is narrated in the *Mahāvadāna-sūtra*". Heinz Bechert (2004). Buddha, Life of the. In Robert E. Buswell (Ed.). *Encyclopedia of Buddhism*. Volume I. New York, p. 85.

3   Edward B. Cowell (Ed.) (2003). Book III: The Prince's Perturbation. *The Buddha-carita of Aśvaghoṣa*. Delhi, p. 40.

4   These are referred in Sanskrit as jāti-jarā-vyādhi-maraṇa and, in Tibetan, as skye rga na 'chi (W.) (Ph. kye ga na chi). Tibetan terms will appear transcribed according to the Wylie system indicated by "W." and followed by a phonetic approximation indicated by "Ph".

categories of clinging objects."[5]
(Bold emphasis added).

It is the cultivation of the Buddhist eight-fold path that may put an end to such suffering when final liberation (nirvana) is attained.[6] In this context, the end of the suffering of sickness usually refers to the perception of the experience of illness in terms of affliction, not to the biological condition itself.[7] There are, though, other instances where that seems to be the case. Scholar Bhikkhu Anālayo refers to several texts where the cultivation or even the mere recitation of the awakening factors (mental qualities to be cultivated by practitioners) result in the healing of patients.[8]

Other narratives take a less soteriological approach, and focus on sickness, its etiology, and cure in a worldlier fashion. For example, the *Sivaka Sutta* explains the 8 causes of disease as being the 3 humors, their combination, the seasons, lack of care, assault, and the ripening of karma.[9] Even the Buddha himself is depicted as falling sick and asking for a purgative in a version of the Code of Monastic Discipline (Vinaya).[10]

In most cases, though, rather than as a patient, the Buddha is represented as a "Healer", and not only in a metaphorical sense[11], but as someone who in one of his many lives possessed medical knowledge and treated patients with both con-

5   Thera (Tr.) Ñanamoli (2010). Dhammacakkappavattana Sutta: Setting Rolling the Wheel of Truth (SN 56.11). *Access to Insight* (BCBS Edition). June 13. See: https://www.accesstoinsight.org/tipitaka/sn/sn56/sn56.011.nymo.html

6   These are: right view, right intention; right speech, right action, right livelihood; right effort, right mindfulness, right concentration.

7   Nevertheless, the biological condition would not be, logically, re-experienced since nirvana puts an end to the cycle of rebirths. The idea that holy people may still suffer sickness but no associated mental pain, is well attested. Cf. Paul Demiéville (1985). *Buddhism and Healing. Demiéville's Article "Byō" from Hōbōgirin*. Boston, pp. 21-23.

8   Cf. Bhikkhu Anālayo (2017). The Healing Potential of Awakening Factors in Early Buddhist Discourse. C. Pierce Salguero (Ed.). *Buddhism and Medicine. An Anthology of Premodern Sources*. New York, pp. 12-18.

9   See Thanissaro Bhikkhu (2013). *Sivaka Sutta: To Sivaka (SN 36.21). Access to Insight (BCBS Edition)*. November 30. See: http://www.accesstoinsight.org/tipitaka/sn/sn36/sn36.021.than.html.

10   Cf. Thomas Dhivan Jones (2017). Illness, Cure and Care: Selections from the Pāli Canon. In C. Pierce Salguero (Ed.). *Buddhism and Medicine. An Anthology of Premodern Sources*. New York, pp. 3-10.; Hin-tak Sik 2016. Ancient Indian medicine in early Buddhist literature: a study based on the Bhesajjakkhandhaka and the parallels in other Vinaya Canons. (Thesis). University of Hong Kong, Pokfulam, Hong Kong SAR. See: http://dx.doi.org/10.5353/th_b5760924.

11   Demiéville, 1985, pp. 14-15.; Thanissaro Bhikkhu (2013). *Beyond Coping: The Buddha's Teachings on Aging, Illness, Death, and Separation. Access to Insight (BCBS Edition)*. November 30. See: http://www.accesstoinsight.org/lib/study/beyondcoping/index.html .

ventional and supernatural means.[12] Stories about Jīvaka, who worked as a doctor to the Buddha and his monks, are also popular and numerous.[13]

Despite this centrality, and the praise of doctors and those who look after the sick, it has been pointed out that early Buddhist literature was initially reluctant or ambivalent towards having monks (and nuns in particular) habitually engaged in the medical profession, for varied reasons.[14] The situation changed over time, and the development of Mahāyāna brought new medically-oriented literature, an emphasis on healthcare as an act of compassion, and a more important role of deities, rituals, and esotericism in healing practices.[15] Such elements were further potentiated in Vajrayāna Buddhism, finding its arguably greatest expression in the Tibetan system of Medicine (Ph. sowa rigpa, W. *gso ba rig pa*).[16] Exposed to varied influences, especially in its first centuries, Tibetan Medicine evolved alongside its wider religious and political context to become a Buddhist scholastic discipline.[17] Promi-

---

12   Phyllis Granoff (1998). Cures and Karma II. Some Miraculous Healings in the Indian Buddhist Story Tradition. *Bulletin de l'École française d'Extrême-Orient* 85, 288-289. A list of "Stories of Treatments Based on Cases of Diseases", may be found at: Kenneth G. Zysk (2010). *Asceticism and Healing in Ancient India: Medicine in the Buddhist Monastery.* Delhi, pp.84-86.

13   Cf. Thomas S. N. Chen and Peter S. Y. Chen (2002). Jivaka, physician to the Buddha. *Journal of Medical Biography* 10, 88-91; Kenneth G. Zysk (1982). Studies in Traditional Indian Medicine in the Pāli Canon: Jīvaka and Āyurveda. *Journal of the International Association of Buddhist Studies* 5, 7–86.

14   See: David Fiordalis (2017). Medical Practice as Wrong Livelihood: Selections from the Pāli Discourses, Vinaya, and Commentaries. In C. Pierce Salguero (Ed.). *Buddhism and Medicine. An Anthology of Premodern Sources.* New York, p. 105f.; Cf. David Fiordalis (2014). On Buddhism, Divination and the Worldly Arts: Textual Evidence from the Theravāda Tradition. *Indian International Journal of Buddhist Studies* 15, pp. 89-91.

15   C. Pierce Salguero (2018). Buddhist Medicine and its circulation. In David Ludden (Ed.). *Oxford Research Encyclopedia, Asian History.* New York, pp. 2-4.

16   In Indo-Tibetan Buddhist scholasticism, Medicine is considered one of the 5 major sciences (W. *rig gnas chen po lnga*; Ph. rigñe chenpo na), along with craftsmanship, logic, grammar, and Inner science (religion). Cf. Bhagwan Dash (1976). Indian Contribution to Tibetan Medicine. In Dawa Norbu (Ed.). *An Introduction to Tibetan Medicine.* Delhi, p 12.

17   The background of Tibetan Medicine seems to have been widely cosmopolitan, especially in its first centuries, drawing from indigenous, Ayurvedic, Persian, and Chinese sources, among others, though later native representations insisted on the Indian and Buddhist elements as the essential defining features. Cf. Frances M. Garrett (2015). *Religion, Medicine and the Human Embryo in Tibet.* London, pp. 37-44. Its main classical text, known as the *Four Tantras* (W. *gryus bzhi*, Ph. gyu thi), dates form the end of the XIIth century and its historical origins were subject of controversy for centuries. An important tradition (and the text itself) attributes its authorship to the Buddha in the form of the Medicine Buddha (Bhaiṣajyaguru, Tib. W. sangs rgyas sman bla, Ph. sangye nanla). Cf. Frances M. Garrett (2006). Buddhism and the Historicizing of Medicine in Thirteenth Century Tibet. *Asian Medicine. Journal of the International Association for the Study of Traditional Asian Medicine* 2, no. 2, 202-224.; Cf. Janet Gyatso (2017). *Being human in a Buddhist world: An intellectual history of medicine in early modern Tibet.* New York, pp. 143-192.

nent monastic scholars were "expected" to write on *materia medica*, while most doctors were educated in and pertained to monastic institutions.[18] To provide some background, the etiology of Tibetan Medicine is centered on the aforementioned imbalance of the 3 humors, and it places especial stress on channels and winds of energy (W. *rlung*, Ph. lung) that circulate within the body in a complex interconnection of mind, physical body, senses, and the universe.[19] At the same time, it categorizes congenital conditions as karmic afflictions, and includes the influence of malefic spirits within the causes of disease[20]. Most importantly, the distant cause of illness is considered to be primordial ignorance manifested in attachment, anger, and delusion[21]. Within its wide array of treatments, we typically find dietary and lifestyle guidelines, mantra recitation and visualizations, meditation, medicinal herbs (W. *bod sman*, Ph. pö men), rituals, and exorcisms.[22]

Traditional Tibetan Medicine has been the object of Western medical and scholarly interest from multiple angles, ranging from its use of medicinal plants to its holistic approach to the patient and his condition.[23] Its attention to the psychosomatic interface and the benefits of meditation, particularly in stress relief and pain management, have arguably raised the most interest.[24]

2.2   Collective Notions: Plagues, Millenarianism, and Social Welfare

Disease is not only an individual affliction. It also possesses an undeniable social dimension, particularly when its impact and spread reach such a considerable magnitude that it becomes a plague or, in more modern language, an epidemic (W. *nad yams*, Ph. ne yam). It is not uncommon, in this regard, for religious traditions

---

The text has been translated into English: Clark, Barry: The Quintessence Tantras of Tibetan Medicine. Boston 1995.

18   Garrett, 2015, pp. 52-55.

19   Barbara Gerke (2013). On the 'Subtle Body' and 'Circulation' in Tibetan Medicine. In Geoffrey Samuel and Jay Johnston (Eds.). *Religion and the Subtle Body in Asia and the West*. New York, pp. 83-99; Gyatso 2017, pp. 193-250.

20   Tamdin S. Bradley (2013). *Principles of Tibetan Medicine*. London, pp. 40-44, 71.

21   Bradley, 2013, pp. 31-33.

22   Ib., pp. 40-41., 123-160.

23   As sheer examples within an abundant literature, see: Christa Kletter and Monika Kriechbaum (Eds.) (2001). *Tibetan Medicinal Plants*. Stuttgart.; Cf. Craig R. Janes (2002). Buddhism, science, and market: The globalisation of Tibetan medicine. *Anthropology & Medicine*, 9:3, pp. 267-289; Laurent Pordié (Ed.) (2008). *Tibetan Medicine in the Contemporary World: Global Politics of Medical Knowledge and Practice*. London.

24   Again, the existing bibliography is overwhelming. Arguably, the most re-known platform dedicated to the scientific study of Tibetan Buddhist meditation and its benefits, which include performing MRI on practicing lamas, is the Mind & Life Institute, founded by the 14th Dalai Lama and biologist Francisco Varela. See their website: https://www.mindandlife.org/

to assign it a particular meaning within their own world vision and soteriological project that goes further than a mere health issue. The Christian-based Western world is seemingly so familiar with such an ingrained perception that "biblical plague" or "plague of biblical proportions" have become common expressions in everyday language.

In the case of Buddhism, the absence of a potentially punishing God-creator and the assumed lack of an apocalyptic/ millennialist tradition, have deemed it popularly (and sometimes scholarly) unlikely to develop such interpretations.[25] Still, Buddhist literature contains its own depiction of time cycles in which the notion of degenerate times or decline of the Dharma (Buddhist teachings) plays a crucial role.[26] Such scenarios not only allude to a future crisis of faith, doctrine, and practice, but are also typically tainted by wars, famines, and plagues. In the Tibetan version of the *Candragarbha Sutra*, we find a representative take on the matter:

> "Then at the time of the [next] five hundred year [period], as for [the first] three hundred years, the protectors of sentient beings who dwell in the True Dharma —gods, nagas, and so on —will not remain, {but will go [elsewhere] to spread the True Dharma.} {Sentient beings will no longer believe in the Dharma. Even those sentient beings who practice the Dharma will not practice it in accordance with the basic Dharma texts. Because [their] efforts are small, their attainments will be few. The four [principal] colors and those derived from the four will decline, and {smell,}* taste, and so forth will diminish. And **human diseases, animal diseases**, and famine will arise."[27]
> (Bold emphasis added).

Following such a phase of decline, a new prosperous era is often envisioned, though not necessarily.[28] Alternation of periods of flourishing and decay are not exclusive

---

25 Charles F. Keyes has pointed out that some scholars of millennialism have wrongly assumed that in Buddhism the pursuit of nirvana is the only and pervasive soteriological goal, and that karma implies strict determinism, thus mistakenly concluding the unsuitability or irrelevance of apocalyptic and millennialist elements. Cf. Charles F. Keyes (1977). Millennialism, Theravada Buddhism and Thai Society. *The Journal of Asian Studies* 36, N° 2, pp. 285-287.

26 In his classical work, Étienne Lamotte referred to the age as "the Disappearance of the Good Law" and provided a detailed list of the numerous Buddhist texts from different schools and traditions referring to it. Cf. Étienne Lamotte (1988). *History of Indian Buddhism from the Origins to the Śaka Era*. Louvain-la-Neuve, pp. 191-202. For an overview from a Japanese perspective, see Chappell, D. Wellington (1980). Early Forebodings of the Death of Buddhism. *Numen* 27, N° 1, 122-154.

27 Quotation from the Tibetan version as translated by Jan Nattier (1991). *Once Upon a Future Time: Studies in a Buddhist Prophecy of Decline*. Berkeley, p. 241

28 As Jan Nattier points out, it is a peculiarity of Buddhist apocalyptic literature that it contains references to decline with no subsequent redemption. Cf. Jan Nattier (1988). The Meanings of

to sutra literature and may also be found in philosophical treatises like the *Abhidharmakośa*[29]. One popular version of these cycles relates the advent of Maitreya (Pali, Metteya; Tib. W. *byams pa*, Ph. janmpa), a future Buddha representing the coming of a Golden Age, prior to which human degeneration would have reduced life-span to 10 years in a context of constant quarrelling, famine, and plagues.[30] The figure of Maitreya—and the notion of his coming—have historically inspired varied millennialist revolts and political movements in China, Korea, and South East Asia[31], while in the case of Tibet, he is mainly an aspirational figure for mystics and scholars.[32] Even so, the notion of the degenerate times is common in Tibetan texts, particularly in Dharma chronicles (W. *chos 'byung*, Ph. chö jung) and in traditions of revealed treasures (W. *gter ma*, Ph. terma), in which concealed teachings are to be discovered to help restore the Dharma in degenerate times.[33] The idea has been popularly employed when reflecting on the circumstances leading to the Chinese invasion of Tibet, often deemed a calamity prophesized by VIIIth century Guru Padmasambhava, and is very much relevant and alive among contemporary

---

the Maitreya Myth. In Alan Sponberg and Helen Hardacre (Eds.). *Maitreya, the Future Buddha*. Cambridge, p. 39.

29   Composed in verse between the 4th and 5th centuries by Vasubandhu, this highly influential text describes a temporal cosmology of cycles of kalpas comprising the beginning of the world, the rise and fall of humankind, the destruction of the world, and then emptiness. See verses 89 to 102 in chapter 3. An English version of the "classical" French translation by La Vallé Poussin was published by Lokananda C. Bhikkhu (2018). *Abhidharmakośa of Ācārya Vasubandhu. English trad. of La Vallé Poussin by Leo M. Pruden*. Delhi.

30   Cf. Nattier, 1988, p. 27.

31   Cf., among others, Susan Naquin (1976). *Millenarian rebellion in China: The Eight Trigrams uprising of 1813*. New Haven.; Cf. Daniel Overmyer (1976). *Folk Buddhist religion: Dissenting sects in late traditional China*. Cambridge, esp. p. 81 ff.; Cf. Erik Zürcher (1982). "Prince Moonlight". Messianism and Eschatology in Early Medieval Chinese Buddhism. *T'oung Pao* 68, 1/3, pp. 1-75.; Cf. Hue-Tam Ho Tai (1988). Perfect World and Perfect Time: Maitreya in Vietnam. Alan Sponberg and Helen Hardacre (Eds.). *Maitreya, the Future Buddha*. Cambridge, pp. 154-170.; Cf. Keyes, 1977, pp. 283-302.; Cf. Manuel Sarkisyanz (1965). *Buddhist backgrounds of the Burmese revolution*. The Hague.; Cf. Robert Flaherty and Robert Pearson (2011). Korean Millennial Movements. In Chaterine Wessinger (Ed.). The Oxford Handbook of Millennialism. Oxford, pp. 326-347.

32   In the Tibetan tradition, Maitreya is considered to have transmitted his teachings to Asaṅga (Vasubandhu's elder brother, circa IVth century), whose philosophical works are thus referred as *The Five Treatises of Maitreya* (W. *byams chos sde lnga*, Ph. jam chö de na). See: Philippe Turenne (2015). The History and Significance of the Tibetan Concept of the Five Treatises of Maitreya. *The Indian International Journal of Buddhist Studies* 16, pp. 215-233. On the cult of Maitreya in Tibet, see Jonathan Silk et al. (2019). Maitreya. In Jonathan Silk et al. (Eds.). *Brill's Encyclopedia of Buddhism. Volume II: Lives*. Leiden, pp. 308-309.

33   Janet Gyasto (1993). The Logic of Legitimation in the Tibetan Treasure Tradition. *History of Religions* 33, N° 2, 132.

Tibetan teachers.[34] For example, in 2012, Dzongsar Jamyang Khyentse, an important reincarnated lama, referred to our present time as "kaliyuga" (the Hindu Age of Quarrel) and "dark age"[35].

The particular approach to plagues in contrast to regular sickness seems also to be shown in the particular type of response employable. According to the study of P. Granoff on *avadāna* (biographical stories) literature, plagues would be the only clear instances of healing by unabashedly miraculous means, directly or indirectly undertaken by Buddha, either because of—it is hypothesized—their sometimes demonic origin or due to their extraordinary social impact alike droughts and famine.[36]

The communal character represented by plagues or spread diseases also raises the question of healing beyond the singular patient-healer paradigm into the social sphere of what we may contemporarily refer to as social healthcare. In this regard, Buddhist literature typically consigns the provision of medical assistance as a duty of a lawful (Dharma-abiding) king, along with other assistance duties towards those in need, namely, victims of disasters, famine, and poverty. Nāgārjuna's *Precious Garland* is an often-quoted example.[37] Also, Emperor Aśoka, arguably the

---

34 In his autobiographical account, exiled Tibetologist Dawa Norbu writes about the strong beliefs regarding a future Chinese invasion commonly held before it actually took place: "In one *lungten*, written in the middle of the ninth century, King Ralpachen asked the guru Rinpoche what would be the future of Buddhism in Tibet. The guru predicted the advent of Communism, almost in so many words: 'The subjects will rule the kingdom, the king will be made a commoner. A sacrilegious act will be considered a deed of heroism". Cf. Dawa Norbu (1998). *Tibet: The Road Ahead*. London, p. 32. I was exposed to such interpretation during my field work with Tibetan exiles in Kathmandu. Cf. Miguel Álvarez Ortega (2018). Traditional Tibetan Buddhist Scholars on Dharma, Law, Politics, and Social Ethics: Philosophical Discussions in Boudhanath (Nepal). *Buddhism, Law, and Society* 4, 31.

35 We will refer to the figure of Dzongsar Khyentse below. The quotation is taken from a publication on his Facebook page posted on January 12, 2012. https://www.facebook. com/djkhyentse/posts/some-say-the-dark-age-age-of-vice-kaliyuga-is-here-now-or-at-least-coming-soon-s/369588269733327/

36 Granoff bases his thesis mainly on the *Avadānakalpalatā* and the *Avadāna-Śataka*, both translated into Tibetan. Cf. Phyllis Granoff, (1998). Cures and Karma II. Some Miraculous Healings in the Indian Buddhist Story Tradition. *Bulletin de l'École française d'Extrême-Orient* 85, esp. pp. 290, 298, 300.

37 Always care compassionately / For the sick, the unprotected, those stricken / With suffering, the lowly, and the poor/ And take special care to nourish them/ Provide extensive care/ For the persecuted, the victims of crop failure/ The stricken, those **suffering contagion** / And for beings in conquered areas / Cause the blind, **the sick**, the lowly, /The protectorless, the destitute, / And the crippled equally to obtain/ Food and drink without interruption. (...) In order to alleviate the suffering/ Of sentient beings, the old, young, and infirm/ You should establish through the estates [that you control]/ **Doctors** and barbers through the country. (Bold emphasis added). Verses 243, 251, 320, 240, as translated and arranged by Jeffrey Hopkins (1998). *Nāgārjuna's Precious Garland. Buddhist Advice for Liberation explanation*. New York, p. 77.

political figure more decisive for the consolidation and spread of Buddhism, and traditionally regarded as a model king, included provisions in his famous Edicts concerning medical treatment for both human and animals.[38] Regardless of such textual and historical references, it has not been uncommon in the West to label Buddhism as socio-politically uninvolved at least since Max Weber.[39] However accurate or fair the categorization, a need to deepen the social commitment of Buddhist practitioners seems to have inspired Vietnamese Buddhist monk Thích Nhất Hạnh's "Engaged Buddhism" and subsequent advocates and movements aiming at addressing social and political issues from a Buddhist perspective.[40] Along such activism, Buddhist scholarship in both East and West has since developed a wealth of literature on social welfare, healthcare, bioethics, economics, ecology, and other contemporary socio-political issues drawing from Buddhist sources, concepts, and way of reasoning, often aiming at a laicized reading acceptable by the general public. Traditional teachers and monastics have shown a range of attitudes towards such proposals, while some Western scholars have on occasion pointed out the tension existing between said approaches and canonical sources, traditional readings, and conventional praxis.[41]

3.   International Lamas and their Public Discourse

The current situation of Tibetan Buddhism is undeniable marked by the Tibetan diaspora following the Chinese invasion in the 1950s. A positive side effect of the takeover, it is often stated, has been the opening and access to a massive body of texts, teachings, practices, and masters, previously secluded in the Himalayas. Upon the fleeing of the Dalai Lama to India in 1959 and his establishment in Dharamsala, teachers from the different schools of Tibetan Buddhism also went into exile, typically to Nepal and India, where monasteries and centers were thus reconstructed. This relocation not only facilitated the access of scholars and practitioners to Tibetan Buddhist teachers, but eventually resulted in the creation

---

38   Upinder Singh (2012). Governing the State and the Self: Political Philosophy and Practice in the Edicts of Aśoka. *South Asian Studies* 28, N º 2, 134.

39   Max Weber famously referred to Buddhism as "unpolitical and antipolitical". Max Weber (1958). *The Religion of India: The Sociology of Hinduism and Buddhism*. Glencoe, p. 206.

40   See the collective volume: Christopher S. Queen and Sallie B. King (Eds.) (1996). *Engaged Buddhism: Buddhist Liberation Movements in Asia*. New York.

41   Donald S. Lopez's accusation of idealizations, decontextualization, and unfounded scientificism are notorious examples of such criticism. See, e.g. Donald S. Lopez (1999). *Prisoners of Shangri-La: Tibetan Buddhism and the West*. Chicago.; Cf. Donald S. Lopez (2010). *Buddhism & science: a guide for the perplexed*. Chicago.; Donald S. Lopez (2012). *Scientific Buddha - His Short and Happy Life*. New Haven.

of truly international webs along with the development of globalization and new technologies.

Contrasting with the romanticized image of spiritual masters in secluded caves or hard to access monasteries in the middle of the mountains, prominent Tibetan teachers, particularly High Lamas, outside Tibet are often the heads of complex, modern, and resourceful organizations that include traditional monasteries and schools, along with retreat and Dharma centers in both South Asia and Western countries. They provide teachings, empowerments and so forth following the tradition of their school and lineage, and at the same time they often offer courses and teachings to an international audience (both face-to-face and online), and provide social or community services directly or by means of affiliated NGOs. Many of them travel frequently around the world, are active in the social media, have their own Facebook page in English, and have their videos uploaded to YouTube.[42]

The Covid-19 crisis has thus taken place in a context where Tibetan teachers, formerly offering rituals for Tibetan lay followers and education to Tibetan monastics in loco, face an international audience, being able to convey their message, advice, and instructions to students and followers with a varied degree of knowledge and engagement, as well as to the general public, with a global range. To provide just an example, the site of Lotsawa House, a virtual library dedicated to translations from classical Tibetan, offered a list of mantras and prayers recommended by Tibetan masters from different traditions with their corresponding links, so that practitioners could easily locate resources for "protection and healing during the current Coronavirus crisis"[43].

In what follows, the public pronouncements, reactions, and advice from the foremost Tibetan teachers are presented according to their affiliation to the main schools of Tibetan Buddhism: Gelug, Nyingma, Karma Kagyu and Ka-Nying, Sakya, and, finally, Bon and Rime (ecumenical).[44]

---

42   See Gregory Price Grieve and Daniel Veidlinger (Eds.) 2014. *Buddhism, the Internet, and Digital Media. The Pixel in the Lotus.* New York Routlege.; Geoffrey Samuel (2017). Tibetan Religion as a World Religion: Global Networking and its Consequences. *Tantric Revisionings: New Understandings of Tibetan Buddhism and Indian Religion.* New York, pp. 288-316.

43   It included the following warning: "Please note that several of these practices require an empowerment and reading transmission (lung). If in doubt, please consult a lama." Cf. Lotsawa House (2020). *Love in the Time of Covid-19.* March 16. See: https://lotsawahouse.blog/2020/03/16/love-in-the-time-of-covid-19/

44   For an overview of each school, see John Powers (2007). *Introduction to Tibetan Buddhism.* Ithaca.

3.1   Gelug

The Gelug is the most recent among the 4 major Tibetan Buddhist schools, becoming preeminent and politically dominant by the end of the 16th century. Although its formal head is known as the Ganden Tripa, its most important leader is indisputably the Dalai Lama. The 14th Dalai Lama, Nobel Peace Laurate Tenzin Gyatso, is not only a symbol of religiosity, culture, and unity for Tibetans in exile, but also stands as a true international figure, and, as the most globally recognizable Tibetan master, who possesses the widest reach, particularly among non-practitioners. To provide a trivial example of his media impact, his Facebook page alone has 14 million followers.

In mid-February, the Dalai Lama's Office, upon the advice of his doctor and due to the coronavirus, announced the cancellation of all his public commitments "until further notice" in a statement communicated to CNN[45]. Since then, His Holiness has had the chance to express himself in different occasions on the Covid-crisis.

His first reactions, taking place in late March, bore an institutional character. He expressed his support while donating funds to help with the relief of those sick and in need to both the Federal Government of Himachal Pradesh, the State where his residence is located, and the Prime Minister of India Narendra Modi.[46] On March 30, upon "repeated requests from many people around the world," the Dalai Lama conveyed a special message:

> "Today, we are passing through an exceptionally difficult time due to the outbreak of the coronavirus pandemic. In addition to this, further problems confront humanity such as extreme climate change.
>
> Ancient Indian tradition describes the creation, abiding and destruction of worlds over time. Among the causes of such destruction are wars and disease, which seems to accord with what we are experiencing today. However, despite the enormous challenges we face, living beings, including humans, have shown a remarkable ability to survive.
>
> No matter how difficult the situation may be, we should employ science and human ingenuity with determination and courage to overcome the problems that confront us. (...)

---

45   Cf. Tenzin Dharpo and CNN's Sugam Pokharel (2020). 'Dalai Lama cancels all public engagements due to the coronavirus'. February 12. See: https://edition.cnn.com/asia/live-news/coronavirus-outbreak-02-12-20-intl-hnk/h_44c26bc4035ba6d1e0286237b5a19558

46   Cf. The Tribune. Voice of the People. (India). (2020). 'Dalai Lama donates to CM Relief Fund'. March 26. See: https://www.tribuneindia.com/news/himachal/dalai-lama-donates-to-cm-relief-fund-61678; Cf. 2020 NDTV (2020). 'COVID-19: Dalai Lama Donates To PM-CARES Fund, Extends Support'. March 31. See: https://www.ndtv.com/india-news/covid-19-dalai-lama-donates-to-pm-cares-fund-extends-support-2203873

For those with no stable income life is a daily struggle for survival. I earnestly appeal to all concerned to do everything possible to care for the vulnerable members of our communities.

I offer special gratitude to the medical staff—doctors, nurses and other support personnel—who are working on the frontline to save lives at great personal risk. Their service is indeed compassion in action.

With heartfelt feelings of concern for my brothers and sisters around the world who are passing through these difficult times, I pray for an early end to this pandemic so that your peace and happiness may soon be restored.[47"]

Besides such official declarations, the Dalai Lama has been asked for his view and advice by several mainstream English-speaking media. In an article in *Time Magazine*, expressively entitled "Prayer is not Enough," he declared possessing no "magical powers" that could alleviate the crisis, having to face, like all human beings, "the suffering and the truths of sickness, old age, and death." He pointed to the pandemic as an example of the Buddhist understanding of the world in terms of interdependence and appealed to a "universal responsibility" which, beyond prayer, required truly global efforts alongside doctors and science.[48] Answering the petition of *The Call to Unite*, an American-based 24-hour global livestream initiative in response to the coronavirus, the Dalai Lama had the chance to stress this idea of a global response based upon "Our human capacity to reason and to see things realistically [which] gives us the ability to transform hardship into opportunity" in a message read by Archbishop Desmond Tutu.[49] On May 28th, the Dalai Lama gave an online interview to ABC's Dan Harris, in which he declared that his daily life of reading and meditation had not been particularly affected by the crisis. Asked about Trump's management of the pandemic in America, he declared Trump's attitude to be too narrow-minded for the leader of the free world, but that it was ultimately "your (American people's) business". Upon his allusion to the practice of compassion to combat anxiety, the reporter referred to the Dalai Lama as a "major scientific figure" due to his fostering of psychologist Richard Davidson's research on the impact of mediation on the brain, and finished his section with a discus-

---

47   Cf. His Holiness the 14th Dalai Lama of Tibet (2020/1). 'A Special Message from His Holiness the Dalai Lama'. March 30. See: https://www.dalailama.com/news/2020/a-special-message-fr om-his-holiness-the-dalai-lama

48   Cf. Time Magazine (2020).'Prayer is not Enough'. April 14. See: https://time.com/5820613/dalai- lama-coronavirus-compassion/

49   The whole broadcast streamed from 8:00 p.m. EDT on May 1 until 8:00 p.m. EDT on May 2. The Dalai Lama's video may be watched at: https://unite.us/videos/?596. For an overview of "The call to Unite", see the CNBC coverage: https://www.cnbc.com/2020/05/01/the-call-to- unite-organizer-explains-idea-behind-24-hour-livestream.html

sion of the benefits of mediation with the conductor of the program.[50] Finally, BBC Justin Rowland was given an interview on June 13 wherein His Holiness insisted on the "deeper human values of compassion" that are revealed when we face tragic situations, and that currently call for a global scope: "In the past there was too much emphasis on my continent, my nation, my religion. Now that thinking is out of date. Now we really need a sense of oneness of seven billion human beings.[51]"

Other references to the virus crisis were uttered in the context of varied religious events, Dharma teachings, and intellectual discussions, and so have a more tangential character.[52] Also, when expressing his gratitude for the birthday wishes received upon his 85th birthday, he reminded that: "Climate change and the current pandemic, which threaten us all, are challengers that teach us we must work together." Not all statements pronounced during such a period, however, included an explicit allusion to the virus. Arguably the most important ceremony conducted by the Dalai Lama during the pandemic was the 2-days Avalokiteśvara Empowerment (May 29th and 30th 2020), broadcasted with translation in 13 languages along with the participation of tens of thousands of people around the world. At the introduction, His Holiness presented an overview of the context of the empowerment where he referred to current social struggles like racial violence in the USA, or religious discrimination but made no mention to the virus.[53]

---

50   Richard Davidson appeared in the interview himself stating that: "compassion practice is anti-inflammatory, it actually decreases molecules in the body that we know are important in producing inflammation". Cf. ABC News Prime (2020). 'Dalai Lama speaks out on COVID-19'. May 28. See: https://www.youtube.com/watch?v=NEWqRcy-6Wg&t=1s

51   Cf. BBC News (2020). 'Dalai Lama: Seven billion people 'need a sense of oneness'. June 13. See: https://www.bbc.com/news/stories-53028343?fbclid=IwAR3PN2xFONDnm7jK_SR2G4zokQ3gQw KUPPW7KTgcSGbDjDD6otoY6kcAkus

52   For example, during the dialogue with Young People from South-East Asia, the moderator brought out the topic at stake to which the Dalai Lama responded praising the possibilities that technology now offers to share one's experiences with others. His Holiness the 14th Dalai Lama of Tibet (2020/2). 'Dialogue with Young People from South-east Asia'. June 7. See: https://www.dalailama.com/news/2020/dialogue-with-young-people-from-south-east-asia. He also referred to both the medical remedy to the illness, to be found in research, and to the management of anxiety associated to it, which required the cultivation of self-confidence. His Holiness the 14th Dalai Lama of Tibet (2020/3). 'Mind & Life Conversation: Resilience, Compassion, & Science for Healing Today'. June 20. See: https://www.dalailama.com/news/2020/mind-life-conversation-resilience-compassion-science-for-healing-today

53   The Dalai Lama was alluding to the death of African-American George Floyd at the hands of the police on May 25, 2020, leading to massive protests and riots throughout the USA. The empowerment videos are accessible on YouTube: "Preliminaries to the Avalokiteshvara Empowerment" (https://www.youtube.com/watch?v=iUWH3PIjZQ8), and "Actual Avalokiteshvara Empowerment" (https://www.youtube.com/watch?v=Ti-L1BdhLw4). A summary is offered on the Dalai Lama's website under the titles "Preliminaries for an Avalokiteshvara Empowerment" (https://www.dalailama.com/news/2020/preliminaries-for-an-avalokiteshvara-

The fact that the empowerments were to be given online raised its own controversy. Tibetan teacher Tulku Orgyen Tobgyal, former member of the Tibetan parliament in Exile, criticized the Dalai Lama and other Tibetan teachers a few days before the Avalokiteśvara Empowerment maintaining that empowerments and blessings required the physical co-presence of student and master, so that online conferral was a sign of degeneration and implied a violation "destroying the faith." Strong reactions came not only from religious figures, but significantly, from political leaders. The Kashag (Cabinet) led by Dr. Lobsang Sangay, the President of the Central Tibetan Administration, deemed the declarations "regrettable" and "wrong," stressing the Dalai Lama's work spreading Buddhism worldwide and the contextual needs during the Covid-19 pandemic.[54] Comprehensive and sympathetic comments were made on the matter by cabinet minister for Religion and Culture Yuthok Karma Gelek, also a monastic, which sparked a call for his resignation.[55] Eventually, both Tulku Orgyen Tobgyal and Yuthok Karma Gelek ended up apologizing and retracted their comments.[56] Interestingly, during the preliminaries to the initiation the Dalai Lama remarked that the same empowerment had been given online in 2019 as an expeditious way to reach Tibetans in Tibet, thus arguably distancing himself for the consideration of telematic technology as extraordinary means for an exceptional context defined by the pandemic.

Drawing from his dual background as a former Tibetan monastic and a Western scholar, as well as from his experience as translator of the Dalai Lama for a long time, Geshe Thupten Jinpa Langri had the chance to express his views in a live YouTube interview with Asia Society Vice President Tom Nagorski, while aiming to serve as a "medium to channel the Dalai Lama's wisdom and thoughts." The encounter, entitled "Coping in the Time of Coronavirus," focused on the implementation of contemplative practices to psychologically deal with the lockdown and on the need to reflect globally on the circumstances and challenges brought by the

---

empowerment) and "Webcast of an Avalokiteshvara Empowerment" (https://www.dalail-ama.com/news/2020/webcast-of-an-avalokiteshvara-empowerment)

54 Cf. Phayul (2020/1). 'Tulku Orgyen Tobgyal's remarks "regrettable and wrong": Kashag'. May 27. See: http://www.phayul.com/2020/05/27/43492/

55 Ib.

56 Cf. Tulku Orgyen Tobgyal wrote a letter declaring: "At the advice of my root guru, and scoldings I got from Sakya Trichen Rinpoche and Sakya Trizin, Ratna Vajra Rinpoche, they being my masters, I am withdrawing my recent words, and tendering my apology to His Holiness the Dalai Lama, and appeal to him to live a long life." (....) "Following the suggestions of my masters, I will never again in future criticize online teachings and empowerments." Cf. Tibet Sun (2020). 'Tulku Orgyen Tobgyal apologises to Dalai Lama for criticizing online teachings'. May 31. See: https://www.tibetsun.com/news/2020/05/31/tulku-orgyen-tobgyal-apologises-to-dalai-lama-for-criticising-online-teachings.; Cf. Tibetan Journal (2020). 'Kalon Karma Gelek Apologizes and Willing to Resign if Needed'. May 28. See: https://www.tibetan-journal.com/kalon-karma-gelek-apologizes-and-willing-to-resign-if-needed/

pandemic. Jinpa recommended a brief daily mediation practice consisting of not denying or suppressing the negative feelings triggered by the harsh situation, such as anger or frustration, but to observe them, breathe, and thus generate calm and awareness. He insisted on the individual responsibility over our own mental health, both before ourselves and interacting with others, and stressed the need to express gratitude to those in the frontline, like nurses and doctors.[57]

In his general reflection on the pandemic, he underlined how clear the notions of "interconnectedness" and "uncertainty" have become undeniably perceivable by everyone, though they have always been part of the human reality. To the unprecedented global threat that the virus poses, he opposed the equally unprecedented interconnection granted by the Internet and New Technologies; a context in which, he jokingly claimed, "Netflix is our savior!" He concluded drawing attention to the deep social inequalities revealed in the impact of the virus on vulnerable social groups, and the need for socio-political structures which, beyond sheer liberal capitalism, require the protection of basic social services, such as healthcare.[58]

Less known by non-practitioners and yet quite internationally influential, Tibetan teacher Lama Zopa Rinpoche is a pioneer in teaching Tibetan Buddhism to Westerners from his Kopan Monastery in Nepal. In 1975 he created, along with Lama Thubten Yeshe, the Foundation for the Preservation of the Mahayana Tradition (FPMT), an impressive worldwide network currently comprising more than 160 Dharma centers in the five continents, and providing diverse services such as education, the sale of religious objects, charitable services, and online learning.

Within the online site of the FPMT, a special page was created solely to provide "Resources for the Coronavirus Pandemic."[59] The page starts with a series of links to the teachings and statements of His Holiness the Dalai Lama as mentioned above, followed by Lama Zopa's own advice. The latter contain a list of prayers and mantras, the oral transmissions for which can also be received online, and a series of video teachings on "Thought Transformation" given from Kopan Monastery specifically for the pandemic. Practices are divided between those aimed at protecting yourself from the virus, and those aiming at protecting others; e.g. "this prayer from Thangtong Gyalpo is to heal the disease in China and for it not to spread out to other countries. So, it is to protect the country. And anyone in the world can recite this prayer.[60]"

---

57   Cf. Asia Society YouTube channel (2020). 'Coping in the Time of Coronavirus'. April 8. See: https://www.youtube.com/watch?v=n_sc1SDwopg

58   He specifically referred to the disproportionate death rate of black citizens and the lack of universal healthcare in the USA. Ib.

59   Cf. Preservation of the Mahayana Tradition (2020/1). 'Resources for Coronavirus Pandemic'. March. See: https://fpmt.org/fpmt/announcements/resources-for-coronavirus-pandemic/

60   Cf. Preservation of the Mahayana Tradition (2020/2). 'Advice from Lama Zopa Rinpoche for coronavirus'. March See: https://fpmt.org/fpmt/announcements/resources-for-coronavirus-

The Thought Transformation video series consists of a vast collection of 50 sessions (as by mid-July 2020) in English, with translations in Chinese, French, Italian, Russian, and Spanish. The videos are available with summaries and full transcriptions. Drawing from the general idea that the pandemic is a good opportunity for practice, the teachings address both generic Buddhist topics like impermanence, attachment, bodhicitta, and so forth, and the very specific circumstances of the pandemic and how to respond to them. The first teaching, entitled "Advice for Coronavirus Disease (Covid-19)" and given on March 17, begins by referring to how the SARS pandemic (2003) could successfully be tamed by the practice of pujas (offering rituals) performed by an FPMT center in Singapore. A few days later, on March 28, a special puja was conducted in Kathmandu by Lama Zopa and other teachers to mitigate the effects of Covid-19.[61] Most of this teaching focuses on the importance of the awareness of death, usually neglected and now triggered by the coronavirus, and finishes with the advice of daily recitation of the Vajra Armor mantra to "not get the disease" or "recover from it" if already infected.[62] Some teachings in the series present sickness as an opportunity to achieve enlightenment for others, an altruism that is highlighted in the case of nurses and doctors exposed to the virus, who will never be reborn in the lower realms. "We all must die, [he concludes] so to die with compassion for others, this is a very good death"[63]. Other teachings reflect on the ultimate causes of the pandemic,

(...) "not only the virus, but the whole thing came from the mind. It came from the mind. The world coming into existence, and then existing, and then degeneration, the whole thing came from the mind.
Abhidharmakosha (v. 4.1) says: "The various worlds came from karma". (...). "All came from your mind, but also, from there, all the sufferings came from the negative

---

pandemic/advice-from-lama-zopa-rinpoche-for-coronavirus/ The site also contains advice on practices from Rangjung Neljorma Khadro Namsel Drönme focusing on Nölsang "Incense Ritual by the Great Master Padmasambhava Called "The Divine Blue Water Clearing Away Contamination".

61   Cf. Preservation of the Mahayana Tradition (2020/2).
62   Cf. Preservation of the Mahayana Tradition (2020/2).
63   Cf. Preservation of the Mahayana Tradition (2020/3). 'Use Pleasure and Suffering to Achieve Enlightenment and Experience the Virus for Numberless Sentient Beings'. April 18. See: https://fpmt.org/lama-zopa-rinpoche-news-and-advice/advice-from-lama-zopa-rinpoche/use-pleasure-and-suffering-to-achieve-enlightenment-and-experience-the-virus-for-numberless-sentient-beings/; Cf. Preservation of the Mahayana Tradition (2020/4). 'Coronavirus Leaves Us No Choice But to Develop Compassion and 80,000 Eons of Benefits from Making Charity'. April 23. See: https://fpmt.org/lama-zopa-rinpoche-news-and-advice/advice-from-lama-zopa-rinpoche/coronavirus-leaves-us-no-choice-but-to-develop-compassion/

mind, your negative mind. There is individual suffering but there is world suffering, world problems. That is called collective karma.[64]"

"[S]o therefore, we have to be very careful, we have to be very careful. In the past, in the past, if you are very careful of the karma, there is no reason why the virus has to happen, why we have to experience it, why so many people have to die in the world. If you are careful, if from the beginning you are careful, you practice Dharma, you are careful of karma, careful, then you don't need to experience the virus." (...) "For example, there are people, there are many people in the world who don't experience the virus, who don't die due to the virus (...).[65]"

This series of teachings probably constitutes the main initiative of the FPMT before the pandemic, but it is not the only one. The organization also offers several FPMT Online Learning Center programs to "any student or center who would like to use them" free of charge[66]. In May 2020, the International Merit Box Project Fund, created in 2001 as a means to collect offerings for varied Dharma-related purposes, was dedicated entirely to help FPMT centers to deal the crisis caused by the virus.[67]

Other Gelugpa teachers with relatively less reach and influence have also tried to offer specific responses to the Covidd-19 crisis for his international followers. For example, the Abbot of Sera Mey Monastery (Bylakuppe, India) Geshe Tashi Tsering created a series of posts in his personal website called "Practicing Buddhism in a Pandemic," in which he provides updates on the management of the crisis at the monastery and gives commentaries on teachings and prayers (namely the Lam Rim Chenmo and Maitreya's prayer). There is little reference to the virus besides the generic need to not abandon one's practice despite the circumstances.[68]

---

64   Cf. Preservation of the Mahayana Tradition (2020/5). 'All the Problems in the World, Including the Coronavirus, are Telling Us to Practice Dharma'. April 21. See: https://fpmt.org/lama-zopa-rinpoche-news-and-advice/advice-from-lama-zopa-rinpoche/all-the-problems-in-the-world-including-the-coronavirus-are-telling-us-to-practice-dharma/

65   Cf. Preservation of the Mahayana Tradition (2020/6). 'If We Had Been Careful of Karma, There Would Be No Reason for the Virus to Happen'. April 25. See: https://fpmt.org/lama-zopa-rinpoche-news-and-advice/advice-from-lama-zopa-rinpoche/if-we-had-been-careful-of-karma-there-would-be-no-reason-for-the-virus-to-happen/

66   The Free programs offered via the FPMT Online Learning Center are: "Discovering Buddhism: Module 11.Transforming Problems"; Basic Program: Mahayana Mind Training, Wheel of Sharp Weapons", "Living in the Path", "Living in the Path (Spanish)", "Discovering Buddhism (French)". Resources for the Coronavirus Pandemic. FPMT, see: https://fpmt.org/fpmt/announcements/resources-for-coronavirus-pandemic/

67   US$31,368 were distributed in the spring of 2020. Cf. Preservation of the Mahayana Tradition (2020/7). 'The Merit Box Project'. May 15. See: https://fpmt.org/projects/fpmt/merit-box/

68   GesheTashi.org (2020). 'Geshe Tashi's Coronavirus Updates. Practising Buddhism in a Pandemic'. Consulted in July. See: https://geshetashi.org/category/geshe-tashis-coronavirus-updates/

Director of The Tibet Center Austria Geshe Tendhar gave a couple of specific teachings aimed at the coronavirus situation, where he asked his followers to abide by the guidelines and recommendations provided by the Austrian Government. He also provided varied advice for non-Buddhists and Buddhist practitioners with different backgrounds and formative experience, while asking everyone to try to understand the situation as clearly as possible to act accordingly.[69]

Finally, Demo Rinpoche, Resident Spiritual Advisor at Jewel Heart (Ann Arbor, Michigan) on April 16 announced that:

> "In this moment of crisis, we have an opportunity to shift our minds from stress-inducing consumption of upsetting news to the spiritual path. We will be studying and applying the lessons of Shantideva's *Guide to the Bodhisattva's Way of Life* to turn this time of pandemic into a beneficial period."[70]

The eleven teachings, delivered in English and with sparse yet explicit references to the pandemic, can all be accessed online.

3.2 Nyingma

Considered the oldest among the four major Tibetan schools, the Nyingma tradition has never occupied a dominant political position in Tibet, and it has traditionally kept a de-centralized internal structure lacking a single head of the school.[71] The major lineage holders are associated with the main six monasteries (Shechen,

---

69   Geshe Tendhar suggested that non-Buddhists who have meditation training should bring mindfulness to everyday life to protect oneself and others (e.g. being careful with what you touch, being aware of physical distance, not touching your face, etc.). For those who have received teachings on emptiness, he also suggested meditating on emptiness. For those who have studied Traditional Tibetan Medicine, he suggested focusing on strengthening their immune system and avoid negative emotions. To those who have studied Buddhist psychology, he advised to "develop a strong and peaceful mind." Cf. Tibet Center Austria - Institute of H.H. Dalai Lama (2020). 'Lama Geshe TenDhar on the Coronavirus situation- March 2020'. March 18. See: https://www.tibetcenter.at/en/coronavirus-en/ Aspiration prayers dedicated to those fighting the virus and the study of the Lam Rim Chenmo were in general recommended to his followers. Cf. Institute of H.H. Dalai Lama (2020). 'Our practice in difficult times – April 2020'. April. See: https://www.tibetcenter.at/en/our-practice-in-difficult-times/

70   Cf. Jewel Heart (2020). 'SPECIAL TEACHING FOR THE CORONAVIRUS: Finding Relief through the Bodhisattva's Way of Life'. April. See: https://www.jewelheart.org/events/coronavirus-finding-relief-through-the-bodhisattvas-way-of-life/

71   At the request of the Central Tibetan Administration in exile, a representative of the school was appointed by a rotation system of senior lamas from the six-major Nyingma monasteries from the 1960s until February 2020. The last appointee rejected the position and deemed it harmful for the school. Cf. Phayul (2020/2). 'Shechen Rabjam Rinpoche declines the position to head Nyingma tradition'. February 2nd. See: http://www.phayul.com/2020/02/04/42548/

Dzogchen, Mindrolling, Palyul, Kathok, and Dorje Drak), all rebuilt in exile, although this internal relevance does not necessarily imply a major international projection.

Shechen Monastery lineage holder Khyentse Yangsi Rinpoche, a young teacher born in 1993 and reincarnation of the famous lama Dilgo Khyentse Rinpoche, recorded an audio message for his followers that was posted on his Facebook page. He started depicting the context of the virus in terms of the prophesies of Guru Rinpoche on the advent of a degenerate era comprised of a kalpa of war, a kalpa of natural disaster, a kalpa of famine, and a kalpa of major diseases. Even if pandemics are not a new thing – he elaborated – the particular harshness of the current one would be but a result of our own destructive behavior towards ourselves and others, so that "we are seeing now the results of the negative seeds, now ripening upon all of us." Alike other teachers, he advised not to panic and continue with one's daily practice along with the recitation of Medicine Guru Rinpoche mantra. His final reflection dealt with the frustration of not being able to do something for others besides confinement and self-cultivation; he apologized: "I'm sorry I cannot do much. I wish I could sacrifice my life with the right motivation, and physically go and help; but since I'm not able to do that, I'm sorry"[72].

Dzogchen Monastery Dzogchen Rinpoche, Jigme Losel Wangpo, was even more incisive in his degenerate times rhetoric, claiming he had even prophesied the virus. In Mid-March he posted on his Facebook wall:

"I want to offer you my humble and direct advice. I want to support you through this **kali yuga virus**. Things look serious, but we don't need to panic. This event has been **prophesized in ancient texts** and is the result of the **disrespect of mother nature**, being greedy, and the lack of compassion and kindness to one another.

Mother nature is showing supernatural power beyond human, scientific, and political control. This crisis is showing us how to be respectful of mother nature and how to be kind to one another in our one world.

I have been consulted by Tibetan Buddhist Leaders to give my thoughts.

This **virus will end soon**. We must confess to mother nature and request reverse of conditions by practicing Ekazati. **I had mentioned this three or four years ago in my teachings**, and I have made a joke about how you would all survive without toilet paper, and this is now happening.

Make sure you all take care of yourselves and your health. I feel responsible for taking care of you.

Please take this opportunity as a home retreat or as I'm jokingly calling it a Coronavirus Quarantine retreat. During these days, we will be accumulating as much

---

72   Dilgo Khyentse Yangsi Rinpoche (2020). 'About the current situation with Coronavirus'. *Facebook*. March 21. https://www.facebook.com/shechen.cro/videos/2809514709139867/

of the Ekazati practice as is possible, Barsam Drolsum and Dukshe Sengsum. To-gether with both monastic and international sangha, we will do the necessary prayers and practices for world healing and health.

I encourage you to commit to not disrespect mother nature by just taking and not giving back."[73]

(Bold emphasis added)

Mindrolling Monastery Jetsun Khandro Rinpoche is an influential female teacher having both a monastic and Western education. In early March, she informed that "The Verses that Saved Sakya from Sickness: A Prayer for Pacifying the Fear of Dis-ease" had been recited at the monastery to help tame the virus and recommended it to her followers.[74] In April, at the request of her students, Khandro Rinpoche recorded a video announcing the compliance with the lockdown at her monastery, praising the government and health workers, and hoping everyone was careful and safe. She stressed that Buddhist practitioners should not make a great deal of being isolated, but cherish the opportunity to keep one's practice in a yet deeper fashion: "this is a wonderful blessing and an opportunity". Finally, she encouraged the look-ing out for those in need of support and help[75]; and so, her monastery donated 1.6 million rupees to several Indian state governments and provided food and sup-plies to the local community.[76] The notion that no special practice was needed was stressed on her personal website, where instead of particular instructions, a post entitled "Practicing in Times of Adversity" from 2018, was reposted[77]. Nevertheless, she deemed it appropriate to make teachings on "Turning Suffering and Happiness into Enlightenment" available online, and her summer program was substituted by a 2-week online course on Longchenpa's *The Great Chariot*.[78]

---

73   Cf. Message from His Eminence the 7th Dzogchen Rinpoche (2020). Facebook. March 21. See: https://www.facebook.com/DzogchenBuddhism/ Rinpoche also has international followers and centers in Europe, America and Australia, but there is practically no online informa-tion besides this message. His international groups may be checked at "Gyalwa Dzogchen Sangha", See: http://www.dzogchen.org.in/sangha.

74   The prayer was allegedly composed by Thangtong Gyalpo at the time of a seemingly untam-able infectious disease. Ringpa (2020). 'Dedicating our Dharma Practice to the Coronavirus'. March 10. See: https://www.rigpa.org/rigpa-news/2020/3/10/6civjuaj6w2pt4qtzoopl6rlne71ko

75   Cf. Mindrolling Jetsün Khandro Rinpoche (2020). ,Advice for the COVID-19 situation'. *YouTube.* April 10. https://www.youtube.com/watch?v=uWJWunQgtyc

76   Cf. Khandro Rinpoche (2020/3). 'Mindrolling Aids in Pandemic Relief Effort'. *Facebook.* April 14. See: https://www.khandrorinpoche.org/mindrolling-monastery-aids-in-pandemic-relief-e ffort/

77   Cf. Khandro Rinpoche (2020/2). 'Practicing in Times of Adversity'. (Originally posted on November 21, 2018). *Facebook.* March 24. See: https://www.khandrorinpoche.org/practicing-in-times-of-adversity/

78   Cf. Ringpa (2020/2). 'Online Teachings with Jetsun Khando Rinpoche'. *Facebook.* April 12. See: https://www.rigpa.org/upcoming-events/2020/4/12/online-teachings-with-jetsun-khand

The Nyingma lineage holders from the other three "mother monasteries" were significantly less vocal regarding the pandemic, at least their international followers and public[79]; whereas other teachers with a dual Nyignma and Kagyu affiliation and arguably a more global projection were more active and communicative towards their audience, as we shall see in the next section.

A last figure is worth including here: the aforementioned protagonist of the controversy on the Dalai Lama's online empowerments, Orgyen Tobgyal Rinpoche, who is a Nyingma rituals expert, former member of the Tibetan Parliament in exile, and amateur actor. In his YouTube Channel, he uploaded a video in Tibetan with his "Advice in the time of COVID-19," where he described the pandemic as a result of the 5 poisons disturbing people's minds and thus creating an imbalance in the 5 primary elements. Though he recommended to follow the scientists and doctors' advice, he also argued that:

> "Since the main point is 'mind', if your mind remains relaxed, the outer and inner disturbance of the primary elements and the epidemics caused by the mind will be pacified (...) If your thoughts are pacified naturally, all sickness will also be pacified."[80]

He recommended praying to the Triple Gem, i.e. Buddha, Dharma, and Sangha, and to Guru Rinpoche, as well as reciting "Pacifying the Turmoil of the Mamos," since the kind of disturbance that causes epidemics is caused by an agitation in the minds of Dakinis and Mamos (female spirit-deities). Above all, he concluded, the most important thing is to relax.[81]

---

ro-rinpoche; Cf. Khandro Rinpoche (2020/4). 'Mindrol Lekshey Online: Curriculum Review and Teachings'. *Facebook*. July 13. See: https://www.khandrorinpoche.org/mindrol-lekshey-online-2020/

79   Palyul Monastery Penar Rinpoche's seat in exile, Namdroling Monastery donated Rs. 10 lakh to PM CARES Fund (Cf. Star of Mysore (2020). 'Penor Rinpoche Charity Foundation Donates Rs.10 Lakh Towards PM CARES Fund'. April 17. See: https://starofmysore.com/penor-rinpoche-charity-foundation-donates-rs-10-lakh-towards-pm-cares-fund/); while his international network published a special advice for the 2003 SARS and none for the covid-19. (Cf. Palyul Ling International (2020). 'Advice: Dealing with the 2003 SARS Outbreak'. February 3. See: https://palyul.org/wp/1456-2/). Khatok Monastery Lhoga Rinpoche succinctly recommended the practice of Gotrab during the virus crisis (Cf. Nyignma Kathok Buddhist Centre (2020). 'Practice for the Wuhan Corona Virus'. March. See: https://kathok.org.sg/practice-for-the-wuhan-corona-virus/). Finally, Dorje Drak Monastery (the throne holder of which is still to be recognized in his latest reincarnation), also announced a donation of ₹ 1, 30,000 to HPSDMA COVID-19 state disaster response fund. The official letter may be consulted on the monastery's Facebook page (See April 20, 2020: https://www.facebook.com/dorje-drag/?rc=p).

80   Cf. Orgyan Tobgyal YouTube channel (2020). 'OT Rinpoche's advice in the time of COVID-19'. March 19. See: https://www.youtube.com/watch?v=g4TX8U7BGTw&t=194s

81   Ib.

3.3   Karma Kagyu and Ka-Nying

The Kagyu, literally meaning the "oral lineage" because of its emphasis on direct oral transmission, has the Karma Kagyu as its largest school, arguably thanks to their unbroken line of reincarnate lineage holders known as the Karmapas, relevant and influential figures within the whole Tibetan Buddhist tradition. The recognition of the last Karmapa, following the death of the 16th in 1981, gave rise to a dispute between two aspiring candidates, Trinley Thaye Dorje and Ogyen Trinley Dorje, both of whom have been publicly performing the role within their own organizations and counting on diverse support.

Trinley Thaye Dorje, enthroned in Delhi as the 17th Gyalwang Karmapa in 1994, was probably the first high lama to publicly react before the virus crisis in an official letter published by the end of January. Therein he recommended his followers to stay at home and get together for streaming practice sessions, and argued that:

> "the many and various kinds of obstacles that we face, such as natural disasters, wars, infectious diseases, and famines that keep occurring are the infallible **consequence of our collective and individual karmas**.
> Nevertheless, because of our lack of deep conviction about this, we tend to deny the causality of our actions and their results when we encounter difficult challenges. (...). Or, **we may consider all of the problems we face as the result of bad policies in our societal systems, or erroneous scientific views** or other negative developments. (...) **This is wrong.**
> In general, this all happens as a result of not being able to come to terms with the fact that, no matter how frequently we experience joy and happiness in this world, the suffering of birth, ageing, illness, and death come side by side, just as the body and its shadow walk together. **Whatever suffering occurs, it is important to identify its root**. In the Buddha's teachings, there is the system of tracing **the origin of our suffering in our karma and afflicting emotions** (...).
> Engage in the six sessions practice of day and night, be heedful to sustain yourselves on white food, and spend your time doing practices such as Nyungne, or similar practices."[82]
> (Bold emphasis added).

A shorter official letter was published in March where he stressed the need to take all due precautions and particularly to avoid panicking, since "the core sickness is, in my opinion, both a mind filled with anxiety about the disease, and a tendency

---

82   Cf. Karmapa (2020/1). 'Coronavirus: Karmapa's message for dharma centres and practitioners'. January 29. See: https://www.karmapa.org/coronavirus-karmapas-message-for-dharma-centres-and-practitioners/

to wrongly think that we should never become sick or die"[83]. Other incidental or more direct allusions to the pandemic may be found in a section in his personal website where the Karmapa shares his reflections and provides answers and advice requested by his students. A key idea here is the perception of the virus as a "blessing in disguise" bringing people together; a notion qualified by the lives lost and the harshness faced by countless individuals.[84]

On the economic front, in Mid-April, he announced donations to the Indian and Bhutanese Governments to help address the pandemic and encouraged "everyone to practice whatever form of generosity you can – no matter how limited your financial means may be."[85]

Ogyen Trinley Dorje, enthroned as the 17th Karmapa in 1992 at Tsurphu Monastery (Gurum, Tibet), is endorsed by the Dalai Lama and has more international visibility and political weight. His first public reactions to the virus appeared in a video on his Facebook page aimed at reflecting on the proper response to protect sentient beings from wars, famine, and plagues. He insisted that barely acknowledging the news was not enough, so that one should ask "what can I do to help?" and work "according to our own abilities and capacities," even if they come down to just making aspirations.[86]

His main stance, though, was articulated in Mid-April and built upon the notions of impermanence and prayer. The Karmapa insisted that we are prone to smoothly embrace impermanence when we envisage changes aligned with what we want, but get paralyzed when they take a different turn. Instead, we should contemplate ourselves and "use this crisis to improve ourselves and learn something new." As Buddhists, he proposed a series of prayer sessions to show support and appreciation to those on the frontline, and "for world peace and for the pandemic

---

83   Cf. Karmapa (2020/2). 'Coronavirus: Karmapa's new message'. March 19. See: https://www. karmapa.org/coronavirus-karmapas-new-message/

84   Cf. Thaye Dorje, His Holiness the 17th Gyalwa Karmapa, reflects on the pandemic, and introduces his responses to questions from student". In Karmapa (2020/3). 'Meditations for our Times'. July 15. See: https://www.karmapa.org/meditations-for-our-times/

85   Cf. Karmapa (2020/4). 'Karmapa donates 14.6 million rupees to Covid-19 relief funds'. April 26, See: https://www.karmapa.org/karmapa-donates-14-6-million-rupees-to-covid-19-relief-funds/; Cf. Karmapa (2020/5). 'A further donation was announced in May: "Karmapa donates 500,000 rupees to West Bengal for Covid-19 relief". May 11. See: https://www.karmapa.org/karmapa-donates-500000-rupees-to-west-bengal-for-covid-19-relief/.

86   He also recommended the recitation of Thangtong Gyalpo's prayer, The Verses that Saved Sakya from Sickness: A Prayer for Pacifying the Fear of Disease, the same recommended by Khandro Rinpoche (2020/1). 'The Gyalwang Karmapa's Advice Regarding Covid-19'. Facebook. March 19. See: https://www.facebook.com/karmapa/

to be quelled."[87] Thus, from April 18th, he started leading a series of weekly-cycled online prayers with a different practice each day. The choice of prayers and the corresponding explanation is of interest since esoteric or supernatural elements are given a symbolic contextual value. For example, "A Prayer for Rebirth in the Pure Realm of Sukhāvatī" is not explained as a supplication to be reborn in a joyful and heavenly Pure Land as opposed to our common world, but as a call to reflect on the causes and conditions that create our world and thus develop an environmental conscience and attitude that would help preserve it. Similarly, the malicious spirits targeted by "Appeasing the Discord of the Mamos" "could be understood as the natural environment arising in the form of inner goddesses," so the mantra would represent an aspiration "to remedy our imbalances and disharmony with the natural environment." Interestingly, at the explanation to the same mantra, he claimed that "some experienced Tibetan doctors" can cure the virus, though insisting that prevention was crucial: "A protection cord around your neck or a blessing pill will not be of any help if you then rush off to a large gathering of people[88]."

Besides the Karmapas, as mentioned above, several teachers belonging to both the Kagyu and Nyingma lineages, and thus sometimes referred to as Ka-Nying, have managed to attain a notable international relevance. We shall here focus on Kathmandu-based Yongey Mingyur Rinpoche and Chokyi Nyima Rinpoche.

Mingyur Rinpoche has a wide net of centers around the world (more than 50 Meditation and Community Groups on five continents), managed under the label of *Tergar*.[89] Due to the lockdown, the organization made available online their group practices conducted by instructors, 4-days retreats, and the inclusion of sick relatives in the daily practices of senior lamas.[90] Mingyur Rinpoche's initial reflection

---

87   Cf. Kagyu Office (2020). 'A Message from the Gyalwang Karmapa About the Coronavirus Pandemic'. April 14. See: https://kagyuoffice.org/a-message-from-the-gyalwang-karmapa-about-the-coronavirus-pandemic/

88   Karmapa (Ed.) (2020). Prayers for a Time of Pandemic. Compiled and Introduced by the Seventeenth Gyalwang Karmapa Ogyen Trinley Dorje. Dharma Ebooks, pp. 178-179, 237-238. The whole list of prayers follows this order: 1) The Heart Sutra with the Repulsion of Maras; 2) The Noble Aspiration for Excellent Conduct & The Sutra in Three Sections; 3) Sutras of the Dharani of Akshobhya; 4) Praises on the Twenty-One Taras with Benefits; 5) Supplications of Guru Rinpoche; 6) A Prayer for Rebirth in the Pure Realm of Sukhāvatī; 7) Selected Dharani Mantras, The Prayer that Saved Sakya from Illness, and Appeasing the Discord of the Mamos. Both the English version and the Tibetan original of the compilation may be downloaded from https://dharmaebooks.org/prayers-for-a-time-of-pandemic/?fbclid=IwAR2oF_WucRp-NRV7Eh7unQc88ATA4HruLNY2RsgB15E7ExKDJ4k45qw-EMd8; https://dharmaebooks.org/prayers-pandemic-tibet/?fbclid=IwAR2XMMUvSS4vv8oJuG1ob1N7pcRdoG3bVtqnA2v5uEOH pgGZoc5PSXrZA8o%EF%BC%89

89   It comprises: Tergar Meditation Communities and Practice Groups, Tergar International and Tergar Asia.

90   Cf. Tergar (2020). 'Covid-19 message'. See: https://tergar.org/covid-19-message-2/. The retreats are as follows: Nectar of the Path: Teachings on the Path of Awakening Online Retreat

centered on the idea that no matter the circumstances "the most important thing is our mindset" and to let go without giving up before the ups and downs of life.[91] From the end of March, he started broadcasting a series of teachings addressing spiritual and mental strategies not only to cope with the pandemic and the lockdown, but to turn the situation into a profitable learning experience.[92] The videos turned out to be a success, Rinpoche's YouTube channel reaching almost a quarter of a million subscribers. In a somehow summary session entitled "10 Life Lessons We Can Learn from Coronavirus" (25 May), Rinpoche drew a parallelism between our tendency to focus on our faults while overlooking our qualities, and our need to overcome such propensity and look into positive aspects of the pandemic. According to him, there would be 10 aspects that could actually be better cultivated and improved thanks to the virus lockdown: interpersonal relationships, spirituality, self-discovery, health and cleanliness, the environment, new discoveries, medical treatments, resilience, meditation, and education[93].

From a ritualistic perspective, and despite having declared in June 5th that Buddhism is not a religion but a science of the mind, on July 22nd Mingyur Rinpoche participated with other important lamas in a "42 fire pujas to subdue the Covid virus and the unrest and turmoil in the world, as well as liberate and bless goats from the butchers."[94]

Chokyi Nyima Rinpoche also leads a net of international centers for Buddhist Studies and Meditation known as Gomde Centers and Dharma Houses[95]. His greatest international asset, though, is probably the Kathmandu-based Rangjung

---

(July 25-28); Exploring the Nature of Mind: Deepening Recognition – Online Retreat (August 1-4); Dzogchen: The Path of Natural Liberation – Online Retreat (August 8-11). "Mingyur Rinpoche's Schedule", https://tergar.org/mingyur-rinpoches-schedule/.

91   Cf. Yongey Mingyur Rinpoche (2020/1). 'Message on COVID-19 outbreak'. *YouTube*. March 15. See: https://www.youtube.com/watch?v=DgZETpd9h5s&feature=youtu.be&fbclid=IwAR3 A-LmqPj6EhU4q3kOZBTvTzdlflgOJ41IFFvd8jh66_S4pY26GuM_IFA8

92   The Live Teaching sessions offered on YouTube include: Living with distress (March 29); Transforming Anxiety into Awareness (April 5); How to Turn Tough Times into Growth and Development (26 April); Living in a Pandemic: How to Transform Depressive Thinking (17 May); 10 Life Lessons We Can Learn from Coronavirus (25 May); Equanimity in Uncertain Times (1 June). Cf. Yongey Mingyur Rinpoche YouTube Channel, see: https://www.youtube.com/user/MingyurRinpoche, and Tergar Meditation Community YouTube Channel, see: https://www.youtube.com/channel/UCQPdChAO9IoHRio2WMGJJzA

93   Cf. Yongey Mingyur Rinpoche (2020/2). '10 Life Lessons We Can Learn from Coronavirus'. May 25. See: https://www.youtube.com/watch?v=i9M5odGK4PQ&feature =youtu.be&fbclid=IwAR11eRUs2X4dZCVb7eR9wZbNdu2K2OV-yAhX_DE3NT1T9prNurA43cJjFGI

94   Both quotations extracted from his official Facebook page, see: https://www.facebook.com/mingyur.rinpoche/

95   Cf. its webpage: Shedrub. The Online Home of Chokyi Nyima Rinpoche, see: https://shedrub.org/

Yeshe Institute. Modelled upon Rinpoche's ideal of the "scholar practitioner," it offers academic degrees on Buddhist Studies and Himalayan languages combing modern Western methodology and traditional Tibetan teachings.[96] Rinpoche's first reactions in March focused on encouraging compliance with social distancing and lockdown measures, to take the opportunity to practice and study, and to take "mendrub" (blessing pills) every morning with water on an empty stomach.[97] Public announcements in April turned the attention towards the material relief of local daily workers and their families in dire straits channeled through Rangjung Yeshe Shenpen, Rinpoche's social work organization[98]. In the same month, a collection of teachings was made available online, discounts were offered on the Tara's Triple Excellence Online Meditation Program, and the whole teaching activities of the Institute were also moved online.[99]

Chokyi Nyima's longest and most detailed statement on the pandemic was an online teaching given at the end of June entitled "Kindness is the Best Medicine during Mental and Physical Distress." Rinpoche pondered upon the notion that no matter the level at stake (individual, familiar, social, and so on), problems always arise as a consequence of not following "Natural Law", that is, the 5 Buddhist precepts (no killing, no stealing, no sexual misconduct, no lying, no consumption of intoxicants). In all circumstances, the cultivation of sīla (moral conduct), samādhi (meditaion), prajñā (wisdom), and particularly karuṇā (compassion), are the solution for a life free of suffering. Besides these basic Buddhist tenets, Rinpoche

---

96 Cf. its webpage: Rangjung Yeshe Institute, see: https://www.ryi.org/

97 He particularly recommended reading Buddhist hagiographies and accumulating the mantra of Bhagavatī Parṇaśavari, "who is associated with healing and the curing of contagious disease". Facebook post by Chokyi Nyima Rinpoche, published on March 15, 2020, https://www.facebook.com/Chokyi.Nyima.Rinpoche/; also "Dharma Teaching and Some Short Advice", video posted on March 22, 2020, Ib.

98 E.g., Rinpoche's Facebook page announced the delivery of relief hampers with essential items (April 1st), and expressed gratitude towards those who had contributed to the social project with their donations and volunteering work (April 13th). Ib. Managed by Rangjung Yeshe Shenpen's director Mélanie Létourneau, the campaign can be accessed at "Food relief for poor families in CoVid-19 Lockdown-Nepal", see: http://www.shenpennepal.org/program/covid-relief/

99 Facebook posts dating from April 11 and April 15, 2020. See: https://www.facebook.com/Chokyi.Nyima.Rinpoche/. The compilation of dharma talks may be found at "Shedrub Mandala Online Dharma Resources", April 14th 2020, see: https://shedrub.org/news/onlineresources/?fbclid=IwAR0l4y1TYkdClrJ3pfvPwnOOeFvjuDt5lXhwobmhLypx6AGleS54-XNXunA. Tara's Triple Excellence Online Meditation Program may be accessed at https://dharmasun.org/tte/. Rangjung Yeshe Institute also offered a series of recommendations to deall with "the challenges of online learning", "emotional challenges of the Covid-19 crisis and "a sense of loss during the Covid-19 outbreak", available at "Support during the Covid-19 Crisis", Rangjung Yeshe Institute, see: https://www.ryi.org/support-during-the-covid-19-crisis.

insisted on the importance of respecting other religions while claiming, similarly to Mingyur Rinpoche, that Buddhism would be the religion that matches Science best.[100]

3.4 Sakya

The fourth major Tibetan Buddhist school is called Sakya, meaning "pale earth," a reference to the landscape of its founding monastery near Shigatse. The throne holder of the school, known as Sakya Trizin, is a position hereditarily passed down through male members of the Khön family, which had a leading political role during medieval Mongol rule over Tibet.

The current Sakya Trizin, Ratna Vajra Rinpoche, is the 42nd in the succession lineage and assumed the position in 2017 from his retiring father, Ngawang Kunga Tegchen, under a new appointment system. The 41st Sakya Trizin established relevant monastic and learning centers in Nepal and India, like the Dzongsar Institute, the Sakya College, and the Sakya Institute, and still remains active as a religious public figure. The international net of Sakya centers around the world is particularly strong in English-speaking countries, namely, the USA, where the Sakya Trizins possess a Seat near New York.[101]

On March 12, the Sakya Trizin emeritus gave an oral online transmission of "The Prayer Which Saved Sakya from the Epidemic," recommended by teachers from other schools cited above.[102] The first major pronouncement of the Sakya Trizin took place in an interview for Tibet TV on April 7, in which he stressed the "global effort" required by the crisis, the need to follow medical guidelines, tame our afflictive emotions, and pray for the recovery of all patients.[103] The following day, a donation to the Chief Minister of Uttarakhand was announced.[104]

---

100   Cf. Shedrub (2020). 'Kindness is the best Medicine during mental and physical distress'. June 30 See: https://shedrub.org/news/onlineresources/?fbclid=IwAROl4y1TYkdClrJ3pfvPwnOOeFvj uDt5lXhwobmhLypx6AGleS 54-XNXunA

101   For a whole list of Sakya centers, see: "Sakya Worldwide" at: http://www.sakyaling.de/sakya-asia/.

102   Cf. Sakya Dolma Phodrang's Facebook post, dating form March 15, 2020. See: https://www.facebook.com/pg/sakya.dolmaphodrang/posts/

103   The interview may be accessed at the YouTube page of TibetTV under the title "His Eminence 42nd Sakya Trizin Ratna Vajra Rinpoche on COVID-19". April 7, 2020. See: https://www.youtube.com/watch?v=KuLWyPFWKlQ. A summary may be found at the website of the Central Tibetan Administration under the heading "Sakya Trizin Rinpoche espouses oneness of humanity on the time of Coronavirus pandemic". April 9, 2020. See: https://tibet.net/sakya-trizin-rinpoche-espouses-oneness-of-humanity-in-the-time-of-coronavirus-pandemic/

104   See the Sakya Dolma Phodrang's official Facebook publication from April 8, 2020: https://www.facebook.com/pg/sakya.dolmaphodrang/posts/

In May a special issue of the Sakya periodical publication called *Melody of Dharma* was dedicated to the pandemic-driven lockdown, containing advice from the main teachers of the school and a collection of mantras and practices. The editorial dwelled on the notion of the pandemic context as a "precious opportunity" to both cultivate ourselves and discover new ways to communicate with each other and practice solidarity[105]. In his article, the Sakya Trizin emeritus encouraged people not to panic, to find refuge in the Triple Gem, and to follow medical instructions since, he elaborated:

> "Will prayers, visualizations and mantra recitations be sufficient to carry us through? These, of course, are of huge benefit, but it is also of major importance that we strictly observe the recommended rules of personal hygiene and social distancing. (...) We should pray to these deities, chant their mantras and recite their prayers. I believe that by doing so, we will successfully be saved from this pandemic, and find happiness.[106]"

The current Sakya Trizin, who referred to the Buddhadharma as a medicine for negative thoughts, argued that

> "All these problems are caused by our own karma, and we should respond to them by taking good care of our own health, by cultivating positive thoughts, and by pacifying this virus by reciting prayers and mantras. (...) As the great bodhisattva Shantideva said in his Bodhicharyavatara, we should practice equality, which means that we are all the same and we should care for each other (...); we should extend our focus and pray "May all beings be free from suffering.[107]"

His brother Khöndung Gyana Vajra Sakya Rinpoche was blunter in categorically refuting the idea that

> "just chanting the mantras, we will be cured, or that we can do whatever we want. Thinking that we can just chant the mantra and everything will be fine, is a wrong view. And there are unfortunately some people who hold this view, that if we pray

---

105   "From the Editors", in Melody of Dharma. A Publication of the Office of Sakya Dolma Phodrang Dedicated to the Dharma Activities of His Holiness Sakya Gongma Trichen Rinpoche And His Noble Family. N. 19. Special Lockdown Issue, May 2020; downloadable from: http://hhsakya-trizin.net/wp-content/uploads/2020/05/Mod-19.pdf

106   Gongma Trichen Rinpoche (2020). Bringing Obstacles Into the Path. In *Melody of Dharma*. A Publication of the Office of Sakya Dolma Phodrang Dedicated to the Dharma Activities of His Holiness Sakya Gongma Trichen Rinpoche And His Noble Family. N. 19. Special Lockdown Issue, p. 6.

107   Cf. Sakya Trizin (2020). Courage in the Face of Illness. In *Melody of Dharma*. A Publication of the Office of Sakya Dolma Phodrang Dedicated to the Dharma Activities of His Holiness Sakya Gongma Trichen Rinpoche And His Noble Family. N. 19. Special Lockdown Issue, p. 7-8.

and recite mantras, we will be safe from the virus. (...) We have to start by taking care of ourselves, taking all the precautions necessary to keep safe. Only then will prayers be effective, helping us emotionally and keeping us strong with their blessing[108]".

This value of prayers as an emotional aid or confidence boost did not entail a mistrust in the illness-dispelling efficacy of rituals, since invocations of the Goodness Parnashavari were performed by Sakya teachers from February through April and an online Parnashavari empowerment was bestowed online by Gongma Trichen Rinpoche on April 17th, relying on its "extremely powerful" capacity of "vanquishing of contagious illnesses"[109].

3.5 Bon and Rime

Besides the 4 major schools covered so far, the Buddhist Tibetan world broadly speaking also comprises the followers of the indigenous religion of Tibet, known as Bon, that developed in a reciprocal influence with Buddhism and was recognized as the 5th school by the Dalai Lama and the Tibetan Government in exile in 1988; as well as teachers embracing a non-sectarian or ecumenical approach, known as Rime (W. *ris med*).

The Head of the Bon school, Lungtok Dawa Dargyal, the 34th Menri Trizin Rinpoche, released a succinct message on his website asking his followers no to panic, take precautions and follow the guidelines of the World Health Organization. He also informed that his sangha was praying to the protectors for a swift eradication of the disease[110]. His Monastery in Dolanji made donations to the PM Cares Fund and Himachal Pradesh COVID-19 Response Fund.[111]

The most interesting initiative from the Bon side, however, was the organization of a Cybersangha event hosted by Geshe Tenzin Wangyal Rinpoche reuniting

---

108 Cf. Khöndung Gyana Vajra Sakya Rinpoche (2020). Keeping A Positive Mind In the Midst Of Suffering. In: Melody of Dharma. A Publication of the Office of Sakya Dolma Phodrang Dedicated to the Dharma Activities of His Holiness Sakya Gongma Trichen Rinpoche And His Noble Family. N. 19. Special Lockdown Issue, p. 11.

109 Cf. Office of Sakya Dolma Phodrang (2020). 'Dharma Practices to Counter the Ongoing Pandemic. The Practice of Parnashavari'. In *Melody of Dharma*. A Publication of the Office of Sakya Dolma Phodrang Dedicated to the Dharma Activities of His Holiness Sakya Gongma Trichen Rinpoche And His Noble Family. N. 19. Special Lockdown Issue. May, pp. 19-20.

110 Cf. Lungtokling (2020). 'Covid-19: Message from His Holiness Lungtok Dawa Dargyal, Menri Trizin 34 Rinpoche'. Blog. March. See: https://www.lungtokling.org/index.php/en/blog/159-co vid-19-message-from-his-holiness-lungtok-dawa-dargyal-menri-trizin-34th-rinpoche

111 See the post of April 6, 2020, on the Facebook page of the Yungdrung Bon Monastic Centre Society: https://www.facebook.com/ybmc.society/posts/on-this-day-of-6th-april-2020-his-hol iness-the-34th-menri-trizin-rinpoche-and-me/3411898062171675/

teachers from six different spiritual traditions of Tibet. This ecumenical encounter took place on June 7 2020 via Zoom and was later uploaded to several digital platforms. In his presentation, the host alluded to the will to follow the Dalai Lama's advice to adopt a non-sectarian (Rime) attitude and open a dialogue with other traditions, particularly in a context of growing racism and discrimination.[112] Pönlop Trinley Nyima Rinpoche (Bon) referred to the Tibetan exile as both an opportunity and obligation as religious leaders to spread the Dharma around the world: "if we pray together"—he claimed—"it will transform into something tangible and influence the community". All teachers started by praising the ecumenical initiative and reciting a prayer from their own traditions, after which they gave a teaching concerning the pandemic. Yongey Mingyur Rinpoche (Kagyu), the first to intervene, delivered a teaching on the Bardo (transitional state) of dying and death and the possibility to choose to be reborn in the Pure Land. Sogan Rinpoche (Nyingma) also addressed the topic of the Bardo and thanked technological progress and globalization for allowing the preservation of Buddhist teachings. Khenpo Gyurmey Dorjee (Sakya) labelled the pandemic as a completely new phenomenon caused by human misconduct, not by nature's dynamics, and referred to internal transformation as the only way out since politicians' approaches never succeed. Gyaltsab Rinpoche Choekyi Nangpa (Jonang) recommended approaching the crisis from the perspective of the 4 noble truths, in order to understand our suffering and be able to do something about it. Finally, Yangten Rinpoche (Gelug) sustained that the pandemic was created by an imbalance of the 4 elements and recommended as a solution the practice of the Medicine Buddha sadhana, which are not only words but have a transforming power.[113]

Possessing a wide non-sectarian education, SOAS alumnus, film-maker, prolific author, and sponsor of the most ambitious translation project of Tibetan canonical texts, Dzongsar Khyentse Rinpoche is one of the most interesting and controversial lamas today. Openly expressing political views and frequently resorting to humor and irony, his Facebook page is anything but dull. For example, in late February he posted a video showing how he was celebrating Losar (the Tibetan New Year) by drinking cow urine he had ordered from Amazon to tease PM Modi and Hindu leaders' claims that it served as a cure for the coronavirus. The same tenor was used a couple of months later in a letter to the famous environmental activist Greta Thunberg where, after stating that the virus was "doing the job

---

112   The broadcast in Tibetan (144 minutes long) may be accessed at the CyberSangha website under the title "Teachings & Prayers for the Pandemic from Six Spiritual Traditions of Tibet". See: https://cybersangha.net/prayer-for-pandemic/?fbclid=IwAR1Uer-PGffNFyVMj1XU yDyhsGbEkcjR2VR7p9h1 C4G HEYAE1f1sp6ujsMg. An English audio translation is available at: https://mixlr.com/ligmincha-in-english/showreel/teachings-prayers-for-the-pandemic

113   Ib.

for (her)", since it would sooner or later be over, it would be a great idea to ask everyone to stop drinking Coca Cola every Friday.[114]

Politically, he openly condemned Western countries for their sanctions on Iran in the very fragile context of the pandemic and referred to the US as "lower than a beast"; moreover, he was probably the only Tibetan teacher to publicly criticize governmental measures: upon the announcement of the lockdown in India by Mid-March, he reacted with an "apology accepted" post, asking the government to feed the poor and provide a better internet connection.[115]

Not all of Rinpoche's reactions had this playful character. He also asked his sangha to pray "to pacify physical and mental pain" caused by the virus and thanked those who participated in the project to illuminate the Mahabodhi Temple in Bodhgaya "in this bleak time"[116]. Support to his followers was also shown in the creation of a Spotify playlist to deal with isolation[117]. At the same time, in an interview with Bhutanese Kuensel, Dzongsar Khyentse confessed that, though as a Buddhist practitioner and teacher he had fairly studied and written on impermanence, "when the Covid-19 hit, I saw those teachings hadn't really entered my heart, and that I'd been teaching them without totally believing them".[118] He also admitted living with the "anxiety of the unknown," to deal with which he resorted to his Buddhist practice. From a socio-political angle, he observed how countries quickly resorted to blaming each other, instead of cooperating, and that the statistics show how the lowering of contamination levels in India due to the lockdown "will save far more lives than those lost to Covid-19"[119].

Finally, from a more philosophical perspective, he offered an interesting interpretation of the abovementioned "mamos" in relation to the pandemic. He argued that it is due to our lack of understanding of emptiness and non-duality that all problems arise. This lack of understanding leads to extremist views and to a disrespect of the 5 elements (which are no other than the 5 Dakinis), for example, by

---

114   Posts on the official Facebook wall of Dzongsar Jamyang Khyentse (February 24, April 29). See: https://www.facebook.com/djkhyentse/

115   Posts on the official Facebook wall of Dzongsar Jamyang Khyentse (March 14, March 15, March 21, April 2). See: https://www.facebook.com/djkhyentse/

116   See the announcement on the website of the Dzongsar Khyentse Chokyi Lodro Institute, February 5. 2020. See: http://dzongsarinstitute.org.in/en/2020/02/05/announcement/. Cf. "Illuminating the World", post at Siddhartha's Intent website, April 11, 2020. See: https://www.siddharthasintent.org/about-us-2/news/2020/illuminating-the-world/

117   The list, which includes artists like Sam Cooke and Nina Simone, is entitled "Dzongsar Jamyang Khyentse Rinpoche playlist for lockdown during Covid-19 pandemic", and is available at: https://open.spotify.com/playlist/4vLPkOuyfSBUfgQWuFVwu1?si=vr9hIaN3-QmuXiW S4_1ifow

118   Cf. Kuensel (2020). 'Things aren't looking good. But there's a lot we can do'. April 29. See: https://kuenselonline.com/things-arent-looking-good-but-theres-a-lot-we-can-do/

119   Cf. Kuensel (2020).

means of excessive greed, and that is what is meant by the "wrath of the mamo": "in Buddhism, we don't generally believe in some sort of evil spirit there that's harming the world". He thus advised Buddhist practitioners to be friends with the 5 elements, rely upon the 3 Jewels, and, if having the proper transmission, practice "Appeasing the Mamos," without failing to comply with all scientifically-grounded guidelines.[120]

4.   Conclusions: External Compliance and Internal Non-Excluding Narratives

The data collected in this study show, first of all, a general compliance with the discourse and policies of political institutions before the pandemic, namely preventive measures of social distancing and isolation as established by healthcare bodies and recommended by the scientific community. In contrast, for example, with certain North American evangelical groups, there has been no questioning of the nature and dangers of the virus or of the enforced measures.[121] Tibetan religious leaders' first typical reaction, having their main monasteries in India, has been of endorsement of the state and federal authorities, to which they offered donations (direct material involvement in social action has been less common), support and praise of healthcare workers, and a general request of obedience of official guidelines. In this regard, it is important to consider that Tibetan lamas often made their first public statements at the request of the Tibetan Government in Exile, as explained by the 42nd Sakya Trizin.[122] At the same time, they have emphasized a need of unity, dwelling on the idea of all humankind facing a global threat, and made a call for interreligious and interracial harmony. Consequently, there has not been, at least in the public discourse of the leaders of each and every school, any sectarian or radical attitudes putting the blame of the pandemic on certain religious groups or ethnicities. This contrasts, for example, with the anti-Muslim rhetoric

---

120   Cf. Siddhartha's Intent YouTube Channel (2020). 'Understanding non-duality: advice from Rinpoche for today and beyond'. March 17. See: https://www.you-tube. com/watch?v=RbUp7iGrKqQ&feature=youtu.be&fbclid=IwAR1g46NszzZHBL_p4G-UQjVdGWv9015IPUAb6FFKTXowolEebRq09cs Cx0q8

121   Cf., e.g., Peter McLaren (2020). Religious Nationalism and the Coronavirus Pandemic: Soul-Sucking Evangelicals and Branch Covidians Make America Sick Again. *Postdigital Science and Education*, 1-22.

122   Cf. Sakya Trizin (2020). Courage in the Face of Illness. In *Melody of Dharma*. A Publication of the Office of Sakya Dolma Phodrang Dedicated to the Dharma Activities of His Holiness Sakya Gongma Trichen Rinpoche And His Noble Family. N. 19. Special Lockdown Issue, p. 6. The Government in Exile also encourage their functionaries and Tibetans around the world to contribute to Coronavirus relief funds, see: https://tibet.net/kashag-appeals-cta-functionaries-and-tibetan-worldwide-to-contribute-to-coronavirus-relief-funds/

found in Indian officials or the globally spread anti-Asian racism and xenophobia denounced by the United Nations.[123]

Internally, the discourse developed by Tibetan teachers may be addressed by the alternatives presented and "allowed" by their scriptures, interpretations, and philosophies. And so, regarding the *context* of the pandemic, it may be interpreted as yet another regular manifestation of our impermanent and suffering-marked reality, or as an exceptional scenario, a never-seen-before threat that stands as a clear sign of humanity living in degenerate times. The question of the *causes*, even if ultimately a non-fortuitous problem of human agency, may be tackled from a merely material biological perspective, or acquire clear moral connotations (not following the 10 virtuous actions or the 5 precepts), a philosophical-spiritual dimension (ignorance of the ultimate nature of reality), or an esoteric approach (the wrath of spirit-deities). As a result, *solutions or responses* also vary, including health-care precautions, ethical behavior, calm-abiding meditation, or prayers and rituals.

This plurality is not internally considered as creating tensions or demanding exclusivism. This may be understandable, at least, because of the compatibility of the elements (mishandling of animals is both a biological and a moral issue) or because they simply operate at different levels. Also, depending on the perspective, seemingly excluding characteristics are deemed compatible: the context of the pandemic is both regular and exceptional depending on the point of view. This does not, of course, entail that an external questioning of the employed elements and their correlations may not be undertaken (one may deny the capacity of pujas to tame the pandemic or argue that animal cruelty cannot per se explain a disease), but that is not our concern here. In this study, we have observed how different teachers choose to privilege certain elements in their rhetoric, but they take good care not to explicitly exclude or condemn others. This is especially revealing in the complex matter of esotericism and the value of rituals and prayers, which touches upon deep philosophical and ontological problems within Buddhism. On the one hand, there is this idea that practice helps us be calm and focused, and also gives us courage, but that prayer is no counterfeit to the virus and the "mamos" are but a metaphor for our relationship with nature; on the other hand, there is this call for rituals, for specific prayers that can tame the virus and appease real evil forces unleashed by humans. The fact that both takes can be found in the very same discourse one after the other is telling of the complex situation of a tradition catering

---

123   Cf. New York Times (2020). Indian officials are blaming an Islamic group for spreading the virus, and Muslims have been targeted in a wave of violence. India, Coronavirus Fans Religious Hatred. April 12. See: https://www.nytimes.com/2020/04/12/world/asia/india-coronavirus-m uslims-bigotry.html; Cf. Human Rights Watch (2020). 'Covid-19 Fueling Anti-Asian Racism and Xenophobia Worldwide'. May 12. See: https://www.hrw.org/news/2020/05/12/covid-19-fueling-anti-asian-racism-and-xenophobia-worldwide

for both a native and an international audience in a context where Science arguably tends to hold, so far, the epistemological monopoly.

This intricacy may also be observed in the controversy surrounding the online conferral of empowerments, significantly raised by drawing from accusations of "degeneration". There seems to be room for such an intellectual questioning or discussion within an esoteric tradition based upon master-disciple connections, while canonical sources could potentially allow a millennialist reading of the situation. The explanation of the lack of a backed-up fundamentalist reaction obviously involves multiple and complex reasons, but I would argue that at least two elements bear decisive importance. Firstly, as Keyes pointed out for the case of Buddhist Thailand, "millennial movements are caused primarily by a crisis centering around political power,"[124] which is absent: the Tibetan Government in exile and the Tibetan religious elite promptly reacted in defense of a socio-politically charismatic figure which symbolizes unity. Secondly, as explained above, technology and mass media have been a key feature in the preservation and spread of Buddhism around the world. As the Dalai Lama cared to point out, "going online" was not an exceptional measure for an exceptional time, but an already implemented and widely used resource. What is more, the virus is depicted as a "blessing in disguise" allowing more people than ever to access teachings and practice Dharma thanks to the combination of general Internet usage and confinement.

In conclusion, it may be argued that a religion that fosters introspection and meditative practices in solitude, that encourages a serene acceptance of adversity, and that has been globally consolidated thanks to the Internet and new technologies, may be particularly suited to deal with a pandemic scenario basically calling for people to stay at home, be calm, and wait until everything is over.

Bibliography

Álvarez Ortega, Miguel (2018). Traditional Tibetan Buddhist Scholars on Dharma, Law, Politics, and Social Ethics: Philosophical Discussions in Boudhanath (Nepal). *Buddhism, Law, and Society* 4, pp. 1-52.

Anālayo, Bhikkhu (2017). The Healing Potential of Awakening Factors in Early Buddhist Discourse. In C. Pierce Salguero (Ed.). *Buddhism and Medicine. An Anthology of Premodern Sources*. New York, pp. 12-18.

Bechert, Heinz (2004). Buddha, Life of the. In Robert E. Buswell (Ed.). *Encyclopedia of Buddhism. Vol. I.* New York, pp. 82-88.

Bradley, Tamdin S. (2013). *Principles of Tibetan Medicine*. London.

Chen, Thomas S. N., and Chen, Peter S. Y. (2002). Jivaka, physician to the Buddha. *Journal of Medical Biography* 10, pp. 88-91.

---

124   Cf. Keyes, 1977, p. 284.

Clark, Barry (1995). *The Quintessence Tantras of Tibetan Medicine*. Boston.

Cowell, Edward B. (Ed.). (2003). *The Buddha-carita of Aśvaghoṣa*. Delhi.

Cucinotta, Domenico, and Vanelli, Maurizio (2020). WHO Declares COVID-19 a Pandemic. *Acta Bio Medica* 91, Nº 1, pp. 157-60.

Dash, Bhagwan (1976). Indian Contribution to Tibetan Medicine. In Dawa Norbu (Ed.). *An Introduction to Tibetan Medicine*. Delhi, pp. 12-24.

Demiéville, Paul (1985). *Buddhism and Healing. Demiéville's Article "Byō" from Hōbōgirin*. Boston.

Fiordalis, David (2017). Medical Practice as Wrong Livelihood: Selections from the Pāli Discourses, Vinaya, and Commentaries. In C. Pierce Salguero (Ed.). *Buddhism and Medicine. An Anthology of Premodern Sources*. New York, pp. 105-112.

Fiordalis, David (2014). On Buddhism, Divination and the Worldly Arts: Textual Evidence from the Theravāda Tradition. *Indian International Journal of Buddhist Studies* 15, pp. 79-108.

Flaherty, Robert Pearson (2011). Korean Millennial Movements. In Chaterine Wessinger (Ed.). *The Oxford Handbook of Millennialism*. Oxford, pp. 326-347.

Garrett, Frances M. (2006). Buddhism and the Historicizing of Medicine in Thirteenth Century Tibet. *Asian Medicine. Journal of the International Association for the Study of Traditional Asian Medicine* 2, no. 2, pp. 202-224.

Garrett, Frances M. (2015). *Religion, Medicine and the Human Embryo in Tibet*. London.

Gerke, Barbara (2013). On the 'Subtle Body' and 'Circulation' in Tibetan Medicine. In Geoffrey Samuel and Jay Johnston (Eds.). *Religion and the Subtle Body in Asia and the West*. New York, pp. 83-99.

Gongma Trichen Rinpoche (2020). Bringing Obstacles Into the Path. In *Melody of Dharma*. A Publication of the Office of Sakya Dolma Phodrang Dedicated to the Dharma Activities of His Holiness Sakya Gongma Trichen Rinpoche And His Noble Family. N. 19. Special Lockdown Issue. pp. 5-6.

Granoff, Phyllis (1998). Cures and Karma II. Some Miraculous Healings in the Indian Buddhist Story Tradition. *Bulletin de l'École française d'Extrême-Orient* 85, 288-289.

Gyasto, Janet (1993). The Logic of Legitimation in the Tibetan Treasure Tradition. *History of Religions* 33, Nº2, pp. 97-134.

Gyatso, Janet (2017). *Being human in a Buddhist world: An intellectual history of medicine in early modern Tibet*. New York.

Ho Tai, Hue-Tam (1988). Perfect World and Perfect Time: Maitreya in Vietnam. In Alan Sponberg and Helen Hardacre (Eds.). *Maitreya, the Future Buddha*. Cambridge, pp. 154-170.

Hopkins, Jeffery (1998). *Nāgārjuna's Precious Garland. Buddhist Advice for Liberation explanation*. New York.

Janes, Craig R. (2002). Buddhism, science, and market: The globalisation of Tibetan medicine. *Anthropology & Medicine*, 9:3, pp. 267-289.

Jones, Thomas Dhivan (2017). Illness, Cure and Care: Selections from the Pāli Canon. In C. Pierce Salguero (Ed.). *Buddhism and Medicine. An Anthology of Premodern Sources*. New York, pp. 3-10.

Karmapa (Ed.) (2020). *Prayers for a Time of Pandemic. Compiled and Introduced by the Seventeenth Gyalwang Karmapa Ogyen Trinley Dorje*. Dharma Ebooks.

Keyes, Charles F. (1977). Millenialism, Theravada Buddhism and Thai Society. *The Journal of Asian Studies* 36, N° 2, pp. 283-302.

Khöndung Gyana Vajra Sakya Rinpoche (2020). Keeping A Positive Mind In the Midst Of Suffering. In *Melody of Dharma*. A Publication of the Office of Sakya Dolma Phodrang Dedicated to the Dharma Activities of His Holiness Sakya Gongma Trichen Rinpoche And His Noble Family. N. 19. Special Lockdown Issue, pp. 10-11.

Kletter, Christa / Kriechbaum, Monika (Ed.) (2001). *Tibetan Medicinal Plants*. Stuttgart.

Lamotte, Étienne (1988). *History of Indian Buddhism from the Origins to the Śaka Era*. Louvain-la-Neuve.

Lokananda C. Bhikkhu (2018). *Abhidharmakośa of Ācārya Vasubandhu*. English trad. of La Vallé Poussin by Leo M. Pruden. Delhi.

Lopez, Donald S. (2010). *Buddhism & science: a guide for the perplexed*. Chicago.

Lopez, Donald S. (1999). *Prisoners of Shangri-La: Tibetan Buddhism and the West*. Chicago.

Lopez, Donald S. (2012). *Scientific Buddha – His Short and Happy Life*. New Haven.

McLaren, Peter (2020). Religious Nationalism and the Coronavirus Pandemic: Soul-Sucking Evangelicals and Branch Covidians Make America Sick Again. *Postdigital Science and Education*, pp. 1-22.

Ñanamoli Thera (Tr.) (2010). *Dhammacakkappavattana Sutta: Setting Rolling the Wheel of Truth (SN 56.11)*. Access to Insight (BCBS Edition). June 13. URL: https://www.accesstoinsight.org/tipitaka/sn/sn56/sn56.011.nymo.html

Naquin, Susan (1976). *Millenarian rebellion in China: The Eight Trigrams uprising of 1813*. New Haven.

Nattier, Jan (1991). *Once Upon a Future Time: Studies in a Buddhist Prophecy of Decline*. Berkeley.

Nattier, Jan (1988). The Meanings of the Maitreya Myth. In Alan Sponberg and Helen Hardacre (Eds.). *Maitreya, the Future Buddha*. Cambridge, pp. 23-47.

Norbu, Dawa (1988). *Tibet: The Road Ahead*. London.

Overmyer, Daniel (1976). *Folk Buddhist religion: Dissenting sects in late traditional China*. Cambridge.

Pierce Salguero, C. (2018). Buddhist Medicine and its circulation. In David Ludden (Ed.). *Oxford Research Encyclopedia, Asian History*. New York, pp. 1-28.

Pordié, Laurent (Ed.) (2008). *Tibetan Medicine in the Contemporary World: Global Politics of Medical Knowledge and Practice*. London.

Powers, John (2007). *Introduction to Tibetan Buddhism*. Ithaca.

Price Grieve, Gregory, and Veidlinger, Daniel (Eds.) (2017). *Buddhism, the Internet, and Digital Media. The Pixel in the Lotus*. New York Routlege.

Queen, Christopher S., and King Sallie B. (Eds.) (1996). *Engaged Buddhism: Buddhist Liberation Movements in Asia*. New York.

Sakya Trizin (2020). Courage in the Face of Illness. In *Melody of Dharma. A Publication of the Office of Sakya Dolma Phodrang Dedicated to the Dharma Activities of His Holiness Sakya Gongma Trichen Rinpoche And His Noble Family*. N. 19. Special Lockdown Issue, pp. 7-9.

Samuel, Geoffrey (2017). Tibetan Religion as a World Religion: Global Networking and its Consequences. In *Tantric Revisionings: New Understandings of Tibetan Buddhism and Indian Religion*. New York, pp. 288-316.

Sarkisyanz, Manuel (1965). *Buddhist backgrounds of the Burmese revolution*. The Hague.

Sik, Hin-tak (2016). *Ancient Indian medicine in early Buddhist literature: a study based on the Bhesajjakkhandhaka and the parallels in other Vinaya Canons*. (Thesis). University of Hong Kong, Pokfulam, Hong Kong SAR. URL: http://dx.doi.org/10.5353/th_b5760924.

Silk, Jonathan et al. (2019). Maitreya. In Jonathan Silk et al. (Eds.). *Brill's Encyclopedia of Buddhism. Vol. II: Lives*. Leiden, pp. 302-324.

Singh, Upinder (2012). Governing the State and the Self: Political Philosophy and Practice in the Edicts of Aśoka. *South Asian Studies*, 28, N ° 2, pp. 131-145.

Thanissaro Bhikkhu (2013). *Beyond Coping: The Buddha's Teachings on Aging, Illness, Death, and Separation. Access to Insight (BCBS Edition)*. November 30. URL: http://www.accesstoinsight.org/lib/study/beyondcoping/index.html

Thanissaro Bhikkhu. Sivaka Sutta (2013). *To Sivaka (SN 36.21). Access to Insight (BCBS Edition)*. November 30. URL: http://www.accesstoinsight.org/tipitaka/sn/sn36/sn36.021.than.html

Turenne, Philippe (2015). The History and Significance of the Tibetan Concept of the Five Treatises of Maitreya. *The Indian International Journal of Buddhist Studies* 16, pp. 215-233.

Weber, Max (1985). *The Religion of India: The Sociology of Hinduism and Buddhism*. Glencoe.

Wellington Chappell, D. (1980). Early Forebodings of the Death of Buddhism. *Numen* 27, N° 1, pp. 122-154.

Zürcher, Erik (1982). "Prince Moonlight". Messianism and Eschatology in Early Medieval Chinese Buddhism. *T'oung Pao* 68, 1/3, pp. 1-75.

Zysk, Kenneth G. (1982). Studies in Traditional Indian Medicine in the Pāli Canon: Jīvaka and Āyurveda. *Journal of the International Association of Buddhist Studies*, 5, pp. 7–86.

Zysk, Kenneth G. (2010). *Asceticism and Healing in Ancient India: Medicine in the Buddhist Monastery*. Delhi.

Online Open Sources

Facebook Pages

Chokyi Nyima Rinpoche: https://www.facebook.com/Chokyi.Nyima.Rinpoche/
Dorje Drak Monastery: https://www.facebook.com/dorjedrag/
Dzogchen Buddhism: https://www.facebook.com/DzogchenBuddhism/
Dzongsar Jamyang Khyentse: https://www.facebook.com/djkhyentse/
Karmapa: https://www.facebook.com/karmapa/
Mingyur Rinpoche: https://www.facebook.com/mingyur.rinpoche/
Sakya Dolma Phodrang: https://www.facebook.com/pg/sakya.dolmaphodrang/posts/
Shechen Croatia, Buddhist Society: https://www.facebook.com/watch/shechen.cro/
Yungdrung Bon Monastic Centre Society: https://www.facebook.com/ybmc.society/

Official Websites

Cyber Sangha: https://cybersangha.net
Dzongsar Institute: http://dzongsarinstitute.org.
Federation for the Preservation of Mahayana Buddhism: https://fpmt.org/fpmt/
Geshe Tashi: https://geshetashi.org/
Gyalwa Dzogchenpa. Sangha: http://www.dzogchen.org.in/sangha
His Holiness the 14th Dalai Lama of Tibet: https://www.dalailama.com
Jewel Heart: https://www.jewelheart.org/
Khandro Rinpoche: https://www.khandrorinpoche.org/
Lotsawa House: https://lotsawahouse.blog/
Lungtokling's Blog: https://www.lungtokling.org
Mind & Life Institute: https://www.mindandlife.org/
Nyignma Kathok Buddhist Centre: https://kathok.org.sg/
Palyul Ling International: https://palyul.org
Rangjung Yeshe Institute: https://www.ryi.org/
Rigpa: https://www.rigpa.org
Sakya Ling: http://www.sakyaling.de/sakya-asia/
Shedrub. The Online Home of Chokyi Nyima Rinpoche: https://shedrub.org/
Shenpen Nepal: http://www.shenpennepal.org/
Siddhartha's Intent: https://www.siddharthasintent.org
Tergar Meditation Community: https://tergar.org/
Thabye Dorje. His Holiness the 17th Gyalwa Karmapa: https://www.karmapa.org
The Karmapa: https://kagyuoffice.org
Tibet Center Austria: https://www.tibetcenter.at/en/coronavirus-en/

Online News

ABC News Prime (2020). 'Dalai Lama speaks out on COVID-19'. May 28. URL: http s://www.youtube.com/watch?v=NEWqRcy-6Wg&t=1s

BBC News (2020). 'Dalai Lama: Seven billion people 'need a sense of oneness'. June 13. URL: https://www.bbc.com/news/stories-53028343?fbclid-=IwAR3PN2 xFOND nm7jK_ SR2G4z0kQ3gQwKUPPW7KTgcSGbDjDD6-ot0Y6kcAkus

CNBC (2020). 'The call to unite organizer explains idea behind 24-hour livestream'. May 1. URL: https://www.cnbc.com/2020/05/01/the-call-to-unite-organizer-ex plains-idea-behind-24-hour-livestream.html

Dharpo, Tenzin, and CNN's Sugam Pokharel (2020). 'Dalai Lama cancels all public engagements due to the coronavirus'. February 12. URL: https:// edition.cnn.com/asia/live-news/coronavirus-outbreak-02-12-20-intl-hnk/h_ 44c26bc4035ba6d1e0286237b5a19558

Human Rights Watch (2020). 'Covid-19 Fueling Anti-Asian Racism and Xenophobia Worldwide'. May 12. URL: https://www.hrw.org/news/2020/05/12/covid-19-fue ling-anti-asian-racism-and-xenophobia-worldwide

Kuensel (2020). 'Things aren't looking good. But there's a lot we can do'. April 29. URL: https://kuenselonline.com/things-arent-looking-good-but-theres-a-l ot-we-can-do/

NDTV (2020). 'COVID-19: Dalai Lama Donates To PM-CARES Fund, Extends Sup- port'. March 31. URL: https://www.ndtv.com/india-news/covid-19-dalai-lama- donates-to-pm-cares-fund-extends-support-2203873

New York Times (2020). 'India, Coronavirus Fans Religious Hatred'. April 12. URL: https://www.nytimes.com/2020/04/12/world/asia/india-coronavirus-mu slims-bigotry.html

Phayul (2020). 'Tulku Orgyen Tobgyal's remarks regrettable and wrong: Kashag'. May 27. URL: http://www.phayul.com/2020/05/27/43492/

Star of Mysore (2020). 'Penor Rinpoche Charity Foundation Donates Rs.10 Lakh Towards PM CARES Fund'. April 17. URL: https://starofmysore.com/penor-rin poche-charity-foundation-donates-rs-10-lakh-towards-pm-cares-fund/

Tibet Net (2020). 'Kashag appeals CTA functionaries and Tibetans world- wide to contribute to Coronavirus relief funds'. April 9. URL: https://ti bet.net/kashag-appeals-cta-functionaries-and-tibetan-worldwide-to- contribute-to-coronavirus-relief-funds/

Tibet Net (2020). 'Sakya Trizin Rinpoche espouses oneness of humanity on the time of Coronavirus pandemic'. April 9. URL: https://tibet.net/sakya- trizin-rinpoche-espouses-oneness-of-humanity-in-the-time-of-coronavirus- pandemic/

Tibetan Journal (2020). 'Kalon Karma Gelek Apologizes and Willing to Resign if Needed'. May 28. URL: https://www.tibetanjournal.com/kalon-karma-gelek-apologizes-and-willing-to-resign-if-needed/

Tibet Sun (2020). 'Tulku Orgyen Tobgyal apologises to Dalai Lama for criticising online teachings'. May 31. URL: https://www.tibetsun.com/news/2020/05/31/tulku-orgyen-tobgyal-apologises-to-dalai-lama-for-criticising-online-teachings.

Time Magazine (2020). 'Prayer is not Enough'. April 14. URL: https://time.com/5820613/dalai-lama-coronavirus-compassion/

The Tribune Voice of the People. (India) (2020). 'Dalai Lama donates to CM Relief Fund'. March 26. URL: https://www.tribuneindia.com/news/himachal/dalai-lama-donates-to-cm-relief-fund-61678

YouTube Videos

Asia Society YouTube channel (2020). 'Coping in the Time of Coronavirus'. April 8. URL: https://ww-w.youtube.com/watch?v=n_sc1SDwopg

Orgyan Tobgyal YouTube channel (2020). 'OT Rinpoche's advice in the time of COVID-19'. March 19. URL: https://www.youtube.com/watch?v=g4TX8-U7BGTw&t=194s

Ringpa (2020/1). 'Dedicating our Dharma Practice to the Coronavirus'. March 10. URL: https://www.rigpa.org/rigpa-news/2020/3/10/6civjuaj6w2pt4qtz0opl6rlne71ko

Ringpa (2020/2). 'Online Teachings with Jetsun Khando Rinpoche'. April 12. URL: https://www.rigpa.org/upcoming-events/2020/4/12/online-teachings-with-jetsun-khandro-rinpoche

Khandro Rinpoche (2020/1). 'The Gyalwang Karmapa's Advice Regarding Covid-19'. March 19. URL: https://www.facebook.com/karmapa/

Rinpoche, Khandro (2020/2). 'Practicing in Times of Adversity'. (Originally posted on November 21, 2018). March 24. URL: https://www.khandrorinpoche.org/practicing-in-times-of-adversity/

Rinpoche, Khandro (2020/3). 'Mindrolling Aids in Pandemic Relief Effort'. April 14. URL: https://www.khandrorinpoche.org/mindrolling-monastery-aids-in-pandemic-relief-effort/

Khandro Rinpoche (2020/4). 'Mindrol Lekshey Online: Curriculum Review and Teachings'. July 13. URL: https://www.khandrorinpoche.org/mindrol-lekshey-online-2020/

Rinpoche, Mindrolling Jetsün Khandro (2020). 'Advice for the COVID-19 situation'. *YouTube*. April 10. URL: https://www.youtube.com/watch?v=uWJWunQgtyc

Rinpoche, Yongey Mingyur (2020/1). 'Message on COVID-19 outbreak'. *YouTube* March 15. URL: https://www.youtube.com/watch?v=DgZETpd9h5s&feature =youtu.be&fbclid=IwAR3ALmqPj6EhU4q3kOZBTvTzdlflgOJ41IFFvd8jh66_S4pY 26GuM_IFA8

Rinpoche, Yongey Mingyur (2020/2). '10 Life Lessons We Can Learn from Coronavirus'. *YouTube.* May 25. URL: https://www.youtube.com/watch?v= i9M50dGK4PQ&feature=youtu.be&fbclid=IwAR11eRUs2X4dZCVb7eR9wZbNd u2K2OV-yAhX_DE3NT1T9prNurA43cJjFGI

Tibet TV (2020). 'His Eminence 42nd Sakya Trizin Ratna Vajra Rinpoche on COVID-19'. April 7. URL: https://www.youtube.com/watch?v=KuLWyPFWKlQ

Siddhartha's Intent YouTube Channel (2020). 'Understanding non-duality: advice from Rinpoche for today and beyond, 17 March 2020'. July 25. URL: https:// www.youtube.com/watch?v=RbUp7iGrKqQ&feature=youtu.be&fbclid=IwAR1 g46NszzZHBL_p4GUQjVdGWv9o15IPUAb6FFKTXowolEebRqo9csCxoq8

Dismantling Prejudices on Muslim Communities in Italy in Times of Pandemic: not just Religious Fundamentalism

Barbara Lucini

Abstract

This contribution aims to offer a reflection on the role that perceptions and cultural aspects of a crisis, such as that cause from the Covid-19 virus can generate in ethnic communities such as the Muslim one. Through a qualitative methodology of online research, the chapter explores the dynamics of perception and interpretation of the relationships between possible exploitation of the pandemic by Islamic extremism and the way in which the Muslim community in Italy is facing the crisis from Covid-19.

Keywords: Covid-19 crisis, Religious fundamentalism, Terrorism threat, Crisis Management

1. Introduction

The current pandemic caused by the Covid-19 virus has put in place important reflections on the latent and previous vulnerabilities and criticalities of the affected societies.

A pandemic as a global crisis highlights the many social, cultural and political characteristics of the management system that must deal with health security. Management systems in each country are affected by the organisational and cultural differences through which the pandemic has been addressed. In this context, Lakoff reminds us that:

> "The objective of global health security is to detect and contain the outbreak of a novel pathogen before it can spread to become a global catastrophe. But the various technical and administrative measures gathered together as part of this diagram should not be understood simply as direct responses to a growing num-

ber of emerging disease outbreaks; rather, these measures function to constitute a given situation as an emergency, one that requires an urgent and rapid collective response. In other words, it is not the inherent characteristics of a given disease outbreak but rather the classificatory schema as it combines with the techniques and politics of global health security that makes the vent a candidate to become an official emergency."[1]

This statement highlights that crisis management systems, particularly those arising from a type of health risk such as the one from Covid-19, have important cultural influences and an impact on the previous vulnerabilities of the affected societies.[2]

Moreover, the current situation of global crisis underlines how an important role in the definition of the concepts of emergency and crisis is also dictated by the subjective perception of the various actors involved, which in turn is influenced by social characteristics and cultural factors.

In this sense, the interpretation of the threat is long a continuum that has at its extreme opposites, the sense of security and the perception of vulnerability.

In accordance with this general perspective of crisis management, it becomes interesting to explore and understand how perceptions of both in and out groups had a specific influence on the definition and perception of religious fundamentalism in Italy in time of pandemic.

Since the end of February 2020, Italy has been one of the European countries most affected by the epidemic caused by the Covid-19 virus.

At the same time, a few days after the first epidemic wave and a convulsive initial emergency management, some news proposed by the media, focused on international scenarios and in particular on how ISIS could exploit this moment of criticality, perhaps planning attacks in Europe.

The theme was very interesting because it shifted the cultural attention of the audience from the national level, of the contingent crisis and located in specific territorial areas, to the international one, while relating two different types of threats, the health one linked to the Covid-19 virus and the one linked to the ISIS organization.

For these reasons, it was considered important to explore the dynamics related to the perception and construction of certain public images, with particular reference to the Muslim community in Italy, with the ultimate aim of understanding whether the association ISIS, terrorism and Muslims were still present or if new narratives present in the different pandemic context had taken place.

---

1   Andrew Lakoff (2017). *Unprepared: Global Health in a Time of Emergency.* Oakland: University of California Press, p. 6

2   Cf. Ilan Kelman (2020). *Disaster by Choice: How Our Actions Turn Natural Hazards Into Catastrophes.* Oxford: OUP.

This exploration and analysis used a qualitative methodology, with specific reference to the virtual ethnography framework. This approach has been chosen for a variety of reasons, including: having a strong multilayer and multi-sited connotation; to focus on the cultural aspects of the definition, representation and interpretation of the pandemic and its side or collateral threats such as those related to extremisms.

The added value of this writing is to explore the dimensions of perception and interpretation of the same phenomenon, at the time of a global crisis such as the pandemic from Covid-19: understanding socio-cultural dynamics: collective perceptions and interpretations is an indispensable tool of analysis to govern a global crisis and its times of uncertainty.

2.   Italian Muslim Community, the Covid-19 Pandemic and its features

The situation of the Italian Muslim community is one of the most complex to delineate, as it serves the double nature present in much of the collective imagination, for which Muslim means terrorism.

Unfortunately, historical references take root on September 11, 2001, when the first associative narratives of being Muslim with being a terrorist settled down[3].

Following that dramatic event, acts of Islamophobia and prejudice against the Muslim community took place, in the United States, but also in other European countries.

In Italy this happened time later, as the largest presence of Muslims was of Moroccan origin, but still first generation.

In 2018 in Italy, it is estimated that there were about 2.6 million Muslims or about 4 percent of the total population. These data come from estimates between different agencies and statistical institutes[4], as the complexity of the legal situation (immigrants, asylum seekers, Italian citizens) of Muslims leads to some different systemizations.

According to the same Author[5] most Muslims come from: Morocco, Albania, Bangladesh, Pakistan, Egypt, Tunisia, Senegal, Macedonia, Kosovo and Bosnia. In particular, there has been a greater presence from Eastern Europe in recent years.

As regards the image of public opinion, it is based on the following socio-political and cultural lines:

---

3   Cf. Lori Peek (2010). *Behind the Backlash: Muslim Americans After 9/11.* Philadelphia: Temple University Press.

4   Cf. Fabrizio Ciocca (2019). *Musulmani in Italia: una presenza stabile e sempre più italiana.* See: https://www.lenius.it/musulmani-in-italia/

5   Ib.

a) a political component that has developed narratives that promote the vision of Muslims as invaders and promoters of a cultural clash between the West and the East
b) a part of the population, which has instead promoted a pervaded vision of welcome, solidarity and coexistence, considering for example in this group those who Italians have converted to Islam and have become a bridge between the various ethnicities and religions as well as part of this group supports the vision of the centrist political component and the radical left wing and
c) a part of the population supporter of the more far-right political component, which supports the invasion and vision of Muslims as largely terrorist people.

This latter orientation is particularly present when new arrivals of migrants or how many terrorist attacks are needed, especially in Europe, as the perception of attacks abroad is different also due to different media coverage.

In this context of public narratives, their perceptions and interpretations, the demands carried out by Muslims in Italy are essentially three:

a) the recognition of certain places of worship and cultural associations as religious bodies
b) to which the construction of new mosques is associated and
c) the contrast to forms of Islamophobia.

With regard to the first two points, various representatives of the Islamic cultural associations and mosques present in Italy, are in dialogue and seeking a solution for the recognition and reference legislation aimed at the management of this issue. This is not an easy action, as is the community, places of worship and mosques appear extremely fragmented and difficult to define legally.[6]

The third point, on the other hand, relates to the socio-political dimensions of the relationship between the indigenous population, Muslim immigrants and converts.

The data presented by the Vox-Osservatorio italiano sui diritti, concerning the Map of Intolerance project, shows us how the theme of Islamophobia expressed mainly through social networks (Twitter in particular) is crucial for the realization of a more tolerant and inclusive society.

The data collected and analysed by Vox-Osservatorio italiano sui diritti related to islamophobia in Italy, practiced through online intolerant and hateful messages

---

6   Cf. Antonio Cuciniello (2017). Luoghi di culto islamici in Italia: tipologie e dati. *Fondazione ISMU Iniziative e Studi* sulla *Multietnicità*. See: https://www.ismu.org/wp-content/uploads/2017/05/Cuciniello_paper_luoghi-di-culto_aprile-2017.pdf

via Twitter, highlights how Muslims are the most affected category after women.[7] Later versions of this working progress project show that the trend related to Islamophobia is constantly on the rise, with specific spikes when dramatic events such as terrorist attacks or crimes committed by Muslims both in Italy and abroad occur.

At the geographical level, the most violent online messages of an Islamophobic nature are present throughout the country, with a greater presence in large cities and a lower spread in the south.

What is interesting to note is that the intolerant or hateful words associated with the interpretation of Muslim as a threat are the following but fundamentalist: jihadist, Moroccan, cutthroat, Bedouin, Abdullah. These words reveal how some part of the collective perceptions on Muslims are based on the cultural interpretation of news and experiences rather than a reflection from a more general perspective or a geopolitical level where it was supposed to place the definition of fundamentalist.

From this overview we can understand how the Muslim presence in Italy is characterized by a multiplicity of currents of perceptions and interpretations, which are partly the mirror of the complexity and multidimensionality of the Muslim community more generally.

An interesting perspective about the sense of Muslim community is provided by Guolo:

"Making community is the most immediate response to the need to reproduce Islam in a cultural and religious context different from the original; but it is also the product of the social construction of groups that self-represent themselves as guardians of tradition and oppose the individual paths of individual Muslims, destined to lead, according to those same groups, to secularization."[8]

According to this definition, the Author[9] also highlights the relevant matter of representativeness of Islam in Europe and it is also valid for Italy and for its political dimensions.[10]

---

7   See: http://www.voxdiritti.it/islamofobia-musulmani-terroristi/

8   Cf. Renzo Guolo (2016). *Sociologia dell'Islam. Religione e politica.* Milano: Mondadori. Original text in Italian: "*La comunitarizzazione è la risposta più immediata alla necessità di riprodurre l'islam in un contesto culturale e religioso diverso da quello originario; ma è anche il prodotto della costruzione sociale di gruppi che si autorappresentano come custodi della tradizione e si oppongono ai percorsi individuali dei singoli musulmani, destinati a sfociare, secondo quegli stessi gruppi, nella secolarizzazione.*" Cf. Renzo Guolo (2001). Il campo verde: strategie islamiche in Italia. *Limes.* See: https://www.limesonline.com/cartaceo/il-campo-verde-strategie-islamiche-in-italia?prv=true, 2001

9   Cf. Guolo (2016).

10   Fabrizio Ciocca (2019). *L'Islam* italiano: *Un'indagine tra religione, identità e islamofobia.* Mimesis. Milano: Sesto San Giovanni.

Furthermore, Guolo offers a systematization of the multidimensional complexity of Islam such as follow:

> »Islam of States«, promoted by the governments of Islamic countries and associations linked to them; That of the »Islam of mosques«, promoted by transnational organisations that are often opposed by the governments of many Crescent countries or who have no close ties to them; »Fraternity Islam« that is structured around the figure of a master or a tradition."[11]

Another specific point of view about the relationship among Muslims, their identities and Italian State is that proposed by Cahouki[12] who reflect on the sense of identity of the Muslim community in Italy, which it recognizes to be complex and fragmented. An important aspect that the Author emphasizes is the relationship with the Italian State, for which he wants continued respect from the Muslim population in Italy, as a religious duty for Muslims.[13]

In these national frameworks it becomes interesting to explore how the perception of "threat" linked to the image of the Muslim was contextualized during the period of the pandemic and what narratives were produced to the virtual environment of social networks and national mass media.

The consideration of transcultural and trans -geographical perceptions makes it clear that the overlapping of the image of the Muslim with that of the terrorist is predominantly determined by the exposure to information related to ISIS and its possible attacks: from a socio-psychological perspective it is interesting to note that this form of prejudice is born not spurious but in the overlap of two images and interpretations such as that of the Muslim and the belonging to ISIS.

A push and driving factor in this overlap has been the focus on the more or less resilient strategies put in place by ISIS as well as statements about Islam's interpretation of the pandemic.[14]

Just as the scientific community appeared divided about the origin, evolution and effects of the Covid-19 pandemic, even experts and geopolitical analysts have been at odds about the concrete possibility of ISIS using the pandemic to organize and carry out attacks around the world.

---

11   Cf. Guolo (2016), p. 190: Original text in Italian: «islam degli stati», promossa dai governi dei paesi islamici e da associazioni a esse legati; quella dell'«islam delle moschee», promossa da organizzazioni transnazionali che spesso sono all'opposizione dei governi di molti paesi della Mezzaluna o che non hanno stretti legami con essi; quella dell'«islam delle confraternite», che si struttura attorno alla figura di un maestro o di una tradizione.

12   Khalid Chaouki (2018). I musulmani d'Italia vogliono essere italiani. Roma: Limes, Gedi.

13   Ib.

14   See: https://www.wilsoncenter.org/article/isis-offensive-exploits-pandemic

For instance, Hanna[15] sustains the effective exploitation of pandemic and its consequences by ISIS, depicted also a sophisticated level of the attacks in Iraq and Syria.

The same was valid for Williams looking at a wider international framework and capacity of exploitation:

"A U.S. Department of Homeland Security bulletin in late March warned that the Islamic State's newsletter had called for attacks on U.S. and European health care targets that are strained by the pandemic. The Islamic State has ordered its followers not to travel to Europe, where the virus outbreak is far worse than in the Middle East. But the group has suggested that its followers who are already in Europe exploit the chaos, calling for "new strikes … similar to the strikes of Paris, London, Brussels and other places" where followers have used bombs and firearms to kill dozens of people in recent years.

The Islamic State is even suggesting that killing "infidels" could be a way for followers to protect themselves from the virus, stating, "They should also remember that obedience to God – the most beloved form of which is jihad – turns away the torment and wrath of God."[16]

From the opposite perspective, Depretis[17] highlighted the fact that ISIS was ineffective to exploit the pandemic and its related vulnerability at international level, to plan and carry our deadly attacks.

This view of the issue of ISIS and international Muslims is also reflected in the public image and media coverage during the pandemic in Italy.

An interesting analysis through google trends in the time span 21/02/20 – 23/06/2020[18] shows how the spike in interest in the ISIS and pandemic issue occurred on March 13, when the national press focused on the spread by ISIS of a leaflet for the prevention of contagion.

It is useful to note that the correlation was reported using the word jihadist and therefore connoting according to a precise meaning the news itself and its interpretation.

---

15   Cf. Andrew Hanna (2020). *ISIS Offensive Exploits Pandemic*. See: https://www.wilsoncenter.org/article/isis-offensive-exploits-pandemic

16   Cf. Brian Glyn Williams (2020). *Islamic State calls for followers to spread coronavirus, exploit pandemic and protests*. See: https://theconversation.com/islamic-state-calls-for-followers-to-spread-coronavirus-exploit-pandemic-and-protests-136224

17   Cf. Daniel Depetris (2020). *No, ISIS Isn't Resurging Amid the Coronavirus Pandemic*. See: https://www.defenseone.com/ideas/2020/05/no-isis-isnt-resurging-amid-coronavirus-pandemic/165401/

18   See: https://trends.google.it/trends/explore?q=isis%20coronavirus&date=2020-02-21%202020-06-23&geo=IT; cf.: https://trends.google.it/trends/explore?date=2020-02-21%202020-06-23&geo=IT&q=musulmano,covid-19,ISIS; cf.: https://trends.google.it/trends/explore?date=2020-02-21%202020-06-23&geo=IT-72&q=isis%20coronavirus

The same was true on 12 May 2020, where news about ISIS, Iraq and Covid-19 were released by international agencies.

With regard to the situation of Muslims in Italy, it is confirmed that the characteristics of the context before the pandemic caused by the Covid-19 virus affected not only the perceptions of such crises, but also the interpretations, thus going to better delineate the specific fragmentary and complexity of the Islamic experience in Italy.

3. Methodology

The methodological approach that was used for this analysis is qualitative and mixed, consisting of different types of online methods.

It must be also considered that in the context of the Covid-19 pandemic, no face to face or personal meetings were allowed, for this reason a "distanced research" [19] approach was chosen.

Moreover, due to the inner and complex nature of the issues explored, a virtual multiple – site (Evans, 2010) approach was preferred as well as the *multilayered definition of the virtual world* and the *cross- matching data* provided by Beck (2004).

The main aim of this methodology is to disclose the *webs of meanings* Geertz (1973) and how a social issue have been framed in different cultural contexts (Hine, 2000).

The general methodological approach can be placed under the framework of the virtual ethnography and it is composed of the following tools, methods and analysis:

> An exploratory questionnaire from selected Muslim representatives of Italian Mosques and Italian Islamic cultural centres. Its main aim was to understand the interpretative categories for the analysis of the phenomenon, considering the answers such as a driver for the combined analysis with the other information collected. This perspective was also supported by what Geertz identified such as "webs of meanings".
>
> Desk research, secondary data collection through online open source: articles and documents on the topics of the research; Facebook Page of Mosques and Italian Islamic cultural centres; post on Twitter.

The online open sources were searched according to the following keywords, where possible both in Italian and English: islamophobia; ISIS; Daesh; Covid-19; coronavirus; Muslim(s).

---

19   Leighton Evans (2010). *Authenticity Online: Using Webnography to Address Phenomenological Concerns. New Media and the Politics of Online Communities.* Oxford: Mousoutzanis, Riha, p. 13.

The online open sources were collected in a time span from 20 February 2020 to 24 June 2020.

In addition, the criteria of relevance and relevance with respect to the topic covered by the data were also used for the collection of sources.

A secondary data analysis as well as a manual content analysis about the information collected through open source were carried out.

The virtual ethnography was conducted considering both the open source secondary data collection and the information found out by a key informant, playing also the role of gatekeeper for the collection of questionnaire: his figure was essential to understand and interpret the phenomenon from a cultural perspective of the Italian Muslim community.

4.   Exploratory questionnaire on the topics of the phenomenon[20]

The online questionnaire was sent through the key informant, who is an important figure to connect with the people representing the reference community of the current research fieldwork.

The people were selected to deepen the characteristics of the fieldwork and those of the themes that were to be studied. In addition, they were chosen in accordance with increased activity in the Italian mosques and Islamic cultural centers in Italy as well as according to the role they have in the environments of mosques and cultural centers.

The questionnaire was divided into two parts:

one on the socio-demographic aspects and
the other on the aspects of the Covid-19 pandemic.

The total number of responses is 20, 4 people are women and 16 are men and represent from a geographical and cultural perspective, the fragmentation of the Muslim community in Italy.

Starting with the analysis of the socio-demographic section, interesting aspects emerge.

The most representative country of origin is Morocco with 15 responses; 1 Egypt; 3 Italy; 1 Tunisia/Hungary. This trend is also present in the more general statistical data, which report that the Moroccan community is one of the most present in Italy.[21]

---

20   See **Annex 2 - Outline of the Exploratory Survey**.
21   See: https://www.lavoro.gov.it/documenti-e-norme/studi-e-statistiche/Documents/Rapport i%20annuali%20sulle%20comunit%C3%A0%20migranti%20in%20Italia%20-%20anno% 202018/Marocco-rapporto-2018.pdf

These data have to be compared with the following, which relate to the years lived in Italy, specifically:

14 years, one person
15 years, two people
20 years, four people
36 years, one person
24 years, one person
32 years, one person and
ten people born in Italy.

Two important aspects emerge from these answers:

the trend of the Moroccan community is also confirmed by the years in which people live in Italy. In fact, the Moroccan community is one of the oldest located in Italy many decades ago and
the discrepancy of the data, between the ten people born in Italy and the three who indicate as the country of origin Italy, find their explanation in being of Moroccan origin.

The third question concerned the city of origin and the answers represent the variety and landscape of the Muslim community in Italy:

a person from Arezzo
a person from Avellino
a person from Belluno
a person from Torino
a person from Oleggio
two people from Pesaro
two people from Verona
two people from Ravenna
two people from Roma
three people from Torino
a person from Treviso
person from Umbertide
a person from Vicenza and
a person from Volla.

The data demonstrate the geographical variety of the Muslim presence in Italy and highlight the absence of reply from Lombardia Region. This can be explained in two ways:

a) Lombardy was the most affected region since the Covid-19 epidemic started and had difficulties in managing the emergency and crisis. It is possible that people, even if they received the questionnaire, did not intend to answer.
b) The absence of a region such as Lombardy, refers to the pattern of the presence of the Muslim community in small towns in Italy, which will occur in a special question in the next section.

The last question of this first section concerns the role played within the mosque or cultural centers, which is in direct relation to the selection of the profiles of the interviewees.

17 people replied in total:

three volunteers
one imam
one member of the youth group
one board member
two people without a role. One of them specified by writing that there is no role in the Muslim community because they are all children of God
three presidents
one youth spokesman
two secretaries
two vice-presidents and
one spokesman.

The second section specifically covers some aspects of the perception of the Muslim community from the outside and from newspaper in relation to the Covid-19 pandemic.

The first question concerned the definition of a pandemic, which was defined from 14 people as follows:

a virus
frustration
restrictions of displacement freedom
a moment of reflection
a mercy and a blessing of Allah
a crisis that caused irrationality
a test
a challenge of humanity
a global emergency
a pandemic.

The answers demonstrate a variety of thinking within the Muslim community, with multiple nuances of definition and interpretation that vary from more scientific to religious aspects.

The second question concerned the consideration of ethnic minorities (e.g. in linguistic and cultural aspects) of religious minorities during the crisis management of the pandemic.

19 people replied and 47.4 percent answered that religious minorities were not considered, while 52.6 percent considered religious minorities.

The rift in the answers to this question is understandable in light of the knowledge of the difficulties faced by the Muslim community for two reasons:

Measures of restrictions for the management of the pandemic have prohibited meetings in mosques and places of worship: this situation similar to so many other collective activities.

The problems and difficulties faced by the Muslim community for the burial of their members in relation to the procedures promoted after the pandemic.

These reasons are therefore the basis of this division in the responses.

The third question was more generally about the perception and assessment of the effectiveness of crisis management in Italy.

The answers are thus divided: 20 percent believe that it has been inadequate, 50 percent think it has been adequate; while 25 percent considered it effective and 5 percent ineffective.

The number of responses for the most positive, which consider crisis management effective and adequate for 75 percent is in line with the previous question where a majority of respondents said they had not noticed discrimination against religious minorities during the first months of the pandemic.

A very interesting topic is the one introduced by the fourth question, which focuses on the fact that some international and Italian media, in the early days of the pandemic, talked about how and if ISIS could exploit the pandemic for possible attacks.

The answers to this question have been very varied, bringing out the complexity of mutual perception on this specific and important issue.

In particular, this phenomenon has been considered as follows:

a defamation campaign
an attack by the media
ignorance
the target wants to be told this
never heard of it
never heard of it, indeed positive focus on the Muslim community
to divert public opinion

because they're ignorant, ISIS isn't all Muslim
because Islam is being exploited
they always try to connect something to Muslims
typical journalistic terrorism
want to make listens and focus attention on a well-known theme
they had nothing else to write about and
the attempt increase fear.

The variety of responses highlights some interesting aspects including:

Six people have never heard of it and this can be explained in the dual meaning
that either they are exposed differently to traditional international and national
media or had no interest in the subject of this question.
Other responses reveal some of the best-known theories of media communication, such as the gate keeper function, the agenda setting or the way in which
news (both linguistically and stylistically) is presented to the public.
Another reflection concerns the role of the audience which appear to be passive
and waiting to meet previous expectations.
It is also interesting the talk about the purpose of putting fear, referring to the
terrorist framework especially for the language used.

The fifth question is related to the previous one and wants to be more precise about
the possibility of ISIS exploiting the crisis moment due to the Covid-19 pandemic to
carry out attacks in European countries. The 19 answers are 73.7 percent no, while a
26.3 percent yes: this percentage of responses are in line with those of the previous
question and especially with the broader overall picture that wants to consider ISIS
as one of various types of extremist threats.

The sixth question aims to focus on the phenomenon of solidarity on the part
of the Muslim community, which has spread as a phenomenon through social networks and where it has been most widespread.

The result is the following: "55 percent think in small towns, while 45 percent in
large cities", representing the dual soul of the Muslim community in Italy and its
presence even in the small provincial realities.

Linked to this question is the following that wants to bring out the definition
of solidarity:

70 percent believe it is a universal human act
25 percent think it is a religious action and
5 percent see it as an act of belonging to the nation where you live.

The answer that defines solidarity as a universal human act is interesting, because
in addition to obtaining the majority of responses, it also indicates the neutrality
of cultural or ideological visions that could guide the previous definition.

The penultimate question focuses on the perception of prejudice by the Muslim community during the first months of the pandemic: 75 percent said they did not feel prejudiced; 15 percent do for their religion and finally 10 percent yes for their ethnicity.

Although the majority of responses indicate a lack of perception of prejudice, 25 percent indicate some form of prejudice related to either their ethnicity or religion: communication in this context played a fundamental role.

The last question concerns the role that solidarity actions promoted during the pandemic may play in reducing and limiting prejudice towards the Muslim community. 95 percent think they are useful for this purpose, while 5 percent do not.

The analysis of this exploratory survey reveals some important dimensions, which will be the common thread and the interpretive lens of the next open source analysis:

Mass media (mainly international) narratives in time of pandemic: connecting ISIS and the Covid-19 pandemic. Especially, the possibility by ISIS to exploit the Covid-19 pandemic for their attacks.

Ethnic and cultural crisis management: few considerations of ethnic groups during crisis management

Ethnic and Muslim Identity; national sense of belonging

the Covid-19 pandemic and its interpretation both religious and cultural and Muslim community solidarity.

All of these listed aspects have been addressed and analysed in the open source analysis of social media and social networks.

5.   Findings from open source and secondary data analysis[22]

The exploratory analysis of the questionnaire revealed some interesting trends, which will be discussed then in light of the results that emerged from the open source analysis.

Online open source data collection focused on various types of data, such as those from newspapers in their online editions and those instead of social networks.

The collection of online open data was possible through the use of certain keywords such as: *ISIS, pandemic, Muslims, Covid-19, coronavirus, terrorism, extremism.*

There are 105 items collected, including some in English by relevance criterion. The harvest took place in the period of time from February 20, 2020 to June 24, 2020.

---

22   See **Annex 1 – Online News.**

From a methodological perspective, a manual content analysis was conducted, looking for the recurrences not only of words, but especially of themes and content.

Moreover, the theoretical background of this analysis lies on the key principles of news framing, social media coverage and agenda setting applied in the online environment.

This is especially valid with regard to the way in which the social media and social networks users narrate certain phenomena and events, especially referring to the issues of prejudice, ethnic and religious differences.

For instance, *Hostile media bias describes how people with strong attitudes about an issue believe that media intentionally slant stories against their side or in favour of the other side* (Vallone et al., 1985). [23]

This topic is in line with the narrative dynamics of the treatment of discriminatory phenomena against Muslim people, as well as hate speech or hate online.

As Weberling McKeever[24] points out, the role of the media in the perception and interpretation of immigrants is real: *Mass media have a role in shaping people's perceptions of immigrants and immigration* (Kellstedt, 2003), *serving as sources for learning about national trends and policy proposals* (Kim, Carvalho, Davis, & Mullins, 2011).[25]

Furthermore, despite different tools made available to the new online communication environment and different figures such as that of the influencer, certain communication strategies and narrative methodologies find themselves applied also to the wider context of social media and social networks.

The theme in question is aimed at a specific area such as that of a correlation, between being Muslim and being a terrorist, in the potential development of prejudices and stereotypes. The news in this case can be a push factor: *News about terrorism may increase prejudiced attitudes toward outgroups.*[26]

---

23   Robert P. Vallone; Lee Ross and Mark R. Lepper (1985). The hostile media phenomenon: Biased perception of media bias in coverage of the Beirut massacre. *Journal of Personality and Social Psychology* 49, 4. Cited in Brooke Weberling McKeever, Daniel Riffe, & Francesca Dillman Carpentier: Perceived Hostile Media Bias, Presumed Media Influence, and Opinions About Immigrants and Immigration. *Southern Communication Journal*, Vol. 77, No. 5.

24   McKeever, Riffe and Carpentier, 2012, p. 3.

25   Cf. Paul Kellstedt (2003). *The mass media and the dynamics of American racial attitudes*. New York: Cambridge University Press.; Cf. Kim Sei hill, John P. Carvalho, Andrew Davis and Amanda M. Mullins (2011). The view of the border: News framing of the definition, causes, and solutions to illegal immigration. *Mass Communication & Society* 14, 292 - 314.; Cf. McKeever, Riffe and Carpentier, 2012, p. 3.

26   Enny Das; et al. (2009). How terrorism, news reports increase prejudice against outgroups: A terror management account. *Journal of Experimental Social Psychology* 45(3), 453-459; cf. Luwei Rose Luqiu, and Fan Yang (2018). Islamophobia in China: news coverage, stereotypes, and Chinese Muslims' perceptions of themselves and Islam. *Asian Journal of Communication*, 28:6, 6.

As for the polarizing dynamics that promote Islamophobia and the influence of media coverage:

"Many studies attempt to trace the origin of Islamophobia by examining representations of Islam and Muslims in the news media. One study on the British media suggests that British Muslims are portrayed as 'un-British' and 'deviant', themes that can be linked to the development of racism (Saeed, 2007). The British media tend to focus on British Muslims as a terrorist threat (Moore, Mason, & Lewis, 2008). A study on British newspapers from 1994 to 2004 concludes that Muslims were portrayed as a threat to Western values (Poole, 2004), and British newspapers have been criticized for biased reporting, disseminating propaganda, and promoting Islamophobia, practices that lead to anti-Muslim sentiment (Richardson, 2004)."[27]

This general mass media frame points out theoretical orientations, which are proper also in the context of virtual and online communications.

Especially, two aspects need to be taken onto account:

how the information is framed by the online users;
how information, beliefs or thoughts are disseminated through social media and social networks, in reference to what can be defined as a diffusion chain:

"Media attention lends legitimacy to the voices and frames – the conceptions and organizations of information that help us understand the world around us —that are chosen to be featured (Bekkers, Beunders, Edwards, & Moody, 2011). Media coverage also amplifies incidents and ideas by providing a platform to spread certain positions and perspectives to a broader audience (Bekkers, Beunders, Edwards, and Moody, 2011). This platform is further expanded by members of the public disseminating media amongst themselves (Nacos, 2002)."[28]

After having combined both theoretical and methodological insights, the analysis demonstrates the recurring themes and narratives, which go to implement the per-

---

27   Ib..; Cf. Amir Saeed (2007). Media, racism and Islamophobia: The representation of Islam and Muslims in the media. *Sociology Compass*, 1(2), 443-462.; Cf. Kerry Moore, Paul Mason and & Justin Matthew Wren Lewis (2008). Images of Islam in the UK: The representation of British Muslims in the national print news media 2000 - 2008. *Cardiff School of Journalism, Media and Cultural Studies.*; Cf. Elisabeth Poole (2004). Islamophobia. In E. Cashmore (Ed.). *Encyclopedia of race and ethnic studies.* New York: Routledge.

28   V. Bekkers, H. Beunders, A. Edwards and R. Moody (2011). New media, micromobilization, and political agenda setting: Crossover effects in political mobilization and media usage. *Information Society*, 27, 209-219.; Cf. Brigitte L. Nacos (2019). *Mass-mediated terrorism*. Oxford: Rowman & Littlefield.; Cf. Erin M. Kearnsa, Allison E. Betusb and Anthony F. Lemieuxb (2019). Why Do Some Terrorist Attacks Receive More Media Attention Than Others? *Justice Quarterly*, Vol. 36, Issue, 6, 6

ception and interpretation of the audience and those who are exposed to it, are as follows:

a) The correlation between the pandemic and new attacks by ISIS.
b) The Islamic definition of the pandemic, especially linked to the vision promoted by ISIS.
c) The international security and geopolitical situation, with a particular focus on stopping the international mission against ISIS in Iraq.
d) The ability by ISIS to exploit the pandemic and the emerging vulnerabilities of the affected societies to organize and carry out attacks in Europe.
e) Donations made by Muslims in Italy especially to Italian agencies. Instead, news and information about donations by Muslims to other Muslims, for example from mosques or cultural centers, are most prominent among social networks.
f) The burial of Muslims who died in Italy for Covid-19 or their repatriation to countries of origin.
g) The impact of restrictive measures during the lockdown for the management of religious services related to Ramadan.
h) The communication by the Muslim and ISIS communities compared to the personal protection measures against the Covid-19 virus. As for information on the protection measures against Covid-19, attention was also reported about the communication of ISIS to its foreign fighters, who were traveling in areas critical of the epidemic.
i) The focus on the migration flows, which shifts the main narrative from the "Muslim" category to the "migrants" category in general, avoiding ethnic connotations as well as in the same area the focus has shifted from the meaning of ISIS to the "Islamist".
j) The way in which Islam defined that the dead of Muslims for Covid-19 is martyrdom.

These themes highlight some essential dimensions to understand the double phenomenon of perception in-group and out-group.

In particular the features of narratives built around specific themes: especially interesting are those relate to solidarity actions promoted by Muslims towards Italian agencies or institutions; the supposed resilience effect, of reorganization of ISIS and affiliates, but which divides scholars and analysts at an international level.

The narratives differentiate their topics according to the dissemination and localization of the media or communication media that promote them: at the national level, more attention is devoted to international scenarios and therefore to the treatment of threats from ISIS and their developments; at regional and local level, the focus is on how Muslims are dealing with the crisis from Covid-19, the problem of burials of Muslim people who died for Covid-19 and the management of Ramadan-related rituals, considering that mosques were closed for lockdown.

As for the perception at the temporal level, the spread of the news focused, as it was to be imagined[29], on the cultural aspects related to religious practices only in the weeks following the emergency. This is relevant because it insists that it is now considered a specific feature of this current pandemic, which is also valid in other contexts, that is the definition of the event, the type of crisis and what was needed had an important time frame. In particular, all this is to be referred to the lack of knowledge on the part of both the scientific community and the public, about the type of biological – health risk that has occurred.

Continuing with the analysis, an interesting perspective and for this reason treated individually is the one that emerges from the analysis of some of the most interesting Facebook and Twitter pages of Italian mosques or Italian Islamic centers. To give an example these are the ones most considered during the same time span used for the collection of other open sources:

Associazione Islamica Italiana degli Imam e delle Guide Religiose[30]
Centro Islamico Culturale d'Italia – Grande Moschea di Roma[31]
CII Confederazione Islamica Italiana[32]
COREIS Italian Muslim Youth[33]
Islamic Relief Italia[34]
UCOI- Unione delle Comunità Islamiche d'Italia.[35]

From this analysis emerge the trends confirming the complexity and fragmentation of the Muslim community present in Italy.

It is also interesting to note how the proposed narrative of the pandemic, its impacts and effects reflects the vision and cultural orientations of the environments, be they mosques or cultural centers, to which they relate.

Similarly, the tones and communication modes often reveal internal divisions and tensions, which broaden their references beyond the context of the current crisis from Covid-19: this has been particularly noted for those cultural centres, associations or mosques that refer to polarizing visions of Italian or European society.

---

29 Cf. Marco Lombardi (2005). *Comunicare nell'emergenza*. Milano: Vita e Pensiero.
30 See: https://www.facebook.com/Associazione.ImamItalia/
31 See: https://www.facebook.com/centroislamicoculturale/
32 See: https://www.facebook.com/confederazioneislamicaitaliana/
33 See: https://www.facebook.com/coreis.giovani/
34 See: https://www.facebook.com/islamic.relief.italia/
35 See: https://www.facebook.com/UCOIIUnioneComunitaIslamicheItalia/

As in any context of crisis, the pandemic from Covid-19 deserves to be interpreted according to two dimensions: the spatial and the temporal[36].

The first in this particular narrative context, confirms what the results of the questionnaires have already emphasized: a difference between centers and mosques in large cities and those present in the Italian provincial areas. Diversity covers issues considered where, for example, during the pandemic more information about personal protection measures against Covid-19 were provided and discussed in provincial contexts; similarly, actions of local solidarity between Muslims and Muslims and Italians are more communicated through social networks with a local physical basis.

At the national level, on the other hand, more attention was given to broader issues such as the international situation and some interpretive orientations related to the pandemic.

As for narratives from a temporal perspective, communications were often posted at the beginning on issues that focused on the practical management of the crisis, but there was also a phenomenon of simultaneity, for which often some practical information was posted or re-discussed even if already published in previous days and weeks.

Finally, one difference that is interesting to point out is the narratives according to the social networks used: through Facebook, news is discussed in a more open and inclusive way; Via Twitter, however, there is no shortage of clashes, tensions and tendencies to polarization. This predisposition had already been noted in other hate speech contexts such as the aforementioned Map of Intolerance.

The narrative and dissemination of communication has different images depending on the cultural and political orientations of mosques and Islamic cultural centers in Italy: there are in fact those that emphasize the link with Italian national identity and therefore approach a dialogue and cooperation with Italian institutions and agencies; there are those of more traditional Islamic orientation, which outline a specific Muslim identity, being nevertheless aware of the national context.

Finally, there are those of cultural-religious orientation who take less part in relational life with other national institutions.

For the purpose of this analysis, it is interesting to point out a trend about the solidarity actions that were promoted during the emergency and in the first months of the pandemic: at the local level among Muslims, while at the national level the offers have also spread to Italian institutions and organizations. Another evidence that emerges from this analysis is the lack of explicit reference to Islamic fundamentalism: the most used and recurring words are those of Islamic extremism or Islamic terrorism. As far as it can be understood, Islamic fundamentalism in

---

36   Cf. Lombardi (2005).

its dual semantic and cultural identification seems to refer primarily to the events of 9/11 and the social phenomena related to them.

6. Future Perspectives: Italian Islam and the Covid-19 pandemic

One of the most interesting findings of this analysis is that there is not only religious fundamentalism as a cognitive and interpretive category. In reality, there are multidimensional cultural components, more or less broad where conflicts, tensions and polarization find their expressive spaces.

In this sense, the pandemic caused by the Covid-19 virus has unearthed these dynamics, often latent or confined to delimited spaces and realities, putting in place what can be defined as the Italian Islam of the two-faced Janus: this means that the diachronic aspect is given not by the temporal dimension of the phenomenon between the past and the future, but also by a cultural perspective that encompasses and makes coexisting different tensions of the same cultural perspective.

Online ethnographic analyses conducted confirmed the variety of cultural positions also present in the Italian Muslim community. Certainly, these are related to the different ethnic backgrounds and especially with regard to the analysis of social networks emerges the multiplicity of visions and interpretations.

This different cultural background and, at least for a certain component, the lack of inclusion of people of Islamic faith has produced perceptions of the pandemic with an interesting cultural perspective. In turn, the interpretations have resulted in social practices and behaviours, which have resulted in compliance with rules and measures during lockdown, but also for some violations.

It also emerged that, the juxtaposition between Muslim people, Islam and terrorism and ISIS exists, although not explicitly and not necessarily targeting.

What is interesting for the future development of this study are the latent or composed of references that emphasize areas of tension and conflict between the same belongings to mosques or Islamic cultural centers in Italy.

Finally, three aspects concern a necessary reflection that comes from a preliminary lesson learned from the impact of this Covid-19 pandemic:

> The inclusion both from a cultural and linguistic point of view of Muslim people and like them of other ethnicities present in Italy, in the management of the crisis, understanding how cultural aspects influence adherence to the methods of crisis management or instead produce social frictions.
> How a national sense of belonging and individual identity are shaped during an emergency like the current one.
> Extremist currents linked to forms of Islamic terrorism were not found to be ex-

plicit either within the Muslim community or for example by scholars studying the phenomenon. It is certain that they also exist in the context considered here and that their manifestations are mainly latent and need for further analysis.

Finally, the context built by the pandemic has given the opportunity to put at the centre of the discussion some important points for Muslim community in Italy, such as the construction of new mosques, the recognition of some Islamic cultural centers and the fight against forms of prejudice, Islamophobia and hate speech.

The future challenge facing crisis management, at least in Italy, is to include all these socio-cultural factors within it, so that the management of the crisis reaches the desired levels of effectiveness, thus avoiding to feed potential threats and conflicts from the most conflicting fringes of the various communities.

Bibliography

Allport, Gordon (1979). *The Nature of Prejudice*. New York: Basic Books.

Beck, Liav Sade (2004). Internet Ethnography: Online and Offline. *International Journal of Qualitative Methods* 3, (2), 45-51.

Bekkers, V.; Beunders, H.; Edwards, A., and Moody, R. (2011). New media, micromobilization, and political agenda setting: Crossover effects in political mobilization and media usage. *Information Society* 27, 209- 219.

Ciocca, Fabrizio (2019). *L'Islam italiano: Un'indagine tra religione, identità e islamophobia*. Mimesis. Milano: Sesto San Giovanni.

Ciocca, Fabrizio (2019). *Musulmani in Italia: una presenza stabile e sempre più italiana*. May, 14. URL: https://www.lenius.it/musulmani-in-italia/

Cuciniello, Antonio (2017). Luoghi di culto islamici in Italia: tipologie e dati. *Fondazione ISMU Iniziative e Studi sulla Multietnicità*. Milano. URL: https://www.ismu.org/wp-content/uploads/2017/05/Cuciniello_paper_luoghi-di-culto_aprile-2017.pdf

Das, Enny; Bushman, Brad J.; Bezemer, Marieke D.; Kerkhof, Peter, and Vermeulen, Ivar E. (2009). How terrorism, news reports increase prejudice against outgroups: A terror management account. *Journal of Experimental Social Psychology* 45(3), 453 – 459.

Depetris, Daniel (2020). *No, ISIS Isn't Resurging Amid the Coronavirus Pandemic*. May 15. URL: https://www.defenseone.com/ideas/2020/05/no-isis-isnt-resurging-amid-coronavirus-pandemic/165401/

Esposito, John, L. (1995). *The Islamic Threat: Myth or Reality?* Oxford: Oxford University Press.

Evans, Leighton (2010). *Authenticity Online: Using Webnography to Address Phenomenological Concerns, New Media and the Politics of Online Communities*. Oxford: Mousoutzanis, Riha, pp. 11–20.

Geertz, Clifford (1973). *The Interpretation of Cultures: Selected Essays by Clifford Geertz*. New York: Basic Books.

Gottschalk, Peter, and Greenberg, Gabriel (2008). *Islamophobia: Making Muslims the Enemy*. Lanham, Maryland: Rowman & Littlefield.

Guolo, Renzo (2001). Il campo verde: strategie islamiche in Italia. *Limes*. April 20. URL: https://www.limesonline.com/cartaceo/il-campo-verde-strategie-isl amiche-in-italia?prv=true

Guolo, Renzo (2016). *Sociologia dell'Islam. Religione e politica*. Milano: Mondadori.

Hal, Lindsey (2002). *The Everlasting Hatred: The Roots of Jihad*. New York: Oracle House Pub.

Hanna, Andrew (2020). *ISIS Offensive Exploits Pandemic*. June 8. URL: https://www.wilsoncenter.org/article/isis-offensive-exploits-pandemic

Hine, Christine (2000). *Virtual Ethnography*. London: SAGE.

Kearnsa Erin M.; Betusb, Allison E., and Lemieuxb, Anthony F. (2019). Why Do Some Terrorist Attacks Receive More Media Attention Than Others? *Justice Quarterly*, Vol. 36, Issue, 6, 985 – 1022.

Kellstedt, Paul (2003). *The mass media and the dynamics of American racial attitudes*. New York: Cambridge University Press.

Kelman, Ilan (2020). *Disaster by Choice: How Our Actions Turn Natural Hazards Into Catastrophes*. Oxford: OUP Oxford.

Kim, Sei hill; Carvalho, John P.; Davis, Andrew. G., and Mullins, Amanda M. (2011). The view of the border: News framing of the definition, causes, and solutions to illegal immigration. *Mass Communication & Society* 14, 292 – 314.

Lakoff, Andrew (2017). *Unprepared: Global Health in a Time of Emergency*. Berkeley: University of California Press.

Lombardi, Marco (2005). *Comunicare nell'emergenza*. Milano: Vita e Pensiero.

Luwei Rose Luqiu, and Fan Yang (2018). Islamophobia in China: news coverage, stereotypes, and Chinese Muslims' perceptions of themselves and Islam. *Asian Journal of Communication* 28:6, 1-22.

Moore, Kerry; Mason, Paul, and Lewis, Justin Matthew Wren (2008). *Images of Islam in the UK: The representation of British Muslims in the national print news media 2000-2008*. Cardiff School of Journalism, Media and Cultural Studies. Cardiff University, pp. 1 – 41. URL: http://orca.cf.ac.uk/53005/1/08channel4-dispatche s.pdf

Nacos, Brigitte L. (2002). *Mass-mediated terrorism*. Oxford: Rowman & Littlefield.

Juergensmeyer, Mark (2003). *Terror in the Mind of God: The Global Rise of Religious Violence*. Berkeley: University of California Press.

Peek, Lori (2010). *Behind the Backlash: Muslim Americans After 9/11*. Philadelphia: Temple University Press.

Poole, Elisabeth (2004). Islamophobia. In E. Cashmore (Ed.) *Encyclopedia of race and ethnic studies*. New York: Routledge, pp. 24–47.

Saeed, Amir (2007). Media, racism and Islamophobia: The representation of Islam and Muslims in the media. *Sociology Compass* 1(2), 443 – 462.

Said, Edward, Wadie (1997). *Covering Islam: How the Media and the Experts Determine how We See the Rest of the World*. New York: Vintage Books.

Richardson, John (2004). *(Mis)representing Islam: The racism and rhetoric of British broadsheet newspapers*. Amsterdam: John Benjamins.

Jerita, Jennifer; Zhaoa, Yangzi; Tanb, Megan, and Wheelerb Munifa (2018). *Differences between National and Local Media in News Coverage of the Zika Virus, Health Communication*. Oxfordshire: Taylor and Francis.

Weberling McKeever, Brooke; Riffe, Daniel, and Carpentier Francesca Dillman (2012). Perceived Hostile Media Bias, Presumed Media Influence, and Opinions About Immigrants and Immigration. *Southern Communication Journal*, Vol. 77, No. 5. Oxfordshire: Routledge.

Vallone, Robert P.; Ross, Lee, and Lepper, Mark. R. (1985). The hostile media phenomenon: Biased perception of media bias in coverage of the Beirut massacre. *Journal of Personality and Social Psychology*, 49, 577–585.

Williams, Brian Glyn (2020). *Islamic State calls for followers to spread coronavirus, exploit pandemic and protests*. June 23. URL: https://theconversation.com/islamic-state-calls-for-followers-to-spread-coronavirus-exploit-pandemic-and-protests-136224

Online Open Sources

https://www.facebook.com/Associazione.ImamItalia/
https://www.facebook.com/centroislamicoculturale/
https://www.facebook.com/confederazioneislamicaitaliana/
https://www.facebook.com/coreis.giovani/
https://www.facebook.com/islamic.relief.italia/
https://www.facebook.com/UCOIIUnioneComunitaIslamicheItalia/
https://trends.google.it/trends/explore?q=isis%20coronavirus&date=2020-02-21%202020-06-23&geo=IT
https://trends.google.it/trends/explore?date=2020-02-21%202020-06-23&geo=IT&q=musulmano,covid-19,ISIS
https://trends.google.it/trends/explore?date=2020-02-21%202020-06-23&geo=IT-72&q=isis%20coronavirus
http://www.voxdiritti.it/islamofobia-musulmani-terroristi/

Annex 1 - Online News

https://www.affaritaliani.it/coffee/video/cronache/covid-19-musulmani-italia-per-noi-manca-spazio-per-sepoltura.html

https://www.agensir.it/italia/2016/11/17/in-italia-1-251-luoghi-di-culto-islamico-panorama-fluido-privo-di-una-normativa-quadro/

https://www.agensir.it/quotidiano/2020/3/31/coronavirus-covid-19-sapienti-musulmani-di-europa-emanata-una-fatwa-sul-lavaggio-del-defunto-in-caso-di-morte-per-malattia-infettiva/

https://almaghrebiya.it/2020/05/31/notizie-dallestero-finalmente-trovata-la-cura-contro-il-coronavirus/

https://www.americansecurityproject.org/how-covid-19-has-emboldened-the-islamic-state-part-1-isis-operations/

https://www.analisidifesa.it/2020/03/per-lisis-il-virus-e-un-flagello-di-dio-contro-gli-infedeli/

https://www.ansa.it/sito/notizie/mondo/2020/03/13/isis-come-proteggersi-dal-coronavirus_fa12e803-1fee-4598-9d65-beb5761dc187.html

https://www.ansa.it/sito/notizie/politica/2020/04/09/coronavirus-dalla-lega-musulmana-1-milione-di-dollari-allitalia_5274a393-4523-426b-9702-6fd67e70f12c.html

https://www.arab.it/almarkaz.html

http://www.asianews.it/notizie-it/Kirkuk,-nellemergenza-Covid-19,-lIsis-sferra-nuovi-attacchi--49889.html

http://www.asianews.it/notizie-it/L'ira-degli-islamisti-per-le-moschee-chiuse.-Il-Covid-19-come-strumento-di-propaganda-49654.html

http://www.asianews.it/notizie-it/Dhaka,-per-lEid-musulmani-in-preghiera-per-la-fine-della-pandemia-di-Covid-19-50176.html

https://asiatimes.com/2020/05/isis-eyes-covid-19-weakness-in-indonesia/

http://assadakah.com/qatar-combattiamo-lisis-nonostante-le-rigide-misure-anti-covid-19/

https://www.avvenire.it/mondo/pagine/pakistan-aiuti-per-conversione

https://www.blitzquotidiano.it/cronaca-mondo/coronavirus-isis-pandemia-attacchi-3170479/

http://www.bolognatoday.it/cronaca/coronavirus-sepolture-morti-musulmani.html

https://www.brainfactor.it/il-think-terrorist-dellisis-durante-la-pandemia/

https://www.brainforum.it/controvirus-terrorismo-e-covid-19/

https://www.businessinsider.com/coronavirus-isis-issues-travel-advisory-for-europe-to-its-fighters-2020-3?IR=T

https://www.bznews24.it/politica/isis-e-hamas-covid-soldato-di-allah/

https://www.centromachiavelli.com/2020/05/13/isis-covid-ritorno-rinascita/

https://www.corrieredellosport.it/news/attualit/cronaca/2020/03/28-68301368/
coronavirus_per_l_isis_e_flagello_inviato_da_dio/

https://www.crisisgroup.org/global/contending-isis-time-coronavirus

https://www.cdt.ch/mondo/isis-coronavirus-e-un-flagello-mandato-da-dio-
MD2511385

https://www.dailymuslim.it/musulmani-e-covid-19/

https://www.difesaesicurezza.com/difesa/isis-usa-il-coronavirus-per-la-propaga
nda-ma-e-unarma-a-doppio-taglio/

https://www.difesaesicurezza.com/difesa/iraq-siria-probabile-epidemia-di-
coronavirus-tra-isis-e-i-miliziani-pro-iran/

https://www.dw.com/en/coronavirus-islamic-state-seeks-to-profit-from-pande
mic/a-52886753

https://www.egic.info/isis-time-of-coronavirus

https://etrurianews.it/2020/03/13/i-terroristi-dellisis-hanno-paura-del-coronavir
us-sospesi-gli-attentati-nelle-zone-rosse-linvito-ai-militanti-di-non-andare-
nelle-aree-infette/

https://it.euronews.com/2020/06/09/covid-19-musulmani-in-italia-salme-in-
attesa-di-sepoltura-e-mancanza-di-spazi

https://it.euronews.com/2020/05/13/covid-19-frontiere-chiuse-i-musulmani-in-
europa-non-sanno-dove-seppellire-i-loro-defunti

https://www.firenzepost.it/2020/03/15/coronavirus-ferma-anche-lisis-ma-non-
blocca-i-migranti/

https://www.focusonafrica.info/mozambico-precipita-elicottero-militare-isis-
rivendica/

https://formiche.net/2020/04/se-i-jihadisti-incoraggiano-il-virus-e-uno-dei-
soldati-di-allah/

https://it.gariwo.net/rubriche/riflessioni-sulla-mente-e-la-ricerca-scientifica/
terrorismo-e-covid19-22015.html

https://www.giornalelavoce.it/trino-coronavirus-i-musulmani-donano-per-
lemergenza-378967

https://formiche.net/2020/06/sepolture-islamiche-coronavirus/

https://it.gariwo.net/persecuzioni/diritti-umani-e-crimini-contro-l-umanita/in-
india-il-covid19-riaccende-l-ostilita-verso-i-musulmani-22026.html

https://www.globalist.it/intelligence/2020/03/13/anche-l-isis-ha-paura-del-cor
onavirus-e-pubblica-le-direttive-su-come-difendersi-dal-contagio-2054397.
html

https://www.ict.org.il/Article/2542/ISIS_in_the_Age_of_COVID-19#gsc.tab=0

https://www.ilfoglio.it/esteri/2020/03/31/news/l-isis-esulta-per-la-rappresaglia-
di-dio-307421/?underPaywall=true

https://www.ilgiornale.it/news/mondo/lisis-festeggia-covid-19-punizione-allah-
1842647.html

https://www.ilgiornale.it/news/mondo/covid-19-predicatore-dellislam-invita-sui-balconi-i-canti-1845960.html

https://www.ilgiornale.it/news/cronache/coronavirus-emergenza-sepoltura-i-musulmani-1849173.html

https://www.ilgiornale.it/news/cronache/coronavirus-islamisti-gioiscono-sul-web-castigo-allah-1820111.html

https://ilmanifesto.it/jihad-in-tempi-di-coronavirus-proteggetevi-e-colpite-niente-pieta/

https://www.ilmattino.it/primopiano/esteri/coronavirus_isis_guida_anti_contagio_ultime_notizie-5109336.html

https://www.ilmessaggero.it/mondo/coronavirus_isis_flagello_dio_infedeli-5138842.html

https://www.ilmessaggero.it/mondo/ramadan_2020_fine_coronavirus_musulmani_islam_news_oggi-5243972.html

https://www.ilsecoloxix.it/italia-mondo/esteri/2020/03/15/news/il-coronavirus-ferma-anche-l-isis-stop-agli-attacchi-in-europa-1.38595718

https://www.ilsussidiario.net/news/il-decreto-di-allah-isis-al-qaeda-talebani-istruzioni-per-usare-il-coronavirus/2011068/

https://insidearabia.com/in-syria-isis-capitalizes-on-coronavirus/

https://it.insideover.com/religioni/lindia-mette-sotto-accusa-i-musulmani-per-la-diffusione-del-coronavirus.html

https://www.ismu.org/coronavirus-e-morte-migranti-di-fede-islamica-emergenza-nell-emergenza/

https://www.isis.stfc.ac.uk/Pages/Coronavirus-(Covid-19)-and-the-ISIS-Neutron-&-Muon-Source.aspx

https://www.ispu.org/journalists/

https://www.lagazzettadelmezzogiorno.it/news/mondo/1211579/isis-come-proteggersi-dal-coronavirus.html

https://www.lastampa.it/topnews/primo-piano/2020/04/08/news/l-isis-arruola-il-coronavirus-e-un-soldato-di-allah-1.38691504

https://www.lastampa.it/topnews/primo-piano/2020/03/26/news/i-morti-islamici-per-il-coronavirus-sono-dei-martiri-1.38639633

https://www.lavocedelpatriota.it/paragoni-pericolosi-per-islam-morti-di-covid-19-sono-martiri/

https://www.leggo.it/italia/cronache/bergamo_coniugi_musulmani_morti_sepolti_vicini_coronavirus_oggi-5142631.html

https://www.limesonline.com/coronavirus-carceri-medio-oriente-detenuti-isis-siria-assad-iran-curdi-iraq-libano/117433?prv=true

https://www.limesonline.com/coronavirus-radicalizzazione-islam-jihadismo-stato-islamico/118036

https://www.lindro.it/isis-rinasce-grazie-al-coronavirus/

https://linserto.it/lisis-festeggia-il-coronavirus-e-una-punizione-di-allah-uid-2/

http://www.meteoweb.eu/2020/03/coronavirus-isis-flagello-dio-colpisce-nazioni-infedeli/1413187/

https://www.militarytimes.com/news/coronavirus/2020/05/08/isis-exploits-covid-19-with-little-success-us-troop-deployments-to-iraq-on-track-despite-pandemic/

https://www.money.it/ISIS-coronavirus-stop-attentati-Europa-consigli-anti-contagio

http://moschee.tuttosuitalia.com/

https://www.nbcnews.com/think/opinion/isis-using-coronavirus-rebuild-its-terrorism-network-iraq-syria-ncna1215941

https://it.notizie.yahoo.com/nuovo-leader-isis-video-covid-19-grande-tormento-121422007.html?guccounter=1&guce_referrer=aHR0cHM6Ly93d3cuZ29vZ2xlLmNvbS8&guce_referrer_sig=AQAAADUH71ZjwDQMavN0Mk9Lb09sOFVRRH0K30XYQEmYswuuZRyiFh40-TtIZP4sRZVT-3Fjw2KN4mqFn72ues8xLTOElyeOLQq3X6HO0Hbya2j-RC1fgdnNwdYkhhWeDSzk09HOIKOdSdNnJXiMx9KySwG-rpi_BgbEIRbPZmW1N74048

https://www.oasiscenter.eu/it/le-autorita-religiose-islamiche-al-tempo-del-coronavirus

https://www.open.online/2020/03/13/coronavirus-anche-isis-teme-contagi-direttive-religiose-contro-pandemia/

https://www.open.online/2020/04/22/coronavirus-il-mese-sacro-del-ramadan-tra-lockdown-e-moschee-chiuse/

https://openmigration.org/analisi/per-la-comunita-musulmana-il-covid-mette-a-rischio-anche-la-sepoltura/

https://www.orientecristiano.it/all-news/medio-oriente/17961-kirkuk-nell-emergenza-covid-19-l-isis-sferra-nuovi-attacchi.html

https://www.orizzontipolitici.it/come-il-coronavirus-ha-rafforzato-il-terrorismo/

https://www.politico.eu/article/coronavirus-isis-terrorists-europe/

https://www.rainews.it/dl/rainews/media/musulmani-piangono-morti-coronavirus-a489433f-1a9f-44e7-a6d0-4ac7b89f08ba.html

https://reliefweb.int/report/syrian-arab-republic/virus-fears-spread-camps-isis-families-syria-s-north-east

https://www.repubblica.it/esteri/2020/03/28/news/coronavirus_per_l_isis_e_una_punizione_agli_infedeli-252504501/

https://www.repubblica.it/solidarieta/emergenza/2020/03/20/news/migranti_musulmani_covid-19_emergenza_per_i_defunti_musulmani_rimpatri_bloccati_salme_stipate_in_obitori_-251799423/

https://www.repubblica.it/solidarieta/immigrazione/2020/02/26/news/musul
mani_in_italia_coronavirus_aperta_una_colletta_per_aiutare_i_centri_piu_
colpiti-249641198/

https://sicurezzainternazionale.luiss.it/2020/05/29/audio-dellisis-coronavirus-
punizione-divina/

https://smallwarsjournal.com/blog/isis-seeks-comeback-under-cover-covid-19

https://www.splcenter.org/intelligence-report?keyword=&amp%3Bpage=1&page=
151

https://www.tempi.it/isis-coronavirus-iraq-siria/

https://www.terrasanta.net/2020/04/se-il-coronavirus-diventa-una-opportunita-
per-lisis/

https://www.tgcom24.mediaset.it/mondo/coronavirus-isis-pubblica-direttive-su-
come-difendersi-da-contagio_16086497-202002a.shtml

https://thediplomat.com/2020/04/islamic-state-terror-in-the-maldives-as-covid-
19-arrives/

https://www.theguardian.com/world/2020/apr/16/opportunity-or-threat-how-
islamic-extremists-reacting-coronavirus

https://theintercept.com/2020/04/19/coronavirus-isis-advice/

https://timgate.it/news/esteri/coronavirus-terroristi-islamici.vum

https://time.com/5828630/isis-coronavirus/

https://www.tpi.it/esteri/coronavirus-isis-militanti-via-europa-20200316566565/

https://www.tuttomercatoweb.com/altre-notizie/emergenza-coronavirus-arrivan
o-le-raccomandazioni-dell-isis-proteggetevi-dal-contagio-1360162

https://www.tuttosport.com/news/attualit/cronaca/2020/03/28-68301603/per
_l_isis_il_coronavirus_e_un_flagello_inviato_da_dio_colpisce_apostati_e_
infedeli_/

http://www.ucoii.org/emergenzacovid19/

https://www.ucoii.org/wp-content/uploads/2020/03/VADEMECUM-RITUALITA-
FUNEBRE-PER-LA-COMUNITA-ISLAMICA-IN-ITALIA-1-1.pdf

https://www.ultimavoce.it/isis-sfrutta-il-covid-19-per-rafforzare-la-sua-propaga
nda/

https://www.unionesarda.it/articolo/news/mondo/2020/03/13/anche-l-isis-teme-
il-coronavirus-le-direttive-religiose-per-prote-137-997089.html

https://varesepress.info/europa-mondo/covid-19-soldato-di-dio.html

https://www.jpost.com/middle-east/behind-the-lines-isis-and-the-virus-624913

Annex 2 - Outline of the Exploratory Survey

Socio - demographic section

1. What is your country of origin?
2. How long have you been living in Italy?
3. Which city do you live in?
4. What is your role within the organization of your Islamic center?

The Covid - 19 Pandemic

1. What is the pandemic caused by the Covid-19 virus for you?
2. Considering the pandemic from Covid-19, according to you the management of the crisis in Italy is...
3. How do you view the management of the crisis caused by the Covid-19 virus in Italy?
4. Why do you think the media during the first months of the pandemic mostly talked about the Islamic community, referring to the possibilities of ISIS to exploit this moment for attacks?
5. The press, especially the foreign press, has often communicated that ISIS would use the pandemic to strike European countries. Do you think such an event is possible?
6. Social networks have reported acts of solidarity by the various Muslim communities in Italy. According to you, there were more:
7. According to you, solidarity is...
8. Do you think you were prejudiced during the first months of the pandemic by Covid-19 in Italy?
9. Do you think solidarity actions can reduce prejudice against Muslim people and communities in Italy?

Religious Fundamentalism – A Misleading Concept?

Peter Antes

Abstract

The chapter shows that Fundamentalism is more than an interpretative term. It does not describe reality but evaluates and even produces it. Therefore, it is a misleading concept with consequences for the addressees who discover themselves as being part of a global protest wave against modernity. Local reasons are thus totally neglected as it was the case in Iran, Algeria and Chechnya.

Keywords: Category Creation, Fundamentalism, Religious Fundamentalism

1. Introduction

Florian Zemmin comes, in his article on *The Problem of Salafism*, to three important observations:

> "First, language does not only describe reality, but it also evaluates reality, since the central concepts we use hold a normative dimension, too: just consider "terrorism" or "freedom". Secondly, our language not only describes and evaluates a given reality, but also helps to produce it. For it should be clear, after the linguistic turn, that "reality" is always reality as interpreted and mediated by language. Scholars produce reality not least by grouping disconnected phenomena in certain categories. These categories, thirdly, have an impact on the social identification and self-identification of actors, as do narratives available for understanding and interpreting a given situation. Of course, it is not only scholars producing such categories and narratives, but also other societal actors. Moreover, the academy forms part of society, and thus in a dialectical process takes up and impacts on societal categories."[1]

---

1   Florian Zemmin (2020). The Problem of Salafism, the Problem with 'Salafism'. An Essay on the Usability of an Academic Category to understand a Political Challenge. In Klaus Hock & Nina

The intention of this article is to show that Religious Fundamentalism is such a category which not only describes reality but also evaluates and produces it.[2] Therefore, the article starts with a reference to the original meaning of Fundamentalism in religion, and it then widens its use to a much broader understanding of the term in order to finally come to some of the consequences of such a narrative. Consequently, the conclusion expresses a strong warning to all not to be too quick with those general interpretative terms but to pay attention to local peculiarities as well.

2.   The original meaning of the term

In 1983 Wilfert Joest published his article on *Fundamentalismus* in the 11th volume of the "Theologische Realenzyklopädie (TRE)" wherein he exclusively deals with the American Protestant Group of the end of the 19th and the beginning of the 20th centuries. Fundamentalism in this context refers to a collection of 90 texts published between 1910 and 1915 by the Bible Institute of Los Angeles under the title of *The Fundamentals. A Testimony To The Truth*, often quoted simply as *The Fundamentals*. The aim of these publications was to reject liberal tendencies in the Protestant theology of that time and to insist instead on the traditional teachings of the Christian creed. *The Fundamentals* are opposed to the idea of an evolution of the human being in line with other species of animals and primates as suggested by Darwin. They also maintain the classical understanding of the virgin birth of Christ and his bodily resurrection and physical return. They confess Christ as the Son of God and hold true all miracles as described in the Bible. Consequently they reject modern exegesis with its historical critical method and are opposed to all modern interpretations of the Holy Scriptures by insisting on the inerrancy of the biblical texts for which, according to them, there is no need for reinterpretation in order to reconcile them with modern natural sciences by giving up the literal understanding of the texts.

The Fundamentals were welcome and particularly successful in American Protestant milieus of those who were social losers in the process of modernization. They fight for the old vision of the world, of which the classical values and norms were put in jeopardy through modernization.

The fundamentalist vision of the world and of religion was thus an anti-modern attitude opposed to all kinds of modernization and addressed to those who felt left behind, and marginalized, in the modernization process.

Käsehage (Eds.). 'Militant Islam' vs. 'Islamic Militancy'? *Religion, Violence, Category Formation and Applied Research, Contested Fields in the Discourses of Scholarship.* Wien: LIT, p. 119.

2   For the following cf. also Peter Antes (2004). New Approaches to the Study of the New Fundamentalisms. In Antes, Peter / Geertz, Armin W. / Warne, Randi R. (Eds). *New Approaches to the Study of Religion, Volume I: Regional, Critical and Historical Approaches (= Religion and Reason).* Vol. 42 [Paperback-Edition 2008]), Berlin-New York: W. de Gruyter, pp. 437-449.

3.   A broader understanding of the term

In 1995 the 4th volume of the 3rd edition of the "Lexikon für Theologie und Kirche" was published. There we also find an article on *Fundamentalismus*. Beinert and his co-authors have a completely different understanding of the term compared with *Fundamentalismus* in the TRE. They say that fundamentalism is a trend in all living religions. It is opposed to another more open-minded and liberal trend, so that contemporary religions embrace at least two opposite trends, an anti-modern and a modern one.

In comparing the two mentioned encyclopaedias, the question arises regarding how the term came to have such a difference in meaning. The answer lies in the Islamic Revolution in Iran when in January 1979 Ayatollah Ruhollah Khomeini came back to Tehran from his exile in France in order replace the Shah of Iran as Head of State, after the latter had fled from the country leaving it to Khomeini and his followers.

It is noteworthy that the Shah's regime was fully supported by the West and equipped with the most modern weapons. Therefore, it was an enormous shock for the West that such a system could not survive against protesting masses led by Khomeini from exile. Neither politicians nor scholars of Islamic studies had foreseen that such a wave of protest could be successful. They all had confidence in the Shah's modernization policy, and they thus totally underestimated what was going on as a consequence of protest-encouraging sermons and pamphlets in the mosques. Khomeini's victory was therefore not only a surprise but a real shock for the West. For the first time in modern history, a revolution was successful based on a religion that, unlike revolutions in the name of nationalism, communism, marxism or socialism, had its roots not in Western thoughts but in a religious setting that seemed to reject modernization.

The predominant question of the time was how to cope with such a reality. Journalists in France began to see parallels in the anti-modern Christian thoughts of integrism while in the German and English-speaking worlds the reference to Christian Fundamentalism came to the minds of those in search for an explanation. The term fundamentalism was so successful that in France it replaced that of integrism and led in most countries to serious academic discussions, such that Martin Riesebrodt could write a PhD thesis to compare American Protestant Fundamentalists (1910-28) and Iranian Shiites (1961-79).

Thanks to the new meaning of the term, other protest phenomena could be identified and interpreted. This holds true for the "Islamic Salvation Front" (Front Islamique du Salut = FIS), which won parts of the general elections in Algeria in 1991, with the result that France felt the need to stop the elections in order to avoid an Islamist victory. Commentators like Gilles Kepel saw in all that a revenge of God, thus bringing religion back to the public floor by making a political factor out of it.

Kepel's and others' use of "fundamentalism" with reference to Islam along with similar references with regard to Christianity and Judaism opened the way to a broad use of the term so that for instance the Hindu fight against the Babri mosque in Ayodhya (India) in 1991 was also labelled as fundamentalist, as was the 1982-founded Shiite Hizbollah (Party of God) in Lebanon or the 1985-founded Sunnite Hamas in Palestine.

The few examples mentioned here show what Zimmer has stated saying that "our language not only describes and evaluates a given reality, but also helps to produce it." This means that it puts local forms of protest with very different local aspects into a general interpretative framework that makes a world-wide trend out of them

More concretely speaking, one might wonder what the Islamic Revolution in Iran from above might have in common with the resurgence of the FIS members in Algeria from below. The same applies to the comparison between the Hamas fighters in Palestine and the Hindu fundamentalists of Ayodhya. Yet, in spite of obvious differences in these forms of protest compared with one another, the term was ideally suited to inspire a large research project to study religious fundamentalisms worldwide. Martin E. Marty and E. Scott Appleby engaged a large number of researchers to show that "fundamentalists seek to replace existing structures with a comprehensive system emanating from religious principles and embracing law, polity, society, economy, and culture."[3] And this seems to be obvious for the editors although the contributions about Buddhism and Judaism in the book have difficulties seeing any similar phenomena in these religions. That, however, does not hinder the editors from claiming at the end of the book that fundamentalisms can be found in all world religions and thus represent a dangerous religious thread opposed to all attempts at modernization that might be needed in the religions.

The only relevant differences are in the strategies. So, we find groups that are in favour of democratic elections as long as they see chances to win while others reject elections if they think that majorities do not vote for them, others again try the long march through institutions to come to power whereas others declare violent acts legitimate in their attempts to reach their goals.

Samuel Huntington goes even one step further. He does not see two different trends in each of the religions but identifies religions as a whole with their role in the process of modernization. In his book *Clash of Civilizations* he declares that Islam is totally opposed to modernization and the modern world; it is thus in absolute opposition to what the West stands for. All the other religions are situated somewhere in between these two contradictory poles of Islam on the one side and the secular West on the other. According to Huntington, the clash of civilizations

---

3   Martin E. Marty & E. S. Appleby (Eds.) (1994). *Fundamentalisms Observed*. Paperback ed. Chicago [et al.]: University of Chicago Press, p. 824.

is the most dangerous potential conflict after fights between aristocratic families, then nation states in the 19th century and the first part of the 20th century. Then came an ideological conflict between the East and the West after World War II. Its end does not mean the end of conflicts; on the contrary, the clash of civilizations could turn into an even more dangerous battle field where Islam is the most prominent enemy.

Looking at the battle fields in the Gulf region and the Near East one might come to the conclusion that such a clash of civilizations is indeed going on. Jan Joffe asked in an article whether Huntington is right or not. He came to the conclusion: "There is no war of religions, but of powers that fight for supremacy." And later in the text he says: "In Syria, the Tehran theocrats are fighting along with the Orthodox of Russia. The Saudis and their Sunni cronies are part of the US-led coalition, and the Muslim Turks are bombing Muslim Kurds who are not allowed to have their own state. A silent alliance connects Israel with Riyadh, Amman and Cairo. It's not about fervour, it's about interest."

4.   The consequences

There are at least four major consequences of such general interpretative terms: the addressees, protest as a moral claim against the economy worldwide, the local differences, and the historicity and ambiguity of terms and texts.

4.1   The addressees

A major research project like Martin Marty's and Scott Appleby's *Fundamentalisms observed* cannot be published unnoticed by those who are dealt with in these volumes. They thus understand that their protest is not a local feeling of dissatisfaction with certain developments in the area but is rather part of a much broader trend of protest typical of all major religions in the world. They thus see themselves involved in a worldwide protest wave due to the victory of capitalism after the break down of an alternative economic system as it was for decades propagated by the Soviet Union and the Eastern bloc, but had obviously failed and led to the end of the East-West confrontation in 1989.

Most willingly, the addressees took the external designation of fundamentalists over for themselves as a self-designation in the following years. And the books on fundamentalism moreover made it easy for them to make contact with other so called fundamentalist groups because all the addresses and their email connections were given in these books, so that contact only needed to be established to create a worldwide network of protest against all the injustices produced by the capitalist unlimited-exploitation policy.

The term fundamentalism was so successful that it was also literally translated into the different languages of the addressees. This led in Arabic to the consequence that the literal translation of $u\!\!\!\!\!\!\!\:s\bar{u}liyya$ evoked in the context of religion an immediate association with $u\!\!\!\!\!\!\!\:s\bar{u}l$ $al\text{-}d\bar{\imath}n$ (= the principles of the religion), the classical title of medieval manuals of Islamic theology. Thus such an originally negatively-connoted term as fundamentalism changed now into a positive meaning because pious people could not seriously oppose the principles of the religion. To indicate the negative implications another term was needed in internal Muslims circles. They therefore preferred Extremism or Islamism instead of the negative use of Fundamentalism. With these new terms, however, new realities were also produced. Florian Zemmin writes with regard to that:

> "Thus, it does make a difference whether scholars speak of, and thereby frame and to some extent construct, a problem as Islamic Extremism or Extremist Islam. The first wording suggests Islamic Extremism to be one variety of different types of Extremism. Consequently, it ought to be viewed together with other such types, and the competencies of experts on Extremism are central for understanding the causes of the problem of Extremism. The second wording suggests Extremist Islam to be one variety of different types of Islam. As such it is primarily to be understood as an articulation of Islam. And, in the last consequence, Islam is framed as the problem, for all articulations of Islam could potentially evolve into the Militant variety. The issue becomes ever clearer from the misleading wording of Radical Islam, in distinction from Moderate Islam. This distinction, voluntarily or not, suggests that the former is Islam in the fullest sense, whereas the latter makes certain concessions."[4]

These examples underline the importance of terms as reality-producers, and this holds true for Islamic Extremism and Extremist Islam or Radical and Moderate Islam as well as for Fundamentalism.

4.2   Protest as a moral claim against economy worldwide

Since left-wing politics had no chance anymore, their followers often changed into religious fundamentalists to formulate the same claims as before, but now in religious or more precisely moral claims against a world that marginalizes them and leaves no chances of participation to them.

The moral claim was particularly successful because the new economic situation produced a total change as concerns the groups struggling in the economy with each other. While the communist and Marxist ideologies were based on the

---

4   Zemmin, 2020, p. 119-20.

opposition between exploiters and exploited who both were part of the production process, the new situation is the gap between those who are involved in the production and those who are outside. Pope Francis in his Apostolic Exhortation *Evangelii Gaudium* of 2013 says: "The excluded are not the 'exploited' but the outcast, the 'leftovers'."[5]

Strikes are not the appropriate means to fight for more justice and participation. It seems that money alone reigns in the world and the individuals do not count in this economic system, or to quote once again the prominent headings of Pope Francis' Apostolic Exhortation *Evangelii Gaudium*:[6]

"No to an economy of exclusion
No to the new idolatry of money
No to a financial system which rules rather than serves
No to the inequality which spawns violence."

In this respect it is quite understandable that religious leaders join the protesters and support their moral claims against an economic system that appears to be the contrary of what human beings are expected to be.[7] So we find monotheists and polytheists in the same wave of protest. Hindus as well as Muslims and Christians wish to return to traditional moral values and classical ethics to avoid the negative effects of the prevailing capitalist system.

It is obvious that those protests are addressed against the system as such; they refer to general claims of traditional values and do not specify particular areas with their regional peculiarities.

4.3 The local differences

General interpretative terms like fundamentalism explain the ongoing processes as being part of a global phenomenon and consequently do not often see the local peculiarities of protest. In the case of the Islamic Revolution of Iran, for instance, the protest was mainly addressed against the oppression system of the Shah's regime, which imposed specific types of modernization on an Iranian people who preferred a much more moderate introduction of new mechanisms, while in Algeria the "Islamic Salvation Front" articulated the protest of the poor and of well-educated jobless intellectuals who did not see any chance of improving their situation.

Most striking is the unspecified explanation of terrorism for what happened in Chechnya over the last decades. Islam there is a quite recent phenomenon. It

---

5   Cf. Pope Francis (2013). *Evangelii Gaudium, Rome.* November 24, Nr. 53.
6   Ibid., Nr. 53-60.
7   Cf. Peter Antes (1996). *Religions and Politics. Facts and Perspectives.* In Religioni e Società. Rivista di scienze sociali della religione. Nr. 26, Anno XI, Settembre-Dicembre, 5-13.

became the official religion in the country in the first half of the 18th century. It is a combination of traditional forms of law (*Ada*) and Muslim traditions in their Sufi form. Brotherhoods led by *Ustas* tell their followers or students (*Murids*) in their gatherings (*wird*) how to behave and what to do. The main purpose of those religious orders (*tarikat*) is to fight for the interests of the community and not to concentrate on one's individual desires. For centuries the Chechnyan population was engaged in a fierce fight for independence from the Russian dominance but suffered enormously under the devastating attempts of Russian troops to keep total control in the country.[8]

Two wars were thus led by the Russians against the Chechnyan people. Between the first war (1994-96) and the second war (1999-2009) Wahhabis from Saudi Arabia came into the country and, supported by former Muslim fighters in Afghanistan, tried to propagate their strict interpretation of Islam among the local Muslim population, so that it came to a split in Muslim circles. "The religious division triggered by Wahhabi extremists extends right into the families. Fathers curse their sons because they have joined the Wahhabis, and sons break away from their fathers because they live an 'impure' Islam according to Wahhabi understanding of salvation."[9] The Wahhabi's influence was such a bad one that this label soon became synonymous with terrorists.[10]

On the other hand, as concerns the second war,

"Putin used the war to create for himself the image of the 'iron fist' in the fight against Russia's enemies. This helped him to win the presidential elections on March 26, 2000. After taking office as President of the Russian Federation, however, he let the campaign continue, even though he would have had several real chances of ending it."[11]

The continuation of the war was

"lucrative for all involved. Everyone got their share. For the contracting's at the post offices, it meant ten to twenty rubles bribe money at every check, and that around the clock. For the generals in Moscow and Chankala [i.e. a district of Grozny, P.A.] it was 'skimming' money from the 'military budget'. For the middle-ranking officers it was the extortion of ransom money for 'temporary hostages' and for corpses. For the low-ranking officers, it was the looting during the 'purges'. And for all together

---

8   Cf. for that the short history: Anna Politkowskaja (2008). *Tschetschenien. Die Wahrheit über den Krieg.* Frankfurt am Main: Fischer Taschenbuchverlag, pp. 304-319.

9   Politkowskaja, 2008, p. 183.

10   Ib., p. 326.

11   Ib., p. 316.

(the Russian military plus a part of the rebels) it was participation in the illegal oil and weapons business. On top of that came promotions, awards, careers..."[12]

The examples of Iran, Algeria, and Chechnya show very clearly how important it is to have a close look at local problems and reasons for protest, in order to avoid thinking that all is embedded in the interpretative framework of global protest as a general trend typical of each of the great religions in the world.

4.4   Historicity and ambiguity of terms and texts

The last aspect to be mentioned here is the use of terms and texts. Schulze puts the terminology question in the following terms:

"A major problem can be seen in the properties of macro-sociological theories. They are aimed at explaining causes and origins in a very general sense, they comparatively capture 'characteristics' of terrorism and extremism, and they are based on fixed, timeless definitions that are intended as a summary of the observed characteristics. As such, they are often theories about Islam: so, certain concepts such as Islam, Sharī'a, jihād, Qur'ān or the prophetic tradtion (sunna) are defined as real universals constituting Islam. [...] Terms like jihād, sharī'a or Islam are thus considered 'real' insofar as they have a reality that exists as a permanent idea and shapes Muslim identity and Muslim being. It is assumed that the meaning of the terms is fixed and unchangeable once and for all by their use in the Qur'ān or other Islamic canonical texts."[13]

Salafism is a very good example to show how different references to early Islam can be. While Muḥammad Abduh (1849-1905) and others of his time referred to the "pious predecessors" of the first three generations of Muslims in history to justify their modernist interpretation of Islam, Salafists today insist on very traditional teachings of Islam without any ambiguity. Here again is an important difference in interpretation. Thomas Bauer says in this respect:

"Religious texts, which are the subject of this article, are much closer to literary texts than to factual texts. Literary texts, however, have a much higher density of ambiguity than, for example, instructions for use. Above all, however, their ambiguity is intentional, since polyvalence is virtually a defining characteristic that distinguishes literary texts from factual texts. The question whether ambiguity in

---

12   Ib., p. 216.
13   Reinhard Schulze (2020). Beyond Religion - Beyond Islam. The Challenge of Ultra-Islamist Violence. In Klaus Hock & Nina Käsehage (Eds.). 'Militant Islam' vs. 'Islamic Militancy'? Religion, Violence, Category Formation and Applied Research, Contested Fields in the Discourses of Scholarship. Wien: LIT, p. 108.

religious texts is also deliberately sought and desired is left open (for the Qur'ān, according to most classical scholars, it is definitely affirmative)."[14]

A good understanding of a religious text, therefore, needs an interpretation in its historical context for the meaning of its terms as well as being part of ambiguous interpretations syn- and diachronically.

Conclusion

As said in the beginning of this article, Florian Zemmin stated that "our language not only describes and evaluates a given reality, but also helps to produce it." This article has showed with regard to the concept of Religious Fundamentalism that this statement is really true. It explains how certain parallels between obviously highly-heterogeneous phenomena have been drawn and have produced an interpretative term used on a worldwide scale, which has made a global trend out of various protests in different areas, albeit for very different reasons. Moreover it also had an impact on the addressees who learned from these studies that they all belong to a global protest wave against modernity. The change from an external designation to a self-designation had moreover the consequence that the term was translated in other languages and produced the result, in the case of its translation into Arabic, that the term lost its negative connotation and had therefore to be replaced by other terms such as Islamic Extremism or Extremist Islam or Radical Islam in order to express the negative connotation of what was originally meant by fundamentalism in the context of religion and more precisely of Islam.

With reference to Iran, Algeria and particularly Chechnya it has been argued that a global concept such as Religious Fundamentalism runs the risk of interpreting every protest as a global phenomenon and thus does not see the local peculiarities that encourage protests, notwithstanding the global tendencies. The use of macro-sociological theories, finally, suggests fixed and timelessly-used terminologies that exclude historical changes in the vocabulary as well as ambiguous readings of the texts syn- and diachronically.

To draw the readers' attention to such a production of reality is very important in times, like those of the Coronavirus, when conspiracy theories are making the rounds and threaten to obscure the view of local formations and concrete regional differences. It is a strong call to engage in an always-needed reality check before one feels inclined to implement general explanations of a particular term, because the obvious connotations of such a term can inadvertently raise, as in the case of

---

14   Thomas Bauer (2011). *Die Kultur der Ambiguität. Eine andere Geschichte des Islam*. Berlin: Verlag der Weltreligionen im Insel Verlag, p. 56.

Religious Fundamentalism, a misleading concept that impedes correct analysis of what is really going on.

Bibliography

Antes, Peter (2004). New Approaches to the Study of the New Fundamentalisms. In Peter Antes, Armin W. Geertz and Randi R. Warne (Eds). *New Approaches to the Study of Religion, Volume I: Regional, Critical and Historical Approaches (= Religion and Reason).* Vol. 42 [Paperback-Edition 2008]). Berlin-New York: W. de Gruyter, pp. 437-449.

Antes, Peter (1996). Religions and Politics. Facts and Perspectives. In Religioni e Società. *Rivista di scienze sociali della religione*, Nr. 26, Anno XI, Settembre-Dicembre, 5-13.

Bauer, Thomas (2011). *Die Kultur der Ambiguität. Eine andere Geschichte des Islam.* Berlin: Verlag der Weltreligionen im Insel Verlag.

Beinert, Wolfgang; Müller, Hans-Peter, and Garhammer, Erich (1995). Fundamentalismus. In *Lexikon für Theologie und Kirche*, Freiburg [et al.]: Herder, 3rd ed., Vol. 4, col. 224-226.

Hock, Klaus and Käsehage, Nina (Eds.) (2020). *'Militant Islam' vs. 'Islamic Militancy'? Religion, Violence, Category Formation and Applied Research, Contested Fields in the Discourses of Scholarship.* Wien: LIT.

Huntington, Samuel (1996). *The Clash of Civilizations and the Making of World Order.* New York [et al.]: Simon & Schuster.

Joest, Wilfried (1983). Fundamentalismus. In *Theologische Realenzyklopädie (TRE).* Berlin-New York: W. de Gruyter, vol. 11, pp. 732-738.

Kepel, Gilles (1994). *The Revenge of God. The Resurgence of Islam, Christianity, and Judaism in the Modern World.* Cambridge: Polity Press.

Marty, Martin E., and Appleby, R. Scott (Eds.) (1991). *Fundamentalisms Observed. (= The Fundamentalism Project, Vol I).* Chicago [et al.]: University of Chicago Press.

Marty, Martin E., and Appleby, R. Scott (Eds.) (1993). *Fundamentalisms and Society: Reclaiming the Sciences, the Family and Education (= The Fundamentalism Project, Vol. II).* Chicago [et al.]: University of Chicago Press.

Marty, Martin E., and Appleby, R. Scott (Eds.) (1993). *Fundamentalisms and the State: Remaking Polities, Economies, and Militance (= The Fundamentalism Project, Vol. III).* Chicago [et al.]: University of Chicago Press.

Marty, Martin E., and Appleby, R. Scott (Eds.) (1994). *Fundamentalisms Observed.* Paperback ed. Chicago [et al.]: University of Chicago Press.

Marty, Martin E., and Appleby, R. Scott (Eds.) (1995). *Fundamentalisms Comprehended.* Chicago [et al.]: University of Chicago Press.

Politkowskaja, Anna (2008). *Tschetschenien. Die Wahrheit über den Krieg.* Frankfurt am Main: Fischer Taschenbuchverlag.

Riesebrodt, Martin (1990). *Fundamentalismus als patriarchalische Protestbewegung. Amerikanische Protestanten (1910-28) und iranische Schiiten (1961-79) im Vergleich*. Tübingen: Mohr.

Schulze, Reinhard (2020). Beyond Religion – Beyond Islam. The Challenge of Ultra-Islamist Violence. In Klaus Hock & Nina Käsehage (Eds.). *'Militant Islam'* vs. *'Islamic Militancy'? Religion, Violence, Category Formation and Applied Research, Contested Fields in the Discourses of Scholarship*. Wien: LIT, pp. 89-116.

Zemmin, Florian (2020). The Problem of Salafism, the Problem with 'Salafism'. An Essay on the Usability of an Academic Category to understand a Political Challenge. In Klaus Hock & Nina Käsehage (Eds.). *'Militant Islam'* vs. *'Islamic Militancy'? Religion, Violence, Category Formation and Applied Research, Contested Fields in the Discourses of Scholarship*. Wien: LIT, pp. 117-141.

Online Open Source

Joffe, Josef (2016). ,Der Prophet, der brillant danebengriff. Der Terror dominiert die Schlagzeilen – »Kampf der Kulturen« unsere Krisen präzise vorhergesagt. Dabei irrte er jedoch gewaltig'. *DIE ZEIT*. Nr. 1, Dezember 29, Feuilleton.

Pope Francis (2013). *Evangelii Gaudium*. Rome, November 24. URL: http://www.vatican.va/content/francesco/en/apost_exhortations/documents/papa-francesco_esortazione-ap_20131124_evangelii-gaudium.html, accessed on May 22, 2020.

List of figures

Chapter: The Impact of Covid-19 on Orthodox Groups and Believers in Russia
Author: Anastasia V. Mitrofanova

Image 1: *Priest, wearing PPE, gives communion to a sick woman.*

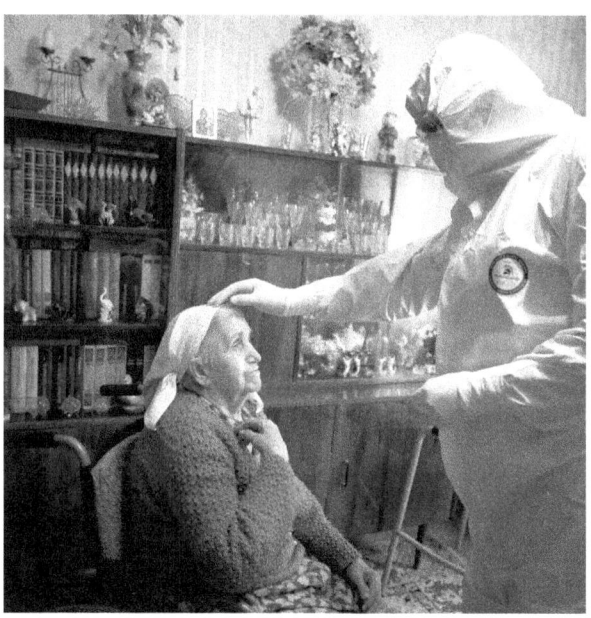

Photo from the public Facebook page of Fr. Vasilii Gelevan. URL:
https://www.facebook.com/padrebasilio/posts/3513566135325185

Image 2: *Naked floor of the Cathedral of Christ the Saviour during the 2020 Paschal Liturgy*

Source: Paskha Khristova. Bogosluzhenie v Khrame Khrista Spasitelya. NTV. 18 April 2020. URL: https://www.youtube.com/watch?v=Himz9wrsUwg

Image 3: *Andrei Kormoukhin's flash mob.*

URL : https ://sun1-88.userapi.com/mzbupVvj1Xs_AbiYYO9540WF9
E8rPPlvt-dYSw/W84mc4bJN90.jpg

Image 4: *Colonel Ret. Vladimir Kvachkov with Schemahegumen Sergii (Romanov).*

URL: https://sun9-44.userapi.com/JEurilNfXohk7dekiDUXSgCaE5s D1dSum8CvRw/ewwXDFzeUGg.jpg.

Image 5: *Aliev, with his son, friends and supporters congratulates war veterans in the evening of May 8th and asks them for forgiveness.*

URL: https://www.youtube.com/watch?v=mc3eJA6pD1c

Chapter: How Central Asian Salafi-Jihadi Groups are Exploiting the Covid-19 Pandemic: New Opportunities and Challenges

Author: Uran Botobekov

Image 1: *Abdul Aziz Uzbeki, the amir of Katibat al Tawhid wal Jihad*

Image posted by Katibat al Tawhid wal Jihad on its *Telegram* channel, May 25, 2019.

Image 2: *Abū Yusuf Muhojir, the amir of Katibat Imam al Bukhari*

Image posted by Katibat Imam al Bukhari on its *Telegram* channel, February 2018.

Image 3: *Ahluddin Navqotiy, the new imam of Katibat al Tawhid wal Jihad, during the Jummah Khutbah tells the Uzbek jihadists about the "invisible soldiers of God"*

Screenshot from the video of Katibat al Tawhid wal Jihad, March 16, 2020, *Telegram* channel.

Image 4: *Taliban doctors distribute masks and drugs for Covid-19*

Official website of Islamic Emirate of Afghanistan (2020/d). 'Essential awareness materials for Prevention of corona virus disease distributed in Badghis'. March 29, 2020. See: http://alemarahenglish.net/?p=34058

Image 5: *The Turkestan Islamic Party's Media Center "Islam Awazi" promoted Covid-19 as "God's punishment" for China*

Screenshot from the video of the Turkestan Islamic Party's Media Center "Islam Awazi", February 29, 2020.

Image 6: *Turkestan Islamic Party believes that Coronavirus is a soldier of God*

Joscelyn, Thomas (2019). 'Turkestan Islamic Party musters large force for battles in Syria.' | *FDD's Long War Journal*. June 29. URL: https://www.longwarjournal.org/archives/2019/06/turkistan-islamic-party-musters-large-force-for-battles-in-syria.php

Chapter: Islamic Fundamentalism Framing Politics in Mali: From the Middle Ages to the Age of Pandemic
Author: Olga Torres Díaz

Image 1: *Abraham Cresques. Atlas de cartes marines*

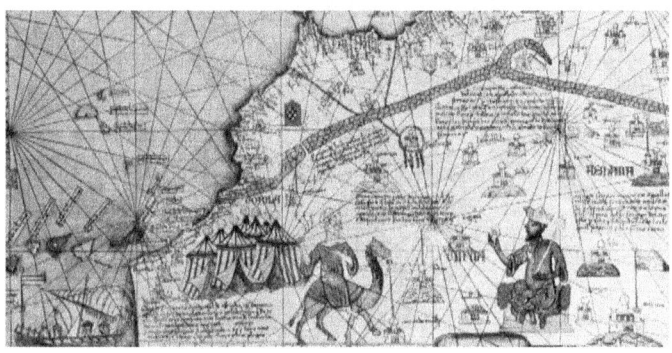

Abraham Cresques (1375) Atlas de cartes marines, dit [Atlas Catalan]. The image inserted is the lower part of the fifth and sixth sections. URL: https://gallica.bnf.fr/ark:/12148/btv1b55002481n.image

List of authors

Miguel Álvarez Ortega is an Associate Professor at the University of Kyoto, where he teaches Jurisprudence, Theories of Justice and Religion and Law. He holds degrees in Linguistics and Translation studies, and Law, and received his Ph.D. in Philosophy of Law in 2007. He has also pursued courses on Buddhist Philosophy and Tibetan language at Rangjung Yeshe Institute (Kathmandu, Nepal).

His initial research was mainly dedicated to contemporary legal and political philosophy, and language rights and policy. His current interests focus on legal, political, and moral philosophy in Buddhist countries, particularly in the Himalayan area.

Current publications: *When Fools Cannot Win: Social Determinism and Political Pragmatism in Bondong´s Reception of Sakya Legshe* (2019), *Traditional Tibetean Buddhist Scholars on Dharma, Law, Politics, and Social Ethics: Philosophical Discussions in Boudkanath (Nepal)* (2019) and *Buddhism and Law* (Oxford Bibliographies entry).

Homepage: https://us.academia.edu/Miguel%C3%81lvarezOrtega

Peter Antes is Professor emeritus of the Institute of Religious Studies at Leibniz University of Hannover (Germany). From 1988 to 1993, Antes has been the President of the *Deutsche Vereinigung für Religionsgeschichte*. From 1995 to 2000, he has been one of the two Vice Presidents and from 2000 to 2005, the President of the *International Association for the History of Religions*.

His main fields of research are Modern Islamic Ethics, Comparative Religion, Interreligious Dialogue and Methodology in the Study of Religions.

He is the author of the publications *Religionen im Brennpunkt; Religionswissenschaftliche Beiträge 1976–2007; Ethik und Politik im Islam* and *Christentum. Eine religionswissenschaftliche Einführung*.

Homepage: http://www.ithrw.uni-hannover.de/peter_antes.html

Yaakov Ariel is Professor of Religious Studies at the University of North Carolina at Chapel Hill and a graduate of the Hebrew University and the University of Chicago.

Ariel's research focuses on Christian-Jewish Relations; Christian and Jewish attitudes towards the Holy Land, Zionism and Israel; Jewish and Christian New Religious Movements and the effect of the modernity and post-modernity on Jewish and Christian groups. He has published dozens of articles and a number of books on these topics. His books, *Evangelizing the Chosen People* won the *Outler Prize* of the *American Society of Church History*.

Ariel's current list of publications include, in addition to three books, and two booklets, a hundred essays (referred articles, and book chapters), and dozens of book reviews and encyclopedia entries.

Homepage-addresses:

http://religion.unc.edu/_people/full-time-faculty/ariel/

http://independent.academia.edu/YaakovAriel

Uran Botobekov is a Member of the Advisory Board of the Modern Diplomacy. In 2011, he received his Ph.D. in Political Science (honor graduate) at the Institute of Philosophy and Political and Legal Studies of the National Academy Sciences of Kyrgyz Republic in Bishkek. Before his work for Modern Diplomacy, Botobekov has been Deputy Director of the Organization and Control Work of the Presidential Administration of the Kyrgyz Republic, Bishkek, Kyrgyzstan and Contributing Analyst for the Carnegie Center in Moscow (USA) and the Institute for War and Peace Reporting (UK) in Bishkek, Kyrgyzstan.

His major research interests include Islamic Radicalization, Religious Fundamentalism, Jihadist Movements and Politics in Central Asia.

He is the author of the publication 'Think like Jihadist: Anatomy of Central Asian Salafi groups' 2019) and the co-author of the book '"Potential for Conflict in the Fergana Valley: Religious Extremism and Drug Trafficking' (2000).

Homepage-addresses:

https://wikipedia.org/wiki/Uran_Botobekovhttps://www.linkedin.com/in/uran-botobekov-phd-96a7b6136/

https://independent.academia.edu/Botobekov

Nina Käsehage is an Historian and Religious Scholar. Since 2017, she is a Senior Lecturer at the Department for Religious Studies and Intercultural Theology (Faculty of Theology) at the University of Rostock. In 2018, she received her Ph.D. for her basic research about the contemporary Salafist and Jihadist milieu in Germany from the Department of Religious Studies (Faculty of Philosophy) at the Georg-August-University of Göttingen.

Her main research interests are Islamic Radicalization, New Religious Movements, Qualitative Religious Research, Religious Fundamentalism, Psychology and Sociology of Religion.

Current publications of Käsehage are: *'Militant Islam' vs. 'Islamic Militancy'*, *Religion, Violence, Category Formation and Applied Research*. *Contested Fields in the Discourses of Scholarship* (2020, co-author Klaus Hock) and *Salafismus in Deutschland - Entstehung und Transformation einer radikal-islamischen Bewegung* (2019).

Homepage-addresses:

https://www.theologie.uni-rostock.de/fachgebiete/religionswissenschaft-und-interkulturelle-theologie/dr-nina-kaesehage/

http://salafismus-forschung.de/en

Barbara Lucini (PhD in Sociology and Methodology of Social Research), is Senior Researcher at Itstime, Department of Sociology, Catholic University of Sacred Heart, Milan. She is adjunct professor of risk management and crisis communication. She has been involved in the scientific coordination of several research projects (European and others) focused on crisis management, risk communication, risk perception, security, resilience, radicalisation and extremisms.

Her research interests are oriented to sociology of disaster, disaster resilience, disaster management, extremisms and radicalisation. Further, the issue of the relation between terrorism and resilience as well as political extremism have been studied.

She is the author of several publications and the "Disaster Resilience from a Sociological Perspective Exploring Three Italian Earthquakes as Models for Disaster Resilience Planning", Springer International Publishing, 2014; The Other Side of Resilience to Terrorism A Portrait of a Resilient-Healthy City", Springer International Publishing, 2017.

Homepage: https://euro3.safelinks.protection.outlook.com/?url=http%3A%2F www.i%2F&data=02%7C01%7CBarabara.Lucini%40unicatt.it%7C86612cacba mp;sdata=0%2FN-ZodaBIDhskf5HkkhsTHihS1IN1hQxMtcPJWNssKamp;reserved=0

Anastasia Mitrofanova is Leading Research fellow at the Institute of Sociology of the Federal Center of Theoretical and Applied Sociology of the Russian Academy of Science since 2019.

She is Professor at the Financial University under the Government of Russia and the Russian State University for the Humanities (RGGU). In 1994, she received her M.A. and in 1998 her Ph.D. from Moscow State University and her Dr. habilitat degree from the Diplomatic Academy of Foreign Affairs Ministry of Russia in 2005.

Mitrofanova´s research interests include: Religious Politicisation, Fundamentalism, Orthodox Christianity and Politics, Nationalism in Postsoviet States and Religiopolitical Movements. Main publications: *Politizatsiia 'pravoslavnogo mira'* (Moskva: Nauka, 2004), *The Politicization of Russian Orthodoxy: Actors and Ideas* (Stuttgart: Ibidem-Verlag 2005).

Homepage: http://www.isras.ru/pers_about.html?id=1913

Olga Torres Díaz is an Arabist and Islamologist. She holds a MA in International Relations and a Postgraduate degree in Analysis of Jihadist Terrorism, Insurgency and Radical Movements. Since 2014, she is a lecturer in Contemporary Arab World and a member of the research group HUM-381: Ixbilia (https://investigacion.us.es/sisius/grupo/HUM381) at the University of Seville (Spain).

Her doctoral thesis at University of Seville deals with the first translation into Spanish of a 12th century Arab mirror for princes – a political and military manual–, identifying its parallelisms with BCE precedents in China and India and contemporary echoes to establish its insertion in a historical and ideological continuum.

From 2015 to 2018, Torres Díaz has been a visiting lecturer at the Army War College, Spanish Ministry of Defence. In 2015, she has been a Visiting Lecturer at NATO Rapid Deployable Corps – Spain Headquarters (HQ NRDC-ESP).

Her major research interest focuses on classical Islamic political thought and its traces on contemporary Islamic fundamentalist movements, primarily in the Middle East, Maghreb, and Sahel area.

Current publications: *Ali ibn Abi Bakr al-Harawi: fe, política y guerra en el pensamiento árabe clásico* (2021), *Islamism and Women in the Sahel: Roots and Evolution* (2020), *La expansion norteafricana del Daesh: repetición de patrones históricos y amenazas en la frontera sur Europa* (2017).

Homepage: https://olgatorres.academia.edu

Social Sciences

kollektiv orangotango+ (ed.)
This Is Not an Atlas
A Global Collection of Counter-Cartographies

2018, 352 p., hardcover, col. ill.
34,99 € (DE), 978-3-8376-4519-4
E-Book: free available, ISBN 978-3-8394-4519-8

Gabriele Dietze, Julia Roth (eds.)
Right-Wing Populism and Gender
European Perspectives and Beyond

April 2020, 286 p., pb., ill.
35,00 € (DE), 978-3-8376-4980-2
E-Book: 34,99 € (DE), ISBN 978-3-8394-4980-6

Mozilla Foundation
Internet Health Report 2019
2019, 118 p., pb., ill.
19,99 € (DE), 978-3-8376-4946-8
E-Book: free available, ISBN 978-3-8394-4946-2

**All print, e-book and open access versions of the titles in our list
are available in our online shop www.transcript-verlag.de/en!**

Social Sciences

James Martin
Psychopolitics of Speech
Uncivil Discourse and the Excess of Desire

2019, 186 p., hardcover
79,99 € (DE), 978-3-8376-3919-3
E-Book: 79,99 € (DE), ISBN 978-3-8394-3919-7

Michael Bray
Powers of the Mind
Mental and Manual Labor
in the Contemporary Political Crisis

2019, 208 p., hardcover
99,99 € (DE), 978-3-8376-4147-9
E-Book: 99,99 € (DE), ISBN 978-3-8394-4147-3

Iain MacKenzie
Resistance and the Politics of Truth
Foucault, Deleuze, Badiou

2018, 148 p., pb.
29,99 € (DE), 978-3-8376-3907-0
E-Book: 26,99 € (DE), ISBN 978-3-8394-3907-4
EPUB: 26,99 € (DE), ISBN 978-3-7328-3907-0

**All print, e-book and open access versions of the titles in our list
are available in our online shop www.transcript-verlag.de/en!**

GPSR Authorized Representative: Easy Access System Europe, Mustamäe tee 50, 10621 Tallinn, Estonia, gpsr.requests@easproject.com